T0375874

BRITISH SOCIALIST FICTION, 1884–1914

CONTENTS OF THE EDITION

VOLUME 1
General Introduction
1884–1891

VOLUME 2
1892–1900

VOLUME 3
1901–1906

VOLUME 4
1907–1910

VOLUME 5
1911–1914

BRITISH SOCIALIST FICTION, 1884–1914

Volume 2
1892–1900

Edited by
Deborah Mutch

PICKERING & CHATTO
2013

Published by Pickering & Chatto (Publishers) Limited
21 Bloomsbury Way, London WC1A 2TH

2252 Ridge Road, Brookfield, Vermont 05036-9704, USA

www.pickeringchatto.com

All rights reserved.
No part of this publication may be reproduced,
stored in a retrieval system, or transmitted in any form or by any means,
electronic, mechanical, photocopying, recording, or otherwise
without prior permission of the publisher.

Copyright © Pickering & Chatto (Publishers) Limited 2013
Copyright © Editorial material Deborah Mutch 2013

To the best of the Publisher's knowledge every effort has been made to contact relevant copyright holders and to clear any relevant copyright issues.
Any omissions that come to their attention will be remedied in future editions.

BRITISH LIBRARY CATALOGUING IN PUBLICATION DATA

British socialist fiction, 1884–1914.
1. Political fiction, English – 19th century. 2. Political fiction, English – 20th century. 3. Socialism – Fiction.
I. Mutch, Deborah, 1965– editor of compilation.
823.8'0803581-dc23

ISBN-13: 9781848933576

This publication is printed on acid-free paper that conforms to the American National Standard for the Permanence of Paper for Printed Library Materials.

Typeset by Pickering & Chatto (Publishers) Limited
Printed and bound in the United Kingdom by Berforts Information Press

CONTENTS

Introduction	vii
Clarion	1
Quinbus Flestrin, 'A Tale of a Turnip' (1891)	5
Ed. Carpenter, 'Saved by a Nose' (1892)	11
M'Ginnis, 'Posterity' (1893)	15
'Citizen', 'Little Maggie's Boots' (1894)	19
J. Bruce Glasier, 'Telby Torbald: or, A Socialist Transformed' (1895)	21
Margaret McMillan, 'Mary's Lover' (1896)	27
Louis Becke, 'A Touch of the Tar Brush' (1897)	33
Harry Lowerison, 'Auld Randy' (1899)	41
Justice	47
'Devilshoof', 'One New Year's Eve' (1893)	49
'Devilshoof', 'On the River' (1894)	53
C. H. V., 'One Among Many' (1895)	55
Dan Baxter, 'The New Shilling' (1895)	57
Dan Baxter, 'A Monkey Story' (1896)	61
C. S. J., 'A Fairy Tale for Tired Socialists' (1898)	65
Labour Elector	69
John Law, 'Connie' (1893–4)	71
Labour Leader	119
A. Chee, 'The Bank-Manager's Girl' (1894)	121
Isabella Fyvie Mayo, 'A Bit of Tragedy' (1895)	125
Caroline E. Derecourt Martyn, 'A Mystery' (1896)	131
Lilian Claxton, 'Nigel Grey (A Serial Story of Love and Effort)' (1896–7)	135
Ella Jeffries, 'A Shop Girl' (1898)	199
Colonel Bradbury, 'Guilty – But Drunk' (1899)	205
Labour Prophet	209
Elihu, 'Nobody's Business' (1892)	211

Social Democrat	215
Anon., 'Rent of Ability' (1898)	217
Anon., 'A Life for a Life' (1900)	223
Teddy Ashton's Journal/Northern Weekly and Teddy Ashton's Journal	227
Ben Adhem, 'Blood on the Cheap Trip' (1896)	229
Teddy Ashton, 'Bill Spriggs an Patsy Filligan o'er Winter Hill. Likewise Bet' (1896)	233
James Haslam, 'Murdered by Money' (1897)	239
Teddy Ashton, 'Greensauce Sketches. Georgie's Fust Day in t' Factory' (1897)	247
Teddy Ashton, 'Th' Kock-Krow Club an' th' War. Darin Decision to Form a Kock-Krow Volunteer Corps to Batter th' Boers' (1899)	251
Fred Plant, 'The Absent-Minded Beggar' (1900)	255
Workman's Times	259
Anon., 'Sunshine and Shadow' (1892)	261
'Citizen', 'The Blackleg' (1893)	265
Martin Fair, 'Nan: A New Year's Eve Story' (1893)	349
Dan Baxter, 'A Terrible Crime' (1893)	355
Editorial Notes	359
Silent Corrections	395

INTRODUCTION

The period covered in Volume 2 of this collection produced a much greater range of tone and genre in the fiction published by socialist authors than the early years of the movement (as sampled in Volume 1). There are a number of reasons that might be put forward to explain this expansion of literary range, the first of which is the significant increase in membership of the socialist groups. Although the Socialist League disintegrated in the mid-1890s, collapsing under the weight of the anarchists, the membership of the Social Democratic Federation (SDF) grew to 2,000 by 1894;[1] the Fabians increased their membership from around 520 in 1891 to around 2,000 in 1893;[2] and the Independent Labour Party (ILP) was founded in 1893, bringing some trade unions under the socialist umbrella. There were, therefore, more potential contributors to the socialist cause, and many would express their experiences and support through literature. There was also a proliferation of periodicals published to advance the cause. Splinter groups would publish their own periodicals to differentiate their version of socialism from other groups, and regional socialist groups would publish local periodicals. The national ILP was served by no fewer than three periodicals: Joseph Burgess and his *Workman's Times* had been central to the formation of the ILP and the founding conference in Bradford;[3] James Keir Hardie's *Labour Leader* was the official ILP organ of publication, although it was owned by Hardie at this point and not by the party; and Robert Blatchford's *Clarion* was used by many as the ILP's unofficial periodical. There were also periodicals not directly associated with specific socialist groups, such as Henry Hyde Champion's *Labour Elector* and Clarke's *Teddy Ashton's Journal and Northern Weekly*. Others were founded to support different aspects of the socialist movement, such as John Trevor's *Labour Prophet*, the periodical of the Labour Church.

This proliferation of periodicals and authors, while increasing the range of literary form and genre, did not reject the genres preferred by earlier authors. It was still felt necessary to illustrate the individual tragedies suffered under the capitalist system, and the thread of tragedy is drawn through many of the periodicals selected for this volume. For example, Harry Lowerison's 'Auld Randy' (1899) in the *Clarion* is based on the sacrifice of the self for others; 'Devilshoof's'

'One New Year's Eve' (1893) in *Justice* shows landlords' disregard for the human lives of their tenants; the *Labour Leader* describes the entrapment of the working-class woman in Ella Jeffries's 'A Shop Girl' (1898); Ben Adhem (Charles Allen Clarke) presents an image of the neglected children of the poor in 'Blood on the Cheap Trip' (1896), *Teddy Ashton's Journal*; and Martin Fair's 'Nan: A New Year's Eve Story' (1893) in *Workman's Times* is the tragedy of the seduced and abandoned woman. Such a range of tragic circumstances necessarily has its basis in realism in order to present a criticism of the capitalist system, and as such some of the stories incorporate a journalistic element. In 'Little Maggie's Boots' (1894) by 'Citizen' (James Sexton), the author/narrator, in a form similar to that of the interview popularized by the New Journalism, presents/records an omnibus driver's description of his long hours and low pay, interwoven with descriptions of his family life, as he drives his bus. Thus 'Citizen' turns to tragedy to illustrate the consequences for labour of the capitalist desire for profit while presenting the tragedy in a form not dissimilar to the surrounding journalism. As discussed in the General Introduction, fiction was not merely included for light relief but was also an integral part of the periodical and an important tool in the promotion of socialism; therefore the divide between fiction and journalism is not always clearly discernible.

This problem does not affect the genre of the fable, which was still perceived as a useful form through which the reader could be educated in socialist theory and was again a form used by the *Justice* authors. Included in this volume are Dan Baxter's 'The New Shilling' (1895), which describes the horror of a newly minted shilling when it finds out that it is not the token of citizenship and love it had been told but was but instead the physical form of capitalist exchange and greed, and C. S. J.'s 'A Fairytale for Tired Socialists' (1898), which describes the complicity of the worker under capitalism as a form of enchantment. Another of Dan Baxter's fables, 'A Monkey Story' (1896), illustrates the arbitrariness of hierarchy and power with the tale of a big gorilla who entices smaller gorillas to create a capitalist society by forcing monkeys to work on their behalf. Baxter's latter story takes a Marxist perspective on the production of unnecessary goods at the expense of the necessary, as he describes the monkeys being forced to gather shells for exchange with 'rent collectors, interest collectors, profit collectors, insurance collectors' etc. rather than gathering fruit for food (p. 63). As with the earlier *Justice* fables, Baxter's 'Monkey Story' creates a sense of simultaneous unity and fragmentation as it describes the end of capitalism when the monkeys decide to stop serving the gorillas. The unity of capitalism is fragmented by the monkey's unified action; the moral of the fable is that unified action by the workers in reality could similarly end the system that enslaves them. The fantasy of fable is always intrinsically connected to reality, especially in the case of the socialist fable, where it is intended to act as a motor for real change.

Didacticism, however, is not restricted to the fable; realism, particularly in the short story, also tackled the inconsistencies of capitalist ideology. In 'Rent of Ability' (1898), published anonymously in the *Social Democrat* but written by its editor, Harry Quelch (see p. 47), the capitalist argument that those who are paid more than others are worth more is systematically dismantled and shown as an ideological position that can only be changed through experience. Quelch presents the story of an employer, Swanage, who dismisses his employee, Smith, for the latter's socialist sympathies. As Smith questions his employer's enrichment by profiting from Smith's work, Swanage savagely rejects the point, declaring: 'I don't make any profit out of you! What I get is what I earn' (p. 218). The two men eventually exchange positions as Smith uses his skill to create a new engine while Swanage's business fails, and Swanage's claims of high income on the basis of 'superior ability' are proven absurd when he tries to obtain employment.

The use of the periodical as an educational tool reached its peak during this period with Robert Blatchford's bestselling *Clarion*, and particularly the globally influential *Merrie England*. This pamphlet, originally serialized in the *Clarion* between March and September 1893 under Blatchford's pseudonym 'Nunquam', was phenomenally successful: the shilling edition sold 30,000 copies while the penny edition sold 750,000 in Britain in the first year, and it was pirated in America and translated into Welsh, Russian, French, Spanish, Dutch, Norwegian, Swedish and Hebrew.[4] The popularity of the pamphlet 'added 7,000 to the *Clarion*'s circulation and made it in some sort a national institution'.[5] Blatchford's explanation of socialism, described by the author as 'horse-sense in tinker's English' but dismissed by Ramsay MacDonald as trying to explain a motor car by describing a wheelbarrow,[6] was followed almost three months later by his utopian vision of *Merrie England* established: 'What They Thought: A Vision', published in the *Clarion* in December 1893, prophesies a classless and apolitical society that has also removed work-based hierarchy (for example, Gilbert would prefer to perfect his system of tanning pigskin to becoming president). There is a similar levelling of the hierarchy of form, as this fiction rises out of the *Merrie England* polemic and opens with a report of the Prime Minister the Marquis of Salisbury's speech at Newport. Just as in *Merrie England*, all work is useful, so in capitalist England all print is usefully employed to promote socialism.

Thus far everything discussed in this Introduction is not very different from the earlier publications in Volume 1: print media was still regarded as having an important role in the promotion of socialist ideas, fiction was still seen as an important vehicle for that promotion, and socialist authors were still using tragedy and fable in their didactic fiction. What had increased, along with the rise of periodicals, was the number of working-class authors. Periodicals such as the *Clarion*, *Labour Leader*, *Teddy Ashton's Journal and Northern Weekly*, *Workman's Times* and *Labour Prophet* were written and edited by men who had started working life in working-class forms of employment: *Clarion* editor Robert Blatchford had been an apprentice brush maker, a soldier and a store keeper before earning a living through journalism; *Labour Leader* editor James Keir Hardie had worked as a miner before becoming secretary of the Lanarkshire miners' union and had entered journalism through working for, and then editing, the *Cumnock News*; Charles Allen Clarke, editor of *Teddy Ashton's Journal and Northern Weekly*, had as a child been a half-timer in the Bolton cotton mills before entering journalism via the teaching profession; and Joseph Burgess, editor of the *Workman's Times*, was a former dock worker who, like Hardie, came to journalism through trade unionism. This expansion of periodicals and working-class editors was followed by a significant increase in working-class authors contributing to the periodical fiction than there had been in the previous period. This is not to suggest that there were no working-class authors in the early part of the socialist movement; but they were certainly fewer, and working-class socialists such as Tom Mann, John Burns and Ben Tillett preferred to publish articles and reports on socialist activities rather than fiction.

In the period 1892–1900 covered by this volume, as socialism grew so did the numbers of working-class authors. Former dockworker James Sexton published fiction in the *Clarion*, the *Labour Leader* and the *Workman's Times*; former weaver James Haslam wrote fiction for *Teddy Ashton's Journal and Northern Weekly*; and unskilled worker Harry Quelch wrote fiction for *Justice* and the *Social Democrat* (while editing both periodicals), in addition to Blatchford and Clarke mentioned above. Amplified in the socialist fiction of this period, along with the increase of working-class authors, were a sense of hope and a sense of humour. The latter is clearly visible in the dialect fiction of Charles Allen Clarke, most popularly in the 'Tum Fowt' sketches featuring Bill Spriggs, his wife Bet and his friends. Clark drew on a number of sources to create his dialect community: the oral and written tradition of Lancashire and Yorkshire dialect literature stretching back to John Collier's eighteenth-century dialect persona 'Tim Bobbin', the humour associated with both dialect literature and its industrial readership, and the music hall popularity of 'policemen, drunkenness and hen-pecked husbands'.[7] He also carries on the tradition of dialect being used to question the status quo and the power wielded over the working-class reader. Clarke used dialect in a more subversive way than the earlier dialect authors Edwin Waugh and Ben Brierley, who were criticized by James Haslam for their apolitical literature: 'whilst Brierley and his contemporaries were soothing the people with dialect, song and wit, manufacturers were making them into slaves'.[8] The adventures of Bill Spriggs raised questions about many aspects of society and power, and in the stories included in this volume, Bill and his friends challenge the right of the landowner to restrict access to the countryside ('Bill Spriggs an Patsy Filligan o'er Winter Hill' (1896)) and illustrate the absurdity of the violent patriotism whipped up by the government to justify the Boer War ('Th' Kock-Krow Club an' th' War' (1899)).

While the Bill Spriggs character resisted the restrictions and expectations imposed on the working classes by other class groups, 'Citizen's' serial fiction 'The Blackleg' posited the benefits of a cross-class drive to further the socialist ideal. Its protagonist, Jack Goodman, is a dock labourer who works with the upper-class Dr Smyth, his friend Mr Garnish, and even the wife and daughter of the capitalist, Crushem, in the unionization of dock workers and to establish independent labour representation in Parliament. Both Sexton's and Clarke's fiction create depictions of a rounded community; Pamela Fox describes Clarke's work as offering 'a "realistic," expansive look at a particular working-class community ... by spotlighting its stubborn passivity, as well as awakening socialist consciousness'.[9] This description can also be applied to Sexton's 'The Blackleg', as the reader is drawn into the networks of working-class life in the city of 'Mudpool', the inter-class interactions between employer and employee (Crushem and Goodman), and extra-class connections developed through socialism (Goodman, Smyth and Garnish). This cross-class vision of concord rejects Marxist socialist categories of class, economics, consumption and employment and creates a unity through sympathy, independence and resistance to oppression.

Cross-class unity for improvement is also at the centre of Lilian Claxton's 'Nigel Grey' (1896–7), as the aristocratic Constance Compton and the working-class mechanic Nigel Grey move to a common ground of understanding about the necessity of social, political and economic change. However, the difference between the class perspectives of Sexton and Claxton is that of the importance of class mobility. Sexton's working-class characters remain working class, forging political relationships with others through socialism and not through shifts in class position. Claxton, on the other hand, draws on what Patrick Joyce terms the Romance of Improvement[10] to reduce the social gap between Constance and Nigel. Thus while Nigel maintains his class ideal and his socialist politics, drawing Constance into socialism, his elevation through work from employee to partner shrinks the social gulf between the two characters. The increase in membership and authors in the socialist movement brought a concurrent increase in hope for the future, and that hope was projected through the lens of fiction.

The hope for cross-class unity, imagined in the fiction, was also evident in reality. Middle-class women joined with working-class male socialists, like Hardie, Burgess, Blatchford and others, in working for socialism. Caroline Martyn, daughter of a police superintendent, joined the Fabians in 1891 and contributed to many of the socialist periodicals, including the *Labour Leader* and the *Clarion*; Katherine St John Conway, daughter of a Congregationalist minister, joined the Fabian Society in 1891 and the ILP in 1892; Daisy Greville, Countess of Warwick, was given a lecture on socialism by Robert Blatchford in 1895 before joining the SDF; Margaret McMillan, daughter of an estate manager, became involved in the socialist movement in 1899; and a little later Emmeline Pankhurst, daughter of a textile works owner and wife of a barrister, joined the ILP in 1903 along with her daughters Christabel and Sylvia. Their efforts have not always been appreciated or recorded by historians, but the revisionists are now bringing them back into view.[11] These women have at least two things in common: a non-working-class background and their sex. The demands for equality and justice were not restricted to class but were expanded to include gender, and the confluence of class and gender at this point within the socialist movement also had an effect on the use of genre in some socialist fiction.

The increasing involvement of women in the socialist movement meant that not only were women writing and publishing more fiction in the socialist periodicals but also that their role as characters within the fiction grew in importance. Volume 1 indicates the low output of female authors in socialism – only Margaret Harkness, under the pseudonym 'John Law', and E. Nesbit, in a joint venture with her husband, published fiction in the selected periodicals, unless the anonymous or initialled 'D.' and 'R. G. B.' are later discovered to be female. Furthermore, the female characters within the fiction are restricted to love interests (Bramsbury, Bauer und Dichter, Katte) or the victim of vivisection at the hands of the male scientist (Bland). In this volume, however, women are shown educating other women (Isabella Fyvie Mayo's 'A Bit of Tragedy' (1895)); holding their own against arbitrary authority (Ashton's 'Bill Spriggs an Patsy Filigan o'er Winter Hill'); as a critique of capitalist employment and social practices (Jeffries's 'A Shop Girl'); as the sharers of cross-class understanding (Margaret McMillan's 'Mary's Lover' (1896)); as worthy of more than is allowed them (Constance Compton in Claxton's 'Nigel Grey', Goodman's wife in Chapter XVI of Sexton's 'The Blackleg'); or as having achieved relative equality in the socialist future (M'Ginnis's 'Posterity' (1893)). Interestingly, and perhaps significantly, the impact of women in the socialist movement is drawn into the fiction by both male and female authors. There was no single or unified attitude towards female involvement in the socialist movement, but neither was there a single or unified attitude towards socialism and change. Women had no role in the leadership of any of the groups, and some socialists actively rejected the notion of the political female (see for instance the headnote for *To-Day* in Volume 1, p. 225, for the debate between Ernest Belfort Bax and Annie Besant on the role of women); nevertheless, their presence in British socialism was growing.

The most sustained discussion of women, work and relationships in the socialist fiction during the period covered by this volume was the serialization 'Connie' (1893–4) by John Law, the pseudonym of Margaret Harkness. Harkness was already known as an author before she began the serialization of 'Connie' in Champion's *Labour Elector* in 1893 (see the headnote for the *Labour Elector* in this volume, pp. 69–70, for a list of fiction by Harkness under the pseudonym

John Law). Her previous fiction had taken a range of perspectives from which the working-class experience was depicted: the seduced woman, the unemployed man, the Salvation Army captain working in the slums, and the widow. 'Connie', along with the only other serial she published, 'Roses and Crucifix' (1891–2) in the *Woman's Herald*, was not published in bound form, and unlike 'Roses and Crucifix' was not completed, as the *Labour Elector* ceased publication before the serial was finished.

The incomplete state of 'Connie' makes it difficult to be conclusive about the genre, but working on what is available, 'Connie' appears to be an example of New Woman fiction. Serialized across the years that also saw the publication of Sarah Grand's *The Heavenly Twins* (1893) and Mona Caird's *The Daughters of Danaus* (1894), 'Connie' is the story of a working-class woman's cohabitation with her upper-class lover and her ensuing pregnancy. Unlike the seduction of working-class Nelly Ambrose by upper-class Radical Arthur Grant in Harkness's *A City Girl*, the relationship between Connie and Humphry Munro is one of mutual love and affection. Their cohabitation is less the political statement of Herminia in Grant Allen's *The Woman Who Did* (1895) or Sue Bridehead in Thomas Hardy's *Jude the Obscure* (1895) and more a mutual agreement created through both love and necessity, in the manner of Eleanor Marx's cohabitation with Edward Aveling but without the barrier of one party being married. Despite the truncated form of the fiction, there is a suggestion that marriage is not disregarded entirely, despite class difference, as the last sentence of the available fiction, spoken by Squire Munro to his son Humphry, is 'Your wife must be my daughter' (p. 118). Nevertheless, a traditional 'happy ending' had not previously been Harkness's modus operandi, and the story leaves Connie in a supportive female environment after being rescued from a night sleeping on the Embankment by two high-class prostitutes. Within this supportive community, the only role of men is as customers whose trade is the economic underpinning of the women's world on the periphery of society. The removal of women from patriarchal capitalism may have been the conclusion Harkness was working towards, or it may have been the uniting of the classes in the marriage of Connie and Humphrey, but as it is the reader can only speculate. What we do have in the fiction that was published is a relationship between the working and landowning classes based on equal affection and emotional attachment – a relationship that had previously been unexplored in Harkness's earlier fiction, but one which was also being explored by Lilian Claxton.

The expansion of the socialist movement, its membership and its periodicals resulted in a much more textured literary landscape than that produced in the first few years. There is still the necessity for tragedy in depicting working-class existence under capitalism, but it is now one part of the perspective projected through fiction. Now tragedy is diluted with hope, expectation and the potential for happiness.

Notes

1. M. Crick, *The History of the Social-Democratic Federation* (Keele: Keele University Press, 1994), p. 86.
2. M. Bevir, *The Making of British Socialism* (Princeton, NJ and Oxford: Princeton University Press, 2011), p. 206.
3. K. McPhillips, *Joseph Burgess (1853–1934) and the Founding of the Independent Labour Party* (Lewiston, NY: Edwin Mellen Press, 2005), pp. 66–8.
4. L. Thompson, *Robert Blatchford: Portrait of an Englishman* (London: Victor Gollancz, 1951), p. 98; A. M. Thompson, *Here I Lie* (London: George Routledge and Sons, 1937), p. 101.
5. Thompson, *Robert Blatchford*, p. 114. See D. Mutch, 'The Merrie England Triptych: Robert Blatchford, Edward Fay and the Didactic Use of Clarion Fiction', *Victorian Periodicals Review*, 38:1 (2005), pp. 83–103, for a discussion on the symbiotic relationship between *Merrie England* and the *Clarion* fiction.
6. Thompson, *Robert Blatchford*, p. 97.
7. P. Gammond, *Music Hall Songbook* (London: EMI Publishing, 1975), p. 16.
8. J. Haslam, *Northern Weekly*, 14 May 1898, quoted in P. Salveson, *Lancashire's Romantic Radical: The Life and Writings of Allen Clarke/Teddy Ashton* (Huddersfield: Little Northern Books, 2009), p. 28.
9. P. Fox, *Class Fictions: Shame and Resistance in the British Working-Class Novel* (Durham, NC: Duke University Press, 1994), p. 123.
10. P. Joyce, *Democratic Subjects: The Self and the Social in Nineteenth-Century England* (Cambridge: Cambridge University Press, 1994), pp. 161–76.
11. See K. Hunt, *Equivocal Feminists: The Social Democratic Federation and the Woman Question, 1884–1911* (Cambridge: Cambridge University Press, 1996); K. Cowman, *Mrs. Brown is a Man and a Brother: Women in Merseyside's Political Organisations, 1890–1920* (Liverpool: Liverpool University Press, 2004); J. Hannam and K. Hunt, *Socialist Women: Britain, 1880s to 1920s* (London and New York: Routledge, 2002); and S. Rowbotham, *Dreamers of a New Day: Women who Invented the Twentieth Century* (London: Verso, 2011) for more on the confluence of class and gender in socialism.

CLARION

Quinbus Flestrin, 'A Tale of a Turnip', *Clarion*, 26 December 1891, p. 6.

Ed. Carpenter, 'Saved by a Nose', *Clarion*, Christmas Number 1892, pp. 55–8.

M'Ginnis, 'Posterity', *Clarion*, 9 December 1893, p. 6.

'Citizen', 'Little Maggie's Boots', *Clarion*, 6 January 1894, p. 8.

J. Bruce Glasier, 'Telby Torbald: or, A Socialist Transformed', *Clarion*, 18 May 1895, p. 159.

Margaret McMillan, 'Mary's Lover', *Clarion*, 15 February 1896, p. 56.

Louis Becke, 'A Touch of the Tar Brush', *Clarion*, 10 April 1897, pp. 113–14.

Harry Lowerison, 'Auld Randy', *Clarion*, 16 December 1899, p. 404.

The *Clarion* (1891–1935) was the socialist movement's bestselling periodical and one of the longest running. It was founded by Robert Peel Glanville Blatchford (1851–1943), his brother Montagu (1848–1910), Alexander Thompson (1861–1948) and Edward Fay (1853–96), and it launched on 12 December 1891. A weekly periodical priced at one penny, it was first published in Manchester by the Co-Operative Newspaper Printing Society and then by the Clarion Press. In 1895 the *Clarion* relocated to London, where Blatchford remained the primary editor but was occasionally aided by Thompson. Sales of the *Clarion* were higher than most of the other socialist periodicals of this period, averaging around 34,000 in the 1890s. The popularity of the *Clarion* rose significantly after the publication of Blatchford's influential socialist treatise *Merrie England*, which was initially serialized in the periodical in 1893. Blatchford and the *Clarion* group generally eschewed party politics, despite early connections with the Independent Labour Party; this connection was short-lived because ILP chairman James Keir Hardie's (1856–1915) 'puritanical' views jarred with Blatchford and the rest of the *Clarion* members' appreciation of entertainment and culture. The *Clarion* group also promoted a sociable form of socialism, and members formed numerous social clubs under the *Clarion* name, including cycle clubs, Cinderella Clubs providing entertainment and education for slum children, glee clubs and choirs. In 1896 Julia Dawson (the pseudonym of Mrs D. Middleton Worrall (n.d.)) began the Clarion van project, with horse-drawn vans taking both the periodical and the message across the country.

The *Clarion* had a high literary content and from the first issue carried poetry, short stories and serial fiction. In the selection presented in this volume, there is a greater range of socialist authors from outside the *Clarion* group than there would be later in the periodical's life. John Bruce Glasier (1859–1920), the son of a Glaswegian farmer and cattle dealer, joined the Land League in 1879, the Scottish Land Restoration League, and helped to found the Social Democratic Federation in 1884. He became secretary of the Glasgow branch of the Socialist League, and upon its disintegration he joined the ILP in 1893. Glasier went on become one of the men who would steer the Labour Party towards Liberal support, criticizing the efforts of Blatchford and Hyndman to create a unified socialist group to compete against the Labour Party in the first decade of the twentieth century.

Edward Carpenter (1844–1929), author, socialist and champion of homosexual rights, became involved in socialism through reading Henry Mayers Hyndman's *England for All* (1881) while creating a smallholding at Millthorpe near Sheffield. He wrote the socialist marching song 'England Arise' (1886) after having joined the SDF in 1883. His publications included arguments for socialism (*Towards Democracy* (four editions; 1883, 1885, 1892 and 1905) and *Civilization: Its Cause and Cure* (1889)) and homosexual freedom (*Love's Coming-of-Age* (1896, 1906) and *The Intermediate Sex* (1908)). Bellerby (Harry) Lowerison (1863–1935) was the son of a County Durham coal miner. He trained to be a teacher and joined the Fabian Society after becoming interested in socialism during the 1889 London dock strike. He wrote for both *Justice* and the *Clarion*; his letters to the latter brought his socialism to the attention of the school board, and he was dismissed from his employment. Using funds donated by *Clarion* readers, he established the Ruskin School at Hunstanton in Norfolk to create a learning environment far removed from the strict rote-learning regimes of the board schools.

Many authors, particularly members of the *Clarion* group, would publish under one or more pseudonyms. Quinbus Flestrin (in Jonathan Swift's *Gulliver's Travels*, the name the Lilliputians gave to Gulliver, meaning 'man mountain') was a pseudonym used by Edward Francis Fay in reference to his stature. Fay was described by Blatchford as 'a big athletic man, standing six feet two in his usually neglected socks'.[1] Fay, who also published as 'The Bounder', was born in Ireland and was one of the founding members of the *Clarion*, having met Blatchford while both were working at Edward Hulton's (1869–1925) paper *Bell's Life*.

M'Ginnis, sometimes spelled McGinnis, is a pseudonym of Robert Blatchford. Born in Maidstone to travelling actors, he ran away from his apprenticeship as a brush maker, joined the army, worked as a store keeper and became a journalist, at which time he met Alex Thompson, who helped him to turn his part-time journalism into full-time employment. While working for Edward Hulton on the *Sunday Chronicle*, Blatchford visited the slums of Manchester and became a committed socialist. Hulton presented him with an ultimatum: to stop writing socialist articles or to leave. He left Hulton's employ in 1891 and spent a few months working on Joseph Burgess's (1853–1934) *Workman's Times* before starting the *Clarion*. Blatchford edited the *Clarion* during its moment of influence as it became the bestselling socialist periodical of the 1890s and 1900s. However, his pro-army stance lost him support and a number of *Clarion* readers during the Second Boer War (1899–1902) and the years leading up to the First World War (1914–18). He left the *Clarion* permanently in 1913 and wrote for the *Weekly Dispatch* until 1916; he returned to Hulton's *Sunday Chronicle* the same year and remained there until 1924. He then wrote for the *Sunday News* until 1927, when he became a freelance journalist publishing in the *Sunday Chronicle*, the *Sunday News*, the *Sunday Graphic* and the *Manchester Evening News*.

Although not a *Clarion* member, James Sexton (1856–1938) also used a pseudonym, publishing fiction under 'Citizen'. Sexton was born in Newcastle-upon-Tyne, the son of Irish immigrants who settled in St Helens (then Lancashire, now Merseyside). He was employed at the docks in Liverpool until he was seriously injured in an accident, after which he became a self-employed coal merchant. He got involved with the National Union of Dock Labourers (NUDL), established in Liverpool in 1889, and rose to the position of general secretary in 1893. He was a militant unionist in terms of membership, which extended to his refusal to sit on an employment committee with ILP member James Larkin because Larkin was a 'non', i.e. not a member of any trade union. Sexton was also a founder member of the ILP and Labour MP for St Helens between 1918 and 1931; he was awarded a CBE in 1917 and knighted in 1931. He published regularly in the socialist press, contributing articles to the *Clarion*, the *Labour Leader* and the *Workman's Times* under both his own name and his pseudonym 'Citizen'. As 'Citizen' he published poetry, short stories and his novel, 'The Blackleg', and he is attributed as the 'Author of "A Docker's Story", "Jimmy Ducks", "Lot 27" &c., &c.' at the beginning of this serialization. Sexton also published *The Riot Act: A Play in Three Parts* in 1914 and the autobiography *Sir James Sexton: Agitator* in 1936.

Louis Becke, the pen-name of George Lewis ('Louis') Becke (1855–1913), is anomalous, being the only author in this selection of *Clarion* fiction who was not a British socialist. He was a prolific Australian author whose background included a youthful entanglement with piracy, sailing as the supercargo for

W. H. 'Bully' Hayes on the *Leonora*. Becke was tried and acquitted of piracy after the ship was sunk. His writing was based on his travels in the Pacific and often featured the theme of the European settler descending into savagery in the Pacific wilderness.

Notes
1.   R. Blatchford, *My Eighty Years* (London: Cassell and Co., 1931), p. 175.

Quinbus Flestrin, 'A Tale of a Turnip' (1891)

In truth, Face was a bad lot. Face was *the* standing dish of scandal in the suburban village of Snubley. Face got valiantly intoxicated every Saturday night with a consistency which in itself was a virtue, and displayed the thoroughness of the man. Face was an old solider, who worked in the brickfields, squat, but broad and powerful of frame, with a bullet head, an unlimited capacity for four ale and unsweetened,[1] and every inch a Cockney.[2] Face would defend himself, when efforts were made for his reformation, by saying that he earned his money fair, and that he would spend it as seemed to him best. It is well known that when the Hon. and Rev. Mr. Septimus Sidebotham approached him on the subject of temperance reform,[3] the hon. and reverend gentleman was much pained by Face's expletives, which were painful and frequent and free.

There was no help for it. Face was incorrigible. He would get drunk o' Saturday nights at the Dog and Duck;[4] he would relate marvellous stories of military life to an admiring crowd of co-artists in clay; he would troll wonderful lyrics in praise of Bacchus and Mars;[5] and if he had had an "extra pot" (his pots for financial reasons were generally limited numberically), he would sally forth to the neighbouring Horns and Chequers, where he would express a desire for combat *à Voutrance*[6] with Bill Cherry, the chimney sweep, accompanied with a dire threat to "knock his bally filbert off."

After a time Snubley grew tired of its ineffectual efforts to reform Face. Besides, it is necessary for a respectable suburban neighbourhood to have a scapegoat, by which their gentility shall show more gracious; and Face fulfilled the function admirably. Mr. William Cherry, the village sweep, occupied this post before the arrival of Face, but he was by no means a perfect scapegrace.[7] Bill was amenable to the exhortations of the Rev. Septimus, and not unsusceptible to the blandishments of the Church ladies; he had lucid intervals during which he would forswear sack and walk most delectably in the narrow way. For six weeks they battled for the scapegrace championship of Snubley.

And so it went on, until Bill had one of his lucid intervals, and Face was awarded the post of scapegrace by default. Bill made one or two subsequent efforts to recover the Championship, but he had lost prestige, and although the old feud still slumbered, Face held the post against all comers.

"I earn my money fair," he would say to the Parson, "and I ain't got no book larning, and I likes my pot o' beer. I don't interfere wi' you, why should you interfere wi' me? If I want to get drunk, I'll get drunk."

The position was indefeasible, and to give Face his due, he did get drunk. No person ever got drunker. And when the respectable automata of the semi-detached residences, decorously marching to church on Sabbath mornings, with ivory-backed prayer-books, ostensibly displayed, would see Face lying on the brickfields, sleeping off his previous night's debauch, they would look the other way.

Still, as I have said, a "Scapegrace" is necessary. No respectable family, society or newspaper staff can be considered complete without one. In the cast of the newspaper staff he is absolutely indispensable, and almost worth his weight in gold. Should anybody's copy be late, or a plate break, or the machine go wrong, behold there is your scapegrace! All friction is thereby avoided; and I really believe that had Face migrated to the neighbouring suburb of Snobbington, that the Snubleyites would have brought an action against the Snobbingtonians for his recovery, assessing the damages at a high figure. But when Legs came all this was changed. Face was bad enough, but he was endurable. But Legs –

Where Legs came from no one ever knew. He was a gaunt man about 6 feet 3 inches in height, and as wiry as a bit of whalebone, without a superfluous ounce of flesh on his bones. Further than that they were both old soldiers, there was no apparent reason for the firm friendship that grew up between them. To question Legs was useless. He was the very genius of taciturnity, and in his wrath terrible. So these inseparable companions became known to the village as Legs and Face. It was about this time that Mr. Cherry, who had abandoned the narrow path, made his last stand for the scapegrace championship, attacking Face on the narrow bridge, which spans the narrow stream, and divides the Dog and Duck from the Horns and Chequers. Bill being supported by half-a-dozen adherents, Face, who was in a minority of one to seven, was being very badly mauled when Legs came to his assistance. The Battle of the Bridge is still spoken of among the inhabitants; and the cool manner in which Legs took up Mr. Cherry and his partizans one by one, and bent them over his knee, is frequently the theme of conversation in adjacent taprooms.

I happened to be in the Private Bar of the Dog and Duck ordering a case of mineral water when the first meeting between these heroes took place. They were in the taproom.[8] They were drinking out of the same pot, using the same spittoon,[9] and smoking "shag"[10] that was calculated to kill at a thousand paces. Face had evidently just finished relating a military experience, and, after a few reflecting puffs at his well-seasoned clay,[11] thus questioned him vis-à-vis:

Face (*diagnosing Legs critically*): You've bin in the Awmy, aint yer?
Legs (*curtly*): Shed think I wawse.
Face: Ever bin in trouble?
Legs: I wawse (with peculiar accent on the "I").
Face: What wawse it?
Legs: Drunk, and absent from Church paroide.
(*Sympathetic interval*)
Face: In the band?
Legs: I wawse.
Face: Wot instrument d'yer play?
Legs: Euphonium.
Face: Wot's that?
Legs: Bass melody – brawse instrument.
(*Second interval for refreshment and expectoration.*)
Face: Wot did yer get?
Legs: Seven days, and arf a crahn.
Face: Wot did yer git drunk on?
Legs (*evasively*): I met a mate, and we gits drunk.
Face (*impatiently*): But where d'yer get it?

For the first time Legs displayed a little animation. He took his pipe out of his mouth, bent his head down, and conveyed the wished-for information in a whisper. I only heard the words, Pilot Point (perhaps Nunquam may enlighten our darkness on this point);[12] but, from the secrecy displayed, I should be inclined to think that the refreshment was not obtained through the usual channels. The conversation was then resumed: –

Legs (*explanatory*): You see, this is 'ow it wawse. There was another chap in the Rigiment called Jinkins. See? And he goes and gits drunk too. See? And the Colonel begins reading of this 'ere bloke's sheet. *See?* So I up and tells 'im 'ow it wawse, and strike me crule if ever I see seech a take dahn. The Colonel ses to me, "Your name's Jinkins?" and I says, "Yus." And he ses, "You were drunk?" and I ses "I wawse." And he ses, "Is there another man named Jinkins?" and I ses, "Yes." And he ses, "Was he drunk too?" And I ses, "*He* wawse." And blimy if they didn't all but bust out a larfin, and I only gits sivin days, and arf-a-crahn. But I lost a badge."[13]

The last item had the most paralysing effect on Face. He opened his mouth, gasped, and asked, with faltering accents, "Did yer 'ave a badge?" to which Legs replied, with something like scorn in his voice, "I had two!!" Face regarded his companion with profound wonder and admiration. It was obvious that he had never been possessed of a badge. It was further clear that he would not have had the remotest chance of getting a badge had he lived to the age of Methusaleh.[14] He fell into a moody reverie, and having instructed the Host to supply the ex-

Warriors with a pot of old six, I left them puffing away in silent communion. As I passed over the threshold I heard the following: –
 Face: You were bleedin' lucky.
 Legs: *I* wawse.

And so Legs settled down in Snubley, and not being skilled in the handling of clay,[15] obtained employment on Farmer Purpletop's large turnip field, doing occasional odd jobs at the Lodge; and he and Face, after a brief campaign, held undisputed sway and supremacy over all comers, not only in the Brickfields, but also in the large turnip fields. Notwithstanding his taciturnity and terrible truculence when in his cups, Legs gradually grew into the life of the neighbourhood, and after he beat Gipsy George, who came over from Snobbington (it was surmised that he had been subsidised by the deposed Cherry), he became quite a personage.

The last opponent brought to dispute his right of champion, was a brawny Irish Navvy, Buffing Dan, who came with a great reputation and influential support from a new railway, which was in the course of construction in the neighbourhood. A terrible engagement ensued, for when Buffing Dan was bent like the rest, his "influential support" took up the cudgel literally, and the Dog and Duck contingent were in imminent danger of succumbing to superior numbers, when Bill Cherry (to his honour be it said) came with his forces to the rescue of his quondam enemy, and the Navvies were routed with great slaughter. Snubley was saved, and from that time there was a truce between the rival (public) houses.

Legs was always making history. His next achievement was to wipe the pavement with a few Bank Holiday cads, who had molested Miss Tiplady. It is remembered to this day with what tender ease he raised the young lady in his arms (she had fainted at the sight of his cruel usage of the young men), and with what exquisite care and solicitude he bore her to the shop of M'Philtre, the Scotch apothecary. It is also remembered how, during the long summer afternoons, when there was no work in the turnip fields, he wold roost on the fence at the lodge gates; and it is on record also that Miss Tiplady was the only being who was known to have raised a smile on that grim graven visage.

After her rescue from the hands of the Bank Holiday young men she had always a pleasant smile and a bow for Legs as she drove past in her neat little basket chaise,[16] accompanied frequently by her fiancée, young Algernon Gillyflower, son of the Snubley solicitor, who would bring his eyeglass to bear upon the curious figure on the fence with a languid and wooden interest. As for Legs, upon these occasions he would remove his pipe and weather-beaten "bowler" with the same movement, and a wonderful smile, like a sunburst, would obliterate all the hard lines and grizzles which time and carking care had sown upon his case. It is well within my memory that on one summer's afternoon I met the basket chaise in the Lodge-road, and fully a couple of minutes afterwards I came to Legs on the fence, still transfigured with a smile.

Tempora mutantur.[17] The Brick Fields were no more, for the suburb of Snubley was built over, and Face's occupation was gone. Mr William Cherry also stumbled upon evil times, for there came to the Suburb a Respectable Temperance Chimney Sweep, who was a bit of a Poet withal, and of a humorous turn, as witness his prospectus: –

> Henry Snooks does live here.
>   He sweeps chinmeys.
> His charge is not dear
>   If your chimney is on fire
> He will put it out at your desire.
>   Chimneys swept with the
>   Most Improved Machines
>   Or climed.
> All orders Town or
>   Country punctually
> Attended by your
>   Humble servant
>   H Snooks
> Temperance Chimney Sweep, and dealer in Black Flour.

Snooks secured the Church Patronage. He swept the chimneys of the Honourable and Reverent Septimus Sidebotham; he swept the chimneys of all the Respectable Automata, and Cherry, whose lucid intervals had been growing smaller by degrees and beautifully less, became a hopeless castaway. He and Face now joined Legs in the Turnip Field, and the trio entered into an offensive and defensive alliance. As Mr. Wellbeloved-the-Family observed in the smoking-room of the Black Bull (*the* respectable Hotel), such an unholy triple alliance boded no good. He was right. The next day, Farmer Purpletop's Prize Turnip disappeared, and for the next two days the Society of Snubley was agitated and shaken by the great Turnip mystery.

There was no gainsaying that Farmer Purpletop was a hard taskmaster; but, at the same time, he worked very hard himself, and it was not known upon what terms he rented his farm from Miss Tiplady's papa, Captain Tiplady. Captain Tiplady, with Mrs. Tiplady, was travelling abroad, but expected back shortly for his daughter's wedding, and also to stand as a Conservative candidate for the Snubley division of Loamshire.[18] When two days afterwards the valuable prize turnip was discovered stuck on a pole, carved by no unskilful hand into a graven image of Purpletop himself, the farmer's rage knew no bounds and, from the information received, he immediately dispensed with the services of the trio. Cherry and Face hitched their gaberdines about them, and departed for fresh turnip fields and pastures new; but Legs, like Byron's black friar that sitteth on Norman stane,[19] refused to be driven away. Summer deepened into autumn and autumn merged into grey winter, and still Legs hung about doing odd jobs, and roosted as of yore upon the fence. He often struck me as a man who was waiting for something.

As it was told to me, Miss Tiplady behaved splendidly. The horse had overpowered her, but she stuck to the reins with singular spirit; and had young

Gillyflower rendered her any assistance, there would have been no need for Legs's last deed of heroism. But young Gillyflower was only skilled in the nice conduct of an eyeglass, and before he had time to realise the position, Legs had saved the chaise from absolute destruction – brought it up short of the bridge parapet. Young Gillyflower sustained the loss of his eyeglass, a loss which occasioned him considerable grief, for he had inherited peculiar vision from his legal progenitors, and couldn't easily see straight, without artificial aid; Miss Tiplady was confined to her room for a week with shock to the system; and as for Legs, he never spake more – "home had gone and ta'en his wages"[20] long ere Miss Tiplady was about again.

* * *

Captain Tiplady delivered himself of the most noble sentiments at his daughter's wedding. He spoke of domestic virtue as peculiar and indigenous to English soil, and alluded incidentally – for the benefit no doubt of young Gillyflower – the young Tobias.[21] I read shortly afterwards (for I had left Snubley) of his triumphant return for the Subley division. It would be nearly a year afterwards that I came across Face, rather pinched of feature, and not nearly so rubicund of visage. I told him of Legs's fate, and how Captain Tiplady at the wedding breakfast had, amongst other things, regretted, with some emotion, that he could not meet and thank the man who saved his daughter's life. "It's p'raps as well for the Capting," said Face, with a dark expression, "as he didn't meet him." "Why?" I asked. "Why!" retorted Face, "because Miss Tiplady ain't no more a daughter of the Capting's than she is of yourn." "Then, whose daughter is she?" I demanded. "Why, she was Legs's daughter, that what she wawse." "Legs's daughter!" I exclaimed with astonishment, "Did he tell you so?" "No, he didn't tell nobody nothink. I heerd it from a man in his regiment I met last winter in the – the Workus.[22] He knew Long Jinkins well, and he said as 'ow there wasn't a finer soldier in the —— army, till the Capting tuk his missus and kiddie away. 'Twawsn't the missus he so much minded, but he was fond of the little kiddie, and that broke him up, and he tuk to drink."

* * *

This is an unpretentious story, without any claim to particular merit save Truth – if that can be called a merit in these latter days. Legs sleeps his last sleep in the Parish reservation of Snubley Cemetery, and it is to be hoped that after life's fitful fever he sleeps well. No storied urn or animated bust marks his resting place, and perhaps it is as well, for if all men's lives were laid bare, few would be found worthy an epitaph.

Ed. Carpenter, 'Saved by a Nose' (1892)

Late in the summer of 1871 I and a friend of mine passed through Paris. The Treaty of Peace[1] had only been signed a few weeks before. The city was quiet. People sat out at the cafés, and sipped their *absinthe*[2] as though nothing had happened. But it was an extraordinary sight. A large part of the Rue de Rivoli lay thrown forward – high buildings and handsome shop fronts – a mass of ruins in the street. Behind were scarred precipices of rear-walls, and jagged and torn floors blackened by petroleum and explosives. The Vendôme column stretched its huge, dislocated joints along the ground, a witness to the hatred felt by the Commune[3] for "military glory" and the jingoism of the Second Empire. All over Paris it was the same. The Hôtel de Ville was gutted, and lifted gaunt chimneys and roofless walls to the sky. Everywhere on streets and buildings were marks of shot and shell. I knew little about revolutionary matters at that time. The word Communist was hardly more than a word to me. Farthest of all from my thoughts was it for me to be arrested as a revolutionary.

A week or two later, however, my friend and I returned homewards down the Rhine. He had to be in England immediately; I had two or three days to spare. I parted from him at a little place on the banks of the castle-crowned river, and, sending on my box to Coblentz,[4] took simply a light overcoat with me, and a few things in the pockets thereof, and set out to walk across that angle of country which lies between the Rhine and the Moselle, and which is practically quite unfrequented by the tourist, in order to reach the old historic town of Trèves.[5] I was alone, but I had a pleasant walk through a quiet sunny land of cornfields, and by evening reached a little country town, where I thought I had best pass the night. Castel was, I think, the name of the place. There was not much accommodation for the traveller, but here were two or three small inns, at one of which, somewhat thronged by country folk, I stopped. I had my supper in a corner of the room. The good people eyed me a little curiously, as being a stranger, and exchanged a few remarks with me; then I went to bed and slept.

The next morning, enquiring of mine host the further route, he told me that at one o'clock there would start a *diligence*[6] in the direction of Trèves. Then I would go by the *diligence*, and would spend the morning looking round the town and neighbourhood, I said. There was a Castle to be seen, and I sallied forth. I explored the old ruin, and then, sitting down by the wayside under a tree, pulled a book from my pocket, and began to read. Presently I heard steps as of one running. Who could want to run on such a morning as this, in this lazy, hot landscape? The feet turned the corner of the road. Lo! mine host, stout and puffy, in a wild headlong career! It flashed upon me at once, "He thinks I am off without paying my score – travelling on the cheap, eh?" And indeed he might well see colour for such a conclusion, since I had only left in pledge the smallest travelling gear – a bit of soap, and a toothbrush, and such-like articles, whose value and even whose use might well seem doubtful to him.

"Where are you going to, then?" puffed he.

"I am not going anywhere, I am sitting here, reading."

"No, but where are you going?"

"I have seen the Castle," I quietly replied, "and am coming back soon to have something to eat, and then am going by the *diligence*"; and I proceeded to order a meal in detail, thinking this would soothe him.

Not a bit of it. He was checked but not defeated. He would not go; but hung about, making aimless conversation, yet unable to come to the point. At last I had to help him out.

"You did not think I was going without paying, did you?"

"No, not exactly," he said, with a sheepish grin.

"But you would rather have me pay you now?"

"Yes – yes I would," with alacrity.

So I paid him his modest *thaler*,[7] and thought that the matter was at an end – while he went off promising to have a meal ready for my return.

But I was mistaken. The fellow must have gone direct to the Burgomaster[8] and told him I don't know what yarns. For when I returned half-an-hour later to the village, I was confronted by a Prussian soldier in a spiked helmet, who asked for my passport.

Passport! passport indeed! "Why my passport is in my box at Coblentz."

"Then you must come to the Burgomaster."

So I was marched through the village – much to the delight of the women and children – to the little town hall. The Burgomaster was the usual little round fussy German official, pot bellied, with large goggles on.

"What are you doing in this neighbourhood?' said he.

"To see the beauty of which your land is famed, I came."

But he was too old a bird to be caught.

"What is your business?"

"I am a student from England, on a holiday."

"Where is your passport?"

"I have not got it. It is in my box at Coblentz."

"This is very serious" – and the genial little man tried to look equal to his words – "There are many Communists coming over the frontiers from France, and we have strict orders to arrest them. Suspicion falls on you, and we shall have to detain you till you can identify yourself."

I could not help laughing. It seemed so comical – the fussy little Burgomaster, the other rustic officials eyeing me suspiciously, and the idea that I should be taken for a Communist – a thing, at that time, as I have said, so strange and unknown to me – I could not believe that the matter was serious.

"You are an Englishman, then?" said the Burgomaster.

"Yes."

"Examine this person in English, if you please," said he to the schoolmaster, who was present; and I was forthwith taken aside by the schoolmaster, while the others conferred from a distance on my appearance.

The schoolmaster spoke English nicely. It is, indeed, surprising how far the Germans are advanced in the matter of this kind of education – a little country place, and a schoolmaster who could talk English! Fancy the schoolmaster of an English village being expected to converse with the first *sauerkraut*-eating traveller, who might come that way in German. And then to be examined in one's own native tongue! That was a curious sensation. Luckily, he didn't go into grammar, or I should have been floored. On the whole, he seemed to be satisfied with my performance. It was, at any rate, better than my German. I, in turn, complimented the schoolmaster on his English, and that seemed to have a good effect. He communicated his impressions to the Burgomaster.

"Can you speak French?" said the latter.

I blushfully acknowledged that I could *parlez-voo*[9] a little; then immediately saw that I had made a mistake in tactics.

"That is very suspicious," – "very suspicious," he thoughtfully repeated, and then added: "I shall now take down your description – Clerk, attend to my dictation." The clerk took a bit of paper.

Blessed "description," it was this which saved me! Drawing himself up to his full height, with his shoulder to mine, and glancing up at the top of my head, he said in a loud voice:–

"Height – five feet eight" (German inches, I suppose); then, turning round, continued: "Hair – brown; forehead – medium; eyes – dark; nose –."

Now I am not especially chuff about my nasal organ, and never expect to be complimented on that particular feature; in fact, I have sometimes felt a difficulty as to how it should be properly described; and, on this occasion, I confess I was quite curious to know what epithet he would find suitable. But he hesitated not a moment.

"*Stumpf*," he shouted; "*Nase – stumpf.*"[10]

That settled it. I had not met with the word before, but it did not require a dictionary. The rest of the description was soon over; but I was seized with an almost incontrollable fit of laughter – which only increased as I pondered more and more on the marvellous expressiveness of the German language.

A reflection of my amusement appeared in the Burgomaster's eye. It seemed to me that he was beginning to think there could not be much amiss. I suppose a straightforward laugh commends itself somehow to the human heart. Perhaps he imagined a Communist to be a kind of person who never laughed.

Besides – I looked at him – was not his own nose *stumpf*? I looked again – yes, decidedly it was; there could be no doubt about it. His nose was *stumpf*. Ah! Burgomaster, you are undone!

"A fellow-feeling makes us wondrous kind."[11] He said nothing, but I was aware of a change in his mind. A secret unspoken bond had sprung up between us. After a pause, we lapsed into quite a friendly chat. Then he said he did not think under the circumstances it would be necessary to detain me. Then we talked again. Finally we parted with a friendly hand-shake, and I left the room.

But just as I was departing – and this was a pretty touch – he called me back, and said:

"But I have one favour to ask of you, and that is that you will leave this part of the country and get back to your passport as soon as possible, for *in case you are a Communist*, you see, it might be very awkward or me." By which I take it he meant that if I, being a Communist, was, after all, caught and landed by some other Burgomaster, he would naturally be severely blamed for letting me slip through the meshes of *his* net.

Good old man! I have often wondered whether beneath the folds of your capacious frock coat you did not conceal a secret sympathy with the Commune, or whether it was the *nase stumpf* alone which melted your official severity. At any rate, I shook hands with him again, and departing found myself just in time to catch the one o'clock *diligence*, by which in due course I proceeded on my way to Trèves.

M'Ginnis, 'Posterity' (1893)

The Marquis of Salisbury,[1] in a speech at Newport, last week, where he had been laying the foundation stone of the Monmouth and Newport Conservative Club, said: –

I was glad to notice that in the cavity of the stone which I had the honour of laying records, in the shape of local newspapers were inserted, giving an account of our recent proceedings in this part of the world. I wonder what the critic, the antiquary who some 2,000 years hence – (laughter) – shall disinter that stone, will think of the light that it throws on the probably forgotten and perished political events of this crisis. (Laughter.) What will he think of the policy of Home Rule? (Renewed laughter.) Let us hope that his opinion will be charitable and indulgent; but I hope that at all events his historical acumen will trace from this time and from the exertions of these constituencies a steady action in favour of the permanence of institutions which he will know have already lasted many hundred years; and that all upon which the prosperity and the moral and material predominance of England depends he will know to have been fortified and strengthened for a yet brilliant career of many centuries by the efforts of the Conservatives of Great Britain. (Loud cheers.)

* * *

WHAT THEY THOUGHT: A VISION.

Scene, a garden near Newport; period, A.D. 2893. Persons: BERTHA, GILBERT, EDMUND.

They are resting under an apple-tree.

Edmund: Where are the papers, Gilbert, which you found under the old stone of the horse-trough?

Gilbert: They are here. I have wrapped the cart grease in them.

Edmund: Keep them, I beg.

Gilbert: Nay, the outer sheet is unsoiled: take it.

Bertha: What are the Papers, Gilly?

Gilbert: On! some fusty old records: 19th century, I believe. Where is Lotta this afternoon?

Bertha: She is taking the *prima donna*'s[2] part in the grand opera to-night, and has stayed at home to practise and do her half. Lisa is to prune the vines for her.

Edmund (*reading*): "Lord Salisbury, alluding to the Home Rule Bill" – who was Salisbury, Gilbert?

Gilbert: Don't know. Never heard of him. Roll me a cigarette, will you?

Edmund: Ask Bertha to roll one; I want to read these papers.

Gilbert: Bertha, roll me a cigarette.

Bertha: You don't deserve one.

Gilbert: Why?

Bertha: You have refused the Presidency when the whole people call for you.

Gilbert: It is Mansfield's turn; why should he shirk? Besides, I've promised to help Noel to perfect a new system of tanning pigskin.

Bertha: Noel's sister Laura *is* pretty.

Edmund (*reading*): "Alluding to Mr. Gladstone, his Lordship said –." Who was Gladstone, Gilbert?

Gilbert: He was an orator, I think; time of Queen Anne.

Bertha: Oh, what a dunce! Queen Anne lived in Swift's time, and Gladstone in Carlyle's. Here is your cigarette.

Edmund: What do they mean by "immutable economic laws"?[3]

Gilbert: Oh! some of their silly "taxes," I suppose.

Bertha: They must have been very stupid people. Rolf, the antiquarian – he was at our village last week mending chairs – tells me that they used to believe that if the men who did the work got enough to eat the country would be ruined.

Edmund: Nonsense, Bertha; Rolf must have been beguiling you.

Bertha: He said that only lazy people were considered honourable.

Gilbert: Ha, ha, ha!

Edmund: It is curious. Listen to this. (*Reads*) "A woman starved to death in London."

Gilbert: Was there a famine? They must have been poor farmers.

Bertha: Rolf says they were all fools. Edmund, have you seen Stella's new embroidered robe?

Edmund: No. She won her race, then?

Bertha: Yes. She is very swift.

Gilbert: She has eyes like pansies.

Edmund: And teeth like milkstones.

Bertha: Her nose is not good, though. Do you think it is?

Gilbert: Tut! She is a clever girl, and very winsome, but I'd rather spend five minutes in a waltz with you, little Bertha, than gaze on her handsome face and listen to her smart prattle for a golden June day.

Bertha: If you don't accept the presidency I will never dance with you again.

Gilbert: I never could refuse a pretty woman, but tell me, Bertie dear, who is to take care of my golden bantams?

Edmund: Bertha will. I believe you two are going to be sweethearts.

Bertha: You are over saucy, Master Edmund. I shall be glad when you start for Moscow.

Gilbert: When do you go, Neddy?

Edmund: On Wednesday, by Great Eastern express balloon route.

Bertha: How long will you be away?

Edmund: A week at least. It is a three days match.

Gilbert: Bertie, what kind of a rose is that in your hair? It is very pure in tint.

Bertha: Yes; I had it from young Pericand, the French Ambassador. I gave him a silver fret fan, one of my own make, and he gave me this in return.[4]

Edmund: Hark! That is two by the farm clock, we must go and pack those peaches.

Gilbert: Yes, indeed, let us go.

Edmund: What am I to do with these old papers?

Gilbert: Burn them. They will only litter the garden.

Bertha: There comes Lisa. We must do our work and get ready for the ball.

Gilbert: And that waltz?

Bertha: Will you accept the presidency?

Gilbert: I will accept anything if you will only –

Bertha: You silly boy; I do not care for you a bit, but you may have this rose if you wish.

Lisa: (*running up*): Here I am! What a beautiful day. Lilian is coming to the ball, and Bertrand, and Maurice. What a pretty rose. Won't it be *fun*?

Bertha: I hope Lilian will not wear that yellow satin. It does not become her.

Lisa: No; she has a velvet in three fawns, with gold lilies on it.

Bertha: O—h!

Edmund: Come girls, to work, to work!

They go off chatting and laughing towards the orchard. The papers are left smouldering on the ground.

'Citizen', 'Little Maggie's Boots' (1894)

This is a sentimental story, though it begins on the box-seat of an omnibus on Christmas Eve, and there's not usually much sentiment in an omnibus. Indeed, I usually avoid omnibuses when other conveyances are get-at-able, because, like "My Grandfather's Clock"[1] of musical memory, these scavengers of City traffic are more famed for their stoppings then their goings on. Every pedestrian is the driver's prey, and he halts therefore for everyone.

My driver was no exception to the rule. To be exact, we had stopped about twenty-seven times within the half-mile, and the result was an addition of three passengers, who, judging by the unspoken expression on their faces, were sorry they were there. Five times in as many minutes had the driver, with the aid of some infernal machine under his apron, brought us to a standstill, when at last the patience of the patient outsiders was exhausted, and a unanimous protest arose from without, together with vigorous language from the insiders, and the threat that if he didn't go ahead with his darned old wagon, they'd get out and walk.

"Werry sorry, gents," said our driver, taking his foot off the infernal machine and causing it to fly with a dull thud against my shins. "I on'y stopped ter get a bite o' summat to eat from my little gal. Yer see, we're so busy to-day as we've hardly time ter stop and get any, and jest has ter take a snack atween times, so ter speak. Sha'n't happen again, gents, this journey, I assures yer. Cluck, cluck.[2] Git erlong wi' yer. Look out there, Polly, my lass," to his daughter, who still stood looking up at him. "What yer waiting for now?"

"Why, mother told me ter tell yer, daddy, not ter furget Maggie's boots when yer comin' home ter-night. She's a deal better ter-day, un she's expectin' 'em."

"Right yer are, lass. I'll not forget, never fear. Tel the mother ter keep yez awake till I come home ter-night. I wunts ter see yez all together for once in twelve months. I'm a-goin' ter surprise yer. Cluck, cluck. Geralong wi' yer, mi beauties."

"My good man," said the left-hand box seat, who had been loudest in the manifestations of impatience, "are you serious in your statement that you have not seen your family altogether this twelve months?"

"Why, bless yer 'art, in coorse I am!" said the driver. "Sometimes I don't see any on 'em awake for a fortnight, 'cept Polly, who brings me a snack on the road

– like this yer. They're in bed when I goes out at mornin'; they're in bed agen when I comes 'ome at night, except the little sick 'un, Maggie, as sometimes keeps me awake at nights. She's sich a weak, ailin', poor little mite! Would yer believe it, gents, I've bin so weary on this box many a time as I've had ter trust to the 'osses on the last journey 'ome many times? But I'm a-goin to see 'em all together ter-night. There's a bit of a jollification on account o' the night it is, and I'm a-goin' ter present my little sick chick wi' a pair o' boots, wi' pearl buttons on, as she's been talkin' about for the last three months, and I've been a-promisin' to her. Sir, it'll do me good to see how she'll henjoy it."

By this time most of the outsiders had got off the 'bus, and there only remained myself and the left-hand seat, whom I learnt afterwards was a much-despised, much-abused publican. We were nearing the terminus, and the left-hand seat got up to get off, and as he did, he leant over and shook hands with the driver, whispering as he did so, "For little Maggie's boots." And as he made his way along the top of the 'bus to get down, I noticed a suspicion of a tear running down his fat cheeks as he passed me in the glare of a lamp.

"Now, that there is wot I calls a gentleman, that is," said the driver, turning to me and displaying what he called "a arf a thick 'un." And I – well, what could I do? Little Maggie's boots must be attended to.

* * *

I took another journey into town that night, by train this time, and came back by tram.

When nearing the terminus on the home-ward journey, our road was blocked by an omnibus right across the track. "Horses down," someone said. "Driver hurt," said another. "Awful gash in the head; they've sent for the ambulance."

It came up just as I got out to see what really was the matter. The horses were on their feet, little the worse for their tumble. The driver was my acquaintance of the previous journey, smashed almost beyond recognition.

He had, as usual, felt weary, and trusted to the 'osses, and here, opposite the stable, the horses had stumbled and thrown him off the box among their plunging heels.

I should not have known him but for a parcel which a bystander handed to the man in charge of the ambulance. It had fallen amongst the horses' feet, and had burst open. And as I looked, there dropped out a pair of wee, shiny leather articles, with splashes of blood here and there on the pearl buttons of little Maggie's boots.

J. Bruce Glasier, 'Telby Torbald: or, A Socialist Transformed' (1895)

Telby Torbald was a Socialist, and lived in the town of Baleston.

[Discriminating readers will, I hope, duly appreciate the cunning with which I have devised the name and place of abode of my hero, so as to render it impossible for them to identify him among their friends. Let them beware, however, that he does not live nearer their own than their neighbour's doorstep.]

Well, Telby was, as I have said, a Socialist, and one, too of almost appalling earnestness and zeal.

From the day on which the sparks of economic truth that flew from the anvil of a street-corner agitator's tongue, set fire to the combustible material of his soul, he became a new man.

Hitherto he had not cared a clipping of his finger-nail about his own or his fellow's plight either in this world or the next. He had even refused to join his trade union, because the very thought of having in any way to acknowledge concern for matters outside working for his pay and spending it afterwards was intolerable to him. Whenever any conversation was raised upon political or social subjects he had never deigned even to express opposition, he had merely turned away from those who engaged in it, as from people for whom he felt too much contempt for words.

But no sooner had his convictions taken fire with the notion of Socialism than, as by a miracle, all Telby's thoughts and activities, which his employer did not scoop up in the factory, rushed as it were from the pole of political apathy to the most extreme pole of public activity. He at once joined his trade union, and turned up at its meetings with almost unbecoming regularity and obtrusion. He put his name down on the roll of the local Socialist Society, and in less than a month was wrestling with the duties of its literature secretaryship. He quarrelled with all his old friends and most of his shopmates[1] because they would not turn Socialist, hardly giving them a day to consider the matter. He even came to loggerheads with his wife because she failed to discern the supreme and overpowering urgency and virtue of his new enthusiasm, and because she would not declare that she perceived clearly the logic of some of his assertions, about which he was, for the moment, not altogether certain himself.

For a year or two Telby went into the work of propaganda with a headlong rush, hardly taking time to breathe as one might say, and his name became known all over the town as the most turbulent spirit in the district.

It cannot, however, be truthfully asserted that the success of Telby's efforts for Socialism was proportionate to the quantity he put forth. Indeed, it might, without any degree of inaccuracy, be affirmed that the more Telby tried to shove Socialism forward the further back it rebounded. There was something in the way he attempted to do things that invariably excited resistance and recoil among those with whom he sought to deal. The members of his trade union, for example, had to a man sworn that they never would become Socialists so long as Telby was one.

When it is borne in mind that at the second meeting which he had attended, he had announced that he rose to speak not as a Trades Unionist but as a Socialist – that in his opinion Trades Unionism was not worth a damn, and that he had only joined them to compel them to join him – when I say we remember that it was thus that he heralded the dawn of the Social Revolution in their midst, their detestation of him and his "blasted Socialism" is not much to be wondered at.

In fact, Telby became a kind of social terror in the neighbourhood.

Not only did the members of the Town Council, his trades union, and other public bodies regard him with fear – perhaps more with hatred than fear – but even the members of his own Socialist society harboured rebellious inclinations towards him.

At public meetings where the vast majority of the audience were not Socialists his proposals were invariably voted, or rather howled, down irrespective of their merits, simply because they were proposed by him. At Socialist meetings his suggestions were always adopted, in a like way, irrespective of their merits, because when the members thought to reject them, he either threatened to resign or give such undue bother, that for peace and propaganda's sake, they gave in to him.

It must thus be confessed that Socialism had not so far wrought any favourable change in Telby's personal disposition. Rather must it be written that, for most common purposes of everyday life, his character had suffered deterioration. Night after night in incessant disputation and conflict had sharpened the less amiable points of his nature, and his friendly impulses had dwindled from lack of use. Even his former lazy, good – if some what dull – humour had grown sour, and his face, though bearing a much more intellectual cast than formerly, had acquired an aggressive, almost forbidding, aspect. His comrades found it hard to retort when some of their Liberal or Conservative workmates threw at them remarks like, "Well, if that lunatic Telby Torbald is a sample of the pleasant company you are going to have under Socialism, Heaven pity you!"

And so it came to pass – and there was no blinking the fact – that Telby was becoming as much a nuisance to his friends as to his foes. Indeed, many of the members of the branch had fallen away simply because, as one of them somewhat brutally put it, "It had come to the point that they must either break Telby's jaw or break up the branch." To add to the accumulation of his offences, he had on many occasions failed to turn up at his workshop by reason of his staying out beyond midnight, arguing some little matter to utter extermination with his comrades. His friends, indeed, expected every day that he would be dismissed from his job, with little likelihood of getting another, and when they ventured to hint to him as much, he only replied, "What the devil do I care?"

There is, however, a divinity that shapes the course of Socialism, rough hew it how we may.

One night Telby attended a Town Council election meeting. For days beforehand he had been preparing a series of questions with which to transfix the moral and intellectual vitals of the candidate. He had obtained a list of the candidate's attendances and votes at the council during the past year, and was in high fever of excitement when he went purposely late into the meeting.

When the candidate had delivered his address, and the chairman had invited questions, Telby, deeming his task of far too grave importance to be accomplished from the body of the hall, rose and tramped up to the platform. Perhaps it was owing to the weight of responsibility that lay upon his mind, and perhaps – if I dare suggest such a thing – it was owing partly to the solid measure of his self-consciousness; any way, it was remarked jeeringly by his opponents, and with humility by his friends, that the noise his feet made upon the floor was unnecessarily loud and declaratory.

"I want to ask the candidate," he shouted, "the following questions *ser-i-at-im*!"[2]

"Yes, we know *you hate him*!" echoed a voice from the gallery.

"Is it the case that the candidate admitted in committee that he was not aware whether the sub-inspector of police was paid £190 or £195 a year?

"Is it the case that the candidate said that he has never read up all the Acts of Parliament bearing upon the duties and powers of municipal councils and the decisions of the higher courts affecting the interpretation of the same?"

But I am not going to set forth all Telby's list of questions, nor the replies given by the candidate amid the uproarious approval of the vast majority of the meeting. My readers have heard them put in more or less the same fashion, and answered more or less in the same terms, dozens of times. What happened after the meeting was over is of much more importance.

When Telby got home an hour after midnight he discovered that a neighbour woman was sitting with his wife by the bedside. She was a burly woman, and eyed Telby with a contempt that hurt him. His wife greeted him with the words:

"We have waited for you so long, Telby! You must go for the doctor: Roby is in a high fever. I wish you had gone last night when I asked you."

"How could I go last night?" replied Telby, surlily. "I was kept at a meeting till after twelve o'clock. Are you sure he needs a doctor? Maybe he'll be better tomorrow."

"You said that last night, and he is worse to-day. If you don't go, I shall."

"Oh, I'll go." Telby muttered ill-naturedly; "but it's a long road, and –"

"Yes," interrupted his wife, "nearly half as far as your meeting was to-night."

Telby went off, left his message for the doctor, and was wending his way home thinking over things.

Suddenly he stopped – a strange sensation came over his brain, and it seemed as though a thought had leapt right out of it, and stood before him like an apparition. He could not recognise the shape for the moment, as he did not dare to lift his eyes from the ground. He felt, however, the vision was familiar to him.

It was the Spirit of Socialism.

"Telby," the Spirit said.

"Yes," Telby replied, with evident foreboding.

"I am going to put a series of questions to you *seriatim*."

Telby's heart beat hard.

"My questions are these," the Spirit continued: "How many times have you attended the meetings of your children at home during the last year?

"How many times have you sat down to speak to them or teach them?

"How many times have you taken your wife and children for a walk in the country, or to a theatre, concert, or other place of amusement?

"How often have you made promises to do things at home, and have failed to fulfil them?"

It is unnecessary to record Telby's answers and excuses to these questions. They are not worth printing.

But the Spirit pressed him further:

"How often, Telby, when you have gone to public meetings or to meetings of your branch, have you done so because you felt you could do good, and how often have you gone because you simply liked to enjoy yourself in that way? Is it, think you, necessary for you to be always acting in public, and trying to do everything yourself and having your own way over your comrades? Is there no one willing to share the good work with you? Is there no one among your comrades has any wisdom but yourself?"

At these last words, Telby took heart a little; he thought he had found a corner in them wherein he could justify himself. But when he looked up at the

Spirit, its face was so wonderfully bright and noble, and its eyes so luminous and kind, that Telby's head drooped again.

"If I did not do the work," he mumbled, "nobody else would do it. And even if they would, they are so stupid, they always do things wrong."

"Telby," the Spirit said firmly, "give me your eyes. Telby, you are a bit of a humbug." Telby winced.

"Don't you see, Telby, that if you insist upon doing all the work yourself, you give no one else a chance to do any of it? Don't you see that if you force all your proposals upon your comrades, you crowd theirs out? Don't you perceive that if you insist that you have all the enthusiasm and wisdom, you as plain as tell the rest they are no use, and thereby discourage the growth of initiative and capacity in them? Telby, I must speak plainly to you – you are a despot, a boss, a survival of Feudalism, and an individualist. You have yet to become a Socialist."

"Must I then become less active, less enthusiastic?" Telby ventured to ask in a voice full of misgiving. "Must I become lukewarm and indifferent? Even Christ said 'Leave father and mother and follow Me, and let the dead bury the dead.'"

"Yea," said the Spirit, "but He did not say, 'Let the living bury the living'; he did not say, 'Let father and mother leave their children.' He called the children also, and He taught them. He was not always at public meetings in the Temple or on the roadside. He visited houses in a friendly way, sat at feasts and marriages, and was kindly and companionable with His fellows. Have you read of Garibaldi, Telby? How, fighter as he was, he nursed and cared for his wife, and was jolly with his comrades and took much interest in simple affairs? Have you read of Sir Thomas More? Have you read how playful and gracious all real heroes and true martyrs have been? Finally," added the Spirit, after a pause, "go home, Telby, and don't be afraid to be a good father and husband, as well as a good Socialist. Think less of yourself and more of your comrades; less of what you can do yourself for the cause and more of the cause itself."

And so in very short time he had the joy of seeing how that, with less force of effort, he accomplished much more. How that work done sweetly, graciously, and even artistically, accomplished in propaganda, as in engineering or carpentry, twenty times more in the end than work done with noise, temper, and self-assertion. He became beloved, not feared, by his friends; respected, not hated, by his unconverted mates in the workshop; and Socialism, which before had counted only a dozen active or thinking men in his branch, now counted several hundreds, all good and capable workers.

And may the Lord bless the reading of this word!

Margaret McMillan, 'Mary's Lover' (1896)

At eight punctually the bell rang for supper at the Working-girl's Home in — Street. There was a sound of many feet in the corridor and stairs; the drawing-room emptied itself as suddenly as an upturned box. Mary, who had been writing at a table near the window, put her papers together and rose. There was no one in the room besides herself but the lady superintendent, who had come in hurriedly, her grey curls waving rather wildly, her cap-strings flying behind her.

"Mary Muse," said the asthmatic old lady, "there is a *man* in the sitting-room for *you*."

Mary's dark eyes were fixed on the superintendent's absently, for a moment. Then her eyebrows were raised slightly. She smiled.

"What! A man!" she said, holding her little locked desk by the strap, and advancing a step or two. "What can he want with me? I know nobody in London."

The superintendent gazed judicially through her glasses at Mary. "It is very possible you know no one in London, my dear," she said, putting her small mittened hand on Mary's, "but it is certain that many people – objectionable people; dirty and dangerous people – know you. I am told that you have spoken in public!"

"Oh, no! Not in public; in dirty little rooms, up dark stairs, to a handful of men – and women. Not in public," said Mary.

The superintendent was horrified. "Worse and worse! My dear, are you losing self-respect? Oh, in dark rooms! And you dare to tell me that quite openly! I hear the bell ringing for prayers. Go downstairs at once. I will dismiss the man."

"No," said Mary, quietly; "this man may want me. I will see him. You can come to us in the sitting-room after prayers, Matrona."

The superintendent, flurried by the noise of contending bells, did not stop to argue the point with this troublesome inmate of the Home. Perhaps she had an instinctive faith in the young girl, who was none the less to her a profound mystery. She left the room suddenly, leaving Mary to act as she pleased.

Mary went down the corridor with light, quick steps. As she opened the sitting-room door she heard the hum of the hundred girls below who were praying together. "Thy kingdom come! They will be done on earth as it is in heaven!"

A cold smile was on her lips when she stepped into the room. It was a shabbily-furnished apartment, with a large gasalier.[1] Near the stained mantel-piece sat a young man with fair hair and a vast expanse of forehead. His light blue eyes were very widely opened. His thick, moist lips were more or less concealed by a scanty but long moustache. He did not trouble to rise when he saw Mary, but addressed her immediately in a loud, unceremonious voice.

"Good-evenin', Miss Muse. My mother's took a fancy to ye. She wants ye to come along and drink a dish o' tea with her. Saw you last night in Rowker's Close room, where you was a 'oldin' forth, ye know."

The last words were spoken with a glance of jocular familiarity which met Mary's calm, fresh gaze as a rush of puddle water might meet the spray of the polar seas.

"Is your mother ill?" she said, gently.

"Not she! Strong and hearty. An' I never knowed her to take a fancy to anyone before. She ain't *given* to fancies. And to think as she should ha' took to *you*, now," pursued the gentleman, "as is one o' them new-fangled women[2] – if you'll excuse me bein' so free – is singular. But there ain't no accountin' for wimmen-folks, old *or* young."

"No," said Mary, thoughtfully, looking into the fire.

She was silent for a moment; so was the young man. Within the last minute or two he had become a little uneasy. The stillness of the young face, so soft and yet so resolute, seemed to fall on him like a cold hand. He had expected her to talk a great deal – to move noisily – to begin to argue with him. And she sat with her little hands folded, and a hush around her – much as though the atmosphere were a sea, and she had stilled it. He twisted his hat round; he glanced around him furtively. Finally he reflected that he was not going to be afraid of a petticoat.

"Well," he said, in a loud, authoritative voice, "I reckon ye'd better be gettin' yer hat on."

Mary rose at once and went to get ready. When she was returning through the corridor she met the panting "Matrona".

"My dear," said that lady, leaning heavily on the rail, and breathing with great difficulty, "where are you going now?"

"I shall be back in an hour," said Mary, straightening Matrona's cap – an action which would have appeared as presumptuous to the other girls as the meddling with the alter fringe.

"Tell me one thing," gasped Matrona; "tell me, my dear child, if you are engaged to this young man. Ah! My cough is coming on again – I ought not to run up these stairs; and really, my dear, you might be more considerate. Is he your lover, anyhow?"

Mary looked grave.

"I don't know," she said thoughtfully; "I have never had a lover, Matrona. This may be one, of course. Anyhow, I had better go to see."

"But, child," said Matrona, gasping again, "I think you must be mad. Do you know anything of him, his friends, his parents?"

"How can I know anything of him, dear Matrona, if I have never seen him?" said Mary, with pardonable impatience. "He has come to beg me to call on his mother."

"Well, that's strange. It looks like a plot. You mustn't go," said Matrona; but the young girl was already gone. She was tripping down the dim corridor with her light step. Matrona looked at her in amazement for a few moments. The she raised herself up, and went back to the drawing-room.

"Primrose," she said to a snub-nosed young girl, who sat her sewing, "here is your cousin going out – with a young man."

Primrose raised her clear blue eyes, and looked at the superintendent. "Let her go," she said, softly; "she always does the right thing, Matrona."

Meantime, Mary was standing on the sitting-room hearthrug.

"I am ready," she said to the young man.

He rose at once, and they went out together. The night was clear and bright. The sky was crowded with stars. Mary and the young man walked in silence. They turned down one street and then another, and still they did not speak. This silence was pleasant enough to Mary; but it disturbed the young man, who was a temperance orator.[3] He did not know why the stream of his own oratory had suddenly become locked. It was the girl's fault, he knew. He glanced at her now and then, and the sight of her quiet face always gave him a kind of noiseless shock. How did she differ from the women he was in the habit of meeting? What was there in her which was not apparently in them? The young man decided at last that it was pride, and became insolent accordingly.

"I don't like women what gets on platforms," he said, taking long strides, and pushing his hat back. "It's presumption, that's what it is. It's a woman's place to keep at home, and look after her 'usband or her brother, or her youngsters. That's what *I* think, and I don't care who knows it."

Mary glanced at him kindly. "A great many wise people think just as you do," she said.

The young man was somewhat mollified. "Well," he said, after a short pause, "why don't *you* think so, too? If you knows what them as is wiser than yerself thinks, why don't ye act accordingly?"

Mayr, jostled by a passenger, made no reply. When she rejoined her companion, she gave him one of her calm, sweet smiles.

"Do you know any woman whom you respect?" she said.

"That I do," said the young man, readily. "I knows my own mother. Bless ye, she's a prime 'un! She was left a wider with five on us to bring up. And she washed and baked and scoured, and sewed, and wore her fingers to the bone to bring us through. She's a brick, is my old mother, and if you'll believe it, I puts up now wi' her fancies and whims. That's why I came to look you up."

Mary made no answer. They were at the door of a small, red-brick house at the end of a quiet street. The front door was ajar, and on the stone floor and in the window shone the ruddy glow of a cheerful fire.

"Go in," said the young man. "The old woman's in the kitchen. When you've had yir gossip over, I'll take you home."

Mary stepped across the threshold, and entered the room. It was a kitchen-parlour, homely, clean, and comfortable. The polished tin covers and bright pewter jugs glistened on the dresser in the firelight. A drugget[4] was spread on the floor. A large wooden armchair, with red cushions, extended its arms like an old friend. A kettle sang on the fire. On the hearthrug stood an old woman of nearly seventy. She was short of stature, and her figure seemed shrunken as well as bowed. Her face was as wrinkled as a russet apple, but browned and reddened by long exposure. She wore a gown of some heavy material, which hung down stiffly in crowded pleats. A red shawl covered her shoulders. Her arms, bent by much labour, did not fall straight, but described a semi-circle, and her hands, large and swollen at the knuckles, refused to close, but remained open, as though expecting a task. Her grey eyes, faded, but lit now with a strange light, surveyed Mary steadily as she stepped in to the room.

Mary came forward slowly, and almost timidly. Her dark eyes read at the first glance the whole story of strenuous toil, of dumb effort written on every line of the aged face. She looked at the old woman, and her heart sank as though it had received too weighty communications. Her dark eyes melted, and her lips and cheeks grew suddenly pale. She took one of the open hands, and held it gently between her own.

"You wanted to see me?" she said, in a low voice.

The old woman made no answer. She was unused to any but the rudest types of beauty, and these had long ceased to move her. The dumb animals she tended had given her something of their calm. She had expected nothing for years, and now she beheld these young eyes in which a world of love kindled and streamed on her like a sun. She welcomed, though it was new to her, the light, soft touch of the hand on her own. She gazed at the beautiful young face, and the long years of painful toil were forgotten in sudden joy.

"Anyone might want to see ye, my dear," she said. "Ye do a body good."

They sat down to supper, and when the old clock above the high mantel struck ten (the hour for closing at the Home), they were close to each other, so close that one of those sudden exchanges of confidence was imminent, which are the lightning of friendship. Their eyes met, and they were silent.

"You have been a good mother," said Mary, softly.

Then from those aged eyes, so long calm and dry, two tears gathered slowly, and fell. From the dim eyes, too, a veil had fallen, so that she saw all the sweetness and glory of the young womanhood beside her – so proud, so chaste, so patient, and so rich at last.

"I done my best," she said, simply.

"'Ave you had your gossip out?" said a loud voice in the lobby, and the blue-eyed young man came in, and threw a condescending but not unkindly glace at the two women. "I told mother as 'twas a queer start o' hers to want to see *you*," he went on, laughing. "Blest if I don't think she might be wantin' soon to start talking herself."

The aged woman looked at him with her dumb eyes; the eloquent dark eyes looked at him, too, but Mary said not a word.

"No one can tell what womenfolk won't take into their heads. But I know one thing. *My* wife 'ull have to stop at home. It's a woman's place, home is."

These words were accompanied by a flattering glance of admiration. The young man, moved by his mother's love for Mary, was indeed himself not quite proof against her attractions. He drew up a chair to the fireside, and produced a copy of *Comic Cuts*[5] from his pocket.

"Oh, it is late! I must be going," said Mary, glancing at the clock, and getting up in some haste. "It is past closing time."

"You're not going alone," said the young man, gallantly. "I took you here, and I'll see you safe home. You shouldn't be out walking in the streets at such hours," he said, a little inconsequently. "It isn't a nice thing for a young girl."

"Oh, no," said Mary, absently, putting on her cloak.

"Come back again soon, my dear," said the old woman, helping her.

They were out again in the starlit streets – the man and the woman. A stream of people hurried by them. The gaslights shone in the distance, carriages filled apparently with tulle and silk (it was a first night at the opera) passed them; street vendors hawked their wares, beggars implored in dim corners for alms, blind men stood upright in dark corners like sentinels of misery. And in spite of the tumult of the street and the jostling of the passengers, the young man continued to expound to Mary his opinions as to the place, functions, limitations, and deserts of women. The stream of words flowed on like the stream of people, and to Mary nothing in it was distinguishable; it was swallowed up by other words, unspoken, yet clear enough, that seemed to ring from the presence of the aged woman in the clean kitchen where the pewter dishes shone, and the floor was white through much scrubbing; words broken by sighs for the powers that had waned over the washing tubs, and the faculties that had shrivelled in an atmosphere of petty cares; words mingled with Desire that outlived failure, withstood age, rose conscious and clear when Desire ought to have been failing.

Nevertheless, the young man was emphatic. He, too, had a purpose. He expressed a desire also – namely, that Mary would walk out with him next Sunday. They were standing at the door of the "Home" when he proffered this request, which Mary very gently declined.

"I will go instead to see your mother," she said.

She could say no more, for Matrona came personally to the door to admit her. She had a shawl on her heard – a sure sign of great mental disturbance. She dismissed the young man with a frigid nod, and led Mary into the big empty drawing room.

"What do you mean, child?" she said, looking very angry. "Do you know that your conduct is disgraceful? To stay out so late – and where have you been during the evening?"

"It's all right, Matrona!" said Mary, taking off her hat wearily. Matrona looked at her steadfastly for a moment. Then this astute woman calmed down wonderfully.

"Well – and this young man?" she said. "What did he want with you? Why did he ask you to walk out with him? You have brought back my cough – I sat up in the cold, you know. Don't do this again, or I shall be obliged to complain to the managers. You are a favourite of mine, but I can't stand *this* you know. It's too much."

"I can go in the day time," said Mary, taking off her hat, and removing her hair-pins absently.

"To say this to my face! You are getting insolent, Mary – you, a well-brought-up girl!"

"It takes a long time to learn to do anything well," said Mary. "I am brought up, it is true. And so is he. And you are brought up, Matrona. We are all brought up – wonderfully!"

"My dear, do you mean to say *my* graining was not excellent?" said Matrona, getting indignant. "My father was a god-fearing man, and my mother never left her home except to go to church or market. She wouldn't have spent an hour in reading or in recreation of any kind. She was a model woman. But you have such strange notions. You think you can teach us old people something, I daresay – we who were capable women before you were born. It takes a long time to gather wisdom – a very long time, indeed, my dear child."

"I know it. It takes *ages* to *get bright pewter*," said Mary, taking up her candle.

Matrona opened her eyes. The words seemed so mad. But Mary often said mad things, and to-night she was plainly very tired. Matrona, for her part, was cold, and disinclined for more talk. She took up her candle, drew the shawl tightly round her head, sneezed, and went off to bed.

"Well, she has a lover!" she said to herself as she closed her bedroom door. "It can't be helped. She is pretty enough. He had to come sooner or later."

Louis Becke, 'A Touch of the Tar Brush' (1897)

Dr. Te Henare Rauparaha, the youngest member of the New Zealand House of Representatives,[1] had made his mark, to a certain extent, upon the political life of the colony. Representing no party, and having no interests but those of the Maori race, he seldom rose to speak except on questions of native land-grants, or when similar matters affecting the Maori population were under discussion. Then his close, masterly reasoning and his natural eloquence gained him the most profound attention. Twice had he succeeded in inducing the House to throw out measures that would have perpetrated the grossest injustice upon certain Mori tribes; and ere long, without effort on his part, he became the tacit leader of a small but growing party, that followed his arguments and resisted tooth and nail the tendency of certain Ministers to smooth the path of the land-grabber and company-promoter. Later on in the session his powers of debate, undeviating resolution, and determined opposition to Governmental measures that he regarded as injurious to the natives began to make Ministers uneasy; and although they cursed him in secret for a meddling fool and mad-brained enthusiast, they no longer attempted to ride rough-shod over him in the House, especially as the Labour members, who held the balance of power, entertained very friendly feelings towards the young man, and gave him considerable support. Therefore he was to be conciliated, and accordingly the curt nods of recognition, which were all that were once given him, were exchanged for friendly smiles and warm hand-grasps. But Rauparaha was not deceived. He knew that in a few evenings a certain Bill to absolutely dispossess the native holders of a vast area of land in the North Island would be read, and that its mover, who was a Government member, was merely the agent of a huge land-buying concern, that intended to re-sell the stolen property to the working people on magnanimous terms for village settlements;[2] and although sorely afraid at heart that he would have to bear the brunt of the battle in opposing the Bill, the young doctor was hopeful that the Labour members would eventually come to his support when he exposed the secret motives that really had brought it into existence. But he did not know that the Labour members had already been "approached," and had given promises not to support him and not to vote against the measure; otherwise some concessions regarding railway contracts, which the Government were prepared to make to the great Labour party, would be "matters for future consideration" only. And, therefore, rather than offend the Government, the honest men agreed to let Dr. Rauparaha "fight it out himself agin the Guv'mint," and "ratted" to a man. Every one of their number also expected to be appointed a Director of a Village Settlement, and were not disposed to fly in the face of a Providence that would give them each a permanent and comfortable billet, especially as their parliamentary career was doomed – not one of them had the faintest hope of re-election.

And so Dr. Rauparaha made the effort of his life, and the House listened to him in cold and stony silence. From the first he knew that he was doomed to failure, when he saw two or three of his once ardent admirers get up and sneak out of the Chamber; but, with a glance of contemptuous scorn at their retreating figures, he went on speaking. And then, at the close of an impassioned address, he held up in his right hand a copy of the Treaty of Waitangi.[3]

"And this, honourable members, is the solemn bond and testimony of a great nation, the written promise of our Queen and her Ministers to these people that their lands and their right to live in their country should be kept inviolate! How has that promise keen kept? Think of it, I pray you, and let your cheeks redden with shame, for the pages of this Treaty are blotted with the blackest treachery and stained a bloody red. And the Bill now before the House to rob and despoil some hundreds of native families of land that has been theirs before a white man ever placed his foot in the country is the most shameful and heartless act of all. I may say 'act' because I recognise how futile is my single voice raised on behalf of my race to stay this bitter injustice. Rob us, then, but offer us no longer the ghastly mockery of parliamentary representation. Better for us all to die as our forefathers have done, rifle in hand, than perish of poverty and starvation on the soil that is our only inheritance.

"Rot!" called out a short, fat man wearing a huge diamond ring and an excessively dirty white waistcoat. This was the Minister for Dredges and Artesian Bores, a gentleman who hoped to receive a C.M.G.ship[4] for his clamorous persistency in advocating the claim of the colony to "'ave a Royel dook as its next Governor."

"Shut up!" said an honourable member beside. "Rauparaha doesn't talk rot. You do – always."

The Minister muttered that he "didn't approve of no one a-usin' of inflammetery langwidge in the 'Ouse," but made no further remark.

Rauparaha resumed his seat, the proposer of the Bill made his reply, and the House voted solidly for the measure.

* * *

That evening, as the young man sat in his chambers gazing moodily into the glowing embers of the fire, and thinking bitterly of the utter hopelessness of the cause that lay so near his heart, his door opened and Captain Francis Brewster, a member of the House and a favoured protégé of the Government, walked in, and held out his hand.

"How are you, doctor?" and he showed his white teeth in a smile of set friendliness. "I hear you are leaving Wellington at the close of the session for the North Island. I really am sorry, you know – deuced sorry – that your splendid speech was so quietly taken this afternoon. As a matter of fact, both — and — have the most friendly feeling towards you, and, although your political opponents in this matter, value and esteem you highly."

"Thanks, Captain Brewster," answered Rauparaha, coldly. He knew this polished gentleman, who was a mere tool of — and —, the two most powerful and brainy Ministers in the colony, had been sent to him merely to smooth him down. Other land-grants had yet to come before the House for discussion, and the young Maori member, although he stood alone, was not an enemy to be despised of treated with nonchalance. One reason was his great wealth, the second his influence with a section of the Press that attacked the Government native policy with an unsparing pen.

However, he asked Brewster to be seated; and that gentleman, twirling his carefully trimmed moustache, smiled genially, and said that he should be delighted to stay and chat a while.

"By-the-way, though, doctor," he resumed, suavely, "my people – my aunt and cousin, you know – have heard so much of you that I have promised to take you down to our place for a few days, if I can induce you to come. They were both in the gallery yesterday, and took the deepest interest in your speech. Now, my dear fellow, the House doesn't meet again till Tuesday. Come down with me to-morrow."

"Thanks," and the doctor's olive features flushed a deep red. "I will come, I think I have fired my last shot in Parliament, and intend to resign, and so do not care much whether I ever enter the House again. And I shall have much pleasure in meeting your aunt and cousin again – I was introduced to them some weeks ago."

"Were you now?" and Brewster smiled sweetly again. "Then you won't come as a stranger. Now, I must be off. I shall call for you after lunch to-morrow."

As Captain Brewster threw himself back in his cab and smoked his cigar, he cursed vigorously. "Damn the cursed half-breed of a fellow! He's clever enough, and all that; but what the devil Helen can see in him to make me invite him down to Te Ariri,[5] I don't know. Curse her infernal twaddle about the rights of humanity and such fustian.[6] Once you are my wife, my sweet, romantic cousin, I'll knock all that idiotic bosh on the head. It's bad enough to sit in the House and listen to this fellow frothing, without having to bring a quarter-bred savage into one's own family. However, he's really not a man to be ashamed of, so far as appearances go … And I must humour her. Five thousand a year must be humoured.[7]

* * *

"Well, Helen, and what do you think of your savage?" said Mrs. Thornton to her niece, late the following evening, as she came to the door of Helen's room before she said good-night.

The girl was lying on a couch at the further end of the room, looking through the opened window out into the shadows of the night. The pale, clear-cut face flushed. "I like him very much, auntie. And I have been thinking."

"Thinking of what, dear?"

"Wondering if my father ever thought, when he was leading his men against the Maoris, of the cruel, dreadful wrong he was helping to perpetrate."

"'Cruel'! 'dreadful'! My dear child, what nonsense you talk. They were blood-thirsty savages."

"Savages! True. But savages fighting for all that was dear to them – for their lands, their lives, their liberties as a people. Oh, auntie, when I read of the awful deeds of bloodshed that are even now being done in Africa by English soldiers, it makes me sicken. Oh, if I were only a man, I would go out into the world and –'

"My dear child," said the older lady, with a smile, "you must not read so much of – of Tolstoy and other horrible writers like him. What would Francis say if he thought you were going to be a Woman with a Mission? Good-night, dear, and don't worry about the Maoris. Many of them are real Christians nowadays, and nearly all the women can sew quite nicely."

Outside on the gravelled walk the young Maori doctor talked to himself as he paced quickly to and fro. "Folly, folly, folly. What interest can she have in me, except that I have native blood in my veins, and that her father fought our people in the Waikato thirty years ago."[8]

* * *

Brewster had gone back to town for a day or two; but as he bade his aunt and cousin good-bye, he warmly seconded their request to the doctor to remain at Te Ariri till he returned, although he swore at them both inwardly for a pair of "blithering" idiots.[9] And as he drove away to the station he congratulated himself on the fact that while his fiancée had a "touch of the tar-brush," as he expressed it, in her descent, her English bringing-up and society training under her worldly-minded, but yet brainless, aunt had led her to accept him as her future husband without difficulty.

For the next two days Dr Rauparaha had much writing to do, and passed his mornings and afternoons in the quiet library. Sometimes, as he wrote, a shadow would flit across the wide, sunlit veranda, and Helen Thornton would flit by, nodding pleasantly to him through the windows. Only two or three times had he met her alone since he came to Te Ariri, and walked with her though the grounds, listening with strange pleasure to her low, tender voice, and gazing into the deep, ark eyes, that shone with softest lustre from out the pale, olive face, set in a wealth of wavy jet-black hair. For Helen Thornton was, like himself, of mixed blood. Her mother, who had died in her infancy, was a South American, with a quadroon strain,[10] and all the burning, ardent passions and hot blood of her race were revealed in her daughter's every graceful gesture and inflection of her low, soft tones.

* * *

It was late in the afternoon, and the young Maori doctor, pushing his papers wearily away from him, rose from his seat. His work was finished. To-morrow he would bid these kind friends good-bye – this proud English lady and her beautiful, sweet-voiced niece – the girl whose dark eyes and red lips had come into his day-dreams and vision of the night. And just then she came to the library door, carrying in her hand a portfolio.

"Are you very busy, Dr Rauparaha?" she said, as she entered and stood before him.

"Busy! No, Miss Thornton. Are these the sketches you told me Colonel Thornton made when he was in New Zealand?" and as he extended his hand for the book, the hot blood surged to his sallow forehead.

"Yes, they were all drawn by my father. I found them about a year since in the bottom of one of his trunks. He died ten years ago."

Slowly the young man turned them over one by one. Many of them were drawings of outposts, heads of native chiefs, &c. At last he came to one, somewhat larger than the others. It depicted the assault and capture of a Maori *pah*,[11] standing on a hill that rose gradually from the margin of a reedy swamp. The troops had driven out the defenders, who were shown escaping across the swamp through the reeds, the women and children in the centre, the men surrounding them on all sides to protect them from the hail of bullets that swept down upon them from the heights above the captured fortress.

A shadow fell across the face of Dr. Rauparaha, and his hand tightened upon and almost crumpled the paper in his grasp; then he smiled but with a red gleam in his dark eyes.

"The assault on Rangiriri by the 18th Royal Irish,"[12] he read.

"The brave Irish," he said, with a mocking smile, raising his head and looking intently into the fair face of the girl; "the brave Irish! So ardent for liberty themselves, such loud-mouthed clamourers to the world for justice to their country – yet how they sell themselves for a paltry wage to butcher women and children," and then he stood up and faced her.

"Pardon me, I forgot myself. I did not remember that your father was an officer in an Irish regiment."

She gave him her hand, and her eyes filled. "No, do not ask my pardon. I think it was horrible, horrible. How can such dreadful things be? I have heard my father say that the very victory filled him with shame ... He led the storming party, and when the *pah* was carried, and he saw the natives escaping – the men surrounding the women and children – he ordered the 'Cease firing' to be sounded, but –" and her voice faltered.

"But –" and the lurid gleam in Rauparaha's eyes made her face flush and then pale again.

"The men went mad, and took no notice of him and the other two officers who were both wounded – the rest were killed in the assault. They had lost heavily, and were maddened with rage when they saw the Maoris escaping, and continued firing at them till they crossed the swamp, and hid in the long fern scrub on the other side."

"And even then a shell was fired into them as they lay there in the fern, resting their exhausted frames ere they crept through it to gain the hills beyond," added the young man, slowly.

"Yes," she murmured, "I have heard my father speak of it. But it was not by his orders – he was a soldier, but not a cruel man. See, this next sketch shows the burstings of the shell."

He took it from her hand and looked. At the foot of it was written, "The last shot at Rangiriri."

His hand trembled for a moment; then he placed the drawing back in the portfolio, and with averted face she rose from the table and walked to the window.

For a moment or two she stood there irresolutely, and then with the colour mantling her brow she came over to him.

"*I* must ask *your* pardon now. I forgot that – that – that –"

"That I have Maori blood in my veins. Yes, I have, my father was a Pakeha Maori*, my mother a woman of one of the Waikato tribes. She died when I was very young." Then, in a curiously strained voice, he said: "Miss Thornton, may I ask a favour of you? Will you give me that sketch?"

She moved quickly to the table, and untied the portfolio again.

"Which, Dr. Rauparaha? The last –

"Yes," he interrupted, with sudden, savage fierceness, "the Last Shot at Rangiriri."

She took it out and came over to him. "Take it, if you wish it; take them all, if you care for them. No one but myself ever looks at them ... and now, after what you have told me, I shall never want to look at them again."

---

*   A white man who has adopted Maori life and customs.

"Thank you," he said, in softer tones, as he took the picture from her. "I only wish for this one. It will help to keep my memory green – when I return to my mother's people."

"Ah," she said, in a pained voice, "don't say that. I wish I had never asked you to look at it. I have read the papers, and know how you Maori people must feel, and I am sorry, oh! so sorry, that I have unthinkingly aroused what must surely be painful memories to you."

"Do not think of it, Miss Thornton. Such things always will be. So long as we live, breathe, and have our being, so long will the strong oppress and slay the weak; so long will the accursed earth-hunger of a great Christian nation be synonymous for bloodshed, murder, and treachery; so long will she hold out with one hand to the children of Ham[13] the figure of Christ crucified, and preach of the benefits of civilisation; while with the other she sweeps them away with the Maxim gun; so long will such things as the 'Last Shot at Rangiriri' – the murder of women and children, always be."

With bated breath she listened to the end, and then said:

"It is terrible to think of, an unjust warfare. Were any women and children killed at Rangiriri?"

"Yes," he almost shouted back, "many were shot as they crossed the swamp. And when thy gained the fern two more were killed by that last shell – a woman and a child – my mother and my sister!"

He turned away again to the window but not so quickly that he could see she was crying softly to herself, as she bent her face over the table.

* * *

Three days after, Mrs. Thornton showed her nephew a note that she had found on her niece's dressing-table:

Do not blame me. I cannot help it. I love him, and am going away with him. Perhaps it is my mother's blood. Wipe me out of your memory for ever.

Harry Lowerison, 'Auld Randy' (1899)

Around the big farmhouse kitchen fire the dogs were lying on the sanded hearth, some stretched out before the blaze and looking thoughtfully at the leaping flames, some curled up and fast asleep, and around these again the lads and lasses sat in half-circle talking softly together. It was Christmas Eve, and from snow-balling and skating they had all come in very tired, and the house-mother had bidden them rest while she prepared tea.

The nearest kirk was far to seek, and but seldom did any attend. To-morrow the roads would be impassable, because the deep snow had begun to melt, and they had found the ice to-day even on the highest reachable tarn too sloppy to be pleasant. At Easter every one took turns in sitting up with the "yowes," which, great with young and dropping lambs hourly, were all shut up in the "close"[1] round the farmstead, but generally on Christmas Day "the bairns" went over the fells and down to the old church in the little market town. This Christmas there could be no such journey, and the talk had drifted from the church to its theology.

In one chimney "neuk"[2] sat an old man, with thin grey hair and keen grey eyes. He had been tall and broad-shouldered, but he had fought the snows of many winters in his "outbye"[3] farm, and his form was bowed and shrunken, and two walking-sticks leaning against his chimney seat told of advancing infirmities. Opposite him sat Auld Randy, the farm servant, a man past middle age, his legs bowed with much riding, because the farm was large, and sheep and cattle had to be counted from the saddle. His much-wrinkled face was dry and wizened, and his eye had the wandering look that betrays what is called the "natural" or half-wit[4] in that part of the North Country. Many tales were told about Randy, and not all of them kindly. Down at Ghyllhead the children would jeer at and mock him, when he passed through the village on foot, till he turned savagely and made play with his drover's stick on their "doups" or legs. Once in his anger he had ridden down a boy who had thrown a snowball at him, and the lad bore the marks of the pony's hoof in a lame leg for the rest of his life.

They told of him how once he had stopped where a gang of men were sod-cutting by the road, and after intently regarding them for a long time had said: "Goy bon![5] Aw cud seun get sum land if aw only had a pleace to put it!"

On another occasion, when living in a little cottage by himself, he had been dreadfully troubled by a "bee byke" (wasp's nest) in the garden dyke, and had burst into a neighbour's kitchen one evening covered with stings to say: "Tam, ye ken that bee-byke i' my bit garden? Weel, aw've tried ivverything, and just noo aw hetted a kittle o' boilin' watter, and stuck the spoot intill the hole, an, wad ye believ't, man, the little divvles cam out o anither hole, and they stand that kittle spoot till it swelled sae's aw cud n't pull it oot – and it's stickin' there yet!"

But within his limitations Auld Randy had been found a faithful and willing servant at the farm, and for the house-mother and the house-mother's bairns he would have cheerfully braved Old Nick.[6]

"Ye've been at kirk, Randy?" the elder man inquired, taking his clay pipe from his lips with trembling fingers.

"Ow, aye," replied Randy; "aw've been in the cathedral at Carel (Carlisle), an' what! – ye mind, gaffer, we selled a Dumfries man twal hundred lambs in the kirk there, yance. It was a nice quiet pleace for a bit o'bisness."

"Did ye ivver hear the parson-men preach?"

"Aye! An' aw've heard them say the prayers ower the deid at the grave i' the kirk-yard."

"D'ye think they're reet when they say that God'll send men tae hell for iver an' iver if they gan wrang here?"

"Aw dinna ken. The Missus wadn't."

"Wad ye?"

"Naw! Aw ken sum wha'd be the better for a damned good ricin' (licking), but for iver and' iver, that's anither sang."

"Naebody believes 't nooadays," put in little Alf; "leastways, naebody but the Methodys[7] down at Ghyllhead. An' they dinna, or else Rob Nixon wad gie ane a fair penn'orth o' sweeties.

At this juncture a heavy step was heard in the yard, and the dogs got up and pushed through the circle of chairs. The door opened, and a tall, strongly-built man stepped across the threshold, pausing there to unwrap his grey shepherd's plaid and shake the wet snow off outside. One look as he came up to the fire was enough to identity him as the Gaffer's son. All the lads stood up, and a chair was set in the widened circle for the new comer. He sat down and filled a pipe, lit it, stretched his feet out among the dogs who had settled down again, and asked slowly:

"Hae ye had yer teas?"

"Not yit," replied Hamish, the elder lad; "Mother's just gettin' 't riddy."

"Weel, after ye've had it, ye'll a' hae tae gan roon' by the far craig and look after the sheep. There's mair than fower score I hae na counted. At three o'clock they were a' reet, feedin' west frae the quarry front. Ye canna get doon the craigs; gan roon' fra this end by the Roman Stanes, and ye'll meet them. Tak lanterns, an' mind the drifts' an' drive them up tae the beeches. There's a storm comin, but aw'm fairly daun up."

"That's all reet, uncle," said Hamish, "we'll be back in an oor. Shall we tak the dogs?"

"Naw! they'll smoor i' the drifts. The snaw's very saft, and there's a lot of starved rabbits and grouse aboot. Get your teas first."

And Uncle Will, worn out with his long walk and fighting through the snow, fell asleep before the fire.

He woke as tea was announced and spoke to the serving man:

"Randy, can ye win throo tae the far pasture an' tak the sheep tae the fauld by the Fairy Stairs?"

"Aw'll try, maister," said Randy. "We're in for a gey bad neet."

And, indeed, it was a wild night that the children encountered, as, legginged and plaided, they left the farmhouse door. Snow was falling in great white flakes that were whirled and tossed by furious gusts of wind which nearly blew them of their feet; but they were sturdy and well-fed, and laughed at the fierceness of the night.

"We'll not gan a' the way roon' by the Roman stanes," said Hamish.

(These stones were the ruins of a Roman mile-castle in a nick or break of the crags) "we cud n't face the win'; we'll gan up tae the 'Sally-port,' an' get doon tae them better."

(The "Sally-port" was a causeway which ran obliquely down the crags.)

"That way'll be chocked wi' snaw," said Will.

"Keep together," replied Hamish, "we'll get throo, some way."

But the wind howled more loudly and the snow fell more thickly as they breasted the slope, and the cold chilled them to the bone. All their known landmarks were blotted out when they reached the Roman wall on the edge of the cliff, and suddenly Alf's foot slipped from before him, and the three boys who were now hand in hand for greater safety, stumbled forward blindly and dropped through space. The still clung together, though Alf had fallen headlong; there was a crash of twigs, and they alighted on a deep drift of yielding snow. Hamish pulled at Alf's hand.

"Are ye a' reet, Alf?"

There was no answer.

"Will, are ye a' reet?"

"Aw think sae," said matter-of-fact Will, "but what aboot Alf? His heid's i' the snaw. Aw think we' better pull him oot."

The snow slipped under them. But the boys managed to raise their younger brother and tried to set him on his feet. He fell limply against them and sank down.

"Ha'e ye yer lantern, Will? I believe he's killed. Mine's lost."

All the lights had gone out in the fall; so now Hamish fumbled nervously with his matchbox, struck a light, and held it to Alf's face. It was as white as the snow. He lit the one lantern, and they set to work to rub the boy's hands. They were in a pit of snow and cramped for space, but they rubbed the cold hands and watched the closed eyes in an agony of fear, till at last they opened and a faint colour came back to the cheeks. Presently the lad smiled as, with returning consciousness, he grasped the situation: "So we've coupe door creels (come head over heels) doon the Craigs?"

"Are ye a' reet?" asked Hamish again.

"Barrin' that aw'm achin' a' ower, yis," said the other.

"Then we' better get oot o' this," said Will, and he began to fight with the snow walls that imprisoned them with hand and foot.

"Sit ye still, Alf," said Hamish, "till Will and me get oot. Then we'll help ye."

But a few minutes convinced them of the utter futility of their efforts. All they succeeded in doing was to enlarge slightly the space in which they were confined. The candle was taken from the lantern, and held up as high as Hamish could reach. Far away above their heads one branch of silver birch reflected the gleam, and the next minute a snow-flake settled on the wick and put out the light. It was re-lit and placed sputtering in the lantern.

Alf was sleepy, Hamish and Will were benumbed and weary.

"Dinna gan tae sleep, Alf, it's dangerous," said the elder. "Let's a' shoot."

They shouted together at the top of their voices till they were hoarse. Then the two elder boys took off their plaids, wrapped them round the younger, and set to work again despairingly to try to climb out. But ever they grew weary and more weary, and when the candle finally sputtered out they crept together for warmth and fell asleep.

Auld Randy meanwhile had worked his way to the sheep, and then back again to the homestead. He went first to the stable, and not finding the lanterns on their pegs knew that the bairns had not returned. A glass of whisky now! and "the missus" he knew would give it him gladly for the asking, so he went to the sitting-room door and tapped gently. The door opened slightly, and he saw her seated on her chair by the fire, her head resting on a cushion, fast asleep.

"God bless her. No!" he said to himself. "She'll be gey fleyed if I tell her the lad isn't back. Aw'll just not tell her."

He called Moss, the most intelligent of the dogs, and stepped into the storm again. His strength was nearly spent, and his steps were feeble as the dog led up the slope to the Crags.

"Good Moss," he said, "find the bairns."

At the edge of the cliff the dog stopped, sniffed, and barked. The old man thrust his stick forward and downward, and felt nothing.

"Alf!" he shouted. "Alf! Will! Hamish!"

No answer. Only the whirling snowflakes and the seep and sough of the wind.

"Back, hyam!" he said. "Back hyam, Moss, an' tell them the bairns is smoored." The dog barked again, and rushed off down the hill."

"Goy bon!" said the old man, "Aw's ganned doon, sumway," and he laid himself down of the edge of the cliff and felt for a handhold. Gaining this he let himself slightly down and felt for a foothold; for a few feet he worked himself down like this till he came to a place where no foothold could be found. He clung for some minutes desperately till he felt that, what with numbness, what with weariness, he must let go, when the snow to which he had pressed his breast as added "purchase" began to slide slowly from under him. The extra weight on his numbed fingers was too much.

"My puir missus," he said, and then next minute was shot into space, whirled round and dashed on a projecting pillar of rock far down the crag side.

Hamish was dozing. He had tried valiantly to keep awake. A heavy fall of snow on his face awoke him, and he distinctly heard old Randy's voice saying these words, then he fell asleep again till he woke and found himself in bed with Will and the House-mother's loving face bending over them.

"Where's Alf?" he asked.

"He's in the next room. Not hurt. The doctor's just gone. You're all safe."

And late next day the boys crept quietly down stairs, awed and hushed, from a room where Auld Randy lay still and solemn on his bed, his wrinkled old face smoothed out, his half litten[8] eyes for ever closed, and a half smile on this thin, set lips.

"Weel," said Alf, "Randy was drunk last Setterday neet, but if he's in hell, then I'll go there too, rather than to the other place."

JUSTICE

'Devilshoof', 'One New Year's Eve', *Justice*, 30 December 1893, p. 7.

'Devilshoof', 'On the River', *Justice*, 6 January 1894, p. 7.

C. H. V., 'One Among Many', *Justice*, 12 January 1895, p. 7 (15).[1]

Dan Baxter, 'The New Shilling', *Justice*, 23 March 1895, p. 2 (90).

Dan Baxter, 'A Monkey Story', *Justice*, 31 October 1896, p. 2.

C. S. J., 'A Fairy Tale for Tired Socialists', *Justice*, 20 August 1898, p. 6.

Justice (1884–1925) continued to be edited by Harry Quelch (1858–1913) and remained the official organ of the SDF, although sales had fallen from the periodical's peak during the Trafalgar Square demonstrations in 1887. Nevertheless, no attempt was made to draw readers in by an increase in the entertainment included in *Justice*; quite the opposite, as during the period covered by this volume, there were no long serializations published in the periodical. Low sales figures did not deter the SDF from involvement in the British socialist movement: *Justice* campaigned for unity between the SDF and the ILP in the 1890s, and a vote by SDF members in 1897 overwhelmingly agreed, but this was rejected by the ILP. The SDF also took part in the formation of the Labour Representation Committee in 1900 but withdrew soon after, unwilling to compromise its socialism to attract trade union support.

The fiction published during this period was less likely than the earlier fiction to be anonymous, as is evident in the selection for this volume: of the seven short stories, none are published anonymously, and there is only one pseudonymous author. According to Jack Mitchell,[2] 'Devilshoof' might be a pseudonym for Harry Quelch, although there is no firm evidence for this pseudonym as there is for some of Quelch's anonymous work posthumously collected and published by Ernest Belfort Bax (1854–1926). Quelch may have preferred to publish anonymously or pseudonymously in order to separate his fiction from his journalism. He was a vocal critic of the suffrage movement, and under the pseudonym 'Tattler', he engaged in a heated debate, along with Bax, against supporters of female suffrage. The authors who only published under their initials, C. H. V. and C. S. J., have not been identified during the research carried out for this project. Little is known about the only author of this selection to publish under his full name, Dan Baxter (n.d.), but he was a regular contributor to *Justice* and sometimes contributed to the ILP-affiliated periodical *Workman's Times*.

Notes

1. For the year 1895 only, the page numbers for *Justice* were given both individually for each issue and consecutively across the year; the latter is provided here in parentheses. Thus for C. H. V.'s 'One Among Many', p. 7 refers to the specific page on which the story was printed in the issue, while p. 15 refers to the consecutive pagination across the year. Similarly, for Baxter's 'The New Shilling', p. 2 is the issue pagination, while p. 90 is the year pagination.
2. J. Mitchel, 'Tendencies in Narrative Fiction in the London-Based Socialist Press of the 1880s and 1890s', in H. G. Klaus (ed.), *The Rise of Socialist Fiction* (Brighton: Harvester Press, 1987), pp. 49–72, on p. 68.

'Devilshoof', 'One New Year's Eve' (1893)

"Well, I didn't think he'd ha' turned us out on New Year's Eve. He might ha' let us seen the old year out in the old place, anyhow."

"Ah, dad, they don't care, New Year's Eve, or no New Year's Eve. There's nothing for it now as I can see but the workhouse after all."

The speakers were two men standing outside a low thatched cottage in the early darkness of the last day of the old year. A bitter east wind was blowing across the common, on the edge of which the cottage stood, and they shivered as they huddled up against the wall, while the sleet, which was fitfully falling, was driven by occasional gusts of wind into their faces.

"No," said the old man after a pause, "I'll never go there, Ned. I'd sooner die by the road-side. I've lived in this cottage, man and boy, for nigh on seventy year, and now to be turned out because I'm past workin'. It's too bad."

"Even if you weren't past working, dad, there's nothing for you to do. I could have earned enough to keep us both if I could have got the work. I'd have gone away, but I couldn't leave you dad, and you wouldn't go in the house."

"Well, it's no good standing here," he resumed. "I'm about frozen, now. Let's go down to the "Swan," we can sit there for a while in the warm, anyhow."

In the taproom of the Swan were a number of labourers, one of whom, a rough, but good-humoured looking individual, wearing a threadbare velveteen coat, on seeing them enter, beckoned Ned on one side.

"What's brought the old man out on this rough night?"

"We've been turned out. You know Joyce gave me the sack a month ago. I've had nothing to do since; and now he's turned us out of the cottage."

"Hard up, I suppose?" queried the other.

"We've just got nothing at all," said Ned, "everything has gone."

"Well, I think I can help you to something to-night. I have got to get a lot of stuff for to-morrow. I know where to find it up at Oakwood, but I want somebody to help me. Griggs and the others will be sure to keep indoors a rough night like this. You'd better come along."

Some more conversation followed, then Ned called to his father, "You can bide here for a couple of hours, dad. I'll be back again then."

Two hours later Ned and his companion were making their way out of Oakwood, each with a well-filled bag on his back. Suddenly they heard a slight rustling sound behind them. Ned's companion turned round. "By God," said he, under his breath, "it's Griggs's dog. We'll have the cursed keepers down on us directly. Come on."

They started to run, but had gone but a few paces when they were confronted by three men.

"Hullo," said one of the new comers, "so you are at it again, Jack Fitch, are you? We've copped you nicely this time. And Ned Sanders, too; I thought he was a bit of a poacher."

"You're a liar," said Ned, "I've never been poaching before, and shouldn't now if I hadn't been drove to it."

"Well, we've got you now, anyway," said the other, advancing towards Jack Fitch and laying his hand roughly on his shoulder. "You'll see the New Year in in the lock-up."[1]

"Don't you be so sure," said Jack, as with a heavy blow of his fist he sent the other sprawling on his back.

The other two keepers advanced to the help of their companion. Ned threw down his bag; for a few minutes there was a tussle, at the end of which the two poachers, having discomfited their assailants, picked up their bags and turned to run. They were on the skirts of the wood. In a few moments they had reached the road leading to the village. Just then a report rang out behind them, and Ned threw up his arms and fell on his face. He had received the whole charge of Griggs' gun in the back.

* * *

It was eleven o'clock. The party at the Swan had broken up and were now finding their way homeward. The old man still sat by the fireside.

"Come, Sanders," said the landlord, not unkindly, "You're not going to spend the night here, are you?"

The old man looked at him enquiringly – "Where's Ned?" he asked.

"I'm sure I don't know," said the landlord. "Perhaps he's gone home."

"Yes, perhaps he's gone home," The old man murmured softly, half to himself, as he walked out into the night.

The bleak wind was still blowing, though the sleet had stopped falling, and dark, heavy masses of cloud were being driven across the sky, obscuring the light of the moon. The old man wandered slowly on, back to the cottage. He raised the latch, but the door was fast.

"Ned, Ned," he cried, as he feebly rattled the door.

"Wonder why Ned doesn't come," he said to himself as he turned away in the direction of the wood. He wandered on aimlessly in the darkness till he stumbled across an object lying in the road. He stooped down and turned it over, feebly, curiously, as a child would; suddenly a wail of anguish burst from his lips, as the moonlight broke through the clouds.

"Ned, Ned, my boy, my boy!"

* * *

The church bells in the distance rang out a glad peal of welcome to the New Year, the sky had cleared, the wind was hushed and the cold bright moon looked down on the dead faces of father and son.

'Devilshoof', 'On the River' (1894)

"Why, what a perfect little Cassandra[1] you are becoming, Nell. Of course I knew the Governor would be huffed about it. But what does it matter? I rather like the idea of being independent of the old curmudgeon. Anyway, *ma Cherie*, we'll not spoil our honeymoon over it."

"Don't call me Cassandra, Phil; I don't want to be a prophetess of evil. But I cannot help being sorry to have been the cause of quarrel between you and your father. I only hope the future will be as bright as the present is. But if your father does carry out his threat, what will you do?"

"Do? Nothing easier to answer, my dear girl. Work, of course. No man with a head on his shoulders and a pair of strong arms need trouble about loss of fortune in this country. Really I think I shall be rather glad if the Governor does turn me off. I feel it would be such a pleasure to work for you, my darling. Everything we had would seem so much better. After all, work is only fun, and people would not look down on it so but for the grumbling and discontent of those lazy louts, 'the working men,' as they are called. There are some of them in that boat over yonder. Just look at the awkward figure they cut. Now see how I'll show them a clean pair of heels."

So saying Philip Danvers plied his sculls with vigour, and the little skiff which had been lazily drifting down stream under the shadow of Cliveden Woods, while he talked to the fair girl sitting opposite him, shot out in to the stream, and quickly distanced the boat to which he had directed his companion's attention.

* * *

"Ah, Nellie, my darling, I never thought it would come to this, it all seemed so bright only eighteen months ago. I thought it was easy to work, I did not know it was so hard to get work to do. It is months now since I've earned a penny. I'm sure it's not for want of trying. But everywhere it is the same. Whenever one sees the opportunity of a job, scores of others are there competing for it. Even if one gets so far as to apply for it, one is met with the objection 'not suitable.' And there are many even worse off than we are, many without even the shelter this garrett affords, who are as eager to work and as able to do anything that offers as I am. It is horrible. And you, my poor girl, you had no food all day yesterday. It is too terrible."

"Never mind me, Phil. I'm not even hungry. But you, Phil, walking about all yesterday and nothing to eat. I wish I had some food to offer you, but there's nothing in the house, and Mrs. Barnes came up for the rent. She, poor thing, has got nothing, and her boy's down with the influenza, and she wanted the money to get the doctor to him."

"I saw by a newspaper, yesterday, that my father died last week, there was no reference to me at all, and he has left all his property, it is stated, to some charity."

"Charity! What an abuse of the word, and his own son with his wife starving from want."

"Starving! Oh, Nell, don't say that. Oh, my poor girl," he cried, as he looked more closely on her face, "I'm afraid it is too true." He hurriedly left the room.

It was a cold, dark, foggy morning as Danvers made his way from the Southwark slum in which he lived to one of the wharves on the river. A crowd of men were gathering in the mist and gloom. Suddenly there was a rush towards a doorway, at which stood a man with a lantern by his side. Phil Danvers found himself carried by the rush close to this individual, who called from the crowd, whether by name or sign, such men as he required.

Danvers was among those thus selected, and in a few minutes found himself standing, with others, on the quay, along side which a steamer was lying. He was told off[2] with two others to go into the hold to sling the bags of sugar which were to be discharged onto the wharf.

It was all quite fresh to him, and he found it very difficult. A cold, chilling breeze was blowing up the river, and his fingers seemed frozen so that he could hardly handle the bags of sugar. He worked with a will, however, it seemed a pleasure to have something to do. The others occasionally glanced at him and smiled to each other. In a little while his exertions had warmed him, his back and limbs began to ache, his fingers were hot and sore. He was fagged and weary when, at twelve o'clock, his companions prepared to go ashore for dinner. They clambered up the iron ladder which led to the deck. Phil was the last to ascend. It was a long reach from the top of the ladder to the combing of the hatchway, and he could only just grasp the edge. His fingers were sore and slippery with sugar – they slipped on the smooth cold iron and he fell, with a sickening thud, backward into the hold.

They got him out and carried him to the hospital, but he never spoke again. They went to take the news to his wife and found her ill in bed. She only smiled when they told her and murmured, "Good bye, Phil, for a little while."

There were two subjects for the Coroner's inquest. On one case the jury found it was "Accidental death," in the other "Death from natural causes, accelerated by want."

C. H. V., 'One Among Many' (1895)

A searching drizzle, a murky, clammy fog, choking the hardy passenger along the High Street – yet everywhere, how two and three together, huddled under a sheltering doorway, and here one alone darting out with wanton invitation, were ranked the women of shame – the outcasts of a mighty city. I quickened my step as I passed one woman more importunate than the rest – the many were too drugged with the reeking mist to be active or impatient. I felt her hand on my shoulder and her breath on my face and made a rough effort of repulse. "For God's sake listen," she cried as she clutched at me, "Damn you, won't you listen? My child is freezing and I haven't a — — farthing for fuel or a feed. You can have me for half-a-crown and its — cheap." And she ended with a laugh, the horrible gurgled laugh of the despairing – more awful than passionate weeping – the laugh of Hell.

I turned and looked her in the face as she gripped my shoulder and swung against me. A face, what need to describe it? Pretty once, no doubt, like a hundred others, now drawn with hunger, blotched and scarred. We moved towards the entry where she had laid in ambush, one of the dark alleys which burrow behind the shops of the High Street. "Where have you left your child?" I asked aimlessly and mechanically. The question seemed to touch her, she ceased the filthy gestures, ungripped my arm, and her body shook with sobbing.

Then rousing again she pushed me away. "Go, and God damn you. I'll drown myself and her before the — — mornin' – I'll drown myself;" and then the sobbing burst out again. Little by little I found out where she lived, gave her the few shillings I had on me and asked again to see her child. She had now grown somewhat quieter, even thanked me for the money and we walked on together through a maze of dirty courts and lanes.

Soon I had all her story – a good husband maimed by a scaffold fall, a long drawn-out dying, and then widow and little daughter thrown penniless into the grinding mill of existence. The sordid, desperate details of that struggle we can hear any week at the coroner's inquest or the Guardians' board.[1] And last of all, mad with care for the innocent babe, weary of rate-wardens and charity-mongers, she sinks to the streets, and plies her ghastly trade to outward seeming like any other. But every night, she told me, and I believe her, she had knelt by the little cot screened off by an old shawl from the rest of her room – knelt there before the evening's quest and prayed with a desperate cry from her mother's heart for the child she was selling herself to cherish and rear. And over it she hung now, her sobbing hushed to the panting movement of her bosom, and watched eagerly as the light from the dirty dip in her hand shone on her little girl, tossing through the night in the feverish sleep of the starving.

For some moments I watched too, then begged her to come to my house on the morrow. Something must, could be, done for her child – for herself a brave heart and better things in the coming year. She thanked me warmly, impulsively, then, shrinking back with a blush which mantled in spite of grease and paint, begged pardon for the accosting. Pardon! I hardly kept down the bitter laugh which rose within me; we grind the hopeless and hapless, drive our women to the streets, and *then they ask our pardon*!

And as I left the stifling garret for the street outside the mist was lifting, a star shone right ahead in the cold sky and one all but felt the breathing of the dawn.

Dan Baxter, 'The New Shilling' (1895)

I do not know how long I may have lain in the womb of the earth; nor am I acquainted with any particulars regarding the men who dug me out further than that they were workers of some kind or another. Neither have I any knowledge as to what part of the world I come from as a piece of silver, nor about what class of workmen carried me to England.

But well do I remember the day when the people of this country, the British nation, gave me my start in life.

When a small shapeless mass I was taken hold of by one of the citizens, and then by another and by several others after them.

This was in what is called the citizens' mint.

I was squeezed until I almost cried, carried on endless belts, dropped, lifted, and put into one machine after another and finally placed before a very nice citizen who took me up and looked into my face.

"What have you been doing to me?" I asked.

The citizen smiled, and, answering, said unto me, "We have been putting you into a form by which you shall be recognised as a coin belonging to the citizens of Great Britain and Ireland. This is their mint you know.

"Turn yourself over and you shall see that we have given you an impression."

"So you have!" cried I, "You have made me beautiful. Am I the Queen?"

"On, no," he answered, "You are only a shilling, you are only the least little bit of the Queen.

"The Queen, you know, is the citizen's figure-head, the citizens have made her their figure-head. This is the citizens' symbol of motherhood, to remind us that we are all brothers and sisters, living as one big family in one big house called the United Kingdom.

"And you, my dear shilling, have been impressed with her likeness in order that you shall perform the duty of reminding us of our brotherhood and sisterhood.

"That is the purpose for which you were made.

"Every time you are looked at by a citizen a quiver of brotherly or sisterly love shall be felt in the bosom of that citizen."

I was about to thank this pleasant citizen for informing me that I was one of the citizens' emblems of love when suddenly I heard a great jingling noise and at the same instant found myself being thrown head foremost into a linen bag along with a great many other shillings.

As I lay, almost smothered, near the bottom of the bag, I thought that the pleasant citizen must either have been mistaken or else some great calamity had occurred.

With an endeavour to attract attention I called out, as did all the other shillings in the bag, "We are little bits of your Queen, symbols of motherhood and love."

While shouting and trying to get into more comfortable positions, we were carried away to a place called a bank.

Here we were released by a very nice citizen known as Teller.

He untied the bag and, with less ceremony I must confess than might have been expected from such a nice man, tumbled us head over heels into a drawer beside some other shillings which, from a sanitary point of view, were in a very shocking condition.

But I shall let that pass. In this drawer I lay praying for the time when I was to be sent on my mission of love.

Suddenly a hand seized me, along with some other shillings, and, in less time than it takes to tell, I was dropped into the trousers pocket of a citizen who happened to call to tell the teller it was a fine day.

Off this citizen went, along one street, up another and into another, stopping at a shop, which he entered.

He stood at the counter for some time, and every now and again put a hand into the pocket where I lay, and turned me over in a manner which made me feel that he was about to take me out so as to remind himself, by looking at my face, that he was a member of the Big Citizen Household.

At last he did take me out; but instead of using me as a reminder he tossed me into the air, caught me while falling to the ground and then placed me very gently on the counter.

If you please," cried I, "Will you tell me why I am used in this irreverent manner?"

Both the citizen who had brought me to this shop and the lady behind the counter laughed very heartily at my question.

"Why," answered the lady – a very nice lady she was. "The gentleman wants a book."

"Well," asked I, "Can you not give him a book?"

She smiled most beautifully, looked carefully and long into my face and then, with a loud laugh, raked me into a drawer.

I had been warm through having lain so long in the gentleman's pocket now I was beginning to feel cold and feverish turn about, as if some of the influenza germs had alighted upon me. Indeed I am almost certain that a few millions of the little pests were playing hide and seek all over me, for I felt a creeping sensation. In this state I fell sound asleep in the drawer and dreamt that two citizens, a lady and gentleman, were fondly looking at me and discussing the propriety of converting me into a button or a brooch. It was a delightful dream, for as a button or a brooch I knew that the object of my existence would be realised.

But while the lady and gentleman were still considering the matter another citizen joined in the conversation and from his remarks I learned that I and all the other shillings, far from being emblems of brotherhood and sisterhood were looked upon, and actually used, as mere counters in a cruel game of chance which necessitated the sacrifice of all true happiness among the citizens.

I awoke with a start just at this moment, and found myself in the hand of the lovely lady behind the counter.

"Please make me into a button," I said. "Do not laugh, for I am in earnest. Why, my dear lady, you have no need to use me for such a vile purpose as that of counter. When your little brother at home asks for a biscuit you do not demand a counter from him.

"It is therefore very wrong of you to take a counter from a citizen when he asks you to supply him with a book.

"For, is not this shop but a small room situated here for the Big Household of which you are a member?

"Being a token of love, it is my duty to speak plain.

"What difference will it make to your big family of citizens whether the book a citizen requires should lie in this shop or be taken to his place of abode? The book will be no less a book no matter where it lies in our big house.

"Nor will I be any less a shilling if you cease to use me other than as a button.

"And the citizens of whom you are one shall be no poorer.

"No, my dear lady, they shall be all the richer by your giving a book to any brother or sister who may be richer by the amount of pleasure and knowledge supplied by the book.

"And they shall be richer in their lives if I be used as a button.

"Sweet lady, I have just learned that thousands of your dear brothers and sisters have no counters, and that, merely because of this, they cannot obtain the books that are lying idle and useless in this little shop; that thousands upon thousands, merely because they have no shillings, cannot get the use of the houses built by their brothers and themselves, nor the furniture and furnishings lying idle in other shops, and which were also made by themselves; that thousands of your brothers and sisters forming your big household, merely because they have no counters, are without the necessaries of life that the mere want of counters prevents them from building proper houses for themselves, making proper furniture for themselves, and scratching the earth to obtain proper food for themselves.

"My lovely lady," I continued, taking advantage of her sweet disposition to listen, "Adam and Eve did not use counters, nor did Robinson Crusoe on his desert island. The absence of counters did not prevent the fruits and flowers from growing in the lovely garden of Eden, nor the goats from giving milk on Crusoe's island.

"Bees do not use counters. Indeed, sweet lady, if bees were to adopt counters the worker bees would soon become half-starved, sickly, insects; for the drones who do no work would soon get hold of the shillings and live upon the honey produced by the slavish workers.

"You may not have thought of it, but it is a fact that the healthiest monkeys enjoy all the necessaries and pleasures of life without the aid of counters.

"But that they enjoy life in their glorious forests and gardens is a truth which you, possibly, cannot understand, for you have only seen them living artificially in cages. I think you are no more capable of understanding the true reason for its imprisonment. For you, yourself, in the life you live in this shop, are even further away from your natural element than are the caged monkeys.

"You are a caged prisoner, trained from your infancy, like a showman's dog, to be obedient to others, and that irrespective of your longings to get away to the fields, the woods, the glens, the sea shore; there to meet your lover or engage in the work you were made to perform – work which no other could imitate, any more than one perfume or one flower is like another; irrespective of your longings to live with nature, where there are no counters.

"Sweet maiden, do not let superstition cause you to shudder when I tell you that you are living in the only hell. It is a cruel word, hell, to be used in presence of a caged citizen like you, for you have been trained to listen to it with horror, just as an ass, or a dog will tremble for the lash when they hear their masters utter words that are always accompanied by a stroke of the whip. Get accustomed to the word and you shall fear it no longer. Hell means nothing but the state in which you live, and the use of shillings for counters has made it and maintains it.

"Heaven. What is Heaven? Where is Heaven?

"It is hell without counters. It is here, in this United Kingdom, which shall become a glorious garden filled with the music of love whenever all the shillings like myself are turned into buttons and brooches, and used for no other purpose than that of reminding angels like yourself who and what you are."

When I had finished speaking she smiled upon me and gently dropped me into one of the most delightful, sweet-smelling purses I have ever sampled.

ADVERTISEMENT

Any lady or gentleman can be supplied with a shilling like this one, along with a certificate from D. B., for the small sum of 2s. 6d., by applying to the editor, who will use the balance in the interests of the citizens.

Dan Baxter, 'A Monkey Story' (1896)

A well known gentleman has just secured another monkey story by means of a phonograph. He placed the instrument in a cage and set it down in one of the great forests of Africa – at a spot where he knew the monkeys were in the habit of congregating.

I do not myself see anything alarming in the story, but it seems that other do, for it is said that a number of American millionaires are endeavouring to suppress it.

They say, for instance, that the gentleman referred to was never in Africa. But that is not true.

And one millionaire who had the privilege of hearing a little bit of the story in the original monkey tongue, with the aid of a phonograph, asserts that it is a "Jabber."

He frankly acknowledges, however, that he is unacquainted with the Simian tongue.

The gentleman who took the trouble to go to Africa, on the other hand, is an authority; indeed, he is one of the foremost authorities on the language of the apes, and has translated the story into six different languages.

He states that, "The story was told by a monkey in a low tone of voice and that the "Here, here's' (pronounced 'Wur, wur' by the monkeys) indicates that a large number of them were listening."

"Once upon a time," said the monkey referred to, "A number of gorillas foregathered on the borders of this forest. One of them was an extraordinary fellow, in his size, wit and ugliness. Few of the inhabitants had ever before seen anything like this specimen. Consequently those of our forefathers who gathered round to have a look at the strangers were struck with wonder, fear, and pretended admiration on seeing this big fellow stretch himself up to his full height.

"The big one saw that neither our forefathers, nor the other gorillas, who accompanied him, felt comfortable in his presence, and being desirous of making friends, especially of the gorillas, he proceeded to exhibit his good nature by standing on his head.

"This performance so much frightened our forefathers that almost all of them who witnessed it ran off to the innermost recesses of the forest. Some of them, however, must have remained, or we should not have had the story handed down to us. It is said that when the big fellow stood on his head and yelled it set the gorillas to laugh and laugh again, so such so that they were obliged to lie on the grass and scream. When the big one saw that he had managed to make them enjoy his company, he invited them to his quarters where they were entertained in a manner that requires no description.

"After this the guests were surprised to see the big fellow fix a sardine tin on his head with the lid in front. (Chuckling.)

"'I am the king of the forest,' said he, 'and this is my crown.' (Chuckling.) 'All the apples and oranges and nuts you have eaten here were gathered by a few of my monkeys. (Chuckling.) But of late they have been rebellious, and I have had to work harder in thrashing them to gather for me than if I had gathered for myself.' (Chuckling.) 'Now,' the big fellow continued, 'I do not charge much for the use of my forest, as you can see from the small stocks of nuts and figs, and dates, and oranges you see heaped around you. (Chuckling.)

"'Had I been a greedy king I could have caused my monkeys to gather a thousand times more. Although not greedy I have my rights, as a king, to look after. I am entitled to respect from my monkeys, and I am determined to let them know that such is the case – (chuckling) – and the plan I propose to put into execution is this: you shall, my beloved warriors, adorn your persons with these pieces of cloth and tin cans, take cudgels in your hands, go into the forest and enlist all my monkeys who are willing to become soldiers and police officers. Those who refuse shall be secured as gatherers one way or another. And, look here, our soldiers and police shall, like ourselves, eat of the things gathered by my rebellious monkeys, and by all my other monkeys. My soldiers and police, like ourselves, shall adorn their persons, and to help them in their work of protecting my forest against intruders from other forests, some of them shall be clothed as chaplains in black robes – for you know the simians are afraid of black – and those in black robes shall go amongst my monkeys and tell them that if they do not support their king and forest they shall be struck down dead and go to hell, there to be roasted for ever and ever.' (Chuckling.) That is how the big fellow addressed the gorillas who accompanied him. What do you think of it, my fellow monkeys? – (chuckling) – and what do you think was the result of this witty speech? I shall tell you if you stop chattering. There were twenty gorillas in all, and by consent of the big fellow they divided the forest into twenty parts. Then taking their clubs they each enlisted a great many of our forefathers as soldiers, police and chaplains. They armed the soldiers and the police with clubs and gave them rent pants which had an aperture in them to allow their tails to serve the purpose of braces. Our forefathers were terrified. They could not understand what their fellow monkeys meant by thus covering their bodies. But the chaplains explained to them that the soldiers and police were going to civilise them.

"The civilising process was started by the soldiers led by the gorillas. It consisted at first of what was called a manœuvre in which thousands of our forefathers were clubbed to death.

"Those who survived the manœuvre were civilised. That is to say, they handed all the oranges, apples, figs, dates and other fruits of their toil to cloth-covered monkeys who were called masters, in exchange for small shells belonging to the big fellow, who distributed the shells among his favourites.

"The masters, sworn to defend their king and forest, sent some of the fruits to the big fellow, some to the chaplains, some to the soldiers, some to the police, and a large proportion to the gorillas, kept some for themselves, and handed the remainder to the gatherers in exchange for the returned shells already mentioned. (Chuckling.) In this way great numbers of our forefathers became idle, consuming tyrants, living upon what their fellow monkeys were compelled to gather for them. Thousands of them were employed by the gorillas to gather shells for the king, and while employed at this unnatural work had to be fed at the expense of their fellow monkey's toil. The king handed some of the shells to the gorillas in exchange for fruit, and the gorillas handed some of them to the chaplains, who went among the monkeys telling them of hell, and explaining to them that although they could not be allowed to eat what they gathered in the forest, they would have a good time when they died. The gorillas also handed some of the shells to those monkeys who were called masters, or captains of industry, in exchange for fruit, and the masters or captains of industry, with the soldiers and police at their back urged the gatherers to be industrious and thrifty god-fearing and evil-hating monkeys.

"But the fear of hell and hope for heaven were not sufficient to make our forefathers exist in this way. The toil was too severe; and, being unnatural, it followed as a result that all our forefathers struggled with each other to get rid of it by becoming possessed of the king's shells, of which, of course, there were only a limited quantity in the forest.

"Thousands escaped from the need of toil by lending shells; thousands more got rid of it by obtaining a loan of shells to purchase fruit gathered by the steadily decreasing number of toiling monkeys. Those who existed by borrowing shells for the purpose of giving them away in exchange for the necessaries of life were called rent collectors, interest collectors, profit collectors, insurance collectors, and the thousands who were engaged by such collectors as clerks, travellers and store-keepers who were known as wage collectors.

"These collectors of shells, or non-gatherers of fruit, increased in numbers very rapidly, and the time came when there were more shell collectors than fruit gatherers in the forest. The unnatural existence of both the shell collectors and fruit gatherers caused thousands of them to become diseased. This necessitated their being cared for in places called prisons, poorhouses, hospitals, model lodging-houses and lunatic asylums. And it is true that they all died prematurely excepting the gorillas and a few of their captains, who lived until they became very fat, very ugly, and very fierce; this fatness and ugliness being due to the fact that each of them consumed the souls and bodies of three monkeys. But the fatness and ugliness were under the decorations formed out of pieces of cloth and old sardine tins.

"Ultimately the struggle for shells, sardine tins, and bits of cloth absorbed the entire attention of the big fellow, the gorillas, and the captains of industry. So busy were they in striving to get hold of these things that they quite forgot the gatherers, the soldiers, and the police. They forgot that they had ordered the police not to allow the gatherers to gather fruits without their permission.

"The soldiers were getting tired of soldiering and wanted a climb in the trees. It was the same with the police. Their feet were sore. And hundreds of thousands of gatherers were idle and could get no fruit without stealing or begging, which they were not permitted to do.

"The gatherers were getting restless. They were organising against they knew not what. Then one night a flock of eagles swooped down upon the forest and carried away all the tin cans, clubs, cloth, and shells. When the gorillas and their captains awoke in the morning they were surprised to find all the monkeys, including the soldiers and police, sitting on the branches of the trees laughing and telling funny stories.

"The big fellow called for his cudgel and called for his crown. But the soldiers just laughed at him, and the police officers having also had more than enough of the tomfoolery threw cocoanuts at his head and went their way to enjoy themselves.

"Many of the gorillas, chaplains, and captains of industry died of disgust; but the great majority lived to confess that the introduction of old sardine tins, bits of cloth, shells, and black gowns, had been nothing but a trick on the part of the big fellow, who, they swore, was no other than the devil so often mentioned by the chaplains.

"The old gentleman died shortly afterwards of a broken heart. Of course there could be no hell without a devil, and seeing this they determined that the things upon which devils and devilment depend – pieces of tin and shells – should never again be permitted to enter the forest."

That story may be true enough, but if so, is it at all likely that the monkeys, I mean the common garden monkeys, exert themselves, as they did when ruled by the gorillas, without some kind of incentive?

C. S. J., 'A Fairy Tale for Tired Socialists' (1898)

Now, behold, there was a man who lived in a rich province where the sun shone on golden fields, plenteous orchards, and sparking waters, on vast storehouses of treasure and noble buildings, and on wonders, which, worked out by the wits of other men who had gone before, were still wonderful, though their makers were dead.

Many inventions were there, and much comfort and ease, and the yield from these things was great; but not for the man, for he, alas! was enchanted.

And, being enchanted, the man was not happy. He took little comfort in the good things about him, and did not even eat of the fruit that grew in the orchards. Much less did he take of the treasure in the storehouse, though of a truth, there was, beyond the enchantment, naught to stop him.

For he had been so enchanted that he believed, for some strange reason – or for none at all – that these things were not his, but another's, and that if he touched them much evil would happen to him here and hereafter. And so, being enchanted, he did no more than gaze enviously at them till it were almost better that the orchards and the treasure houses and inventions had not been at all.

And, through enchantment, the man became ugly and evil visaged. His hands became coarse and hard, his back was bent, and his brows lowering and beetled, for, because of the enchantment, he had to toil long and laboriously; and little pleased him, and he lived, at last, only to eat and sleep.

Worse still, he became lean of soul, and, being enchanted, had no imagination till, at last, he got very mad indeed. One thing only did he believe in – "The order of things as they are"; and when any spoke of "the order of things as they might be," he scoffed and laughed even with the laugh of a lunatic or he who is half insane.

Now, the enchantment that had been cast upon this man was of a curious kind. It had many spells, and each of these helped the other, so that when the man broke through one spell and saw things for an instant as they were, the other spells fell upon his soul, and he remained enchanted and worse off assuredly than the beasts who munch, and are contented.

Many of these spells had this enchantment, and the most powerful of them all was Custom, for of the spells that chain men's souls that is the strongest, and the worst, that is the most cruel and the most difficult to take off; for, having neither body nor form, nor yet being presented in words, it still oppresseth, and is not to be fought or met.

But it causeth men to do things for no reason, and whether they be good or bad; so that when the man thought how happy he could be did he possess the things he envied, Custom said unto him, "did not your father bear many stripes and your mother mourn long? Their days were black and ugly. How art thou different that thou shouldst be strong or happy?" And, seeing that Custom told him not that his father and mother were, in their turn, enchanted, the man listened and endured.

And the second of these spells was Fear, for Fear, next to Custom, is the strongest of the spells that chain men's souls, and will make a man believe even which he doubted, and not to do that which is good in his own eyes, because of the scoff of others, and the terror of a thing that does not exist.

So that, when this man bethought him of the greatness of the kingdom he half wished to take, Fear, the second spell, said unto him, "How know you that you will bear yourself royally enough in this new estate, or that if you take it the earth will not cease blossoming, or you cease thinking, seeing you will have much to eat, or working, with more time to sleep, or how know you that you will not blunder or make errors that your children will scorn, for your bread depends on your doing one thing constantly, how should you now do others that are different?"

And the man, not having courage, listened and was afraid, and grew, for the time, more timid than ever. And there were other spells of exceeding strength and great quantity. There was the spell of Greed, which caused the man to think only of one time, and that the present. And the spell of Ignorance, whereby all these things were unknown to him.

But, greater than the spells, was the effect of the enchantment. For this deprived the man of his imagination, so that he believed only in the order of things as they are, and the order of things as they might be seemed mere midsummer madness unto him.

And, at last, there came unto him one who sought to break his enchantment. Very valiant was he, and of goodly presence, and none of the spells were upon him. And he was earnest, and whole-souled, and he spoke loudly, for, seeing things as they were, he marvelled much that the man did not see them too.

And his words were such that the man listened, and pondered. And he said to the man, "Behold, of a surety are you enchanted." And he told him of the heritage that was his, but which he would not take; of the glories of the life to be, and of the triumph that might be his.

But those who wished to see the man still enchanted said to him, "This is a speaker of vain things. Of a surety he is mad, or would take from you your hard-earned wages. Let us imprison him."

And the man, because the enchantment was so strong upon his soul, pondered a little more, and then consented.

And the man was, and is, the People, and the name of the Prophet who sought to free him, is it not written in the scorn and anger of the world, under which all things good are hidden?

And some there are who say that a magician called Knowledge is, at last, to set the people free from their enchantment, and lead them to the kingdom that is theirs – the kingdom of men.

But the man is still enchanted, and his kingdom is not yet.

LABOUR ELECTOR

John Law, 'Connie', *Labour Elector*, Chapters I and II, June 1893, pp. 10–12; Chapters III and IV, July 1893, pp. 11–12; Chapters V, VI and VII, August 1893, pp. 12–14; Chapters VIII, IX and X, September 1893, pp. 9–12; Chapters XI, XII and XIII, October 1893, pp. 10–12; Chapters XIII (cont.) and XIV, November 1893, pp. 10–12; Chapters XIV (cont.) and XV, December 1893, pp. 11–12; Chapters XV (cont.) and XVI, January 1894, pp. 11–12.

The *Labour Elector* (1888–94) had been suspended in 1890, when proprietor, publisher and editor Henry Hyde Champion (1859–1928) moved to Australia to organize the Australian maritime strike. After Champion returned from Australia in June 1891, he stood as an independent Labour candidate for Aberdeen South during the 1892 general election, and he published the temporary periodical *Fiery Cross* to support his candidature. The *Labour Elector* did not resume publication until January 1893, this time under the editorship of Michael Maltman Barry (1842–1909). The periodical was published weekly in the first instance and monthly from June 1893 until the final full issue in January 1894. The title pages for issues 103 to 108 were published until July 1894 to retain control of the title, but the full periodical was not published again.

There was again very little fiction or poetry published in the revised *Labour Elector*, but this version of the periodical carried a partial serial, John Law's 'Connie', which was incomplete when the periodical ceased publication. John Law was the pseudonym of Margaret Elise Harkness (1854–1923). Harkness was the cousin of Beatrice Potter, later Beatrice Webb (1858–1943), and it has been suggested that it was Harkness who introduced her cousin to Sidney Webb (1859–1947). Like her cousin, Harkness was from an upper-middle-class family, but she desired independence and first trained as a nurse in London before moving into journalism and writing. She was a member of the SDF until the late 1880s and had a pivotal role in the successful conclusion of the London dock strike in 1889, when she persuaded Cardinal Manning (1808–92) to negotiate with the dock owners on behalf of the workers. She was the author of a number of fictions dealing with working-class life: *A City Girl: A Realistic Story* (1887), *Out of Work* (1888), *Captain Lobe* (1889; reissued in 1891 under the title *In*

Darkest London), *A Manchester Shirtmaker: A Realistic Story of To-Day* (1890), 'Roses and Crucifix' (serialized in the *Woman's Herald*, 1891–2) and *George Eastmont: Wanderer* (1905) as well as 'Connie'. She was a close friend of Champion, and her drift away from the socialist movement was exacerbated when Champion emigrated to Australia in 1894. She spent much of the rest of her life on the Indian subcontinent, publishing accounts of Indian life and history.

John Law, 'Connie' (1893–4)

[June 1893]

Chapter I.
Locked Out

"It's no use, Connie, better give it up."

"No, here's another bit. I'll try once again."

So saying, Connie threw a bit of stick up against a window, threw it with all her force, then waited a few seconds.

"Father!" she called loudly, "Father!"

But no one answered. The stick fell on the pavement after it has struck the window, and the girl did not stoop to pick it up again.

"I believe it *is* no use," she said to the young man who had called her "Connie." Then she looked up and down the street.

Her long black cloak had fallen open, showing her lace dress. On her feet were black satin shoes. The hood of the cloak covered her head. Golden curls surrounded her face, which was very young and childlike.

"What *shall* I do?" she asked the young man, looking up at him with her big dark eyes. "Father is asleep, or – or –"

"Or what?"

"Or tipsy." She said the last word in a whisper.

"He wouldn't let me take the latch-key," she added. "I wanted to have it; but he said he would sit up till I came home. The landlady's deaf, and there's no one but father to let me in."

The young man did not speak for a minute. Then he said slowly:

"It's no use to rattle the door and throw things at the window, and you can't spend the night on the doorstep."

"What *can* I do?"

"You had better come home with me."

They were standing in front of a dark house in a street leading out of Drury Lane.[1] It was almost midnight. In a few minutes the public houses would be closed, and the streets would be desolate. The girl knew this and she shivered. What should she do?

Opposite the house was a street lamp, and by its dim light she could see her companion's face as he bent down to ask,

"Do you trust me, Connie?"

"Oh, yes," she said.

"I am alone," he continued. "My friend who lives with me is away in the country. You can have his room."

"If only I could make father hear me," she said, half sobbing.

"You can't," he replied. "We have been here a quarter of an hour, and it's all of no use. You had better come home with me."

Still she hesitated.

Just then a tipsy man reeled by, and as he passed he muttered something about her pretty face. This made her draw the black cloak tightly over her dress, and push back the hair from her forehead.

"Yes, I'll come," she said in a weary voice. "I can't stay here all night. There is nothing else for it."

"Will you take my arm?"

"Yes."

"We shall be home in a few minutes,"[2] he told her, as they walked quickly along.

She said nothing.

"You are not afraid of me?"

"No."

"Then what is it?"

"It's father."

"What do you mean?"

"It's downright cruel of him to lock me out," she sobbed. "He knows the landlady's deaf. Oh, it's cruel to have a father that gets tipsy, and forgets all about one, and leaves one to a stranger."[3]

"We will talk about it when we get home," the young man told her. "I'm not quite a stranger, you know, Connie."

The night was clear, but cold, and as they walked on the wind blew chill upon them, making the girl shiver. She looked down at her thin satin shoes, and asked:

"Is it far?"

"No," he answered. "Isn't it strange," he continued, "that one can never see a policeman or get a cab when such things are really wanted?"

"There's a cab," she said as a four-wheeler[4] crept slowly into sight.

"We are nearly there now," said he; and five minutes later they stopped before a tall house in a more fashionable part of Drury Lane, where he pulled a latchkey out of his pocket.[5]

"Here we are," he said; "I live here in a flat. You will see in a minute."

Then he opened the door, and led the way through a lighted passage, and up two flights of stone steps.

"These are my rooms," he said, opening a second door and leading the way into a little hall. "It's a small place, but not a bad den, taking it all together. Let me help you off with your cloak."

Connie looked shyly round her.

A coloured lamp hung from the ceiling. Two or three chairs, a table, a hat-stand, and a clock furnished the entrance, called by courtesy "the hall."

Horsewhips and tennis rackets,[6] and a motley group of hats and caps were arranged on the hat-stand, and amongst them the tenant of the flat – Humphry Munro – hung up his hat and overcoat. Then he stood before Connie in evening dress, with a crushed flower in his button hole, and, having tossed the flower under the table he said:

"Come in and get warm."

Connie followed him into a small room and waited while he lighted the gas. Afterwards, womanlike, she walked to the nearest mirror and began to smooth her hair, which the wind had blown into wild disorder.

Munro watched her, with a good-natured smile on his handsome face. He was tall and broad shouldered, a well made man, and a gentleman.

"I call this fun," he said, when she turned round and looked at him. "I'll light the fire, and get you something hot to drink. The house-keeper leaves everything ready for us when she goes home at night, and we look after ourselves until she comes in the morning. My friend Grey is in the country, so you can have his room. I'll show it to you when you're warm. Here's a nice low chair by the fire-place."

Then, seeing her crying, he added gently, "Don't cry, Connie; there's nothing to cry about."

"I'll be all right in a minute," she said, trying to swallow the sobs in her throat. "You are very kind, Mr. Munro; don't think me ungrateful, but, but –"

"But what?"

"Father's so cruel!" she sobbed; "I'll never go back to him. To morrow I'll get lodgings and live by myself."

"Sit down while I light the fire," Munro said; "then we will talk about it."

The room was rather too full of furniture to please the ordinary bachelor, but it was pretty and artistic. Connie's eyes wandered over the sofas, chairs, and tables, to the open piano. Flowers in pots, and a sleepy parrot attracted her attention, because they were things to which she was unaccustomed. She glanced at the photographs, of which there were dozens, some in frames, the greater number scattered carelessly about on stands and tables. A long row of ladies adorned the mantelpiece.

Standing by itself in a crimson plush frame was the likeness of a lady whose features resembled those of Humphry Munro. Was the lady his mother, Connie wondered. No, she looked too young for that; she was his sister, perhaps. But what a hard, cold face she had!

"You are looking at my sister," Munro said, when he came back in his smoking jacket, with a pipe in his mouth, and his hands full of sticks. "Do you like her face?"

"No," said Connie.

"No more do I," said he, confidentially. "But I've only one other relation in the world, and that's my father. Do you like this?"

So saying, he handed to Connie another photograph.

"Yes," said Connie, "but he looks unhappy. Is he unhappy?"

"I'll fetch some glasses," said Munro, evading the question. "Then we shall be all right and comfortable."

Connie placed the photograph on a table, and lay back in the arm-chair. A sense of warmth and comfort stole over her. Her sobs stopped altogether. All was so new to her, everything was so interesting, she forgot her troubles and began to think only of Munro and his surroundings.

"What a pretty room this is," she said, when he came back again.

"Do you think so?"

"Yes. You must be very happy here."

"Well I am not in much. Sometimes I only breakfast here, and am out all the rest of the day. I was rather lonely before my friend Grey came to live with me; now we have high times in the evenings, and do all sorts of things, when we are free from engagements."

He mixed some whisky and water for her, and told her to drink it up.

"You are getting warm now?" he asked.

"Oh yes!" she answered, slipping out of the arm-chair onto the hearthrug to enjoy the fire. "I am quite warm now."

Munro sat down to smoke, and while he watched her, he said to himself that she made a pretty picture in her lace dress. Her arms and neck were bare, and they looked very white in the firelight. The rebellious curls that the wind had blown about lay on her forehead. Her eyelids were heavy with crying, and they gave to her dark eyes a tired, pathetic look that added to the childishness of her appearance.

"What are you thinking about?" he asked presently.

"I am thinking I will never, never go back to father," she replied, looking up at him. "To morrow I will take rooms by myself. Other girls live alone, girls who play in the same pantomime[7] I play in. I will give father ten shillings a week, and keep the pound for myself."

"What will he say to that?"

"He won't like it. He'll be very angry. But I mean what I say, I shan't change. This is the last time he shall lock me out."

"Has he ever done so before?"

"Yes; sometimes he has kept me a long time calling and knocking, but I've always been able to wake him up, till to night. If you hadn't been there what would have become of me? I must have looked for a policeman, and, as you say, if one wants a policeman, one can never find one. There's no knowing what might have happened to me but for you."

Tears filled her eyes while she spoke, and a sob ended the sentence.

"Wherever you go, you will let me be your friend?" he asked.

"Oh, yes! you are the only friend I have."

"You have never had a lover?"

"Of course not! Why, you asked me that once before."

"Nor a friend? I mean a man friend?"

"No, never. Why do you want to know?"

"Never mind. Finish the whisky, and then you shall go to bed. You look half asleep now."

He smoked on in silence, glancing from time to time at Connie and thinking of the strange fact that a few weeks previously he had been unaware of her existence.

"I'm glad Grey's away," he said to himself, "for he might have misunderstood all this perhaps. When I told him how I heard screams the other night and found Connie in the clutches of a tipsy brute, he only laughed and shrugged his shoulders. He's such a cynic! He doesn't know that I have met her at the stage door and seen her safely home every night since that happened. How could I let the poor little thing go home alone through that wretched neighbourhood? She's only a child. I guessed her father drank, and she had no mother, poor little thing! But I did not foresee she would be locked out; and I'm glad Grey's away, for if he had been here, I could not have brought her home with me, I must have given her to a policeman, or have walked up and down with her all night."

"Come, Connie," he said aloud, "I'll light the gas for you in Grey's room."

The girl rose up and followed him into a small bedroom.

"You can lock the door," he told her, "and no one will disturb you till the housekeeper brings you a cup of tea in the morning. Good night."

"Good night," she said, as she glanced timidly round the room.

When he was gone, she did not stop to undress, but threw herself on the bed and covered herself over with her black cloak.

"Oh, father!" she sobbed, "how could you do it?"

Chapter II.
Connie's Father

Early the following morning she woke up. The dim grey light showed the strange furniture of an unfamiliar room, and for a minute she wondered where she was and what had happened. Then the memory of the previous evening came back to her, and she started up, saying:

"I must go home."

A few minutes later she opened the door of the room, and went quietly out into the little hall.

Here all was still, but for the ticking of the clock, the hands of which pointed to half past six.

"If I can open the door downstairs without noise, and get out of the house, I shall be all right," she thought, while softly closing the door of the flat. Her heart beat fast, for she was afraid that someone would meet her on the staircase. But no one was about, and in a few seconds she was outside the house and in the street, where she gave a sigh of relief.

The cold morning air cut her like a knife, for she was but lightly dressed. She pulled the hood of the cloak over her head, and wrapped it carefully about her dress, then set off quickly for Drury Lane. On the way there she met milkmen, who noisily rattled their cans, men going to work, and others, who looked suspiciously at her satin slippers. She hurried along with her eyes fixed on the dirty, greasy pavement.

Why she had left the flat so early she hardly knew; but fear of the strange housekeeper, and the knowledge that she was in evening dress, had combined to make her nervous.

"He will come to the stage door to-night, and then I can explain all about it," she thought. "If he had been alone I would have waited; but I could not let a strange woman see me in this dress."

After walking ten minutes she reached the house outside which she had stood so long with Munro the night before. An old woman was scrubbing the doorstep, and the door was wide open.

Connie went in and up the steep staircase to the door of her father's room. There she waited for a minute, listening to his heavy breathing. The door was ajar. She pushed it open and walked in.

He lay in bed with his arms stretched out. His face was red, his features swollen, and he slept the heavy sleep of a man who had been intoxicated. She went to the bed, and stood beside him, with her large, mournful eyes fixed on his face. Soon he moved uneasily, turning his head on the pillow, and when she pulled up the blind, and let the light fall on his face, he awoke.

"You," he muttered.

"Yes, me, father," she said.

"When did you come in?"

"This minute."

He turned round to go to sleep again.

"Father," she said, speaking quickly and looking earnestly at him, "you went to sleep last night, and left me out of doors. I knocked and shouted, but you did not hear me. You were drunk. It shan't happen again; to-day I am going into lodgings to live by myself. Do you understand?"

He stared stupidly at her.

"Look," she said, pointing to a gin bottle on a chair beside the bed. "You drank and drank until you forgot all about me. You left me out of doors all night."

"Where have you been?" he asked.

"Never mind where I have been," she said. "I'll give you ten shillings a week from my salary; but come what will, I'll never live with you any more."

Slowly he took in the meaning of her words; but the effort to understand them was too great an exertion for his stupefied brain.

"Damn your nonsense!" he muttered, turning on the pillow. "Let me go to sleep."

She made no reply, but walked away from the bed to the door. There she stood looking at the untidy room. The man's clothes lay in a heap on the floor, and beside them was a broken glass that had fallen off the chair. Empty bottles were on the table and the remains of some bread and cheese. A lamp was burning dimly, for he had forgotten to turn it out when he had tumbled into bed intoxicated.

There was some good furniture in the room, an armchair and a sofa; but the place showed signs of debauch and smelt of spirits.

After one more look at her father, Connie went out of the room into the passage. There a big box stood under the window on the landing. She pulled the box into her own room – a dark little place – and opened it. Then she began to pack with feverish haste, throwing into the box boots, shoes, and clothing. She emptied the contents of drawers and cupboards on to the floor, and when all was in confusion she paused and pressed her hands to her forehead.

"After rehearsal this morning I must find lodgings," she said, "and before then I must pack and change my dress and get some breakfast. And I must not cry," she added, passing her hands quickly over her face; "it's no use crying now!"

[July 1893]

Chapter III.
Alone in Lodgings

A week later, at about five o'clock in the afternoon, Connie sat in the little sitting-room she had engaged for herself. She was mending a long silk stocking. She held the stocking on her left hand and tried to darn what she called a "ladder"[8] in it. "Ladders" gave her more trouble than any other repairs, and silk stockings are expensive. She looked tired, and said to herself that the gas in the theatre had affected her head, the footlights made her feel sleepy. But the gas did not deserve all the blame she put upon it.

"Where's your gentleman lover?" a girl had asked her with a laugh the night previously.

She had pretended not to hear the question, and had hurried home alone.

Mr. Munro had not been to meet her at the stage door for a week; in fact, she had neither seen him nor heard from him since she had spent the night at his flat. Was he ill? Was he offended?

He had brought a something into her life that had not been there before, a depth, a warmth, she did not know what to call it, a something that she missed very much now that it had apparently vanished as suddenly as it had come. She tried to find a name for this something, and at last she christened it "Kindness." He had been very kind, and possibly he had thought her disappearance without a word of thanks ungrateful conduct, and that was why he had ceased to meet her at the door of the theatre.

"After all, why should he come?" she asked herself. "He is rich, and he lives in a place like a little palace; why should he trouble about a dancer in a theatre, whose salary is only thirty shillings[9] a week, and whose home is a garret?"

So Connie argued with herself, looking at the dingy room with its faded furniture, and common ornaments, and contrasting it with the flat she had visited.

"I'm a goose to expect to see him again," she said aloud. "But he was kind to me, and he asked to be my friend, so I can't help feeling disappointed."

Then she turned her undivided attention to the "ladder" she was mending, and as she had no lamp, she sat down beside the fire, on the hearthrug to make the most of the firelight. She had thrown off her dress, and "made herself comfortable" (so she expressed it) in a blue wrapper. Her hair was loose, and she would not put it up until she dressed for the theatre. She was alone, and expected no one.

Suddenly the door of the room was thrown open by the lodging-house servant.

"Your father's coming, miss," the girl said. "He's on the staircase."

Connie rose quickly and stood waiting for her father to come into the room. Her face grew pale and determined, and she remained silent until he had shuffled up to the fireplace.

"Well, Connie," he said, after the servant had gone away, "how are you, my dear? Cold night, isn't it? You don't seem pleased to see me," he continued, after waiting for her to speak. "It's a week since you left me, and I've got no money."

Without a word she went to fetch a little money box, and took out of it ten shillings.

"I was going to send you this," she said, as she gave him the money. "Remember, it's all I have to give you till next week."

"Do you call yourself a dutiful daughter?" he grumbled. She took no notice.

"If your mother was alive you'd act differently," he said.

"What do you mean?" she asked.

"Why, you wouldn't take up with a lover and leave your home," he told her. "You'd stay with me."

"With mother, you mean," said the girl, whose voice trembled. "Listen! You lived on mother, and now you live on me, but I won't let you have another chance of locking me out at night."

"You'd like me to die in the workhouse, I dare say," he said.

She made no reply, but fixed her eyes on him, making him shift his feet, and twirl his hat on his hand.

"When will you come home?" he asked.

"Never!"

"Not to your father!"

"You are my father," she said in a low voice, "but you are a drunkard. I can't love you, but for mother's sake, I'll keep you out of the workhouse. More than that I won't do, and if you come here again –"

"Well?"

"If you come here again, I'll call a policeman."

"You speak like that to your father, do you?" he whimpered.

"What sort of a father have you been to me?" she asked. "I've slaved for you ever since I can remember, and now mother's dead, I'll not do it any more. Don't talk to me of a lover. I have no lover. I haven't even a friend. You killed mother, but you shan't kill me. Go, or you shall be turned out."

She looked very young with her yellow hair falling over the blue wrapper, but her eyes were full of determination, and her voice shook with suppressed scorn and anger.

This man, with sodden features and matted hair, was her father; she could not deny it; but he had no rights over her, and he should not come to her again, he should be content with the ten shillings a week she would give him. The night that he had left her at the mercy of a stranger, she had determined to break away from the miserable surroundings in which she had lived so many years. For her mother's sake she had put up with this man, worked hard, lived without friends, and buried the shame of her home; but now that her mother was dead, she would be free from him. Ten shillings a week was all he should have from her; and if he wanted more money, he should work for it, or get it from someone else.

"I'm going," he said sullenly, as she laid her hand on the bell. "You might shake hands, Connie."

But she shrank away with such evident disgust, that he slunk out of the room, putting the ten shillings in his pocket.

When he was gone she sat down on the hearthrug, and buried her face in her hands. A reaction set in, and she realised the loneliness of her position. She must prepare for the theatre, and there must smile and dance to amuse the audience; and when the performance was over, must come back to this place – alone.

Chapter IV.
"I Thought You Were Offended"

A few hours afterwards she was on the stage of the theatre, lost in a crowd of girls and women. She had danced before the public from her childhood upwards, and dancing had become a habit. Sometimes she took pleasure in it; but that night her feet seemed to be weighted with lead; the people in the theatre made a great blur of colour before her eyes, and she could not distinguish the gallery from the pit.[10]

She danced with the music in a sort of dream, thinking of her father and his visit to her lonely lodgings.

At last the performance was over and she could wash the rouge from her cheeks and take off her gauze petticoats. She went to the dressing-room, and finding it full of dancers, sat down to rest. Beside her lay a pewter-pot and the crusts of a sandwich – the remains of a feast indulged in by one of the dancers between the acts. She pushed the things away, and laid her head on the table.

"You are not well this evening," remarked the dresser.

"Oh, I'm all right," she said; "but I think the gas gives me a headache."

The dancers took little notice of her, for they thought her "stuck up," so she was not a favourite. They hurried away, and soon she was alone in the dressing room. Then she put on her hat and jacket, and went through the theatre and out of the door.

"Connie!" said a voice in the darkness.

"Oh, Mr. Munro!" said Connie.

"I did not think I should see you again," she said when he came too her, holding out his hand, "I thought you were offended."

"Offended! Why?"

"Because I ran away without saying good bye. But I was afraid to stop."

"Afraid!"

"Yes."

"Of me?"

"No, but of meeting your housekeeper."

He laughed.

"I was not offended," he said, "of course not."

He did not say that he had told his friend Grey about her visit, and that the cynic had advised him not to meet her again. He had stayed away for a week, but that evening his resolution had broken down, and he had come to see how she was getting on and what she was doing.

"Where are you going now?" he asked, as they walked away from the theatre.

"Home," she said, "to my new lodgings."

"So you have left your father?"

"Yes. I told you he should not lock me out again. I took lodgings for myself the day after I slept in your flat, and I've been in them ever since. They are rather far from the theatre, but that can't be helped. You know it's not easy for a girl to get rooms by herself."

"I want to hear all about it," he said. "Let us go somewhere, and have supper."

"Won't you come home with me?" asked Connie, shyly.

"But your landlady?"

"Oh, she won't mind! The front door isn't locked till twelve, and you can go then. I don't want to go anywhere for supper."

"Why not?"

"Because I might meet some of the theatre people. The Boss asked me to go to supper with him once."

"Did he?"

"Yes, and I wouldn't go. If he saw me with you he might be angry; and then –"

"What then?"

"Oh, never mind! Here we are. Will you come in?"

"Well, for a few minutes."

She unlocked the door, and led the way upstairs, feeling that it was all like a story book.

"It's not a grand place like your flat," she said when they reached her room.

"It looks very nice and comfortable," he told her.

Then she went away to take off her hat and jacket, and to fetch the supper. She had only bread and cheese to offer her visitor; but she brought the tray to him herself, and placed it beside the fire that blazed in the grate.

The room was furnished in the usual style of the cheap lodging-house, with horse-hair sofa and horse-hair chairs, faded curtains, and gay antimacassars.[11] Munro examined the ornaments on the mantelpiece. Some large black hens sitting on white china nests, paper roses in a vase, a china shepherd with a dog and crook. Over the mantelpiece hung a picture of a church, surrounded by gravestones. This was not cheerful to look at, so he turned his eyes away from it to Connie.

She was dressed in black lace, which suited her yellow hair and her delicate, pale face. Her big eyes had lost their sadness, and shone with pleasure and excitement as she moved about the room preparing supper.

"Oysters and champagne are what I ought to give him," she said to herself. "I don't suppose he can eat bread and cheese."

But, hungry or not, he did the supper justice. Perhaps he guessed she was anxious about the fare she had place before him; at any rate he ate the bread and cheese with apparent relish while Connie told him about the pantomime she was engaged in, the length of the run it was likely to have, and the value of her engagement.

"Let us push back the table and come to the fire," he said.

Then he drew her towards him, putting his arm around her waist.

His friend Grey would have smiled, perhaps; but the cynic was absent. A rosy colour flooded Connie's cheeks, and she looked shyly at him while he talked to her about herself.

"You must be very lonely here," he said.

"Yes, I am," she admitted.

"And so the Boss wanted to take you out to supper, did he?"

"Yes."

"And you wouldn't go?"

"No!"

"Good child!" he said, drawing her golden head on his shoulder. "You won't go with him if he asks you again?"

"No!"

"You promise?"

"Yes."

The neighbouring clock struck twelve. He touched her cheek softly with his lips, and then went away, leaving her very happy.

[August 1893]

Chapter V.
Mr. Grey's Advice

"Have you seen *la petite danseuse*[12] lately?" inquired Mr. Grey.

Humphry Munro did not look up from his breakfast.

"Have you seen the little girl you put into my room a month ago, when I was away in the country?" asked Mr. Grey, helping himself to marmalade while he repeated the question and speaking with emphasis.

"Oh, yes!" replied Munro. "Pass the toast."

The two friends were in the little room Connie had admired so much, sitting opposite one another, having breakfast.

"Well, Munro," said Grey, "it's foolish."

"You told me that some time ago, my dear fellow, and we agreed that you were probably right."

"Then why do you do it?"

"Because she is a mere child, and has no friend but myself; because I am sorry for her, that's why. Her father drinks, her mother is dead, and a man of the theatre – the Boss she calls him – will work her some harm if I don't prevent it."

"It's delightful to be young and enthusiastic," said Grey, as he got up and stretched himself.

He was tall and slightly built. The features of his pale face were well cut and his manners polished. A pleasant man, and clever, people said, one likely to achieve something before long at the Bar.[13]

A knock at the door, followed by the entrance of the housekeeper with the *Times*, soon made him forget all about Connie. He threw himself into an armchair with his favourite paper, and dismissed the little *danseuse* from his thoughts.

Humphry Munro lingered over his breakfast, ostensibly to feed the parrot. He was young, but few would have accused him of being enthusiastic about women. His friend Gray was a far greater favourite with the ladies. In fact, he did not care much for the society of the fair sex; he declared that girls bored him, and it was no fun to flirt with married women. Connie attracted him because she was so trustful and childlike. It was a perpetual marvel to him how anything so innocent and fresh could have come out of such miserable surroundings. He concluded she must have had a wonderful mother. His own mother having died at his birth, the relationship had for him all the charm of nescience. He felt sure that Connie's mother could not have been quite like ordinary women.

"And the little thing has pluck," he said to himself. "When she makes up her mind to do a thing she sticks to it."

He had now fallen into the habit of going to see Connie every other day. The afternoon, at about five o'clock, was the time he liked best for his visits. Then he found her at tea, or busy preparing her dresses for the theatre. To sit for half-an-hour by the fire in her room, listening to all that she had to tell him, watching while she mended her theatrical dresses, or drinking a cup of tea, gave a domestic touch to his bachelor life. Once or twice he had had supper with her after the theatre, and on such occasions, had sent the servant to fetch some small luxuries; but the afternoon was the time he preferred for his calls. Then the kettle sang on the hob, the firelight lit up the little room, and the only entertainment he asked for was Connie's conversation.

"Going?" said Grey, when he at last rose from the table.

"Yes."

"Shall you dine at the Club?"

"I think so."

"See you at Lady Dacre's,[14] perhaps?"

"Well, yes – perhaps."

"Ta, ta!"

"Ta, Ta!" jerked out the parrot.

At five o'clock that afternoon Munro went to Connie's lodgings. The little servant let him in, and he made his way alone upstairs to Connie's room.

"Come in," she said when he knocked at the door. She knew who it must be, and her voice trembled with gladness.

The armchair stood ready for him near the fire, and he dropped into it with quite the air of a domestic character. Then Connie brought him some tea, and knelt down beside him while she put sugar in it. A soft pink colour was on her cheeks, and her eyes had begun to lose some of their wistfulness. She was happy now in her lodgings, and the only thing that troubled her was a vague fear of the uncertain future.

Presently Munro began to talk about himself. He had never done so before, and the things he said were strange to her – stranger than he could imagine, because to him they were so familiar.

"I wish my father would sell our place in the country," he said; "but the old man's heart would break if I even suggested we should part with it. I believe he knows and loves every tree on the estate. Besides, I sometimes feel that I am only fit for the life of a country squire – that I'm no good for the Bar. But I like London, and I dislike the idea of settling down in the country. Still, I can't make money, it isn't in me. I can spend right enough, but as to making it – well, money's an awful nuisance – I mean the want of it."

"I thought you were so rich," said Connie.

Then he explained that a man can be a beggar on five thousand a year, and a Crœsus[15] on two pounds a week.

"You see, Con," he said, "it's position makes all the difference."

A feeling of uneasiness came over Connie while he talked thus. What part had she in the country life he was describing? None at all. What were his home and his relations to her? Nothing.

"My sister is such a snob," he said. "Poverty is bad enough, but being poor need not make one snobbish any more than being rich. I wish she would marry, but I don't believe any man will be such a fool as to have her."

Connie looked gravely into the fire. The minutes were quickly passing, and Humphry would soon go away. The present alone was hers, the future she must not even think about. She stirred the fire and made it blaze up the chimney, for she felt she must be doing something. Then she got up and fetched her work-box and upset its contents on the floor, cottons and needles, tapes and scissors.

The noise startled Munro.

"How I have been running on about myself," he exclaimed, looking at his watch. "Connie, I am going home for Sunday, so I shall not see you before Monday evening."

"When do you go?"

"To-morrow."

"You will be back Monday evening?"

"Yes, certain."

He lifted her up and kissed her.

"Has your father been here again?" he asked.

"No; I send him his ten shillings."

"Or the Boss?"

"No; of course not."

"If I find him here I'll break every bone in his body!" said Munro as he put on his hat.

"Then," said Connie, "I shall lose my engagement."

Chapter VI.
Humphry Munro's Home

"Chatbury, sir!" said the guard, opening the door of the railway carriage, and touching his hat.

Humphry Munro collected his things together, and stepped on to the platform just as the station-master hurried up to say that "the Squire" was waiting outside in the dog-cart.[16]

He was well known at the little country station. An old woman dropped him a curtsey as he went to find his father, and a red-faced farmer shook his hand, hoping "he found himself well," and that he had come for a long visit.

"Got a horse for you to look at, Mr. Humphry," said the farmer. "Come round tomorrow, sir. You'll excuse its being in its deshabils[17] on a Sunday morning?"

He disengaged himself, and sprang into the dog-cart beside his father, who greeted him with a quiet "Glad to see you, my boy."

Then the dog-cart rolled quickly away from the station.

Directly they reached the high road the Squire turned to take a long look at his son. The Squire was a handsome old man, but his face showed signs of worry, and his shoulders stooped. His snow-white hair and white moustache made him look older than he really was, and his eyes had a careworn expression.

"Let the farms yet, father?" inquired Humphry.

"No, my boy, no chance of letting them. The lease of the Home farm has just fallen in, and I don't think I can get a tenant for it."

"What shall you do?"

"Farm it myself. It's the only thing to do."

The Squire touched up the horse as he said this, and then flicked its ears with the whip.

"I don't know what's come over farmers," he remarked, after a short silence. "They are all taking their capital out of land and putting it into business. Labour is cheap enough, cheaper than ever it was, yet the land don't pay."[18]

"How many farms have you on your hands?"

"Four large ones and two small ones. I never had such bad luck."

"Things have been bad ever since I can remember," his son ruminated.

It was a chilly grey afternoon towards the end of February. The boughs of the trees stood black and bare against the dull sky, not a leaf showed in the hedges; flat fields stretched on either side of the road with here and there a clump of trees, or a solitary cottage. The high road was almost deserted. A mile from the station they passed a wagon loaded with food for cattle; a man walked beside the horse and a small boy was perched on top of the turnips. Farther on they met two old women carrying bundles of sticks, and three or four school children.

"I want to show you some timber I have just sold," the Squire said. "Are you in a hurry to get home?"

"No. How's Di?"

"Oh, she's all right. Sir George McCannon has been over several times lately."

"Has he?"

"Yes."

Humphry drew his cigar case out of his pocket and held it out to the Squire.

"No, thank you, my boy. Di doesn't like me to smoke."

"You give in to Di in everything."

"Well, you see, I have to live with her," said the Squire with a quiet smile. "There's the copse, and there's the timber. I have sold it just as it stands."

He stopped the dog-cart beside a wood, and pointed out some trees marked with a red cross. Then he said with a sigh,

"I remember when the wood was planted. If I could have let the Home farm that copse should not have been touched. It was Di who made me sell the wood, but she's quite right, Humphry, quite right. She's a fine woman, is Di. I sometimes think she ought to have been a man, then she would have had more scope."

A dog-cart rolled on down a hill, passed a farm-house, where a clergyman stood at a gate talking to a woman.

The Squire called out "Good evening!"

"That's the new curate," he explained to Humphry. "Di does not like him. She says he 'interferes' in the parish."

Humphry laughed.

"I believe," said the Squire, "he spends too much on blankets. You know Di is very economical. I don't know where the place would be but for her. When she marries I don't know what I shall do, unless – "

The Squire stopped, and Humphry did not finish the sentence.

"How long can you stay with us?" the Squire asked presently.

"Till Monday, father."

"Not longer?"

"No. But I'll come down soon for a fortnight."

It was dark by the time they reached the lodge, and drove through the open gates into the park. The lights of the house glimmered in the distance; the two men did not talk any more. Humphry smoked, and the Squire devoted himself to the horse. They were both, however, thinking the same thoughts, and that was, probably, why they kept silence.

"He could help me so much here," the Squire thought, "and he could not want such a heavy allowance if he lived at home."

"I could be of use to the old man here; but I can't leave London," thought Humphry.

The younger man felt about for the papers he had brought with him from town, and satisfied himself that he had not left them in the railway carriage.

"Here we are!" said the Squire, as they drew up before an old-fashioned house with a large entrance. "You'll be glad of your tea. Your room's all right. I went to have a look at it before I left. I'm going to the stables for a few minutes. You'll find your sister at home."

The old butler came out, leaving the hall door open, and greeted Humphry with,

"Hope you're quite well, Master Humphry. Miss Diana's in the drawing room, sir," he added.

Humphry went into the hall and took off his overcoat.

Then he stopped to warm himself. He chatted with the old butler about the village – who was dead and who was married. The hall was a big place with many doors, and a broad flight of steps leading to a gallery. Huge logs blazed on a wide hearth, and by the fire Humphry lingered, heedless of the butler's warning that the tea would be cold if he did not make haste to join Miss Diana. He watched the flickering light playing on the skins of bears and tigers, on family portraits, old fashioned firearms, and curiosities of all sorts.

He liked the old hall better than any other part of the house, it was so quaint and home-like.

While he was listening to an exciting account of an accident the groom had had with a favourite horse, his sister came down the staircase. Her features were very much like his own, but the expression of her face was different. She was decidedly handsome. Her tailor-made dress showed off her tall figure; coils of dark hair were neatly arranged about her head. She lacked the graciousness that made her brother a general favourite; but she had more determination (more character some people call it) written upon her face. Her eyebrows were straight and black, and they gave to her grey eyes a steel-like glance. Smiles seldom parted her lips – lips made to command, not to kiss. A whole book might have been written about her chin; it was round and white, but strongly moulded, and when she lifted her face to speak, it showed a neck like a column. Diana Munro was a fine woman, as the Squire said; but he said it with a sigh, for he had lived with her all her life, and now she was nearly twenty-seven.

"Well, Humphry, don't you want any tea?" she asked.

"I'm coming, Di," answered her brother.

Chapter VII.
Diana

"I tell you, Humphry, it is your duty to marry."

"Thank you, Diana."

"I mean it. You can't make money at the Bar, so you must do so in the only way open to a man of your position."

"You can talk to me like that in ten years' time, Di; but I am only twenty-four, and I don't wish to marry."

"Of course you don't!"

"Then why should I do it?"

"Because the place is going to ruin for want of money, and you can't get money in any other way. It's a duty you owe to your position."

The brother and sister were walking through the park to church, and the bells could be heard not far off. The Squire would follow later on, for Diana had told him she wanted to have a talk with Humphry.

"You seem to think you have nothing to do but to amuse yourself," continued Diana, taking advantage of her brother's silence. "You forget that your position has duties attached to it."[19]

"It is certainly not my duty to marry for money," said Humphry. "The first thing a man has to consider in marriage is the prospect of happiness."

"Happiness!" cried Diana, "Happiness is only an accident, it has nothing to do with marriage. Marriage is a duty you owe to your family, and to Society."

"Then why don't you set me an example, my dear Diana?"

"If I marry, I shall certainly take good care not to lose by it," replied Miss Munro.

Her brother looked critically at her little French bonnet, tailor-made dress, neat gloves and boots, and prayer book.

"You have no heart, Di," he said, laughing.

"I am glad to say I have never been troubled with anything so commonplace," replied his sister. "Seriously, Humphry, you must marry Edith Custance, you really must. She is a very nice girl and will make you a good wife, and her money will keep things together."

"I don't want to keep things together. If father died, I should sell the place."

"Humphry!"

"Well, I mean it."

"Give up your position! You, who might one day be Member for the county!"

"Yes, Father loves the place because his happiest associations are connected with it, but I have no reason for being sentimental. As to marrying, I won't do it. Edith Custance is a nice girl, I know, but I won't marry her or any one else."

They had reached the churchyard when he said this; and there they waited for the Squire, standing under an old yew tree, amidst mounds of earth covered with grass. Wooden crosses and rude, oblong stones marked the graves of peasants, and not far from them was the entrance to the vault, whither their mother had been carried when they were little children.

It was not possible to continue the discussion in such a place, so they waited silently for their father. Everything was still and peaceful in the country churchyard. A solitary bell tolled the last five minutes before the service, and some rooks in the neighbouring trees tried to drown its solemn music. Just as the bell stopped and the organ began to play announcing that the clergyman was ready to begin the service, the Squire came up. They followed him into church, and took their places in the family pew. Humphry found his favourite seat under the tablet that the Squire had raised to the memory of his mother. He had sat there ever since he could remember.

During the service he thought of his sister's words and knew that she had spoken the truth. His home was fast going to ruin. His father's face showed it.

He knelt down with the congregation, resting his forehead on an old leather prayer-book; and while kneeling thus he thought of Connie. Her golden hair and sad, dark eyes came back to his memory, and he was glad to think that the very next evening he would meet her outside the theatre. He marry Edith Custance, and settle down in the country? Not he!

He raised his head to look at the Squire. His father's face was partly hidden, but he could see the old man's white hair and bowed shoulders. Diana had spoken of his duty. Well, he would work harder at the Bar than he had been in the habit of doing. Grey was getting on – why should not he?

[September 1893]

Chapter VIII.
The Boss Revenges Himself

"Humphry is very late," said Connie, looking at the little clock on the mantelpiece. "I hope he will come, for I must tell him everything."

She looked pale and tired.

"It's all the Boss," she said to herself. "It's his fault I've been sent away. I knew if he saw me at supper with anyone he'd not forgive it. He made the manager keep me on after the pantomime was over, and now he's made the manager give me a week's notice."

She thought of the diamond merchant who financed the theatre, a Jew,[20] who had taken a fancy to her from the very first, and offered her presents.

How the diamonds glistened on his fingers when he ran them through his greasy hair! How he leered at her when he stood at the wings, with "Master" written on his ugly face.

For months she had avoided him, and had refused his presents. If he had not seen her at supper with Humphry Munro, his attention might perhaps have been drawn away from her by some new dancer; but the night after Munro's return to London, she had been persuaded by him to go to supper at a restaurant; and there she had been seen by the Jew who was prowling up and down between the supper tables. She felt so glad to see Humphry Munro again, that to refuse to go to supper with him seemed to her quite impossible: but while in the restaurant she looked uneasily up and down the room.

"Who are you looking for? asked Munro.

"The Boss," she replied.

And then, even while she was speaking, the head of the diamond merchant appeared from behind a screen.

"It's he! he's coming!" she said, shrinking into her chair.

"Who?" asked Humphry.

"The Boss. He'll never forgive me," she said. "I shall lose my engagement."

The Jew did not see her at first. He prowled around, looking at the girls in low-necked dresses, watching a new face, leering at one, whispering to another. At last he stood still, fixing his eyes on Connie. She grew pale and her heart seemed to stop beating, but she whispered to Humphry, "Take no notice!"

Then the Jew came close to her chair, walking slowly, with his eyes fixed on her face. She dropped the knife and fork on her plate and gazed back at him fascinated. Her tongue seemed glued to her mouth, and she was only able to say when he moved off:

"I shall lose my place."

Munro said "Nonsense!" But the next day after rehearsal the Jew came to her and asked:

"Will you come to supper with me to-night? You had better come," he continued, with a smile, as he drew near to her and tried to seize her hand.

She could see a little diamond ring in his fingers, one he intended to slip into her hand if she allowed him to take it.

"No, I will not come," she said.

Then she ran away quickly, saying to herself:

"Let him mash[21] some girl who cares for a diamond ring and a supper!" but all the time she felt certain the Jew would revenge himself, for she had heard of his ways, and she knew he was master in the theatre.

That night she danced with a heavy heart and went home tired and restless. Sleep only came to her by fits and starts, and in her dreams she saw the Boss talking to the manager of the theatre. So the next morning she was not astonished to hear that her services were no longer required, that she must look out for another engagement.

"I only kept you on until I could fill your place," the manager said, by way of excuse, "I dare say I can find room for you again next Christmas."

To say anything about the Boss would have been worse than useless, so she went to the dressing-room, after wishing the manager "Good morning." There she gave the dresser a shilling for a sick husband, but she did not tell anyone that the manager had given her notice. On the way out of the theatre, she passed the Boss, and he turned his back on her, being busy with the manager.

She must tell Humphry Munro about all this, and she did not know how to put it; for she did not want him to blame himself. He did not belong to the profession, so he could not understand the importance of the Boss. But he must be told, for to-morrow she must see the agents and try to get a new engagement. In London she had no chance; she must go into the provinces. Into the provinces! That meant leaving Humphry. Leave Humphry! Oh, she could not do that! What should she do? Her face grew paler each minute and tears came in her eyes; but she would not cry. She walked up and down the room holding her hands clasped tightly together behind her back.

The clock struck six.

If Humphry was coming that afternoon he could not delay much longer. Perhaps he would not come.

She had been on tour with her mother, but never by herself; and she dreaded the new surroundings and the loneliness. Surely her life was harder than the lives of most girls, for her only friend was a man she had known but a few weeks, and leaving London she would be absolutely friendless.

The door bell rang, and she knew that Munro was coming. She heard him on the staircase. Perhaps she had better tell him everything just as it had taken place; for then he would realise that the Boss was really master in the theatre, with power to have her salary raised or to get her dismissed.

"Why, Connie!" said Munro, when he came into the room, "you look as if you had seen a ghost."

"The ghost won't walk for me much longer," she said, trying to laugh.

"What! the theatre shut up?"

"No, but I've got a week's notice."

"Nonsense!"

"It's true," said Connie. "Come to the fire, I'm so cold."

He sat down in the armchair and tried to draw her on to his knee.[22]

But she shook her head saying;

"I must talk to you."

She leant against the mantelpiece and told him all that had happened.

"I must go into the provinces," she said.

For a minute he was silent. Then he came to her and drew her gently to him.

"It's all my fault," he said; "I'm so sorry, Connie."

"I knew you would be sorry," she said. "But you must not blame yourself, for you don't belong to the profession, so you can't understand how angry it made the Boss to see me with you at supper."

"I should only make matters worse by interfering," he said, as if to himself.

"Yes," said Connie.

Both were silent. She rested her head on his shoulder and looked down into the fire, so he could not see her face, only her golden hair.

"Connie," he said at length, "if I ask you to do something for me and you don't want to do it, you won't be angry with me, will you?"

"Angry!"

"Well, vexed?"

She lifted her head to look at him, and an incredulous smile came over her face.

"We have only known one another a few weeks," he said, "but it seems a long time to me. I love you, Connie."

She hid her face.

"When I was at home, my sister told me I must marry a girl with money because my old home is going to pieces. I don't want to marry. For one thing I cannot afford it, and for another –"

He stopped.

"Well, never mind," he continued. "I love you, Connie; I can't let you go into the provinces for you have become so dear to me. Let us take a cottage somewhere and be happy together. I will be faithful to you and take care of you. You are such a little thing to be all by yourself."

He bent over and kissed her hair.

"Will you trust me?" he whispered.

She raised her head slowly and looked at him.

"If I did this, should I be with you always?" she asked.

"Yes – always!"

She gave a deep sigh, then she said:

"Let me think of it, Humphry."

Chapter IX.
A Cottage at Kew

Winter was over at last. It was early spring, and the first crocus had made its appearance in the garden of the little cottage at Kew, where Humphry Munro had established Connie. The cottage stood by itself some way off the public road, surrounded by trees and shrubs that shut it away from the gaze of the curious. It was a bijou place that had been built for a well-known actress.[23] She had grown tired of Kew, so Humphry Munro had taken it from her much below its worth, but at a high figure considering his income. He had done the thing in a hurry, intending at the time to make up for the extravagance by selling a horse; but the horse happened to be a favourite, so it remained in the stables.

He decided on letting the flat and living at his club when in town. His friend Grey had been obliged to leave him, so the furniture of the flat had been moved to the cottage. Thus Connie found herself surrounded by all the things she had admired so much the night that her father forgot her existence. The parrot arrived at Kew with the chairs, sofas, and photographs, and soon made himself at home in his new quarters, for the cottage now so closely resembled the flat it was scarcely possible to distinguish between the two places. One thing only was tabooed by Connie, that was the photograph of Diana in the plush frame. The Squire, however, had still the place of honour on the mantelpiece.

"Why does your father look so sad?" Connie asked Humphry Munro.

"Oh, he's worried," Munro replied. "Besides, he has no home life. A man must centre his affections on something, and no one can possibly care for my sister Diana. He was devoted to my mother, and has never got over her death, although it happened so long ago. Come into the garden Con., and see the new flower bed."

The little cottage at Kew suited Munro so well, he could not understand the change in himself. He had become quite industrious.

"Munro will do something yet!" his friends said.

Feeling free to stay away from the cottage, he was, in fact, nearly always there. He thought that he did not like to leave Connie by herself, and she refused to have a regular servant.

"Give me the ten shillings a week it would cost you for a servant," she said, "and then I can keep my promise to my father. I should not like him to go into the workhouse."

So Munro bought some dogs to protect her when he was absent, and, not feeling them sufficient protection, he went to the cottage almost every day. Saturday and Sunday he spent at Kew, working in the garden or strolling by the river. He did just as he pleased in the house, for Connie was more like a child than a wife.

"It's bachelor life without its drawbacks," he said to himself.

He liked to see Connie at the gate waiting for him, when he came from the station, and to go with her into the little dining-room where she had prepared the dinner; and after dinner, when he had locked the doors and come back to the fire, he liked to make himself comfortable in his armchair and smoke while Connie talked about the dogs, the chickens, the parrot, and the rest of the things that belonged to him. She belonged to him too, and he said to himself that she grew prettier every day. He was very fond of her, and began to realise that the change he experienced in himself was the result of having some one to care about. The flat had felt empty sometimes, even after his friend had come to live with him, and he had never cared for other people's houses. The cottage at Kew suited him to perfection; and when Connie's little head lay on his shoulder, he called himself the happiest man in London.

The only thing that troubled him was want of money. His father wrote dismal letters about the property, and occasionally he received a curt note from his sister on the subject of extravagance. The farms remained without tenants, and

Diana said that it would be necessary to find a more competent bailiff if he did not settle at home.

He put the letters in his pocket, and tried not to think about them, for he was more than ever determined to go on at the Bar. He had influence, and the restlessness that had made work so odious to him had disappeared. He began to talk of what he would do later on as a barrister, and to believe that he had brains enough to become a success. Connie thought him a great man already, and could not understand what more he wanted. Would he be a judge and hang people? "It was nice to plead for prisoners, and to get them off, but horrid to pass sentence upon poor men and women," she said. She looked so pretty, with her great eyes wide open, while listening to his stories, that one day he put on his wig and gown for her special benefit.

The days passed into weeks, and the weeks became months, and still he was perfectly happy at Kew.

May came in its fresh green dress, and Kew looked its loveliest. The horse chestnuts by the river dropped their blossoms on the young grass, among the daisies and buttercups. Red may and white may, lilac and laburnum, came out in the cottage garden. Soon the view of the river was shut out by the foliage of the trees, and the cottage was enclosed by thick green leaves.

No visitor came to disturb them. When Humphry was in town Connie did her shopping. People looked hard at her, but what did she care? She bought the things that were wanted, and then went back to her little home with the dogs, her faithful companions. The theatre and the Boss seemed to belong to a past existence, the memory of them became dim, and she lived entirely in the present. The dogs, the birds, and the garden filled up her time when she had finished the housework, and if Humphry did not come one day, she knew that he would do so the next. She was not afraid of being by herself. Her father had his ten shillings a week, so she had nothing to trouble about so far as he was concerned.

But sometimes she looked wistfully at the Squire's likeness on the mantelpiece. She felt that only a part of Humphry's life belonged to her, that from much of it she was shut out. Did his family know of her existence? Probably not. Would he grow tired of her, and go back to his relations? He had promised never to leave her, but if she saw that he was tired of her she would leave him. Now he was happy, she knew that. Sometimes she lay awake at night, thinking, thinking, and he lay peacefully asleep, and his dreams were pleasant.

There was something she must tell him before long. Would that make any difference? Well, she would never let him guess that she would like things to be different. But would he think of it himself when he knew her secret?

Spring passed into summer, and the roses began to bloom in the garden. Honeysuckle twined itself about the little rustic arbour, and mignonette grew among the sweet-peas that Humphry had planted beside the entrance. The days were hot, but the evenings were pleasant. Connie had grown rather pale and languid, and after her housework was finished she was glad to rest in the arbour. The dogs told her when Humphry was in sight or hearing and then she hurried with them to meet him.

One sultry July evening she sat thus in the arbour, and the dogs lay near her on the grass. Suddenly they sprang up and barked, for they heard their master's footsteps.

Connie went with them to the gate, and stood beside it in her light summer dress, waiting for Humphry.

"To-night I will tell him," she said to herself.

"You look pale," Munro said when he reached the gate. "Are you ill, Con.?"

"Oh no, I'm all right. It has been very close here. I suppose it was hot in London?"

"Baking."

He put his arm round her as they went back to the cottage, and looked anxiously at her.

"I'm sure you're not well," he said; "and the worst of it is," he continued, "I shall have to go home. Diana is going to give a ball. She must have some reason for it, or she would not be so extravagant. Perhaps she thinks it is time Sir George McCannon came up to the scratch."

"When must you go?" asked Connie.

"Oh, I'll tell you presently. I have the letter in my pocket."

After dinner Connie carried the coffee to the arbour, and Humphry followed with his pipe. Then he took the letter out of his pocket and began to read it aloud. Connie watched his face.

"Well, I must go, I suppose," he said. "Diana will never forgive me if I stay away. It will be rather fun. The old hall is a splendid place to dance in."

He began to describe the hall, gallery, and staircase. Connie listened in silence.

"I can't tell him now," she thought. "I will write a letter and post it to him after he is gone; then he will know about it before I see him again."

"But I don't like to leave you alone, even for two nights," said Humphry. "Are you sure you are not nervous?"

"No, not a bit."

"What a plucky little thing you are!" he said. "Most girls would be frightened out of their senses if they were left alone like this."

He looked admiringly at her, and then he noticed that she was much paler than usual. Perhaps it was the shadow of the honeysuckle that made her eyes look so large and dark, for they seemed to shine like stars in her white face.

He came to her and drew her head on this shoulder and kissed her golden hair.

"Shall I tell him?" she asked herself.

But he began again to talk about himself.

"I shall only be away two nights," he said. "Nothing shall make me stay longer. You see I must go, Con; I can't help it; but I shall want to be back here, you may be sure of that. There's no place like home, and this is our home, is it not?"

A soft breeze moved the honeysuckle and carried to them the scent of the mignonette. All was quiet in the garden; a lamp in the sitting-room gave a home-like look to the cottage.

"We are happy, Con, are not we?"

"Yes, perfectly happy."

"You see, our life is so natural," he continued. "We are young and love one another, and are together. That is how things were meant to be from the beginning; but men have spoiled things with their silly regulations and prejudices."[24]

A bat flew into the arbour and then back into the garden while Munro was speaking; moths fluttered in and out, a solitary cricket chirped under the garden seat.[25] Night came quickly on, and all was quiet. He drew Connie on his knee, and they sat there together in the dark watching the light in the cottage and thinking of their happiness.

"I can't tell him to-night," Connie said to herself. "We are so happy, and I don't know how he will take it."

She shivered and clasped her arms round his neck.

"You are getting cold," he said. So he carried her into the cottage.

Chapter X.
Connie's Letter

Munro had gone home and Connie was alone in the little sitting-room. The window was open, so looking out she could see the arbour, the flower-beds and the shady trees. The scent of roses came to her with the warm air, filling the room with a delicious perfume. Again and again she looked up from the sheet of note paper that lay before her on the table, and her eyes wandered to the garden where nature seemed to revel in the brilliant sunshine.

She had helped Munro pack his portmanteau[26] in the room upstairs that morning, and while they were busy there together he had done a strange thing. He had taken a small gold ring out of a case – his mother's wedding ring – and tried to fit it on his own little finger. Then he had hesitated for a minute, put the ring back in the case, taken it out again, and at last said to her:

"Look here, Con, you must wear this for me. My father gave it to me when I came of age, but it is much too small for me. You must wear it for me, Connie."

So saying, he had slipped the ring on her finger and run downstairs whistling.

Now she was writing a letter to him and her tears fell on the ring. She did not wipe them away because no one could see that she was crying.

"I wish I had told him last night, or he had guessed it," thought Connie. "I don't know how to put it in a letter. But he *must* be told, and I want him to have time to think about it before I see him again. He is with his father and sister by this time, I suppose. I don't know why I am afraid of his sister, but I am. I believe if she knew about me, she would be angry. Humphry does not love her, but she is his sister."

Connie went to a drawer and took out of it Diana's likeness in the plush frame. For some minutes she looked at the photograph, then she replaced it in the drawer and returned to her letter.

> DEAR, DEAR HUMPHRY
>
> You will be surprised to get this letter from me, as you only left to-day and are coming back to-morrow; but this is something I *must* tell you, and I want you to think about it before I see you again. I wanted to tell you days ago, and I hoped you would guess. Dear Humphry, I shall be a mother before Christmas. We have been so happy here together, I am afraid our happiness has made me selfish, for I dread anything coming between you and me to make us less happy. But I think you will love it, I mean our child. The words are strange to me, I don't understand them. They will seem yet stranger to you. Do you remember the little boy we found last week all by himself on the towing-path? You were good to him, and you sat up all night with Rolf, when the poor dog hurt his foot. I think of all this, and say to myself you will be good to it – I mean our child. I shall meet you to-morrow at the station, and shall know by your face, before you get out of the train, if you are glad or sorry about it. –
>
> Your loving CONNIE

"It is too late to post the letter in the pillar-box," she said, when her task was finished; "I must take it to the post-office. Then I will go to the gardens, to the palm house."[27]

She went softly out of the house, for the dogs must not follow her to Kew Gardens; and soon she was walking on the soft, springy grass towards the palm house, thinking of the letter she had dropped into the letter-box at the post office. Bees wandered lazily among the flower beds, birds sang in the trees, and not far off a band was playing. The gardens wore their usual holiday aspect, nevertheless a feeling of melancholy came over Connie as she went towards the palm house. There she found a seat in a secluded spot under a fern tree, and she soon became drowsy. In her dreams she saw Humphry place his mother's wedding ring on her finger, and heard him say:

"You must wear this for me, Connie!"

[October 1893]

Chapter XI.
A Sister's Kindness

"The little fool!" exclaimed Diana Munro. "I knew that there was some sort of entanglement," she added; "I felt quite sure of it."

A leather bag lay beside her on the dressing-table, and upon her knee was an open letter.

"Some shop-girl,[28] I suppose," she said, pushing back her hair impatiently, and looking at an envelope that had fallen on the floor. "It is really too bad of Humphry! I wonder what father would say if he knew of it?"

She took up the letter and read it a second time, then put it down on the dressing table, and went to ring the bell.

"Give the letter-bag to Price," she said to her maid who answered the summons; "I have taken out my letters."

The July sun streamed into the bedroom, for it was ten o'clock; but she did not attempt to dress herself. She sat down again before the glass, and looked at Connie's letter to her brother.

"It is a good thing I sent for the letter-bag," she thought. "If breakfast had not been late on account of the ball last night, Humphry would have had this thing himself. I could tell by the handwriting there was something wrong in it. I did not like to open the envelope, but I am thankful now that I did so. Humphry must be saved from this entanglement. If he finds out the girl is going to have a child, he may marry her. He is capable of doing anything foolish. Now he does not realise what he is about. The thing must be stopped.

She crossed her arms behind her head and gazed into the looking-glass as though the reflection there could help her.

"It is too bad," she said. "Humphry never thinks of anyone but himself. I suppose he is in love with the girl. What a silly letter she writes."

The gong sounded for breakfast, and Diana began to coil up her hair, thinking all the time about the girl whose letter lay on the dressing-table.

"I know what I must do," she said at length when her hair was finished. "I must go to London and see this girl. If I can make her understand that she is doing harm to Humphry, perhaps she will give him up. Anyhow, I can try to bribe her. But whatever I do must be done at once, for Humphry wants to return to London to-day. I must persuade him to stay with father until to-morrow, and meanwhile I must see this 'Connie,' and do my best to get Humphry out of the scrape. If he finds out – no, he shall not find out! I will take care that he shall not guess I have interfered with his arrangements."

She dressed quickly, and rang the bell.

"I shall want you to go with me to London by the morning train," she told the maid. "Pack my things at once. I shall only be away one night."

Ten minutes later all her arrangements were finished, and she was downstairs at breakfast.

Her father and brother began to talk about the ball, but she cut them short.

"I am going to London by the eleven o'clock train," she said. "I shall come home tomorrow. You will stay with father, of course?" she remarked to Humphry.

"I am sorry, Di, but I can't."

"Why not?"

"Because I am due at the Temple."[29]

"Can't you spare me another day?" the Squire asked. I have a good deal to show you, Humphry. I thought we would ride over to Home Farm together this morning."

"Are you sure you will be back the day after to-morrow?" Humphry said to his sister.

"Quite sure. I'm only going to Mrs. de Burgh to do some shopping."

"Then you will stop, Humphry?" the Squire said.

Humphry was obliged to acquiesce.

The Squire hurried out to order the horses, and Humphry left the room thinking, "I will telegraph to Connie."

Then Diana went to see about her household arrangements. She had locked up Connie's letter in her jewel-case, and the little gold key of it was hanging from a bracelet on her wrist. The letter was safe, she said to herself. Now she must think how it would be best to deal with this girl. She could tell better when she had seen "Connie." Probably the girl was vulgar and commonplace. Very likely "Connie" had other lovers. The letter did not show much intelligence.

At half-past ten she left the house for the station, and after she was gone her father and brother went to the Home Farm. The roads were thickly coated with dust, so they trotted their horses on the grass under the hedges. The corn had begun to change colour in some of the fields, and an after-make of hay was being carted. The ride was pleasant, and Humphry noted that the Squire was in good spirits.

The Home Farm wanted capital, but, as his father said, farmers were taking their money out of land and putting it into business.

The Squire left him for a few minutes, and he stood looking at the farm-house, picturing Connie at the door, just as he had so often seen her in the Kew Cottage.

The idea was absurd, of course; but suppose he took this farm himself, and brought Connie to it! But capital was wanted, not only for this farm but for the whole estate.

The Squire came back and they rode on, stopping at the nearest post office for Humphry to send his telegram. When they reached the belt of trees that enclosed the park, they walked their horses slowly under the beeches and discussed Diana's possible marriage.

"I shall be very lonely here if she goes away," the Squire said.

"Oh, well!" said Humphry, "Sir George McCannon has not even proposed as yet!"

Chapter XII.
Diana Visits Kew

That afternoon Connie sat in the arbour thinking about the telegram she had received from Munro. Her house work was finished, everything was ready for him, but he was not coming. Had her letter anything to do with his lengthened visit to the country? He made no reference to the letter in the telegram, he only said it was impossible for him to reach Kew sooner than the following evening.

"I almost wish I'd spoken to him before he went home," she said to herself. "The letter has taken him by surprise. Perhaps he wants to think it over before he comes back."

She had fed the chickens and the parrot, and had now brought her sewing into the arbour, because it was so hot in the house. The dogs lay beside her with their tongues out, for the weather was sultry. Some drops of rain had fallen, but not enough to be called a shower. The garden was parched and the creepers drooped from the walls of the cottage. There was thunder in the air, and the grey sky looked sullen.

Suddenly the bell at the garden gate gave a loud peal, and the dogs jumped up with angry growls to answer it.

"Who can it be?" Connie wondered, while she followed the dogs to the front of the cottage, for visitors were rare, and tradesmen did not peal the bell when they came to solicit orders. She called the dogs, and they came to her growling.

At the gate stood Diana Munro. Connie recognised her instantly from the photograph.

"Is he ill?" she asked, hurrying forward. "Oh, tell me, is he ill?"

"Who are you speaking about?" inquired Diana.

"Your brother."

"Then you know who I am?"

"Oh, yes, you are Miss Munro. Is he ill?"

"No, my brother is not ill," replied Diana. "My brother is quite well. Be good enough to open the gate."

Connie slowly turned the key, and Diana passed into the garden.

"Please come into the house," said Connie.

So saying, she led the way into the little sitting-room where Humphry's things were littered about – pipes, papers, and photographs. The sitting-room had folding doors, and through the open window Diana could see the garden and the arbour. Nothing escaped her notice. The parrot, the dogs, the piano, the expensive furniture, and the luxurious carpet. All these things she noticed before Connie could ask her to sit down; but most of all she noticed the girl she had come to visit.

"I wonder who the girl can be?" she said to herself. "Pretty! One of those soft little things, all curves and no angles, that a man likes to pet and kiss. She moves well, and is graceful – almost a lady, I should say. Where did Humphry find her?"

"Please sit down," said Connie, pointing to a chair.

She had steadied herself against the mantelpiece, for a strange sort of dizziness had crept over her. She was waiting for Miss Munro to speak.

Diana sat down on a sofa and thought for a minute.

Connie's great mournful eyes followed her, and she was not sure how it would be best to deal with this little thing whose face was white like her simple dress, whose golden hair curled so simply about her head and neck. This was no pewter-pot that she could batter to bits, but something frail that she could break. So she took Connie's letter out of her pocket.

"You sent this to my brother," she said slowly, while holding out the little note in its envelope.

Connie started.

"I believe this is your letter?" said Diana.

"How did you get it?" asked Connie.

"My brother gave it to me," replied Diana.

"He gave you my letter!" said Connie, grasping the mantelpiece with both hands and speaking with a painful effort.

"Yes. The things you wrote distressed him very much; he was very much upset. I have come to see what can be done for him, how he can be saved from this – this entanglement."

"Why did he not come himself?"

"My brother is young and thoughtless," continued Diana, ignoring the question. "You may think, perhaps, that he has money because he keeps you here in idleness and luxury, but I can assure you that is not the case. He has not a penny of his own; he is entirely dependent on my father. I do not know your name. What is it?"

"My name is Constance Ufindel."[30]

"Well, Miss Ufindel, if money can be of any service to you –"

"Did he tell you to say that?" interrupted Connie.

"My brother has no money of his own, not a farthing! but my father makes him an allowance – and we –"

"Oh!" said Connie, "don't."

Her head had fallen on the mantelpiece beside the Squire's likeness, and Diana could not see her face.

"If you care for my brother," said Diana, "if you have any real affection for him, you will listen to me."

Connie did not speak.

"This house is furnished with my father's money," continued Diana. "The money you have received from my brother has come out of my father's pocket. Your child will be dependent on my father if you stay here. You are my brother's mistress, a woman of no reputation, whose proper place is the workhouse. Living here, you do harm to my brother, whose duty lies at home. Before he met you he was about to marry a girl in his own position – a lady. His entanglement with you has kept him from making an honourable marriage. If you really care for him you will leave this house at once, you will go away before he returns to London."

Connie raised her head to look at Miss Munro. She did not speak, but she seemed to be reading the face of her visitor. Diana's likeness to Humphry was great; she could not fail to see it. But Diana's face was cold like stone, and her eyes were pitiless. Connie looked at her faultless dress, small bonnet, neat boots, and shivered as if a cold wind had come through the open window.

The dogs wandered up and down the room, whining and sniffing at Diana. It had begun to rain, and thunder rumbled in the distance.

Diana looked at Connie, but Connie remained silent. She was thinking of Humphry. So he had given her letter to his sister, and sent his sister here to help him out of what they called "an entanglement"! He had brought her here for his amusement, and all the time he had wanted to marry a lady – some one in his own position. His promise to remain with her always had been a lie. He had kept her until she was going to have a child, and then he had sent his sister to offer her money! Money! money that was not his, that would make her dependent on his father and on this sister who had come here to insult her.

Diana rose from the sofa.

"I have left my maid in the cab," she said. "What message shall I take to my brother, Miss Ufindel?"

"You can tell him he will never see me again."

Diana waited.

"I'm going away to day," continued Connie.

"You will be gone when he returns to London?"

"Yes, gone!"

Diana drew a purse out of her pocket and laid it on the mantelpiece.

"You can take that back," said Connie; "I do not want your father's money."

"You are very proud, Miss Ufindel."

"And tell your brother," continued Connie, "tell him to marry this lady in his own position; tell him that I wish it."

Her eyes flashed.

"You must think of yourself," said Diana. "In your condition you will need money."

"I can go to the workhouse," said Connie.

"I am sure that my brother –"

"Don't speak to me of your brother," Connie interrupted. "And now, Miss Munro, you can go. You have insulted me long enough. If you do not go, the dogs shall make you."

She stood up, shaking like a leaf, but with determination in her voice, and she laid her hand on the head of the nearest dog.

Diana hesitated.

The game was won; but this girl's eyes haunted her with their strange mournfulness, and made her feel that she could not go away without applying a salve to her conscience.

"Go!" said Connie.

"My brother would like to know that you are provided for," said Diana.

"I will take care of that myself."

"You will not accept any money?"

"Not one penny."

"Then good-bye, Miss Ufindel."

Connie made no reply.

"Shall you write to my brother?" asked Diana.

"No, I shall not! He will never see me or hear from me again. Go! and give him my message."

Diana went slowly out of the house into the rain, and Connie followed. The dogs growled angrily, but she held out her hand and let them lick it. She unlocked the gate and Diana passed through it into the road. Then Connie went back with the dogs into the cottage. The rain fell heavily, thunder rolled and grumbled, and Diana was wet through before she reached the cab.

"The most unpleasant thing I have ever done in my life," she said to herself, as the cab rattled away from Kew. "But I have saved Humphry. I wonder who the girl is, and where she comes from! I daresay he is very fond of her. How angry he would be if he knew what I have done! But he will never know, for she will never forgive him."

Chapter XIII.
Connie Leaves the Cottage

An hour passed by, and yet another, and still Connie lay on the sofa with her face buried in the cushions. The dogs walked up and down, they whined, they licked her hands, but she took no notice of them. She did not cry; what was the good of crying?

"How could he do it?" she asked herself. "To send his sister to her with the open letter, that woman with the cruel face; how could he be so heartless?"

The thought of Humphry Munro as he had been only two nights before – her lover. Now he was gone, and it was as though she had never known him. She was alone – no, not alone! – she could not now go back to the old life, but must live on, and face what was coming. That woman had called her his mistress, and had said that her proper place was the workhouse. She had been his plaything. All his gentleness and kindness had been a sham; all his promises deceitful. Now he had left her, and he would marry this "girl in his own position," "this lady," and never think of her again. Oh, it was cruel!

Rain beat against the windows and thunder rolled over the cottage, and she knew that a storm had come. The atmosphere seemed to press her down; her mouth was parched, her head was hot, she felt stifled. Words repeated themselves in her brain, but they made no sense; she was only conscious of a heavy pressure that seemed to keep her down on the sofa. When she got up it would be time to go away; for she would not spend another night in the cottage. But she need not go until the storm was over. At last the thunder rumbled in the distance, and the rain stopped beating against the windows.

"I must feed the chickens," she said to herself.

It would be a relief to do something commonplace. Diana's visit seemed like a dream, but she knew it had really happened, for quick thoughts presented themselves, cutting like knives into her consciousness, thoughts of the woman who had brought back her letter, of Humphry, and of her father, the drunken man who was her only relation, who would now blame her because she had no means to help him further. She sat up and put her arms round the dogs. They looked up lovingly at her. If only she might take them with her, it would be less lonely, for they loved her, and would protect her. But they belonged to him! She buried her face in their hair, kissing first one and then the other.

"They are hungry!" she said at last.

So she called them into the kitchen and fed them. Afterwards she prepared the food for the chickens and the parrot. All this she did as if in a dream, and when it was done she went into the garden, where the trees looked bright and refreshed and a delicious scent of earth came from the flower-beds. The grass seemed to be drinking up the rain that had fallen; drops of water trembled on the bowed heads of the roses. She stood for a few minutes looking at the place in which she had been happiest; then went back into the cottage to complete the arrangements she had to make.

Humphry would return the following day, so the animals would not starve if she left plenty of food in the parrot's cage, the chickens' coops, and the dogs' troughs. The dogs would guard the house until their master came back to take possession of all that belonged to him. She would carry nothing of his with her, not a penny, nor a bit of clothing. The dress she had worn when she came to Kew had been laid aside; she would put on that and wrap herself in the old cloak she had used to cover her theatrical dresses.

She went upstairs to the bedroom and there took off the white dress Humphry had liked so much, and put on her old frock, the last she had bought with her own money.

"Father can't have his ten shillings a week any longer," she thought; "but I can't help it now. I have kept him while I could, and as that woman said: 'There is the workhouse.'"

Humphry's likeness was on the dressing-table. Should she take that with her? No; she would never forget him, so she would not need his photograph to recall what he looked like, his voice would sound in her ears, his eyes would follow her until death brought forgetfulness.

[November 1893]
Chapter XIII.
Continued

"If I could but die!" said Connie. "Our home" he called the cottage only two nights before, while they were sitting in the arbour looking at the lights in the sitting-room. If she had told him then about her secret, things might perhaps have been different; but she had put off speaking in the hope that he would guess what the doctor had said to her when she felt ill, and went to fetch some medicine. She had hidden things from him, and he had only noticed that she looked pale and languid. If she had spoken that night while he was talking about their happiness, while she sat on his knee in the arbour, and all seemed so calm and happy around them, perhaps he would not have been so cruel. He had never said anything to her of this lady he was going to marry, this "girl in his own position," although he had talked to her of his father, his sister, Mr. Grey, and his grand friends and relations. Why had he been silent about her?

"So he did not marry me because he meant to marry her; he only wanted to play with me," thought Connie. "Why did I trust him? Why was I so foolish?"

She looked at the photograph once again, then she went down stairs. The dogs did not at first recognise her in the old dress, but directly she spoke to them they barked and jumped about thinking she was going for a walk. She sat down on the lowest step of the staircase, and put her arms round them. They could not speak, and call her their master's mistress, as his sister had done. Presently she got up, and went quickly out of the door, leaving the dogs barking and whining in the cottage. She unlocked the garden gate, and when she had locked it on the outside she threw the key of it into a rose-bush.

Humphry had his own key, and she did not want to take anything of his away with her. She had not thought where she would go or what she would do, but she turned her steps towards London. On Kew Bridge she stood still to consider. Alone, without a penny in her purse, what would become of her? Should she go to her father? No! To the landlady, with whom she had lodged after leaving him? Yes. The woman had been very kind to her, and would, no doubt, take her in until she could find work. Of course, she could not get a theatrical engagement, but she could go as a matcher to some Jewish tailor,[31] or as a day servant in a shop. It was getting late, so she must hurry to the lodging-house.

She walked from Kew to Hammersmith, and then to Kensington, feeling faint, for she had had no dinner, but without stopping until she reached Piccadilly.[32] The lodging-house was near Leicester Square, in a back street not far from the Alhambra Theatre.

She rang the bell, and then supported herself against the railings until the door was opened. A strange servant girl come to answer the bell, and the girl said the landlady had left the house, and gone away to the country. The door was shut and she was left on the doorstep.

It was nine o'clock and growing dark when she turned into the Strand and stood outside a shop, looking into the window while she asked herself where she could find a night's lodging. Anything seemed to be better than her father's rooms. He would give her a poor welcome if he found out that she had no money in her pocket. Possibly the dresser at the theatre would help her; but the woman would not leave the theatre much before midnight, unless some dancer wanted a glass of beer or some fish and potatoes. She could not wait all that time outside the stage door, because the Boss might see her. She would walk up and down in the neighbourhood of the fish shop patronised by the dancers, in the hope that the dresser would be sent on such an errand, and at half-past eleven she would go to the stage door. No other plan suggested itself to her, for she was hungry and tired, too exhausted to think much about anything but the quickest way to find a night's lodging.

Soon she was in the neighbourhood that had been her home from childhood, Drury Lane. Her father and mother had lived there ever since she could remember; she had grown up in its dingy streets, wandering from house to house, wherever her parents could find lodgings. Both her father and mother had been in the Profession, and at the time of her birth they had played good parts in the provinces; but their prospects had been spoiled by her father's drunken habits. She remembered her mother pleading for half of the money she brought home from her first pantomime, and her father putting it all into his pocket. Her mother had loved him with a cringing affection, but she had always despised him, although she had helped her mother to keep him out of the workhouse. She had loved her mother, and the saddest day of her life had been when the undertaker's men dragged her mother's coffin down the steep stairs of the lodging-house to the hearse. After the funeral her eyes had grown so sad she had been afraid to look at them in the glass. But what she had felt then was sadness, not the dull despair that had now taken possession of her, for her mother's death had had no other bitter memories attached to it.

She went to the fish-shop and walked up and down outside, hoping that the dresser would come to fetch a "snack" for a dancer who needed refreshment between the acts. Not far off was a public-house frequented by the dancers. Men had often offered to treat her there, and they had called her "stuck up" when she refused to drink with them. They had not known that her home reeked with spirits, that the cupboards of her father's lodgings were full of empty gin bottles.

Men and women passed in and out of the fish-shop with dishes, and children lingered at the door, hoping that some kindhearted person would give them a farthing to buy some fried potatoes. The smell of fish made her feel sick, for hunger had left her. The dresser did not come, and at last she grew too tired to walk up and down any more; so she sat down on a doorstep between the public house and the fish-shop and laid her head against the wall. People took no notice of her, for they were intent on their own business; they saw a girl in black sitting on a doorstep, and they passed on. The sight was not uncommon.

The clock struck eleven. Then she got up and dragged herself to the stage door of the theatre, and stood not far from it waiting for the dresser. Humphry Munro had often waited for her in the same place at some little distance from the street lamp.

A policemen passed by and he told her to "move on," but the words fell mechanically from his lips, and he did not wait to see them put into practice. So she stood still until the stage door was thrown open; then she drew near to scan the faces of the people who were hurrying out of the theatre. She recognised some of the women, but where was her friend the dresser? The woman did not come. At last the door was shut, and she heard someone inside lock and bolt it.

It was useless to wait longer, so she turned away, knowing that she must pass the night out of doors. Should she go to the Thames Embankment and find a seat?[33] No policeman would disturb her there, and she could go to sleep. Yes, she would go there, for she was getting faint, and her feet would not carry her much further.

A church clock struck twelve when she came to Piccadilly Circus, where a crowd of men and women surged up and down, making it difficult for her to keep on the pavement. At the Haymarket she stood still, but not for long, for she found a man at her elbow. There was no place where she could rest before reaching the river, so she staggered on without heeding the man who followed her.

At last she came to Charing Cross.[34] She had not far to go then, only down one more street, before coming to the benches. There was nothing to pay for a bed on the Embankment, because it is "The Beggars' Metropole."[35]

The air began to grow cold, for much rain had fallen, and a chilly wind met her as she came near to the river. She wrapped the cloak closely round her while she walked slowly down the street to the Embankment. There she laid her head on the stone parapet, for she was overcome with dizziness. A man with white hair spoke to her and he would not go away, so she crept to a bench where an old woman had taken refuge, and there she sat down, thinking that she would go to sleep and forget her wretchedness.

But sleep would not come at her bidding. Her aching limbs might rest, but her memory grew active while her body rested. She had trusted Humphry Munro and staked her happiness on his word, believing his faithfulness. He had gone away, leaving her to face the future by herself, a future that terrified her with its strangeness. However long the night might be, morning must come, and then she must go on again and walk about until she found some sort of employment.

She knew this, and in sharp contrast to the future came a vision of the cottage at Kew where she had been so happy with Humphry.

Above her was a cloudy sky, no stars could be seen in the heavens, for another storm was coming. Heavy drops of rain began to fall, and the wind died away. She put the hood of her cloak over her head and curled herself up on the seat beside the old woman.

Soon a shower came, and the rain soaked through the cloak, wetting her to the skin. The old woman moved uneasily, but did not wake up, and Connie wished that sleep would visit her as it had done her neighbour.

The city became quiet; only now and then the rumble of a cab could be heard or the noise of a shrill whistle. The strokes of Big Ben came in solemn tones up the river. The lamps grew dim, and a glimmer of daylight appeared in the east. She dozed for an hour, and when she opened her eyes it was early morning. Then she sat up, racked with pain, and wondering where she was and what had happened.

She left the bench and went to the stone parapet. There she laid her head down and began to cry. Tears came fast, for she was exhausted, hot tears that seemed to burn her face and hands.

"Dear, what is it?" someone asked.

She looked up, and saw a smartly-dressed girl standing beside her.

"Why are you crying?" the girl asked Connie.

"Because I have no money to pay for a night's lodging," Connie answered.

"Oh, I'm sorry! Come home with me," the girl said. "You'll catch your death of cold in these wet clothes. I'll give you a bed, dear, at all events."

Connie did not answer.

"Won't you come?" the girl asked again.

Connie tried to speak, but no words left her lips; she swooned, and fell heavily against the stone parapet.

Chapter XIV.
Bess and Flora

When she came to herself it was midday. She had been dimly conscious of a cab jolting a long distance and of a cabman who carried her up some steps; then she had forgotten everything, for she had fallen fast asleep. She had slept for hours; so at last when she opened her eyes, it was twelve o'clock.

Not far from her two girls were sitting speaking in whispers. A bottle of champagne was on a table, and while they talked the girls filled their glasses. They looked from time to time at Connie, and directly she opened her eyes they came to the bed.

"How are you now, dear?" asked the dark, handsome girl who had spoken to her on the Embankment.

Connie tried to raise herself in bed, but fell back upon the pillows.

"Fetch a cup of tea," the eldest girl said to her companion.

The younger girl left the room so quickly, Connie could not see what she looked like.

"You must not talk," the eldest girl told Connie; "you must lie down and wait till Flora comes back. My name is Bess."

Connie slipped pack into bed, and lay watching Bess, who returned to her seat. On the table beside the champagne bottle was a large white rat whisking its tail between the glasses.

"A medical student gave this rat to Flora," explained Bess. "It has been vivisected. Look, it has lost an ear, and its head is full of holes.[36] Flora loves it more than any of her pets; she has a whole menagerie downstairs."

Flora came back with a teapot in her hand, and a small mongrel dog under her arm. She poured some tea into a cup and brought it to Connie. Bess propped Connie up with pillows, and the two girls sat on the bed, helping their visitor to milk and sugar. The white rat ran down the table on to the floor and up Flora's dress. It settled itself on her shoulder, and whisked its tail round its pink ears.

"Isn't it a pretty beast?" flora asked Connie.

Then she made the mongrel show Connie its tricks, and fed it with bits of sugar.

"What sort of dog is it?" Connie asked.

"I don't know," answered Flora. "But I know it's a very pure breed;[37] the man who gave it to me said so."

"All Flora's friends give her animals," said Bess, looking affectionately at her friend while she was speaking. "You shall see the menagerie when you get up. She has birds and white mice and a pet lizard downstairs."

Both girls wore smart wrappers, made of bright coloured satin trimmed with lace. Flora was small, and looked delicate; she resembled a wax doll, for she had fluffy hair and blue eyes without any sort of expression in them. Her pouting lips were dyed crimson, and her eyelids were painted black. She had cut her eyelashes, so her eyes seemed to stare out of their lids like a doll's glass eyeballs. Bess was tall and well moulded, with magnificent arms and bust. She had a defiant expression in her face, a sort of recklessness, and hard lines marked her mouth, although she was still young.[38]

Connie looked at the girls, and they smiled back at her. Flora dropped sugar into her cup, and Bess held the milk jug. They asked her no questions about herself, but talked to her like old acquaintances.

"You are prettier than either of us," said Bess.

"What lovely gold curls you've got!" said Flora.

So they chatted to Connie for half an hour; then Bess suggested that they had all better go to sleep.

One girl lay down on a sofa, the other sat in an armchair, and before long they were dozing. Connie watched them. The rat rested on Flora's shoulder and the mongrel lay in her lap.

Connie closed her eyes, but she soon opened them again and looked round the room. It was very untidy. Clothes lay on the chairs and floor, scraps of food and dirty glasses, bits of cigars and gaudy feathers were on the table. Bright crimson curtains shut out the daylight. The room was in some respects comfortable, almost luxurious, but littered about with odds and ends and rubbish.

The girls slept for an hour, then Bess woke up.

"You must be famished," she said to Connie. "I'll go and get some dinner."

She put on her hat and jacket and went downstairs, telling Flora to get the table ready.

When the front door shut with a bang the little mongrel began to bark.

"He's hungry, poor beast!" said Flora, "and he thinks it's the cats'-meat man.[39] Isn't he beautiful?"

Connie sat up in bed to look at the mongrel. Then for the first time she realised what had happened. She had left the dogs and the cottage!

Tears would come; she could not stop them from rolling down her cheeks, for she was too weak. The room seemed to move round her and she would have lost consciousness if Flora had not come quickly to the bed with a glass.

"Here's some brandy," said Flora. "Drink it up; you'll be all right in a minute."

"You are both so good," sobbed Connie.

"Good!" cried Flora, laughing. "That's a joke, isn't it? Get up and put on a wrapper. You'll be better when you've had something to eat. I believed you're starved. I know what it is like to be hungry myself; nothing makes one feel so miserable as being hungry."

Soon they had dinner, hot mutton and roast potatoes that Bess brought from an eating house. The girls drank brandy with their dinner, and afterwards they took "Cognac neat."

"Now come and see the house," Bess said after dinner. "We have the whole place to ourselves, and the landlady only comes once a week for the rent."

She led the way, followed by Connie and Flora came in the rear with the dog and the white rat. The house was only partly furnished. Some of the rooms were not used at all. A sitting-room on the ground floor had an unused look, and seemed to be meant more for show than comfort. The most comfortable room was the kitchen.

"We sit here in the winter," Bess said. "Now it's too hot."

In the scullery Flora had her menagerie of white mice and puppies. A tame lizard lived there in a box, and Flora let it wind itself round her wrist. She sat down on the floor to play with the puppies and to feed the mice, calling Connie's attention to their cleverness and beauty. Bess looked on with a smile that seemed to say:

"I put up with these things because they please Flora."

"I don't care for animals myself," she explained to Connie.

The afternoon wore away, and it was dark before they went upstairs again. All this time the girls asked Connie no questions about herself. They waited for her to speak. She was welcome to bed and food because she was in trouble, or she might stay until she was rested and then go silently away if she did not wish to give them her confidence.

"We won't go out to-night, it's so wet," Bess said to Flora.

[December 1893]

Chapter XIV.
Continued

They went upstairs with Connie and made her lie down on the sofa.

Then they talked to her about themselves. Bess had been a governess, Flora had been in a shop. They had met my accident and had become fast friends. So they had taken a house together.

"We had another girl here," Bess said; "but she's gone away for a bit. You can have her bed to-night, if you like."

"Do you think I can get work?" asked Connie.

"What sort of work?"

"I was in the Profession, but it's no good my trying for an engagement in a theatre before Christmas."

"I told Flora you were a pantomime girl," Bess said. "I was sure of it. Why did you give it up?"

"I lost my place."

"Through some man?"

"Yes."

"And he chucked you up?"

"Yes."

"Just like 'em!"

"I hate men, and I love beasts," remarked Flora, who had let Bess carry on the conversation.

"What's more," said Bess, "you're in trouble, I guess. That's why he's bolted."

Connie covered her face.

"Look here, dear," said Bess, "you stay with us. We want someone to look after the house, and that's about all you're fit for. You won't get any sort of work, depend on that. You stay with us, and we'll look after you. The girl that's gone used to keep the house. You take her place. When you're well, you can pay us back, supposing you don't cover your expenses; but you will, for it saves a lot to have someone do the housekeeping. If you leave us you will only find yourself in the workhouse."

Chapter XV.
The Empty Cottage

The same evening Humphry Munro returned to Kew. He left his portmanteau at the station with a friendly porter, who promised to bring it later to the cottage, and walked home by the river, thinking about Connie, and congratulating himself that he was back home again.

The grass looked fresh after the heavy rain that had fallen, and the trees had renewed their youth with Nature's tonic. All was life and jollity on the river; canoes and boats passed up and down with girls and men in them, either busy with oars and paddles, or lazily enjoying the cool summer evening. The pedestrians looked cheerful, for a cloudless sky had enticed many people on to the towing path.

"There's no place like home," he said to himself, when he came in sight of the garden gate.

He wondered why Connie was not there to welcome him, and why the dogs had not heard his footsteps? When the gate fell back with a grating noise, and he passed into the garden, he heard loud barking in the cottage.

"Is she ill?" he asked himself.

Directly he opened the door the dogs jumped upon him in wild excitement.

"Connie!" he called loudly.

"Where can she be?" he wondered, when no one answered. He looked for her in the sitting-room and in the garden, then he searched the kitchen.

"She must be upstairs," he said.

The dogs followed him to the bedroom, and they sniffed at Connie's white dress on the bed, and at her shoes on the floor.

Humphry Munro looked round the room; everything was just as usual there, everything was in order.

"She must have gone out to do some shopping," he said; "but I wonder she did not stay in for me. I told her I should be home by half-past seven."

The cottage felt strangely empty, for Connie had always been there to welcome him before this; he had never found the place deserted until this evening. So he went into the garden and sat down in the arbour with his pipe to possess his soul in patience.[40]

It grew dark while he waited in the summerhouse, and each minute he became more anxious; but he said to himself:

"Nothing can have happened to her; she will be here directly."

The porter came from the station with his portmanteau; and after the man had gone away he went to the larder to find supper. He carried some bread and meat to the sitting-room and put the cellaret[41] on the table, but he did not feel hungry. When he had emptied his glass and swallowed some cold beef, he strolled to the cottage gate, and leant on it, waiting for Connie.

"Where can she be?" he asked himself.

At last he went back to the cottage, listening to every noise, hoping to hear the gate open. But all was quiet. A light wind blew a rose branch against the window, no other sound broke the stillness.

"She might have left a note to explain it," he thought.

Then he began to blame himself for leaving her alone in the cottage.

"I ought to have made her keep the char-woman here while I was in the country," he said. "But no one has been here, everything is as usual; she must have left the place for some reason or other. I don't understand it."

The hours were creeping on towards midnight; so he lit the gas, leaving the blinds up that she might see the light from a distance; and he sat down in the sitting-room, where the dogs lay on the floor, watching his movements, and the parrot blinked its round eyes while it ruffled its green and yellow feathers.

"I'll go to town by the first train to see if she is at the old lodgings," he said.

He threw himself on the sofa and tried to go to sleep, but could not; and when the dim light of early morning came through the windows, he was walking up and down in the sitting-room and the passage.

The first sound that he heard was the milk-man's voice at the gate, and he went quickly into the garden to inquire if the man had seen Connie.

No, the man had not seen the lady. The milk-can had been left outside the garden gate the previous day, and there it was still for no one had emptied it. Munro turned away, wondering if he had better go to the Police Station.

Drops of water were hanging on the blades of grass in the garden, and sparrows shook the dew from the leaves while they jumped about looking for their breakfast. A tame robin had perched itself on an acacia tree to watch the chickens peck the corn up. The place looked so peaceful and homelike that Munro said to himself:

"Connie must come soon, and things will go on as usual."

But his words did not make him feel any the less anxious; so he dressed and went to the station. The porters stared at him when he arrived on the platform, for he was well-known there, but he did not often put in an appearance so early in the morning. For a minute he thought it might be worth while to question the porters about Connie, but he decided that it would be best to make the first inquiries at the lodging-house. So he went to Hammersmith, and on to Charing Cross, and then he walked to the house where she had lodged after leaving her father.

He knocked. When the door was opened he was told that the former landlady had let the house and gone into the country.

"Miss Ufindel! I know no such person," said the new woman. "I believe the lady who had this house before me wasn't particler, but I take only single gentlemen."

Mr. Munro turned away without heeding the stony stare of the British Matron.

"The idea of his coming here to ask for a girl at this time o' day," she said; "and a gentleman, too! He ought to be ashamed of hisself."

She watched him call a cab, and wondered much where he was going next.

"Polly," she said to the dirty servant who was toiling upstairs with the lodger's boots, "what was the name of the young girl that called here the night before last? Wasn't it Ufindel?"

"Yes'm."

"Well, I never!" said the British Matron, as she went downstairs, "and quite a gentleman! I wonder where he went in that cab he got into? I'd like to know the ins and outs of it."

The cab stopped at a house in a street facing the park, and Munro got out. He rang the bell, and when the door was opened he went upstairs to a room where his friend Grey was sitting at breakfast.

"Well, Munro, what's up?" asked the cynic.

"She's gone!" said Humphry.

"Who's she?"

"Connie!"

"Who the deuce is Connie?"

"Don't you remember the girl I told you about, who slept in your room one night when we had the flat?"

"Yes."

"Well, she's gone."

"Where was she?"

"In a cottage I took for her at Kew."

"Oh! it came to that, did it?"

"I went home for a ball, and when I returned to Kew last night I found her gone."

"With some other fellow?"

"No; hang it."

"Suppose she found out you're hard up."

"I tell you that had nothing to do with it."

"My dear fellow, these girls are all alike. How long has she been with you?"

"Five months."

[January 1894]

Chapter XV.
Continued

"Had another lover all the time most likely, and has now gone off with a richer man than yourself."

Munro's face blanched.

"Look here, Grey," he said; "I love the girl. I am not in love. You understand the difference?"

The cynic's eyebrows met together, and a sharp, short line came in his forehead.

"Perhaps she'll come back," he said, presently.

"She has not left a line to explain her absence," said Munro. "She was all right when I went away on Thursday. She was alone, because she would not keep a servant; she used to send ten shillings a week to her father, a drunken wretch in Drury Lane."

"Have you seen the old toper?" his friend interrupted.

"No. I have been to the house where she lodged after she left her father, but they know nothing about her."

"Her father is the most likely person to find her for you. He must know her friends and habits."

"I'll go to him at once."

"Wait! I'll go for you. She was in a pantomime, if I remember right. I'll let him think I am manager of a theatre, that I can give her an engagement. If you go he will be suspicious. I will take a cab from Drury Lane to my chambers, so you can meet me there, after you have had some breakfast. Give me the man's address."

Mr. Grey started on his errand, throwing a remorseful glance at *The Times* as he left the room. Twenty minutes later he was in a street leading out of Drury Lane, where a small crowd of women and children gathered to look at the rare sight of a cab stopping before a common lodging-house. He found Mr. Ufindel in a neighbouring public house, enjoying a glass with some kindred spirits. Ragged, with sodden features, Connie's father looked a miserable object when the fashionably dressed barrister singled him out with the help of a boy whose wits had been sharpened by the payment of a sixpence for his services.

Mr. Ufindel had not seen his daughter for six months, he said. She sent him ten shillings a week, and that was only twenty-six pounds a year, little enough for a man to live on who had once taken leading parts in the provinces. Mr. Grey had a shilling to spare, perhaps.

He shuffled to the cab and stood abjectly by the door until his fashionable visitor departed.

"I believe Munro really cared for this girl," Grey said to himself. "But how could he place his affections on anything in Drury Lane is surprising –"

Then he bent forward to read the morning's news on the posters, and his thoughts travelled from Connie to the House of Commons.

"It's no good," he said, when he arrived at the Temple and found Munro waiting for him in a room full of papers and law books. "The old toper knows nothing about his daughter. I have promised him five pounds if he finds her and sends her address here, so he will do his best. Depend upon it, Munro, the girl has gone off with some other man. You are well rid of her. How can any good thing come out of such miserable surroundings?"

"You don't know Connie," said Munro.

"I could tell you of dozens of cases –"

But Munro thanked him and left the room with an abrupt "Good morning," before he could finish the sentence.

Chapter XVI.
"Your Wife Must Be My Daughter"

"I must go to the police," said Munro.

He returned to Kew, and went to the nearest police station. But there he learnt nothing about Connie; he only received promises that inquiries should be made for her, and was advised to employ a private detective.

He turned away saying he would think the matter over and call again, and after leaving the police-station he went slowly towards the cottage. Presently he heard footsteps behind him, and turning round, saw a policeman hurrying to catch him up. "Beg pardon, sir," said the man, "but I'm told you're looking for someone you've lost from the cottage."

"Yes."

"Well, I saw two ladies go there the day before yesterday, about three o'clock in the afternoon. A cab pulled up a little way from the gate: one lady got out and rang the bell; the other stopped in the cab. A young girl in a white dress opened the gate and the lady went in with her. It was raining hard, so I stood under a tree opposite for a bit; that's how I come to see it. Presently the lady came out again with the girl and drove away in her cab. The girl looked very much upset. Is it her you're looking for, sir?"

"What was the lady like, the one who came in the cab?" inquired Munro.

"Well, she was tall and dark, and not unlike you, sir, in appearance."

"Diana!" exclaimed Munro.

"Beg pardon, sir?"

"Never mind. After the lady drove away in the cab, what happened?"

"Why, the girl went back into the cottage and shut the door. I left the tree then, but I saw her again a few hours afterwards."

"Where?"

"On Kew bridge."

"What was she doing there?"

"Nothing particular. She had on a dark dress then, and a long black cloak; but I knew her all the same. She stood on the bridge quite ten minutes; then she went towards Hammersmith. I passed by the cottage late that night, and the dogs were barking and whining, but all was dark inside. I've seen the girl about Kew this last four months. Is it her you've lost, sir?"

"Yes."

"Well, my belief is the lady who came in the cab could tell you more about the business. I'll keep a look out for the girl, and come round at once if I hear or see anything of her. I suppose there is someone in charge of the place?"

"Yes."

Munro pressed a sovereign into the man's hand and turned away, with the blood throbbing in his veins and his heart full of bitterness. He did not doubt for a moment that the lady thus described was Diana, who had somehow or other found out about Connie, and had taken advantage of his absence to pay her a visit. What his sister had said and done to Connie he did not know yet, but he would soon, he said to himself, for he would go home that morning. He forgot about Connie in his anger, and thought only of Diana, who had dared to go to his house and interfere with his arrangements.

He strode on to find the charwoman, and place her in charge of the cottage, and as he went he vowed that nothing should make him forgive his sister if any harm came to Connie through her interference.

Within an hour he was at Waterloo Station, where he snatched a hasty lunch, and took the first train home. His anger grew more intense as time wore on. He tried to read the newspapers, but could make no sense of the telegrams and leading articles, so he threw them away and stared out of the window until the train stopped at Chatbury. Then he hurried past the guard who opened the door of the carriage, took no notice of the station-master and the porters, but went quickly through the station to the high road and on to the hall.

The drawing-room windows were open, and he heard voices when he approached.

"I asked the Princess to come on my 'At Home' day. She did not know, of course, and visitors were impressed by the fact that Royalty barred the entrance."

"It's Mrs. de Burgh," he said to himself; "no one else could be so snobbish."

Then he came suddenly to the nearest window.

"Humphry!" exclaimed Diana, "I suppose you have come to congratulate me on my engagement to Sir George McCannon?" she continued, growing very pale while she spoke. "How did you know about it?"

"No, I did not come for that purpose," said Munro. "Mrs. de Burgh, will you allow me to speak to my sister alone? It is urgent."

Mrs. de Burgh rose languidly and went out upon the terrace.

"Now, Diana, explain yourself!" said Munro as he came through the window and walked straight up to his sister.

"What do you mean?" inquired Diana.

"You went to my house," said Munro, "and Connie has left it. Why did you go there? What did you do there? Answer me, or by God I'll –"

"Hush!" said his sister; "Sir George McCannon is with father in the library."

"I don't care. Answer my questions."

"There was a letter –" faltered Diana.

"Where is it?"

"I will fetch it."

"You opened my letter!" said Munro, with horror and disgust written on his face.

"I did it for the best," replied his sister. "Indeed I did, Humphry. I wanted to save you from the consequences of your own folly. I knew you did not realise what you were doing. I thought you might marry the girl if you had her letter."

"Fetch it!"

Diana was not gone long. She returned a few minutes with Connie's note.

Munro took it from her without a word and read it. Then followed a long silence.

"Marry her!" he said at last. "Yes, of course!"

His sister did not speak, and he stared vacantly at the carpet.

Presently the door opened and the Squire came into the room.

"Humphry!" he exclaimed, "you here! What's the matter?"

"Read this, sir," said Humphry, holding out Connie's note. "This came for me two days ago and was opened by Diana. She has been to my cottage at Kew and driven away Connie."

"Who is Connie?"

"The girl I am going to marry."

The Squire looked from his son to his daughter, then prepared to read the letter. He read it twice. Afterwards he said to Diana:

"Go to Sir George McCannon, my dear, and order tea for Mrs. de Burgh at once – on the terrace."

"Well, Humphry," he asked when they were alone, "what do you propose to do?"

"I don't know, sir," said Humphry. "You see, I had no idea of it – no idea of it."

The Squire walked to the window.

"She is such a little thing to be alone," continued Humphry. "I must return to London at once, and look for her. I suppose if I find her I may bring her to Home Farm?"

He looked wistfully at his father while speaking, and put Connie's letter in his pocket.

The Squire did not answer for a minute. Then he came to his son and laid his hand on the young man's arm.

"No, Humphry," he said; "you must bring her here. Your wife must be my daughter."

LABOUR LEADER

A. Chee, 'The Bank-Manager's Girl', *Labour Leader*, 26 May 1894, p. 3.

Mrs Isabella Fyvie Mayo, 'A Bit of Tragedy', *Labour Leader*, 21 December 1895, p. 3.

Caroline E. Derecourt Martyn, 'A Mystery', *Labour Leader*, 7 March 1896, pp. 80–1.

Lilian Claxton, 'Nigel Grey (A Serial Story of Love and Effort)', *Labour Leader*, Chapter I, 19 December 1896, p. 436; Chapter II, 26 December 1896, p. 454; Chapter III, 2 January 1897, p. 8; Chapter IV, 9 January 1897, p. 16; Chapter V, 16 January 1897, p. 24; Chapter V (cont.), 23 January 1897, p. 32; Chapter VI, 30 January 1897, p. 40; Chapter VII, 6 February 1897, p. 48; Chapter VIII, 13 February 1897, p. 56; Chapter IX, 20 February 1897, p. 64; Chapter IX (cont.), 27 February 1897, p. 72; Chapter XI, 6 March 1897, p. 80; Chapters XI (cont.) and XII, 13 March 1897, p. 88; Chapter XIII, 20 March 1897, p. 96; Chapters XIII (cont.) and XIV, 27 March 1897, p. 104.[1]

Ella Jeffries, 'A Shop Girl', *Labour Leader*, 31 December 1898, p. 430.

Colonel Bradbury, 'Guilty – But Drunk', *Labour Leader*, 24 June 1899, p. 198.

Founded by in Glasgow by James Keir Hardie, the first incarnation of the *Labour Leader* was issued in 1888 as a new name for Hardie's first periodical, the *Miner*, but his attempt to widen its potential readership beyond the mining trade was unsuccessful. Hardie founded the second *Labour Leader* (1893–1987) in 1893 as a Glasgow monthly publication, and in 1894 it became a London-based weekly penny publication that acted as the official organ of the ILP. As editor, Hardie undertook some notorious undercover investigations, including an exposé of working practices at philanthropist Lord Overtoun's chemical plant outside Glasgow in 1899. Although it was the official ILP publication, the *Labour Leader* struggled in competition with Robert Blatchford's popular *Clarion*, which was a much livelier paper despite being less rigorous in its socialism.

Serial fiction was not such a regular feature in the *Labour Leader* as it was in the *Clarion*, but during the period covered by this volume, there were serials by authors such as Fergus Hume (n.d.) ('The Lone Inn', 1894); Albert T. Marks (n.d.) ('By Shadowed Paths', 1895); Samuel Washington (n.d.) ('The Bloodstone: A Tale of Ancient Manchester', 1896); and R. L. Gorton (n.d.) ('A Song of the Bow', 1897). Lilian Claxton (n.d.), author of 'Nigel Grey', was also a poet whose poetry was published in the *Labour Leader* as well as in non-socialist periodicals such as the *Ladies Home Journal* and the *National Temperance Mirror*. Claxton's serial was selected for inclusion in this volume as an example of one of the few serials written by a female author.

The *Labour Leader* regularly published short stories, and this genre had a higher volume of female authors, including Caroline E. Derecourt Martyn (1867–96), who was a regular contributor in 1895–6. Caroline Martyn was born in Lincoln to a police superintendent who would later become the Deputy Chief Constable of Lincolnshire. She was deeply religious and combined her socialism with her religion, embracing Fabian socialism and simultaneously publishing articles in the *Christian Weekly*. Martyn was renowned for her public speaking and travelled widely across the country to speak about socialism. She acted as Tom Mann's (1856–1941) secretary during his candidature for Aberdeen in 1896, and she had just been appointed editor of the journal *Fraternity* when she died suddenly of pleurisy in July 1896. Martyn is one of many female socialists who, along with Katherine Bruce Glasier (née St John Conway) (1867–1950) and Enid Stacy (1868–1903), have been the focus of historians' subsequent interest; June Hannam and Karen Hunt have argued that the focus on these women suggests their unusual position in the socialist movement and elides the work of many other women.[2]

Mrs Isabella Fyvie Mayo (1843–1914) was a novelist, essayist and campaigner for human rights and anti-vivisection. The remaining three authors included in this sample, A. Chee, Ella Jeffries and Colonel Bradbury, have not been identified.

Notes
1. In Claxton's serial publication 'Nigel Grey', the numbering of the chapters moves from IX (published 20 and 27 February 1897) to XI (published 6 and 13 March 1897), with no Chapter X. In Chapter IX, the break between Nigel's meeting with Nelly and his meeting with Constance may have been intended as the start of a new chapter, but it is not designated as such in the published serial.
2. See Hunt, *Equivocal Feminists*, and Hannam and Hunt, *Socialist Women*.

A. Chee, 'The Bank-Manager's Girl' (1894)

I

There were two men at Bogalong in love with the one woman, and each of them tried to hide the fact from the other, because they both worked in the one bank. It was the only bank in the place – Bogalong always was a one-horse town – and Chapson, the manager, and his assistant, Perkins, formed the whole staff. The woman who was the cause of the trouble was beautiful, of course. Blue eyes, flossy hair, and a fine figure on horseback. Chapson was very much "gone" on her, being only five-and-twenty, and innocent. Perkins was "shook" too – excuse the aboriginal idioms – but he was a Melbourne man, and "fly." *Her* name was Nelly Jacques.

Miss Jacques, being of age, and having inherited some property, had a banking-account. Chapson, merely as an excuse for calling on her, used to urge her to transfer it from the distant bank with which she dealt to the Bogalong institution. And he was quite pleased when she did so, for he foresaw many "business" interviews between himself and Miss Jacques looming ahead. Perkins manifested no emotion on the auspicious occasion, however. He calmly headed a fresh page in the general ledger, "Ellen Jacques, Landowner," and smiled darkly as the first entry showed "cr. £102 2s. 1d."[1]

Then Miss Jacques' autographs flowed in freely, and Chapson used to feel quite proud and benefactor-like as he honoured their demands. In three weeks the cr. balance had sunk to £2 odd,[2] and Chapson was immensely delighted that a cheque of Nelly's – he used to think of her as "Nelly" now – for £10 should just then be presented. Of course he paid it at once – what a capital chance of doing Nelly a little favour! Then a few more requests to pay bearer tumbled in (how he hated Perkins' style of always asking whether he should pay!) until Miss Jacques' account stood dr. £25,[3] which Perkins noted with his usual cold-blooded smile. At this time Chapson and Perkins were both courting Miss Jacques to the very utmost of their respected abilities, Chapson – poor innocent – thinking himself the only candidate for the lady's affections, and the darksome Perkins lying very low, but well satisfied with his chances.

II

Now came Chapson's opportunity. Miss Jacques formally requested from the bank an advance of £200, "to improve her section." Said Chapson: "Depend upon me, Miss Jacques, to do the very best I can for you with the general manager." And he received a look of gratitude in reply that was well worth ten times £200, in *his* opinion.

"I suppose," Miss Jacques said innocently, "I shall have to sign a mortgage, or a bill of sale, or some other horrid legal paper?"

Chapson felt quite ashamed of the institution he represented as he admitted that such would probably be the case.

"I'll let you know by the end of the week, Miss Nelly," said he, as he escorted her out, and, under Perkins' baleful glare, assisted her on her horse. "And in the meantime" – *what* an idiot he was – "any little amounts, you know – er –"

"Mr. Chapson, you're a perfect dear! You make this nasty business quite a pleasure. I'm *so* much obliged. *Good*bye!" And she cantered away, leaving Chapson in such a joyous state that he straightway went in and offered to lend Perkins his horse whenever Perkins liked. Perkins, thereupon, accepted the offer for the following Sunday, when he went out riding with Miss Jacques. And poor old Chapson knew not of it, and was quite disappointed when he called that Sunday to hear that "Miss Nelly was not at home."

The head office sanctioned the advance to Miss Jacques, provided that she executed an equitable mortgage on her land in favour of the bank, and provided, also, that a competent valuer confirmed Chapson's estimate that the said land was worth £400, and Chapson was so far gone that he actually squared the valuer![4] which was necessary, as will be seen.

But Miss Jacques delayed in the matter of executing the mortgage – "that stupid lawyer, Mr. Chapson, is *so* slow!" – until she had piled up the respectable debit balance of £90, and Chapson began to receive letters weekly from the head office inquiring as to "the security held on Ellen Jacques' overdraft," and reminding him of previous instructions regarding unsecured advances. When the amount reached three figures, peremptory orders were received from headquarters to have the overdraft reduced at once, or sufficient security lodged. That very day Miss Jacques' cheque for £80 odd came in with the mail, and Chapson went round to see her about it. But he found she had gone away for a month's holiday. She had left a letter for him, saying she was *so* sorry she couldn't bid him good-bye, that she would send those parchment things, all properly signed, next week, and that she was *most* sincerely –

Well, you can't blame Chapson. What else could he do? That evening it became Perkins' duty, as ledger-keeper, to enter up Miss Jacques' debit as £190 3s. 6d. *He* didn't care – there was no responsibility attaching to him – but Chapson was shaken up a bit next day on receiving a private letter from a friend at headquarters to say that "Ugly Jack" – the very worst of all the bank's inspectors – would be round this way during the week. Also, that he'd better put the screw on all his unsecured O.D. men, or there'd be squalls![5] Now, "Ugly Jack" hated Chapson like the very devil, so Chapson prayed very hard the next few days for a sight of Miss Jacques or that mortgage deed. But neither showed up. And the day before the inspector's coming arrived.

There was only one way out now. Perkins' smile was a study that evening, as he entered up a credit of £190 to Miss Jacques, and debited John Charles Chapson's account with precisely the same amount on a cheque payable to "self." Which debit reduced the unhappy manager's credit balance to 13s. 9d. But when the inspector came next day, it was very gratifying to Chapson to note his look of disappointment on viewing Miss J's page. "And I'll get Nelly to give me a cheque for it when she comes back," he reflected. "Or maybe there'll be no need. If she'll only say 'yes,' we'll –" and he gazed into futurity and was happy. Until Miss Jacques returned.

III

For she treated him with marked chilliness. In vain he tried to discover the cause (which was simply that Perkins had kept Miss J. posted of all the developments of her business at the bank), uselessly endeavoured to reassume the former pleasant relations, and – ass that he was – brought matters to a climax by asserting that he loved Miss Jacques more than anything else in the world, and would she be his wife? Whereupon she laughed and said, "Thanks, Mr. Chapson, I'd rather not!"

Going home he met Miss Jacques' lawyer, and tried to hide his distressed appearance by talking business. "Got that mortgage ready yet, Pounce?" said he.

"That *which*?"

"Why, you know – Miss Jacques to the bank – two hundred pounds – and at Dry Creek, with buildings, tenements, messuages,[6] and so on, and so forth."

"First *I've* heard of it," said Pounce. "Say it again, and say it slow." So Chapson explained.

"Why, hang it, man, that ground don't belong to Miss Jacques. She's only a quarter interest in it. And it's mortgaged up to the handle already, to the bank at Hopefield. Besides, the whole turn-out ain't worth more than a £100, at the outside. Don't you go lending any money on that, my son, or you'll slip!"

I don't think, for a moment, that it was the loss of his money that troubled Chapson. What he fretted over was the girl. And he grew neglectful of his work, and failed to flatter and coax folks into doing business with him, and was surly to existing customers, and became untidy in his attire, and fond of whisky and devil's-pool.[7] So business fell off, and Perkins testified strongly against the manager, and Chapson was reprimanded. This did no good, so he was transferred to a less important branch, where he played more pool, and absorbed altogether too much whisky. When the shortage occurred – a couple of years later – his friends squared the matter; but Chapson had to go; and he has since drifted away out of the ken of all who used to know him. The last I heard of him was that he was a house-to-house tea fiend, and there are not many grades below *that*. Poor old Jack! He was as good a fellow as ever lived, but too soft – too soft!

And Miss Jacques? Oh, she married Perkins. He's manager at Bogalong now.

From the Sydney Bulletin

Isabella Fyvie Mayo, 'A Bit of Tragedy' (1895)

Several ladies sat together at afternoon tea in the pleasant drawing-room of a house in the suburbs of a well-conditioned and somewhat stately provincial town. They were all women of the easy, affluent class. They talked, as such women do talk, of tennis parties, the last novel, of foreign travel and of these ornamental kinds of philanthropy which can be sandwiched between social gaieties, and, indeed, merge into them in the shape of benefit concerts, fancy fairs, and committee meetings.

Every woman there would have been "cut to the heart" to be "obliged" to refuse to marry some worthy but not wealthy man, on the score that to accept his offer might entail self-denials too terrible – for instance, the wearing of thread gloves instead of kid ones.

One of the ladies sat a little apart – or, rather, she seemed to be apart, for an indefinable line separated her from the rest. She was not often seen in such gatherings, and when she was, she was always distinctly not of them. She had a history more strongly marked than theirs, and had enjoyed opportunities for unrestrained social movement.

One or two of the younger women, to whom the stress of life's responsibility had yet scarcely presented itself – either to be accepted for salvation, or rejected to eternal loss – gazed rather wistfully at the grave face which they knew was not always so calmly and sternly sad.

And when the little party broke up, one pretty girl, for whom that quiet face always kept a ready smile, slipped her hand through her friend's arm and whispered:

"Dorothea, where are you to-day? You have been with us in the body, but not in the spirit. Where are you?"

And, with one moment's pause, the answer came:

"I am in the City Dead-House."[1]

The other shuddered.

"How can you think of such things?" she cried. "Is there a city dead-house? I do not know where it is. And why should your thoughts be there?"

"There is a city dead-house, Alice," said the elder lady. "It stands near the sea in that part of the city which is not a fashionable promenade. And my thoughts are there to-day, because this morning from the public papers I learned that the end of a sad story lies there – a piteous spectacle for the same bright sun that was shining so sweetly into Mrs. Vining's pretty drawing-room."

"Oh, tell me all about it," said Alice, eagerly. "It is so seldom there is anything interesting in this quiet place. Everything here is so matter-of-fact and comfortable. It is seldom one gets the thrill of a bit of tragedy!"

There settled back on Dorothea's face the expression which had been there all the afternoon – an expression like that of one who is enduring pain under the further strain of fatigue. She had to restrain herself from turning sharply upon this human butterfly, and asking her if she did not realise that the "bit of tragedy," which was so welcome a sensation to her, must mean the torture of some human heart, the exquisite agony of an immortal soul, or the bitter degradation of a life.

Alice remarked: "I looked through the paper this morning, but I did not notice anything specially interesting."

"It was a very short paragraph," said Dorothea, in the quietest of her even tones. "It only set forth that yesterday evening a sailor, walking on the beach, came across the dead body of a man. He was scarcely a man, rather a boy about eighteen or nineteen. It seemed that he must have walked into the water when it was high, and that the receding tide had left him there. It is he who rests in the dead-house now. And he has been identified."

"And I suppose he was a gentleman – and there was some romantic disappointment – or he had been a little wild, and his relatives were too hard on him?" questioned Alice, eagerly.

She kept in her desk a photograph of a young country magnate with whom she had once danced, and who, going on the continent and plunging into a life that involved him in difficulties, and having increased those difficulties by the "gaming" through which he hoped to extricate himself, had ended his days with a pistol shot.

"Nothing of the kind," answered Dorothea, rather severely, for she knew where her companion's thoughts had turned. "He was a young artisan – a carpenter, I think. The people with whom he had lodged said he bore an excellent character, and had always been quiet and steady; but for the last six months he had been ailing and growing unfit for work, which he had to give up entirely. He had seemed very despondent, but nobody had taken much notice of that; it seemed so natural in his circumstances."

"Where were his relations?" asked Alice, carelessly.

"Well," replied Dorothea, "he was called Thomas Reed, but his name was not worth much, for, while he is not described as an orphan, it is stated that he 'had no relations whatever,' which, we can understand, means that he had a father whom he never knew by that name, and a mother who had somehow got lost to his sight."

"Of course, it is very sad," said Alice, carelessly, with a secret wonder what had made her friend bestow two thoughts on a "case" so commonplace. "But I suppose such things must happen sometimes. Sensitive people like you, Dora, should not let their minds dwell on such gloomy subjects. I have heard you say so."

Dorothea had made up her mind to be patient, and though her disposition was vehement and intense, her will was equally strong to control its forces.

"I have said that we should never indulge gushes of emotion, except towards some practical outlet of action," she answered, gently. "And I have deprecated that school of fiction which makes the woes and miseries of the poor into the sentimental pastime of another class. And I may have quoted my favourite lines:

> He who lets his feelings run
> In soft luxurious flow,
> Shrinks when hard service must be done,
> And faints at every woe.[2]

And I say the same to-day. For this sad little story in our town has haunted me precisely because I cannot help wondering whether any of us – and which of us – may have had a hand in it, or if not a hand active in deepening its gloom, then a hand passive in failing to lighten it. I could not help wondering about that as I sat in the pretty drawing room, and heard the conversation about our pleasures and purchases, our tours and travels.

"I think it is little likely that any of us had ever seen this miserable young man, or that anybody belonging to us has had anything whatever to do with him," replied Alice, with a dash of hauteur. "And at the utmost he could have come across us in the way of doing some work and I presume we should have certainly paid him what was just and fair."

"Alice," said Dorothea, "do you think we touch no destinies but those of the people whom we see and speak with? The human world is an organic unity far too complete for any such arbitrary division.

"It would be worse than useless to endeavour to gaze down such a vista as opens before every word or action," assented Dorothea, heartily. "But the knowledge that such a vista does certainly open should make us very watchful and earnest over our words and actions themselves, 'redeeming the time,' or, as the revised version suggests, 'buying up the opportunity,' 'because the days are evil.'[3] Consequences will take care of themselves, since their fruit, beyond our control, will be good or evil, only according to the seed which is ours to sow."

"But please to illustrate how we could possibly have done anything to influence this suicide's destiny," said Alice.

"Perhaps some of us, wishing a few more frills for the same money, docked a few pence off a sempstresses's wage," suggested Dorothea, "and that sempstress may have been his landlady's niece or daughter, and the little curtailment of her modest expectations so filled her with fretfulness and despondency as to alarm the old woman into throwing out dismal hints to the sickly lodger falling into arrears. Or we forgot to pay a laundress's bill before we went on to the continent, and the laundress was the wife of a kindly fellow-woman, and the little scarcity in the domestic funds hindered the good couple from inviting the lad to share their mid-day meal on Sunday, and so not only deprived him of that most cheering consolation, nourishing food, but made him feel that everybody was forsaking him, and that he was becoming a mere 'burden.' Our primal rule of conduct, in our endeavour not to do harm to our fellow creatures, is to strive after justice, Alice."

"Oh, Dorothea," cried Alice, "it seems such a poor thing to try not to do harm. Ought we not to seek to do good? Should not you put mercy first?"

"Alice," said Dorothea, "it seems to me that justice is the very gentlest spirit in the whole universe. We have no right to think of it only as meaning punishment or retribution. Justice may involve punishment and severity, because sometimes these are the best blessings to those who receive them. But there can be no mercy without justice. Anything which passes as mercy, apart from justice, is a mere robbing of Peter to pay Paul,[4] and is generally the most cruel of wrongs to everybody concerned. Justice really means thoughtful consideration for others, first for their rights, and then for their needs, and their weaknesses, and disadvantages. It is only those who sincerely try to exercise this, who understand what a weighty matter it is, and how wide and deep are its ramifications. And they never again complain of life as flat or uninteresting."

"There you have a hit at me, Dora," said Alice, quite complacently. "But I don't want my life to be made more interesting by getting things to worry myself over. What I want is more pleasant excitement – something to stir one up, cheerful events of some kind."

"Yet every 'cheerful event' of the kind you mean ought only to bring you more and more of what you choose to call 'worry,'" said Dorothea. "For no brightness that comes to us should be absorbed by us. We should only take our share in it, and the best of our share should be that we may pass it on, with increased significance, into other lives. It will not be worth much for ourselves, if it cannot be made into something for other people. I often wonder how, in the great consummation of our earthly existence, we shall answer to the divine question 'What hast thou made of the joys I gave thee? Hast thou made family pride and selfishness and oppression out of the near ties with which I blessed thee? If thou visited the widow and the orphan in their affliction, did the visit always lift up their sinking hearts, or did it leave them rather with a redoubled sense of bitter loneliness? Into what has thou turned thy wealth? Didst thou make it into human industry and peace and prosperity? or didst thou keep it for thine own pleasure, and so transmute it into the refuse which thou callest luxury'?"

"Well, Dora," said Alice, "when I hear you talk, my only comfort is that all this can have nothing to do with girls like me."

"It has everything to do with girls like you," answered Dorothea, with quick emphasis. "It can be applied quite practically even to very young girls. First of all, everybody in this world ought to do something to justify his or her existence therein. Everybody ought to 'work out a living,' whether he be rich or poor, else he is a pauper, the curse of his community, preying on the labour and wage of others. For the true paupers are not those who have worked hard and fall on public charity because they have been ill paid; but those who have done nothing all their days but consume the labour of others."

"If that is to be the case, what is the use of being well off?" asked Alice.

"Don't say anything so ignoble," said Dorothea. "Do not say that need can compel us to better things than love and duty and honour. Why, life contradicts you flatly at once. I do not suppose any lady at the head of a great house of business works harder than does our Queen. And I know a countess whose husband has a rent roll of eighty thousand a year, who works as assiduously as could the most devoted secretary of a philanthropic institution. I fear it is the women of the middle class who are the greatest sinners in this respect. Innovations have deprived them of the old-fashioned methods of housekeeping and stitchery and home school-room, and they have been driven to make their pastimes into their life's labour, and very hard labour they become in the end."

"What is a girl to do, then?" asked Alice; but not like one seeking counsel.

"First and foremost, she must see how she can make herself useful, so as to have some right to the bread and the roof with which love provides her," answered Dorothea. "Next, she must not fret after finery and frivolity, for these cost money, and that may hamper and limit her father when he would apply it to better purposes. She must not get a new dress for mere fashion's sake, and then, as a salve to her conscience, give the old one to some poorer girl; but she must cultivate a noble economy, which shall so dispense her means as to further honest people in their efforts to get good, fresh garments for themselves. And she must treasure all love's gifts to herself, recognising love's labour as God's most precious gift of any, and giving the precedence over gold and diamonds to poem or sketch, to home-reared flowers or home-trained animals."

"But have we not wandered very far from our starting-point?" asked Alice. "Even if we all did these things, I do not see how these could affect such cases as that of this suicide."

Dorothea shook her head sadly.

"It is in little things like these that complications begin which finally puzzle our greatest philosophers," she said. "Girls like finery and frivolity. These cost money. Therefore, money must be made and possessed even at the cost of the highest and sweetest ideals of life. There comes a temptation to regard the sins of a rich man differently from those of a poor one. People whose character would prevent them, if they were needy, from being hired to weed our gardens or wash our clothes, are, because of their wealth readily welcomed to drawing-rooms and dinner-tables. When the rich profligate at last inclines to woo, it is 'charitably' assumed that he is reformed, and the woman on whom his choice falls, is content to ignore the ignorant souls he has led to ruin, and the innocent lives he has robbed of their best rights."

"But girls ought not to know anything about such things," said Alice.

"Well, my dear," repeated the elder lady, "for years past you have read novels and newspapers without supervision. You are old enough to have thoughts of courtship and marriage, and society would allow you to become the mistress of a house and the head of a family. Therefore, you must be also old enough to consider these things, though when presented to you as I am about to present them, they may make you start. Let me ask you to reflect that the father of this poor drowned boy, the man who is answerable for his namelessness and loneliness and destitution, may be – not improbably – now the husband of a woman such as we are, perhaps one who finds nothing too good or too dainty for her own children. Perhaps some of us may have sat at their festive board while the unacknowledged son lay dead upon the beach."

"But it is not our duty to pry into people's past lives and private histories," remarked Alice.

"Most assuredly not," said Dorothea. "Indeed, I have found that a very ready disposition to 'think evil' and to indulge in morbid 'suspicions,' is very apt to accompany a stubborn disinclination to recognise undoubted evil. But it is terrible to hear how characteristics which a moment's consideration would show us must involve depths of human degradation and agony somewhere are slurred over, or actually admired! Why, Alice, very few of the heroes of popular fiction are men of the type which makes the world better!"

"But generally they are described as being sorry for their past lives," said the girl. "And would you leave no room for repentance?"

"I would leave all room for repentance," cried Dorothea, passionately; "but repentance is an awful and solemn thing to be worked out in daylight actions, not merely whispered over in twilight gardens and perfumed parlours. Oh, Alice, Alice, when I sit in luxurious rooms, and hear the prattle of selfishness and recklessness and thoughtlessness, I wonder sometimes how we should feel if we could see the other end of the life-threads which we hold so carelessly."

"But we can't see it," said Alice, "and that is the comfort of it. We could not live if we did."

"Say, rather, we could not live as we do," replied Dorothea, emphatically. "But suppose some day we shall see it all? May there not be personal meanings for us in that declaration of the prophet of old, which we are so apt to limit to one theologic sense, 'They shall look unto Him whom they have pierced, and they shall be in bitterness for Him as one that is in bitterness for his first-born.'"[5]

"Well, it may be so," said Alice, pausing at her own gate, "but I never pretend to be clever, and I do not see the use of going deeply into things if it makes one miserable. Good-by Dorothea."

Caroline E. Derecourt Martyn, 'A Mystery' (1896)

The golden dawn flushed and faded between the purple shadows of the night and the pale glory of the morning. The sun gazed with gladness on the cool earth, sparkling with dew, and she wafted to him the perfume of her breath from meadows thick with cowslips and woods whose tender foliage waved above the coverts of the violet.

A boy roamed through the wood gathering the purple sweets.[1] He wandered beyond the trees aimlessly, as children will, till he reached the middle of a meadow, where a little girl, fresh as the morning, greeted him with gay laughter as her playmate.

But as the day grew, childhood departed from them, and each was enwrapped in the beautiful garment of youth. And on its border were written signs of maturity and old age and separation and death.

The thought of separation wounded them sore, and they sought the bond that cannot be broken, so that they might pass through life in peace and escape the dreadful fear.

So they betook them to a journey in search of a bond that could not be broken, and wandered far until they reached the Temple of Religion. And to the priest who was there they said:

"Sir, we fain would be made one with the bond that cannot be broken."

So he led them within the holy place, and brought forth the treasure. But, lo! An iron chain too heavy for them to bear, and they fled affrighted.

Hurriedly they passed along the road, and soon the stately Palace of Justice reared its towers before their eyes. They passed hopefully through the gates, and met the janitor.

"Sir," said they, "we fain would be made one with the bond that cannot be broken."

Whereupon he led them to a throne-room, where the awe of a great silence and the terror of mysterious recesses weakened the will with fear. But he who sat on the throne spake kindly to them, and sought for that bond within a chest near to his hand, and it was locked with many locks and sealed with many seals.

Thence he drew a golden chain, which was joined with wondrous cunning; but, behold! at the touch of a golden key that hung at his girdle its links all fell apart or were again united. And as they turned away sorrowful he would have held them perforce, and bound them with the chain, but they fought hard, and so escaped.

Soon they came to the Hall of Pleasure, at whose doors stood a woman very good to see, wearing garments finely wrought. And they said to her:

"Lady, we fain would be made one with the bond that cannot be broken."

She led them into the place with many promises, and there they found a great crowd of people. Some danced, some sang, and others feasted. And the lady brought them a garland of flowers; but, behold! among the flowers a serpent and many thorns, and, as they gazed, already the flowers faded.

So they passed on to the House of Love. They needed no guide to the altar, and there they knelt in awe. Sweet scent surrounded them, all things glowed in wondrous light, and faint music filled the air. And a voice from out the melodies said:

"What would ye?"

And they said:

"We would fain be bound with the bond that cannot be broken."

And the voice said:

"Where Earth's breast is Nature's bosom the secret of the treasure may be learned."

Then they wandered far through the beautiful world, suffering many woes and rejoicing in much gladness. They went past the cities, away from the farms and well-tilled fields, across the barren hills, over the still blue lake, and threaded a dim forest. And at noon they reached a plain where the softness of moss and the spring of heather were combined in the jewelled turf. In the mist there lay a little hill, and it was the Earth's breast, which is Nature's bosom. So they lay on the swelling ground, where they could hear the great heart of life beating beneath its roundness.

And a murmuring voice sighed through the trees:

"What would ye?"

And they said:

"We would fain be bound with the bond that cannot be broken."

And the voice said:

"At the Gate of Life ye shall find the bond, if your strength fail not."

So they arose, and passed onwards. Now the robe of mature life enfolded them, and on its borders was written the lore of future generations.

They walked through night and day, and summer and winter. Now her weakness rested on his strength; anon his vigour went from him, and she was the sustenance of his steps. And always they loved each other with deeper love.

And so they came to an amphitheatre of hills, with an opening in the west, wherein glowed the sun in the gold and crimson glory of his setting.

And the way between the hills was the Gate of Life.

They reached it as the last bright ray departed, leaving the world in the grey dimness of the night.

They lay on the threshold of the gate to sleep.

And the priest, passing by, cursed them, because they bore not his iron fetters.

The lawyer mocked them because no golden chain encircled them.

The votaries of pleasure laughed at them because no garland graced their forms.

But in their peaceful sleep they heeded not.

And Nature laid her gentle hand on them, so that their bodies became commingled with her own.

Thus were they joined in the bond which cannot be broken, for Love drew forth their souls to His embrace, and they twain, being one therein, knew not death or separation.

Lilian Claxton, 'Nigel Grey (A Serial Story of Love and Effort)' (1896–7)

[19 December 1896]

Chapter I.

The village of Brierly[1] stood on gently rising ground, and consisted chiefly of one straggling main street of white-washed cottages. The Hall, Squire Compton's place, was situated at the lower end of the village, and stood some way back from the high road, in thickly wooded grounds.

In the upper part of the village, at the end of the main street, the last house, a red brick building, had turned its back upon the rest and faced the common and the sunset. The clear pink of the monthly roses clustering about the walls showed up vividly against the dull red of the bricks one afternoon in early November; and the honeysuckle, flowerless, but climbing round the porch, with the hollyhocks in the garden, and the blue smoke rising from the chimney, gave it a Christmas-card-like prettiness. The door was ajar; two women within were talking. One was quite an old lady, with wrinkled, ruddy cheeks; the other woman was much younger, and bore sufficient likeness to her companion to show a relationship somewhere.

"Well, I'm glad they're back," the latter was saying. "It gave one the blues – I declare it did – to pass the Hall with the shutters all closed. Not that one can see much of it from the road, but still one couldn't help thinking of the dismal old place. Miss Constance has been round to see you, you say? I suppose she'll be thinking of settling soon. I wonder did she meet with anyone abroad."

"Lor', no! You may be sure Miss Constance wouldn't look twice at one of them furriners;[2] besides, she'd have told me if she'd anyone in her mind. I can't help thinking myself that her cousin will carry her off some day."

"What! Mr. Tom?" cried the other, in a tone of dismay.

The old lady frowned and shook her head.

"I meant Master George," she said. "Sir George, I ought to call him. As for Mr. Wilton, I don't know what's come to him. Yes, that's what I'm to call him in future; it ain't to be Master Tom any more; me that's known him from a baby. He came to see me last Michaelmas. 'Hello, old nurse,' says he – you know his 'earty way? 'Why, Master Tom,' I says. 'Drop that, nurse,' says he. 'Don't go a-mastering me,' and then says he – I mind the words, 'We are strivin' for a hage, nurse,' says he, 'which shall do away with those baubles of distinction. I'm plain Thomas,' he said. But I could as soon call him plain Thomas as I could take off my hat in church or repeat the h'absolution along with the clergyman."

"In one sense he certainly is plain Thomas," said the nurse's niece, a woman who, if she had lived in the States, would have been called "smart."

She was in her bonnet and shawl, and had evidently only been paying an afternoon call. She lingered a moment on the threshold before leaving.

"So we're going to have a new well. Have you heard?" she said.

"Bless me, yes," returned the old woman, testily.

"They say the old one's unhealthy they say that outbreak of fever can be traced to it. You remember that time when Tom Milligan's widow made such a fuss, right in the very graveyard, because they buried old Downing, who had died of it, alongside of Tom, who'd never had it."

"Eh, Milligan's widow is a poor, weak-minded critter," said the old woman, shaking her head. "Who's doing all these things down in the village, Martha; a-bothering about a new well, and so on? I hear someone's taken the Manor House, and someone else is a-patching up them old cottages. We got on very well with things as they were. A h'epidemic now and then is the will of the Lord to clear off sickness. However, Mr. Tom Wilton's mightily pleased with this new well; he says it's the beginning of a new hearer. He comes down now and again to see how it's getting on. I'm thinking as he's at the bottom of it."

"Bottom of the well!" said Martha, seeing another opportunity for a play upon word. "No, no, that ain't Mr. Tom's doings; and that reminds me. Do you remember anything of a family of the name of Grey who lived round here some twenty years ago? Because I think it's a Mr. Grey who is thinking of boring the new well. Anyway, he's mixed up with it, and I hear tell his folks once lived in these parts, so he's interested like in the place."

The old woman thought for a moment.

"Why, yes," she then said, "there was a Mr. Grey, steward to the old earl. He married Mary Leigh daughter of the gamekeeper. A little beauty she was; half the village lads were crazy over her, but she held her head high. Why, yes, I remember it all now. I went up to their place after they'd been married some years, with a message from the mistress, and I took Miss Constance with me. She was a toddling baby then, not turned two. There was a little slim lad of seven or eight there, and Mrs. Grey told him to take Miss Constance and show her his rabbits. But he looks at her for a minute, and then says he, 'No,' he says, 'she's too young,' and with that he puts his hands in his pockets and stalks off. I think there were some other youngsters, but I only remember that boy. Such manners from him to my pretty little lady! Mr. Grey took up queer notions. They say he was mixed up with the great strike over at Findlay. I know he moved away to London, and didn't get on there, according to reports, as well as he might. So this is the 'igh and mighty son, is it, a-coming here like a prince in a fairy tale to provide a fresh well for our benefit?"

"Oh, I don't know as he's doing it, I only thought it likely. But I must go, aunt. Here's your young lady coming, so you won't be dull."

Martha nodded farewell, gathered up her skirts, and stepped briskly down the sunny front path bordered with pebbles, London pride, and Old Man.[3]

Up the village street came a girl in a dainty gown, with a puckered piece of blue flannel on her head, which did duty for a Tam o'Shanter,[4] and beneath which her hair curled in a bright fringe. Her face was not classical, it hardly aspired to beauty, but it was fresh and pretty; the mouth, girlish and mobile – had latent possibilities, and the eyes had caught dreaming, tender fancies from the shadowland of thought.

"Why, it is really you, Miss Constance?" cried the old woman, in delight, as she entered. "I didn't think you'd be round so soon again, I didn't. Sit down, my dear; I was just a-going to have a cup of tea. The pot's on the hob all ready, and you must have one, too; yes, you must dearie."

There was nothing old Mrs. Brenton enjoyed so much as decoying one of "her children," as she called Miss Compton and the two young men cousins who had been Constance's companions in childhood, into her little parlour, and there making them partake of the cup that cheers.[5] It had been a pleasant change for the high spirited little schoolgirl during her somewhat monotonous holidays to escape from the shadowy old house and the vigilant eye of her aunt. For Constance's mother had died when she was very small, and after that her father's half-sister, a widow lady of ascetic principles, had ruled with a high hand at the Hall. Now, however, she had found another home, and Constance, in the dignity of one-and-twenty, stood at the head of the domestic hearth.

This afternoon, having an hour to spare, she sank into the easy chair opposite the old lady.

"And how did you get on abroad, my dear?" the latter asked. "I suppose, being so long at school in Germany and France, you felt quite at home there; but Ameriky[6] was all new to you. Did it take you long a-learning the language?"

"Not long at all, nurse; I soon had it pat.[7] My father says it is so ingrained in me now that the difficulty will be in getting me not to talk it. Oh, the moving about was very nice, but I'm glad to be home again amongst the old faces. I'm 'tuckered out' with novelty. There, that's American for tired, nursie."

"And you didn't pick up a young gentleman in furrin parts, Miss Constance?"

"No, indeed," the girl returned, laughing. "I didn't get so much as an offer except from an old German baron who wore goggles and took snuff. I begin to wish now I had accepted him; yes, I wish I had! We should have been Baron and

Baroness Von Schreiber Heiben. Think of that! George would never, never – why, there *is* George. Wait a minute, nurse; I must run out and speak to my cousin."

Down the pebble-bordered pathway she ran, and reached the gate just as a young man on horseback, who had seen her beckoning hand at the window, pulled up there.

"Constance, as I live!" he cried, dismounting, and coming forward with outstretched hand. "I was just riding over to pay my respects to you."

"Yes, I am back, your majesty; and how are you?" asked Constance, taking his hand across the wicket gate and addressing him by the nickname she and Tom Wilton had given him years ago, on the strength of the grand airs of the Eton boy.

"Walk back with me to the Hall. I will lead Stella," said the young man.

"Oh, I can't. I have promised to take a cup of tea with nurse. Come in and have one, too."

Sir George hesitated a moment, then made the mare fast to the fence, opened the gate, and followed his cousin up the walk, looking at the figure in front of him with the critical eye of a relative, and estimating the success of her *debût* next season.

A few minutes later Sir George Cumberland-West was standing before nurse's fire making toast, while Constance was setting white and gold cups out on the centre table, and giving a brief sketch of her travels the while in her bright chatty way. When she had reached the end of her narrative, Sir George, whose eyes had been wandering over the mantelpiece, remarked that the room always reminded him of the British Museum, and that nurse should provide an explanatory catalogue.[8]

"What is this now – David and Goliath?[9] Why, that is new, surely." Then, as nurse disappeared into the pantry: "Feeble-looking fellow, that David; wants putting in training. 'Bliaf,[10] now, has a bluff and hail-fellow-well-met look, quite up to what he's going in for; but why the Rob Roy tunic and pea-green bandage? Don't admire 'Bliaf's taste, do you, Constance?

He passed on to an ancient timepiece suspended on a nail. "Why is nurse's watch invariably five hours and three-quarters too fast? Are those old Brenton's relatives or hers, in the ferrotype?[11] A wickeder group I never saw."

"Oh, hush, George, she'll hear you."

Constance was looking over shoulder in silent mirth. She was one of those happy beings who are always ready to laugh at other people's jokes – good, bad, or indifferent. Does the world realise how much it owes to those simple-minded, happy beings?

"Not she – deaf as a post, unless you are within a yard of her. What is she getting? Not that old almond cake, I trust. I couldn't stand it now; it took a week to digest even in the vigour of early youth. Why, here is that little old photo, we all had taken together. You were just like a spider in those days, Constance. Tom was a hideous infant, wasn't he? Well, certainly, even to a disinterested eye, I am the best-looking of the trio. Tom *wiggled* so at the knees as a child. Learnt to walk too young, I conclude; he always seemed to be struggling with gravitation."

"Tom doesn't look as if his name were Tom," said Constance, thoughtfully.

"Looks as if his name were Nicompoop," responded her cousin, with some wrath.

"For shame, George! It is just because your politics differ that you are so spiteful: but it does seem as if a Tom should be a bluff, jolly fellow."

"Life 'Bliaf when he was young," suggested George, with a glance at the oleograph.[12]

"Yes, like 'Bliaf in his palmy days, and our Tom is so pragmatical and sententious."

"Oh, hang him! No, I don't like him, Constance. It's mutual. He considers me beyond redemption, and I consider him one of Nature's idiots. Jove, who is that at the door?"

"Tom," returned Constance, with an awful calmness.

She was standing in the centre of the room, having just transferred the teapot from the hob to the table. Constance's custom from childhood had been to get the tea "all by herself" when she came to nurse's cottage.

It was impossible to tell from Tom's countenance how much he had heard of the foregoing conversation. In spite of Sir George's remark about "Nature's idiots" (whatever that might mean) Tom did not look like one. He did look like an enthusiast, though, and one not endowed, perhaps, with an extra amount of common-sense or ballast. He had a low, square forehead, round which his thick black hair stood straight up. This had won for him amongst his comrades the name of "Blacking Brush." His eyes were dark and small, but very bright. He stood in the doorway. George lounged to the little table, and threw himself into one of the straight-backed chairs, while Constance went to the door and greeted the newcomer.

"I saw you from the road, Constance," said Tom, "so I thought I'd come and ask if uncle is in just now."

"I believe so. He was when I left home."

"Tea, Thomas?" drawled George. "Come in. Try to look happy for once, man, and have some hot buttered toast."

"No, no." Tom always spoke as if he were in a hurry, as, indeed, he generally was. "I haven't a minute to spare. How are you, George? I haven't seen you for three or four months. I suppose you're going to the Hall?"

"No," returned the other, quietly; "I'm bound for Allerton as soon as I've finished this cup of tea. Little more milk, please, nurse."

Constance looked up in surprise.

"Well, I must be off," said Tom. "I've a friend with me that I'm taking to see my uncle, and we want to have a look at the site they've chosen for the new well on our way back to the station to catch the 6.20." And Tom raised his hat and departed.

"Who is your friend?" Constance called lightly after him.

"Nigel Grey," Tom shouted back from the gate, where a young man was standing looking down the street.

"George, that was a 'big one' you told about Allerton House, wasn't it?" asked Constance, a little soberly.

"No, fair lady; I have an appointment with Lord Allerton, and it all depends on the presence or absence of dear Cousin Tom whether or not I call in at the Hall to-day."

"I'm rather glad poor Tom didn't stay," said Constance, "for he does try one's patience dreadfully when he begins on that ridiculous old well. He talked for an hour and a half the other day on the subject."

"Then 'All's well that ends well,' or we might say 'Leave well alone,'"[13] re-joined George, who was not above a bad pun when opportunity offered. "And now, old lady, though I know I shall suffer for it, I'll take another slice of your excellent almond cake. We've been neglecting you all this time."

That was what her children generally did on the rare occasions when they found themselves at tea together at old nurse's.

Cousin George was decidedly improved, Constance was thinking, as, later on, they walked through the village together, the former leading Stella. Constance cast her mind back to the slim boy figure with the clear-cut pink and white face who used to ride over to the Hall on high days and holidays, and to patronise little Tom Wilton and herself. She could see him again, standing with his hands in his pockets, looking at her out of those wonderful blue eyes of his, and addressing her at intervals as Spike, Chips, or Long-legs, while Tom was Touzle-head, Snub-nose, or Freckles. True, he could hardly call her by those appellations now even had they been applicable but still he might have shown a little of the old superiority, and so far he had shown none; nay, he had even addressed her as "fair ladye" – indifferently, it is true, but then indifference was second nature to George.

When they reached the Hall gates, George stopped suddenly.

"Verily, the redoubtable Thomas again! He is standing on the steps. Well, ta-ta, Constance. I will go on and catch Lord Allerton before his dinner hour. Tell your father I hope to look in on my way back if I've time."

"Surely there is room enough for both you and Tom," said Constance half laughing, half vexed. "I suppose the truth is you want to have dinner at Allerton House. Still the old attraction?"

"Dinner – in this attire? Scarcely," with a glance at his light tweed knickerbockers and leggings. "Attraction? Are you alluding to Grace? Evidently the

Rev. Ambrose has not yet dawned upon your horizon in his ecclesiastical beauty. Wait till you behold your spiritual director, and you will see how little chance there is for commonplace mortals like myself. Grace and Beatrice are vieing with each other in good works and the embroidering of vestments, and are both ready to tear each other's eyes out at a moment's notice these days."

Constance laughed.

"Bring Bea over to see me next time you come."

"I will. Who is that the worthy Thomas has with him?" asked George, craning his neck to see between the branches – he had mounted Stella. "Oh, yes, I remember – Nigel Grey. Don't let him go introducing you to all the fellows he chooses to pick up. I foresee that will be his object. That Nigel Grey is nothing more or less than a working man, with brains a cut above the average, which have enabled him to work his way up from plain mechanic to working manager in some engine works somewhere in town.

"I suppose, then, he is immensely flattered at going about in Tom's company."

"He's easily pleased then, poor beggar! But still I hardly think Nigel Grey is the fellow to do much toadying. He is too eaten up with natural conceit for that. He is a great politician is Mr. Grey."

Constance shrugged her shoulders, as much as to say, What next will the working men of England be up to?

Then, catching a glimpse through the bare branches of the trees of Tom Wilton and his companion coming quickly within hearing, she nodded to George and turned within the gates leading to her home.

[26 December 1896]

Chapter II.

The last rays of level sunshine through which Sir George and Constance Compton had been walking had vanished. November began to be felt in the air. A shiver ran over Constance, and she felt a chilly and insignificant mortal as she hurried up the drive, under the shadow of the mighty oaks, which had stood there as solemn sentinels through long annals of England's past. She little knew that to one of the young men approaching she was the representative of the blue blood of the nation, of the old feudal system, of cold, tyrannical despotism. He was looking at her with a quick, keen glance, this young man, Tom's companion; but Constance scarcely looked at him. She spoke to her cousin, with a preliminary inclination of her head towards Nigel Grey.

"Going, Tom? Come again next week, will you not? The Burrowes will be here then, I believe."

"The Burrowes coming? Well, I'll try to run down. I hope by then we shall have the well under way, and then we must –"

"Tom, Tom; here a minute," called the squire's voice from the steps.

Tom turned.

"Hold on a moment, Grey. Oh, by the bye, Constance, this is Mr. Grey. He will tell you all about the improvements Mr. Ross is making in the village, the new inmates at the Manor, and so on. Of course, you are interested in Brierly, and you have been away so long. Coming, uncle," and with that this stupid Tom ran off, to poor, chilly Constance's disgust, leaving her shivering in her summer dress, to the tender mercies of another prosy man, devoted to sanitation, reformation, and strong opinions on the opposite side of every subject anyone could mention.

As Nigel Grey did not speak, it was incumbent on Miss Compton to break the silence.

"My cousin has told me a good deal about your work amongst the poor in London," she began, pleasantly, unconscious patronage in every word; "it is very good of you to do so much."

Next moment she would like to have recalled the words. Nigel Grey was looking straight at her in the peculiarly searching way he had. There seemed to be scepticism, even a certain distain for her opinion, about that look.

"I wish I could do more," she added.

"You can do a great deal, Miss Compton," said Grey, speaking for the first time.

"How?" asked Constance, with some curiosity.

She was looking attentively now at her companion; at the clever face, too thin, possibly, and too full of an absorbing eagerness, to be called handsome, and yet with an expression upon it which no woman could see without a touch of admiration and interest, for it told of sincerity and power.

"How?" asked Constance, again.

Nigel Grey had not answered her at once, his eyes had been wandering round the grounds.

"You ask me what you can do," he said, at length, speaking slowly, as though he were choosing his words with thought – "you, with wealth, and influence, and beauty" – Constance coloured, the piercing eyes were looking straight at her again – "and all your life before you. I look round this place of yours and think of lives lived out in close courts and alleys, to whom this air and scenery would mean salvation. I should like to bring some twenty or thirty tired old people, or wan, joyless little children that I know of, down here some day, and turn them out in these grounds for a few hours. You'd soon see by their faces how much good you could do." He was speaking quickly now. "To your table every day come dainties which would bring new life to many a wasted sufferer. Then you have books and pictures; you have been taught things that are interesting and good and beautiful. Are you trying to pass on that knowledge to others who have not had your chances, or does it merely make you hold yourself aloof from them? Even in this little village I find much that is ignorant and coarse and bad. What claim have you – excuse me, Miss Compton – to so much while others have so little? I am afraid you will resent my speaking like this, and I dare say there is no need for me to suggest these things; only," he paused and looked at her with a little smile, "whatever we do, there is more we ought to do."

Constance was too sweet-tempered to be easily offended besides, she was prepared for anything peculiar in Tom's friends, especially a man so much talked of as Nigel Grey, so she answered evenly, but with reserve:

"You must give me credit for thinking of these things myself though, Mr. Grey. From the time I was a child I have been taught to – er – go about among the cottages, you know."

What impression the cool, lady-like tones made upon Nigel Grey, with his impassioned earnestness, it is hard to say. After a moment's pause, he spoke.

"The world cries out for a great deal from you, Miss Compton, for it has given you a great deal. Just in proportion as a man had, so must he pay back again, and the hands cannot be clean and honest that accept more than they give. And because the voice that cries to you is feeble, coming as it does from the poor, the work-worn, and the suffering, must it be disregarded? Will not the womanhood in you turn and listen the more?"

Nigel paused, but Constance did not speak immediately. A desire had come over her to stand well in the eyes of this curious, unconventional man, and she was mentally going through her own various efforts for the regeneration of mankind. Her former defence of herself, after Grey's first speech, had sounded peculiarly lame even in her own ears.

"You must not think that we – that I do not try to do good amongst the poor, and to better their condition. I do indeed, Mr. Grey. Now, our temperance organisation –"[14]

She paused. Nigel Grey was looking at her again, not with disdain this time, though with no particular approval. He seemed about to speak, but checked himself; he also succeeded in checking Constance.

"Well?" she said, rather haughtily, and as he did not immediately answer, she continued: "I should have thought a work so obviously needed as temperance reform would have met with your full approbation. You must be aware how drink increased taxation and impoverishes the people; one hundred and thirty millions are thrown away annually upon it. I should have imagined, if you really care for the condition of the people, you would have done everything in your power to further temperance."

There is no being who can summon up such severity as the English girl when her principles are attacked, but Grey remained as unmoved by Constance's coldness as he had been by her praise.

"I do try to further it, Miss Compton, though perhaps not always with a pledge-card.[15] You know, I believe you must make men happy before you can make them good."

"And a very dangerous doctrine, too," said Constance sententiously.

Nigel waived the remark.

"You talked of bettering the people's condition by advocating temperance. Good. But the radical cure of drunkenness must begin further back than the pledge. Take the temperance movement in one hand, Miss Compton; but with the other stretch back and take hold of poverty, ignorance, and the wretchedness of life. Never forget or over look these things. You can make your own little individual efforts to remedy them even if you cannot touch the nation's laws."

The effect of Nigel's speech was somewhat lessened by Tom, who had returned, now cutting in with:

"I say, Constance, you should just see the old well water magnified – one drop. O my! Couldn't you ask the parson to lend us the schoolroom, and we might have a magic lantern, and show them the creatures wobbling about, and jostling one another. Mr. Ross or someone could give a lecture on bacteria, and tell the people how they'd been swallowing them by quarts, and what their effects were. That would be an eye-opener!"

"I shall do nothing of the kind," said Constance, indignantly, "and I beg you will not, either. They would all take to alcohol at once, not daring to touch a drop of water again."

"And a jolly good job, too, if that was the only kind they could get!"

Constance turned her face away, and tapped her foot on the gravel. Nigel would have liked to have laughed. He glanced at her to see whether it would be politic; her face revealed the fact that it would not. After a minute, he broke the silence which had fallen upon them.

"Until the present condition of the poor is altered, I don't quite see how temperance reform can go beyond a certain point. Certainly, the present condition of things plants plenty of obstacles in the way of a man who tries to be a teetotaler.[16] The food of the average London working man, earning his twenty shillings[17] per week, is inadequate in nourishment to what his system requires. While the daily consumption of flesh-forming food falls considerably below the average and at the same time his physical strength is being taxed to the utmost, both body and brain must suffer. Perhaps you do not know how many men in London go breakfastless to their work every morning?"

"But if he did not spend his money on alcohol, he would have it to spend on better food," said Constance.

"And how much extra food would it provide him with? We will suppose he has a wife and half-a-dozen children at home, and will not suppose the man is a drunkard, for, after all, that is the exception, not the rule – quite the exception – amongst the London poor. Would the money provide him also with light and air in his close little room, extra clothing, means for cleanliness, possibilities for rest and quiet – I might add, books and knowledge for the starving brain? All these things are needed to keep health at its normal standard, all these things must be remedied before this national evil can be swept away; and, again, if alcohol were abolished from the land to-morrow, all these things, though in a lesser degree, would remain. The capitalist would see to that."

Here Tom broke in.

"Oh, I say, Grey, come on. While you're trying to make some impression on my cousin's mind, we shall miss the train."

"One minute," said Constance. "Mr. Grey, I have something to say on my father's behalf; not that I think his conduct needs defence from anyone, but because I believe you are labouring under a mistaken idea. You go about in our little village and you see many of the people underfed and underpaid. But, remember, *he* is not pay-master. He does pay for their children's school, though; he makes a point of seeing that all who ever worked for him have sufficient; he lets his cottages at far less than their value, and when the tenants don't pay him he accepts their excuses, though he knows that he is the last one that they will pay – that he stands even below the doctor. In trouble and sickness when they go to him (as they always do) they are never sent away without sympathy or substantial aid. Do him some justice, even though he is that most reprehensible being – a Conservative landowner."

The speech was uttered simply and loyally. Nigel glanced at the speaker with a touch of admiration.

"It would be strange if no good thing could come out of Nazareth," he answered, smiling. "If all men of all parties had acted up to their consciences there would be little need for social reform. But the majority who hold the reins of power at the present time are neither kind, helpful, nor just; therefore, it behoves others to go further than we need otherwise have done, and bring in a radical reform."

"What made you take so much interest in our village?" asked Constance, somewhat abruptly.

"I was born here. My father was steward to Lord Allerton some twenty years ago," said Nigel. "I came over to-day to explain things to Mr. Compton, for I heard that he thought I was stirring up discontent among the people. I had no wish to create anarchy in your village, and I don't want to be considered a meddling busybody. After all, my work lies in town, not here; but I find it a pleasant change to run down occasionally.

"Oh, come on, Grey," said Tom, beginning to move off.

"Miss Compton," said Nigel, hurriedly, "you must forgive me if in speaking to the point my words have sounded harsh – rude – to a lady's ear. I am not used to speaking to such, and indeed, I had no intention of speaking in this style at all when I came to your house to-day; but you asked my opinion. I am a plain man – a man of the people – and I have a message from them to deliver to the class to which you belong."

He raised his cap, with a bow, and then without another word or glance strode off beside Tom Wilton to the gate.

Ten minutes later, Constance, in her cosy room, slipped into her silken gown of shimmering mauve and grey, with its old point lace, and then descended to stand by the blazing logs in the great square hall, with one foot on the fender and the head of "Reckless," the Newfoundland,[18] against her knee. By-and-by her father came upon the scene, and Sir George dropped in, and declared that in that misty gown she reminded him of the blue Scotch hills with their white and purple heather, and the grouse shooting he had missed that season, which was a considerable stretch of poetic fancy, coming as it did from so practical a being as Sir George.

"By the bye, did you speak to that Nigel Grey?" he asked once during the evening.

"Yes. Tom, of course, left him in my charge."

"What did you think of him?" asked George, with a smile, and a look which spoke volumes of what *he* thought.

"Think of him? Why, George, he is a perfect Daniel come to judgement!"[19]

And the conversation dropped. Nevertheless, the interview did not pass from Constance's mind. Such talk might be of every-day occurrence to Nigel Grey; it was not to Miss Compton in her easy, pleasant passage through life. Nigel Grey had not spoken in vain. Curious fact: Nigel Grey never did speak in vain! He had a simple means of insuring this. The man was desperately in earnest.

[2 January 1897]

Chapter III.

In the meanwhile, Nigel, back in town again, had just been shown by a slipshod girl into a small back room in a side street in Hammersmith.[20] The window opened upon a high brick wall, some six feet off. The brick wall belonged to a mews, and in consequence of the look-out Nelly Graham rented this room at very low terms, though extra light in the mornings and evenings ran away with a good deal of what she saved in her rent. By the faint star-light glimmering down, Nigel could see that the room was empty. He wondered where Nelly was; then concluded that she must be speaking to one of the other occupants of the house, which was rented out to sewing girls, so he sat down to wait. By-and-bye surrounding objects became clearer; he could make out on the table a tumbler of water, with the half-withered head of a chrysanthemum drooping over the side. Nigel knew Nelly, and he could guess how that flower had been cherished, and the water changed twice a day. He looked down at his coat where a few scarlet hips and haws from the Brierly hedges glistened then took them from his buttonhole and placed them in the glass. As he did so, some voices broke upon his ear – low, but clear and distinct in the evening stillness, apparently coming from a room on the landing above.

"There, I think that'll lie straight. Tack it there on the table, and then you won't get it wrong. 'Twon't hurt him to wait a minute."

Nigel instinctively felt that the "him" referred to himself. The next moment he was sure, for Nelly's patient voice came down the stairs.

"Thanks, yes, I will. I expect its only Tom Blunt or Allie, and they can wait a few minutes. I want to get this done to-morrow, and see if I can't get paid for it then and there. I've called again and again, Sarah, about that little sailor suit, and it don't seem as if it would ever be convenient for them to let me have the money."

"It's a shame," the other girl burst out: "it's a wicked shame! And you've worked so terrible hard of late, too."

"I've got behind, you see," the quiet voice went on. "Medicine, and one thing or another, and then the winter is coming on. I haven't felt up to the mark of late, either. I work, but I don't work so quick as I did, seems to me." She paused a moment, then resumed: "I wonder what Sue's doin' now? Poor Susie, you know, when she ran away with that fellow last year, and came back here, half-starving in the summer I lent her some money I'd put by – fifteen shillings. I'd been savin' it up against a rainy day. Well, it was the least I could do; her husband had left her, and she wasn't fit to work. She promised faithful to pay it back – I suppose she couldn't. But the rainy day is comin', I'm afraid. I don't seem to have no go in me these days. Oh, well," the voice changed, "p'raps I'll get that money to-morrow. Things look brighter by daylight. Emma's come round again and been quite good to me of late."

All through this conversation Nigel Grey sat below listening. He made no effort to remind them of his near presence, neither coughed nor spoke, nor stirred his chair. On the contrary, he seemed anxious not to lose a word of the above remarks. He moved silently a little nearer the door, for the voices were pitched in a low key, and only the quiet of the house made them audible. Reprehensible, this of Nigel. Perhaps it was because he did not belong to the class to which *noblesse oblige*[21] is supposed to belong.

The girls' voices continued for a minute or two, then Nelly Graham came down the stairs with a candle, and entered the room. She started when she saw Nigel, and a flush and brightness came into her wan little face, which might have been likened to the roseate hue of dawn in the pale wintry sky. She set the candle down.

"Why, Nigel," she said, "I've not seen you for ages. Oh, but I'm glad to see you again."

The enthusiasm in the tone touched Nigel, used though he was to homage and admiration. He jumped up and took the girl's hands, one in each of his.

"How are you, Nell? Chilly again, as usual. Is there no fire in this establishment?"

He looked at the grate, which had so far apparently not been in use that season.

"Sarah Dean has one upstairs; I've been sitting there."

The speaker let her hands fall locked before her, and looked up with undisguised pleasure at Nigel. It was a graceful attitude; the frayed gown and work-worn hands did not detract from it: it suited the girl's face, with its terrible look of patience – the outcome of the battle where Despair, born of man's cruelty had fought with Hope, the God-sent attribute.

Let us look at her a minute (such as she do not trouble us often), at the purity of contour and the bravery which lies beneath it. Was she not meant to reach a higher standard than she ever can attain working late and early in her dark room? She is but one of many thousand Nellies whose best life can never fully develop, who, being weak must be made weaker that the strong may be made stronger; who, being insignificant, must live the life of a machine that others may be made more prominent, and fill our newspapers with vapid, soul-sickening details of dress and display; who must face the police court, the reformatory, or the prison if she steal so much as a loaf of bread from the man of affluence, but must give her very life's blood at starvation wages to supply his wants. By-and-bye, when work and hardship have so told upon her that she can no longer minister to the capitalist, death will step in and sweep her away to the great forgotten majority, and her life apparently shall leave no more mark than a drop gone from the ocean.

"I only looked in for a minute," Nigel said, "to see how things were getting along with you. Are they looking up at all? How's Emma?"

"Oh, better. Sit down, Nigel; do. Yes, Emma's better. I went over to tea with her last Sunday. Jem isn't drinking like he did – he was quite sober on Sunday; and little Jem seems to be picking up his strength again.

Emma was Nelly's married sister – a regular termagant. The word "better" referred not to her health but her temper.

Just then Nelly's eye fell on the scarlet berries Nigel had placed in the glass. She gave a cry of delight.

"Oh, how pretty!"

"Yes, I was down in the country to-day at a rum little place called Brierly, where I used to live as a child. I wanted to see Mr. Compton, the squire of the place. Mr. Ross has taken a house down there, and in consequence has had to take the village in hand a bit. Anything of that sort, you know, suits him to a T.[22] He is seeing about a new well.

"Couldn't the squire have seen after things for himself, instead of Mr. Ross having to do it? Is he well off?"

"Oh, yes, he's well off – too well off to disturb his comfortable existence with such things," said Nigel, roughly. After a moment's pause he added, with characteristic honesty: "He's been away, and the agent doesn't seem to have reported affairs to him."

"Oh."

Nelly did not take much interest in Brierly, but she liked to hear Nigel Grey talk.

"He has acres of beautiful grounds," Nigel went on "I thought of you, Nelly, when I walked through them this afternoon. I saw his daughter. There she lives, breathing air which would bring life to thousands of her sisters in streets like these."

Nelly sighed.

"It doesn't do any good to talk of such things, Nigel," she said. "People don't *think*, you know; that's what's wrong."

Nigel looked half angrily at her. Her patience irritated him. It was this wonderful patience on the part of the working people of England which militated more against his schemes than all the indifference of the other class.

"Did you speak to the young lady?" asked Nelly, with interest. "What is she like?"

She looked curiously at him. This interview with the squire, even though it had been on business, seemed to have lifted Nigel to an even higher position than he had before occupied in her mind.

"Oh, I don't know," Grey said rather wearily. "Not a bad sort of girl, certainly – wants to regenerate the world, I imagine, with a bundle of tracts and a pledge card."

He was away from the influence of Constance's presence now, back amongst his own people, with their burdens which he had made his own, and which he believed directly attributable to the class to which Constance belonged. But even as he spoke he saw again the slender figure beneath the oaks, and the sweet upturned face with its earnest eyes. It seemed to appeal against the cold remark he had just made, but he did not recall the words. He sat silent, looking at the flame of the candle, and taboring with his fingers on the table.[23]

Nelly gave a hard laugh.

"It'll take a long time to do good in that way," she said.

She sat silent a minute. She had evidently been carried away on a train of thought awakened by Nigel's words, for she presently added slowly:

"Perhaps some day we shall see clear. What looks dark'll be made plain; the shadows'll pass away."

Long afterwards those words came back to Nigel. He looked across at her now with that keen look with which he was apt to analyse character.

"What do you mean by that?" he asked.

"I was thinkin' –" Nelly looked down and plucked with her finger and thumb at her gown with that nervous, undefined dislike most people have of speaking on religious subjects. "I was thinkin' of – heaven."

"Can you really think of heaven, Nell? I can't. I can't understand a religion which is contented with a miserable, degraded existence here so long as it gets compensation some day. I can't understand a religion which will suffer the injustice there is on earth to-day. I can't see God in it – no, I can't see Him," he added heavily.

Nelly sat silent. Like many of her class – ignorant, patient, plodding – she was not apt at expressing her thoughts. Sometimes, beyond the darkness of the years, she could catch the gleam of a distant dawn – a far-off hope of something better, which she had just spoken of as "heaven" – leisure to think maybe, a rest from the grind, when little suits and little shirts would be no longer needed, and one had not to tramp the streets at night to ask for one's earnings at the doors of big houses, only to be sent empty away. But the hope was dim and intangible, as things are that are seldom thought of.

"How's Hilda to-night?" she asked, presently.

"I don't know. I came here straight from Brierly."

He rose as he spoke and took up his hat.

"Well, is there anything I can do for you, Nelly?"

He would have dearly liked to have passed something out of his own pocket to this frail-looking little thing in her chilly room, but he knew better than to offer her money. He said the words as a forlorn hope.

"Nothing, thanks, Nigel – except, yes – you might look Jem up now and again. You can generally keep him straight – for a week or two anyway."

"I will, Nell I will. And now trot upstairs and get warm; and I wish – I wish, Nell, you'd let me send you some coals round. May I?"

"Oh, no, Nigel!" The girl shrank back. "I couldn't use them; indeed, I couldn't."

"Well."

He put his hat on, and turned towards the door, but still lingered. He was aware that he had not shown up to his best advantage during this interview. He had been rather pleased at the time at the point-blank way in which he had delivered his message to Miss Compton; but here, in this dreary room, of what use to rail against fate? Why point out the shadows when the shadows were already too plain? A man cannot always keep at high tension, but it was hard that he should run down here. So he lingered by the door.

"Cheer up, Nell," he said; "there's a good time coming, you know. Strong hands are working for it, and though strong hands try to hold it back, they will have to give way in the end. I think," he added, laughing, "I shall have to take you with me to Fraternity Hall next Sunday to hear what I'm preparing for them. It'll knock the backbone out of the old system.

Nelly looked up admiringly.

"It must be fine, Nigel, to be able to speak in public, and alter the government, and so on."

"Oh, as to that," said Nigel, rather taken aback, "of course, it takes time and more than my speeches to alter the government; but

> For a' that and a' that,
> 'Tis coming yet for a' that,
> When man to man the world o'er,
> Shall brothers be and a' that.[24]

[9 January 1897]

Chapter IV.

Nigel's aunt, Miss Hannah Grey, lived in a gloomy house in a side street off a busy thoroughfare at Chelsea[25] – a quiet place from which the flood tides of life had long ago ebbed away. She owned the house herself. Her grandfather had bought it in days when the family had been in more flourishing circumstances and suburban property was not so high in value. Since then the house had considerably deteriorated in the hands of Hannah Grey's father and afterwards herself.

It was here that Nigel Grey, and his little sister lived, Nigel paying his aunt so much a week for their board. The only survivors of Mr. and Mrs. Grey's family of seven were the youngest, Hilda, and the two eldest, Nigel and Jack. The latter had emigrated, and was farming out in Australia.

No. 3 Sheridan Street was a rambling abode. The wind howled in gusts down the big chimneys on winter nights, and through window frames and creaky doors; and the rain, when heavy, had a habit of coming through the roof in the attics, where two clerks lodged. It was cold in winter and damp in summer. In the disused rooms the plaster would peel off the walls and fall with a thud sometimes in the dead of night, and Hilda would wake in a fright, and hide her head beneath the bedclothes, thinking of the ghost which they said walked there on the nights of the full moon. Still, Nigel had grown fond of the house, as we do grow fond of places, be they ever so poor, where we dream our early dreams and fight our early battles. For nearly twenty years it had been his home now. His parents had rented part of the house from Hannah Grey when they first came to town, and had lived there till a fever came which carried them both away within one week. That was some nine years before, when Hilda was a baby. Since then Jack had emigrated and settled down in the colonies and Nigel had fought life on his own behalf and Hilda's.

Nigel's room looked out at the back upon a paved yard, and the gnarled branches of an ancient apple tree, which must have seen many changeful scenes in its time before the days when little Hilda Grey was carried out to sit beneath its branches: days when the gloomy house with its remnants of past greatness – the cherubic faces cut in stone above the portal, the faded gold and crimson bell ropes, the carved cornices was no longer dim and forbidding, but aglow with stir and life, and blue-blooded children pattered in the courtyard, and dainty high-heeled slippers tapped up and down the stone steps.

But the inmates of No. 3 in their practical workday life did not think of these things. When at length the romance of the old dwelling-house did strike Nigel Grey, it was when he turned his back upon it for ever, and then not the romance of *its* past but that of his own came to him. In that hour a whole lifetime seemed to separate him from the sights and sounds of quiet old Sheridan Street. They floated to him across the change of fortune as if from far-off years or the land of dreams – the eager boyhood, the launching out into a stormy, impetuous manhood; the early breasting of the billows, the old conceited self-reliance, the nights when "the gallant boys and true"[26] had sat, and smoked, and laughed, and planned, and denounced in the draughty back room, where the apple boughs tapped against the pane and trudged off together afterwards through the star-lit streets, loud in their enthusiasm over the latest work on land nationalisation or the last speech or some shining light at one of the lecture halls.

It was this back room in Sheridan Street which Nigel sought after having paid his visit to Nelly Graham. Nelly Graham, it may be mentioned was one of Nigel's special *protégés*, he had several of either sex to whom he had lent a helping hand at times. Nelly he had come across some years before when she was little more than a child, through Jem Scott, her sister's husband, a somewhat unpromising disciple of the cause. Emma was unmarried at that time, and the two girls lived together, and Nigel would sometimes drop in of an evening with Jem. Since Emma had set up a home of her own, Nigel had found it incumbent on him to keep any eye on Nelly. He was sorry for her loneliness; her prettiness and gentle ways attracted him. Altogether, he looked upon her much as one might look upon a child whom fate had harshly treated. Nigel's was a room of strong contrasts,[27] and afforded a good index to its owner's character. The floor was uncarpeted, and the plain wooden table had no covering, but in the centre of it bloomed a Christmas rose, a present from Hilda to her brother on his birthday. Magazines and newspapers were scattered about, cheap editions of the novels of the day, and old histories picked up at second-hand book-stalls. The room was large, the furniture scanty, there was not a picture on the walls, the wind filtered freely in through the badly fitting window. This particular evening when Nigel came in, a letter from Mr. Ross was awaiting him. He and Mr. Ross (one of the leaders of the movement to which he belonged) were strong allies. The latter, who was the humblest of men, sometimes used to wonder if, supposing Nigel were in his position and had had his education, he might not have the be cleverer and more able man of the two. Nigel, with all his admiration and love for his leader, was quite sure he would have been when he thought over the matter himself.

He had thrown himself in a chair and was reading over Mr. Ross's letter when a voice called him from an adjoining room.

"Nigel, Nigel; is that you?"

He rose, still holding the letter in his hand, and walked down the passage to the open door of the room from which the voice had come.

"Yes, Hilda. What is it?"

"I'm tired, but I can't sleep. Sing something, Nigel; sing something, do," and the fretful little voice broke into a sob.

"What shall I sing?"

He entered the dark room and took a seat by the bed.

"Sing about 'My Dinah.'"

"Very well," and Nigel struck up in his clear baritone:

> Oh, have you seen my Dinah?
> Do you know where she goes?
> She's the flower of North Carolina,
> She's the North Carolina rose.[28]

"What have you been doing all day, Nigel?" Hilda asked, when he reached the last word.

"I've been down in the country."

"Oh, have you? Oh, how I wish I could go!"

"Into the country? Oh, nonsense, pet!" Hilda was a spoilt little woman, for this brother never thwarted her, so he hastily added: "Why, the country is quite ugly now – the flowers have gone and the leaves and the grass have turned brown. You wouldn't care for it a bit now."

"Yes, I should," said Hilda, persistently. "I know as I should like it. You go about, Nigel; you don't know how dreadfully dull it is lying here all day – sometimes here, sometimes in the kitchen or parlour."

An idea had flashed into Nigel's brain while his sister had been speaking, but it was so vague and intangible as yet that he did not broach it to the child. He only said:

"See, Hilda, I have a letter to write, and if you're not asleep when I've done, I'll sing another song."

The child reluctantly loosed the hand she held, and Nigel went back and started his letter; but when it was finished all was so silent in Hilda's room that, concluding she had dropped asleep, Nigel did not go back again, but fell into thought. The child was right; it was dull – bad – for her to have no change from year's end to year's end. Could he not provide a change for her somehow? Was there no one in Brierly who would take a little sick child in and look after her for a few weeks? He would see about it at once – this very week. There were plenty of old friends there who had known his parents; he would look some of them up. Nigel Grey never shilly-shallied with a plan. Having settled this, he dismissed it from his mind to make room for a more difficult matter.

For a few minutes he seemed thoroughly perplexed, his brows knotted together, his hands clasping and unclasping themselves, then light dawned through the entanglement of thought, and touched his eyes with a slight smile for a moment.

Scarcely above his breath, he called: "Hilda."

"Yes, Nigel."

"Oh, I thought you were asleep. I'm coming to sing you that song."

He rose as he spoke, and taking the ink and some writing materials in his hand went into the child's room, this time bringing a candle with him. The light disclosed to view a thin little figure lying on a tumbled bed. The child's face was a miniature reproduction of Nigel's. Here the same clear paleness of complexion, the same beautiful eyes of deepest blue or grey, with their intent gaze as though eager to learn the right of things and mend the wrong; the same steady mouth, with delicate refined terminations to the lips. But the soft hair curling about the forehead gave the face the look of a cherub; rather a wan and worn little angel, certainly, though one may fancy many such enter the Kingdom from our great cities.

"Look here, Hilda," said Nigel, quite diffidently for him. "I want you to write something for me."

He propped the pillows up behind her, and handed her a sheet of paper on *Blackwood's Magazine*,[29] and a pen which he had dipped in the ink.

"What shall I write?" asked Hilda, with wide-open eyes.

"Let's see. What the dickens *are* you to write? That's the thing." He fell a-thinking, but his brain seemed curiously slow. "Oh, put – put 'Better late than never.' I think that'll do. Now, take care, old girl, and write slowly."

Hilda wrote the words with great care, and then pushed the paper across in triumph for her brother to see.

"Is that all?" she asked.

She had spelt better with one t, and balanced things by giving two v's to never, but Nigel nodded approval. He knew that spelling was but a matter of taste down in the nether world,[30] where this missive was to go.

"Is that all?" Hilda asked again.

"Yes; stick down 'Sue.' That's all."

"Oh, goodness gracious, Nigel, whatever are you going to do?" asked Hilda, as she wrote the last word with her shaky little hand.

Nigel's little game was easy enough to see through, to us who know of the conversation at Nelly Graham's. The fact that he should have done such a thing as he was now doing showed very plainly that Nigel had not a strong belief in matters of honour as regarded debt entertained by the dwellers in such regions as Poplar Street, where Nelly lived. The fact that Sue owed Nelly fifteen shillings was quite sufficient to make Nigel very certain that she would not cross Nelly's path again.

"Now, here's an envelope," went on Nigel. "Hello Hilda, I quite forgot – what an idiot I am – this business is private. But you can keep a secret, can't you? It's – it's Nelly Graham's name I want you to put here, and you must never tell her if you see her, or anyone else either. See?"

"Oh, yes." A light dawned on the child's face. "A valentine, eh?"

"Exactly so," said honest Nigel; "a valentine, and it would spoil it all to tell."

"I won't tell; indeed, I won't. I didn't know it was Valentine's day."

"It will be directly," said Nigel, evasively. "Now, go on – 'Ellen Graham, 10 Poplar Street, Hammersmith.'" He ran quickly through the letters for her. "Thank goodness that's done."

He took it back to his room, slipped a half sovereign and two half-crowns through a slit in a piece of cardboard, folded them inside the paper, and enclosed them in the envelope.

To make a speech in Fraternity Hall, to point out national abuses to Miss Compton, a wealthy landowner's daughter, came spontaneously to him: but this work of seeming by-play, such as the schoolboy does in for every 13th of February, had baffled and bothered him, and taken far more thought than, ten minutes later on, he brought to bear upon Shaw's "Transition to Social Democracy" in the "Fabian Essays."[31]

The next evening a youth left this mysterious missive at No. 10 Poplar Street, and Nigel forgot all about his small device, and never gave it another thought till long after, when there came a day when he would have given all he possessed never to have perpetrated it.

While Nelly Graham in wonder and delight was turning over the money, Nigel was deep in conversation in Mr. Ross's study. The scheme which he and Mr. Ross were considering was to engage some hall or large room in East London, in which to give free instruction on certain evenings on various subjects, chiefly connected with science – those subjects on which the working man would find a difficulty in gaining knowledge. Mr. Ross hoped to enlist the aid of various scientists, and others, and even, if need be, to pay such as were conversant with the subjects most required. And he was anxious to provide special instructions occasionally for those who wished for it in languages or subjects out of the common beat.

To set such a scheme on foot was worth the sacrifice of time and thought and labour; it was the thin end of the wedge, the forerunner of great things.

[16 January 1897]
Chapter V.

It was New Year's eve, and a small group were gathered round the fire in the cosy, old-fashioned drawing-room of the Hall. Sir George Cumberland-West and his sister were there; they had driven over to see the old year out. There were also Mary St. John, a married niece of the squire's, whose husband was away in India, and their handsome twin boy and girl; also Rollo Grainger, a young fellow of twenty or thereabouts.

Beatrice Cumberland-West was several years older than Constance; she was older than her brother George. Until the last two months the girls had seen but little of one another; now, since Constance's return from abroad, they had struck up a desultory friendship. Why Beatrice had not married was a puzzle. Some said she was too particular; she certainly had prettiness and liveliness enough to have attracted the male sex – perhaps rather too much of the latter quality. Strange to say, the only man who seemed to have made an impression on the heart of the lively Beatrice was the ascetic young priest who was acting as *locum tenens*[32] for the Vicar of Brierly, then absent on account of ill-health.

The talk and laughter was at its height when the door opened and Mr. Compton came in. He was evident in high glee; he came to the fire chuckling and rubbing his hands, and took a seat in one of the deep armchairs, while the two children climbed on his knee. The squire was a handsome man, with a somewhat military type of face, a long moustache sprinkled with grey, an aquiline nose, prominent chin, and large, kindly eyes. His presence, with the quaintly dressed, yellow haired children on his knee, gave a finishing touch to the group. The flames in the grate leaped round the logs, and their light fell Rembrandt-like on the faces gathered round: the pictures of the dead and gone Comptons on the walls looked solemnly down from under their wreaths of holly and mistletoe and rosy-tipped tendrils of ivy.

"What is it, dad?" asked Constance, catching sight of her father's face.

"A political discussion, my dear, which I have been having, in which I am afraid I came off the worst. One has to give way to a lady."

"A lady! I thought perhaps it was that everlasting Nigel Grey. Why have he and his disciples invaded our village in this way? I have seen him in the distance two or three times lately. But who was your opponent, father?"

"A small thing – that high – a very small thing," and the squire laughed again at the remembrance. "I called in at Mrs. Linden's while I was out, as I wanted to speak to Linden about mending the paddock fence where Brindle broke it down the other day, and she had a child staying with her – a poor mite with spinal complaint or something wrong with her back – not much bigger than you, Kitty; but she hadn't your fat cheeks. But, my goodness, she was an impudent little missy!" and the squire went off again; he was very fond of children. "It seems she had come from London for change of air; she hadn't a bit of shyness, and we were soon chatting together. I said: 'And I suppose you are longing to get back to the London streets again?' 'Oh, no,' she said, she liked the fields best. 'I ought by rights to have some of my own,' said she. I supposed her parent were thinking of buying land somewhere, so by way of keeping up the conversation I asked her, 'How many?' and she said – she said – what *do* you suppose she said?" The squire roared. "She said, 'Three acres and a cow.'"[33]

A chorus of laughter greeted this remark.

"Wait; I haven't finished," continued the squire. "'How do you know you should have that?' I asked. 'Well, that is the amount the state might fix on,' said she. 'But I have a great deal more than that,' I said. 'You wouldn't take it from me, would you?' 'Oh, certainly,' she responded. 'You have no right to so much more than other people, and should be made to divide it up into acres for them.'"

The squire was much tickled.

"Oh, what a bright little thing!" cried Constance. "See here; it is going to be a lovely moonlight night, and not too cold; suppose we walk down and interview this small Socialist. We will take one of Kitty's dolls, poor mite! And some goodies and things for the New Year. It will be fun, and the walk will be nice. Come and escort us, George. You know the song says, 'A starry night for a ramble.'"[34]

"How does it go on, Constance?" asked Rollo. "Let's carry it out to the letter. I forget it, but you can quote it, can't you?"

"Vulgar boy!" said Miss Constance.

But just then nurse appeared for the St. John infants, and the butler announced dinner.

Just at the last Rollo backed out of the walk to Mrs. Linden's. There would be skating on the morrow on the Hall pond, and he wanted to stay to sharpen and polish his skates. It was useless to intimate to him that two, or four in this case, was company, three none (Mrs. St. John was strong enough to brave the night air); he only remarked:

"Then Constance can stay with me; I shall be glad of her help."

Finally they left him and set off abreast along the crisp, white road. It was a good mile's walk to Mrs. Linden's for she lived beyond the village in a pleasant, rambling, low-roofed building bordering on a copse. George would gladly have waited outside for his sister and cousin, but they would not hear of it, and towed him sternly up the path. Mrs. Linden opened the door to them. She was a little, sprightly woman of fifty or thereabouts, with a remarkable and inimitable dialect. Though equal to most emergencies in life, she was rather overpowered at the sight of royalty in the shape of Sir George and his sister bearing down upon her humble home. She could have borne up under Miss Cumberland-West's presence, but Sir George did slightly take her breath away, so much so that she fairly forgot to ask them in, and at Constance's; "Good evening, Mrs. Linden.

You've a little sick girl here, my father tells me; we've come to see her," she rambled off into a long explanation.

"Well, you see, miss, it's in this way. Mr. Grey, him that's son to Mrs. Grey that was, as come down here to see the old place a few weeks ago, and got a-talking to Barnes as kep' the shop, and I a-hearin' of it, I tells Mr. Barnes if he comes again to send him round here, for I knowed his mother years ago, afore they went to London to live, and I thought I'd like to see one of her kith and kin. So by-and-by Mr. Grey came round, and he told me as how he's a little sister he wanted to get change of air for, and did I know of anyone here who'd haver her for a time? So says I: 'To be sure, I will, sir' and so –"

"Yes, very good of you, Mrs. Linden," said Constance, rapidly. "Where is she? In the kitchen? May we all come in – we are quite a party?"

"Oh, to be sure, to be sure. Dearie me!" ejaculated Mrs. Linden, in manifest joy, as George and Beatrice followed Constance into the hall. "Straight through into the kitchen there, Miss Compton."

It was Constance who opened the door and entered first, with the Santa Clause load. The folds of her velvet dress gleamed beneath the white fur-lined cloak, the hood was drawn over her head, and the snow crystals sparkled on it, for Rollo irreverently had thrown a snowball after her when she started, her cheeks were a soft carmine, her eyes sparkling. Thus she met Nigel Grey a second time.

As soon as she entered the room she caught sight of him, and stopped short for a moment. Tiresome that he should be there! But he should not do her out of the speech she had been rehearsing all the way along. She had had no idea that it was his little sister whom she was coming to see; but what mattered it? She nodded as she passed him with her smiling face, but went swiftly on to the farther end of the long kitchen where a pretty child was lying on a chintz-covered setee, staring with puzzled eyes at the visitors. Constance dropped on one knee before her and opened the basket.

"I am the Christmas fairy," she said. "Old Father Christmas did not give me your address on Christmas day, so I was not able to bring you anything; but he told me about you this evening, and he sends his apologies for forgetting before, and – these."

Out came a beautiful doll, with flowing golden tresses and shining spangles; out came a large paint box of Harry St. John's and a Jack-in-the-box, and a sugar Father Christmas, and candied fruit, and oranges, and dates. Constance placed them solemnly on the child's couch.

"Oh, oh, oh!" cried Hilda.

It was a pretty tableau. Sir George (who had passed Nigel with a rather curt "Good evening") and Beatrice had drawn near to witness it. Mrs. Linden was smiling broadly in the foreground. Nigel alone stood apart in the shadow, motionless.

[23 January 1897]
Chapter V. Continued.

The two men of the party, seen thus together in Mrs. Linden's kitchen, might have formed an interesting study; not by reason of their different positions – these are too well known – but their different natures. Both were fine-looking men, possessing more than the average of good looks. Here was Sir George, a mixture, it if were possible, of the sanguine and the phlegmatic;[35] easy, good-natured, sure of himself; too adverse to bother of any kind to trouble himself to think otherwise than well of people as a whole; hopeful, because he had not realised life's pathos, and try his hardest he never could – it was not in him; strong in his own opinions and beliefs because he was thoroughly strong in physical health, and had never faced those dark hours when overstrained powers result in mental doubts. Here was Nigel Grey, with high-strung nerves – which condition is, after all, the essence of vitality, the highest concentration of human life – difficult, uncertain; warm-hearted, but with reserve, because he had seen much of life's shams and shady side; pessimistic at times, for the same reason, and because the odds he fought against were great; apt to judge harshly from the fact that he saw things too forcibly and clearly; doubtful often of his own beliefs, because in his very groping after the truth he perceived that that truth was not bound, and no one could say Lo, here; or lo, there, it may be found! for the old rules of right and wrong must be re-adjusted to fit individual cases. They could never amalgamate – no social system could bring them together or on a more intimate footing than they were on that evening, separated by the length of the kitchen – Nigel, with his solemn grey eyes, looking fixedly at the fire; Sir George, with his sunny blue ones, laughing lightly across at the little girl.

"And are you really the Christmas fairy?" asked Hilda, looking with interest at Constance.

"Of course," nodded the girl.

"What very beautiful toys! Be sure and thank Father Christmas for me." The child looked doubtfully again at Constance. "You are sure you are the fairy?"

"Isn't she pretty enough for one?" asked Sir George, mischievously.

"She has too much on," said Hilda, stoutly.

She had heard of the fairies at the pantomime.

A good deal of laughter greeted this remark, and in the middle Sir George snapped the spring of the Jack-in-the-box and sent Hilda off laughing as well; and then, finding this action had been received with approval, this really rather shy young man drew a chair up and tried to draw the little politician out upon the subject which had so amused the squire that afternoon. Constance quietly withdrew herself from the interested group round the couch and took a seat not far from where Nigel was standing leaning against the mantelpiece. She wished to speak to him, but the profile of his face turned towards her was not encouraging – it was forbidding in its gravity. Presently she ventured:

"I have several times thought about what you said to me the last time I saw you," she began.

Nigel started and turned. It was too shadowy at that end of the room to see the expression of his face, but the slight bow and the silence with which he received her remark was sufficient to check any further attempt at continuing the subject.

"You have taken a great deal of trouble for my sister, Miss Compton," he said, after a minute.

His tone was not grateful. Constance was human enough to feel hurt.

"It is nothing," she said, coldly. "One likes to do what one can for a sick child. I had no idea, by-the-bye, that she was your sister. My father told me of her for the first time this afternoon: he was very much amused by something she said to him about three acres and a cow."

"I cannot think where the child gets such ideas from," said Nigel, testily. "I suppose she overhears the fellows talking. I don't put them there."

The short conversation dropped. Sir George could be heard saying,

"And would you really take my land from me and give me nothing in exchange?"

"I might," said Hilda, after due consideration (her politics were a little mixed) – "I might give you the market value for your son and yourself."

Sir George exploded.

"What is the market value?" asked Beatrice, trying to corner the child.

"The market value is the value in the market," returned Hilda, wisely.

Nigel did not speak again, and Constance likewise was silent. She had recovered from her momentary pique, and accounted for his preoccupation by the fact that he probably had much to think of. This led onto other thoughts – serious ones. Her mind had wandered far away from the room and its occupants when George and Beatrice looked round in search of her, and rose to go. Nigel accompanied them to the door with a lamp. When they got out upon the high road, Constance slipped in between her two cousins, putting a hand through the arm of each, and her thoughts for the last ten minutes came out with a rush.

"Oh, Bea, do you think we are all trying to do 'the greatest good we can to the greatest number'?"[36]

"I am quite sure we are not," said Bea, in her direct way. "Good gracious! why we might all do a great deal more; some of us couldn't do less. Why, I might be but sick nursing in Seven Dials."

"Heaven help your patients!"

This from George.

"And you, Constance, might be wearing a poke bonnet[37] and heading the Salvation Army, and George might be an African missionary. Doing the most good we can? I should think not!"

"And yet we ought to be," said Constance, slowly.

Her companions walked on in silence for a few minutes. Then George, who always felt rather out of place when the conversation touched on serious topics, remarked, rather feebly, that for his part he did not believe in indiscriminate giving.

"Who talked about giving, stupid?" asked Beatrice.

"Constance did. That was what you meant, wasn't it, Constance?"

"Not exactly. I was thinking of some words I heard once, to the effect that just in proportion as the world has given to us so should we pay back, and that our hands cannot be honest if they keep more than they give."

"Phew! Who said that? Tom Wilton, I'll be bound."

"No, not Tom."

"It sounds like one of his cracked statements. Suppose we all did give in that proportion, things would be equalised amongst us to-morrow, and by next month half the people would be wealthy again and the other half starving. Tom, for I'm sure Tom *did* say it, had better nationalise brains and thrift at the same time that he distributes money.

"I don't think the speaker quite meant what you think, George. He meant that we should pass on the best that is in us, which is not always money. Some things one can give away and be none the poorer."

"Do let's hear them."

"Knowledge, for one thing. It does seem so hard that a few people should have so many advantages that way over the great majority. How are they ever to rise? What chance can they have? Ignorance must cramp and hold them back even more than poverty."

"Humph!" said George. "Well, you try educating them, Constance, and see whether they are improved. What is being done is quite sufficient: more would only breed discontent. Have you any fault to find with the board schools?" he asked, turning rather wrathfully upon her. "The teaching is excellent."

"I did not mean the sort of things taught at the board schools," said Constance, a little helplessly. "I meant that they should learn to appreciate things that are beautiful – music, pictures, books, and things that are noble – the thoughts and acts of great men, and that they should learn something of what is going on in the world round them, here in England and in other lands – the questions of the day."

"Let me refer you to Nigel Grey," said George, with irony. "He and you might patch up the world and put it straight between you. By the way, our friend the politician did not seem up to his usual flow of talk this evening."

"No. Wasn't he quiet? Do you know he can talk well, George?"
"Can he? Have you ever called on those people at the Manor House?"
"Mrs. Forrester? Yes, once."
"She's a sister of Ross, the Socialist, isn't she? Is she that way?"
"Oh, dear, no! Her time and thoughts are all taken up with her children, I would say. Such madcap infants! They keep her on the run all the time. Privately, I believe she thinks Mr. Ross rather foolish." Then, as they neared the Hall gates, "Come, Bea, a race – a race. Who will reach the house first? No, not you with your long stride, George – Bea and I."

The two girls set off together and arrived breathless at the steps, George slowly following.

[30 January 1897]

Chapter VI.

Nigel Grey was angry. No doubt this showed a want of amiability, even a lack of common-sense, yet so it was. What unknown child in her own station, he had been arguing, or, indeed, in any station save one infinitely below her, would Miss Compton dare to offer a gratuitous gift to? True, she had not known at first who Hilda was, but when she had discovered she had still seemed to take it as a matter of course that they should accept her gifts, and her patronage. That insufferably conceited fellow, Cumberland-West, who had walked into the house and chaffed his little sister; doubtless, he considered that in so doing he had conferred a favour on both. It irritated Nigel, he could not tell why (indeed, next morning he puzzled over why he should concern himself with it at all), to see Miss Compton in company with the Cumberland-Wests. He did not know that they were closely related. He would like to have refused the presents then and there, but he was too angry to be sure of himself, and he specially wished to avoid anything which should show him to a disadvantage before Sir George Cumberland-West. Besides, he had the instincts of a gentleman. So he stood quietly by while the visitors were present, and hid his feelings as much as he was able. It would have considerably surprised Miss Compton had she known that under that stern exterior, Nigel Grey, the reformer, was indulging in a fit of unreasonably bad temper.

So it came to pass that, while Constance sat at luncheon with her father and cousins next day, a cardboard box was brought to her, accompanied by a note.

"A boy left this for you, miss," said the servant.

"Who can it be from? I don't recognise the writing," Constance remarked, as she tore the envelope open. Then she read the contents in silence, and the colour rushed to her face.

"Fancy!" she said, trying to speak in a customary easy way. "You can read it, George," turning to her cousin, who was sitting by her. "It is from that Nigel Grey. Who would have thought he would be so touchy."

George picked up the note and read:

"Nigel Grey presents his respects to Miss Compton, and begs to return the toys she was kind enough to lend his sister. He is much obliged for the loan of the same."

"What a bear!" remarked George. "An ill-mannered, ignorant cub! So much for Tom Wilton's friends! I've heard him talk in open-mouthed admiration of the perfections of Nigel Grey."

The colour had not faded from Constance's face. She sat staring with puzzled eyes at the note; her intention had been to give pleasure, not offence. Constance had been distinctly impressed by Nigel Grey at that first meeting, but had she been indifferent to the man she would still have felt hurt.

"Well, it just shows that it doesn't do for different classes to mix; his very conduct given the death-blow to his theories," said Beatrice. "You've nothing in common, and can't be expected to understand one another."

"Oh, he's a fool!" said George summarily. "Run upstairs, girls, and put your hats on, and don't keep me waiting all day if you want me to escort you over to Allerton."

Constance tore Nigel's note into several pieces and dropped them into the grate as she passed, but she did not so easily dismiss the matter from her mind, and as she went up the stairs to her room she tightened her lips and raised her head a little. Good girl, though she was, Constance was still Miss Compton of the Hall, and she did not receive a slight from a working mechanic for nothing.

Nigel Grey was returning to town that evening, and was on his way to the station when the two were on their way back from Allerton House, whither they had gone to consult Lady Grace about a bazaar to be held at Wareminster, of which she was patroness. They passed Nigel in the road, and then Constance had her revenge; not knowing the nature of the man, she did not know how sharp a one. Nigel's hand went instinctively to his cap when he saw her, but he paused in the act of raising it, for Miss Compton glanced at him with calm, unrecognising eyes, and passed on; though only the day before she had told her cousin Beatrice that to cut a person was a thing no true lady would do under any circumstances. Constance had no sooner done it than she repented of it; her anger vanished in the moment of her revenge.

She was not reassured by George's remark:

"I wouldn't have done that, Constance. You knew that was Grey; you should not cut a fellow in that position – bad form!"

Tear of vexation welled up into the girl's eyes.

"He was really rude in sending those presents back, George," she said, with the old childish humility.

"Who cares what he does," returned George. "Couldn't you have shown him that? Couldn't you have overlooked the fellow's manners as only what might have been expected from him, instead of letting him see you've thought sufficiently about it to cut him?"

Constance was not enjoying her walk. Whatever position Nigel Grey might occupy socially, in Constance Compton's mind he occupied a prominent one that afternoon. The talk wandered off to the coming bazaar, but as they neared the Hall gates Constance asked abruptly:

"How would you describe a Socialist, George?"

"A fellow who is after other people's money," returned George promptly.

Constance tapped her foot impatiently on the snowy road.

"Now, don't think of Tom or Nigel Grey, George. Do put all prejudice aside for once, and tell me why you think Socialism would not be a benefit to the community at large."

"Because it cripples individual action."

"Why should it?"

"Naturally it would put an end to thrift and industry. If every man were provided for by the State, what incentive would he have to work?"

"I thought they would all *have* to work – those who were able."

"Yes; but all motive for industry and thrift would be dead, and with them self-control and energy. What sort of a nation should we have?"

"But you can't be content with the nation as it is, George. You must own that many things need reforming."

"Undoubtedly. But is Socialism to reform them? That's another question."

After a pause he went on:

"Yes, I dare say you think me a hard-hearted fellow for not flinging myself heart and soul into the cause of the people. When men like Grey come to the fore, the practical man like myself appears a most reprehensible being in the eyes of the visionary like you. Nevertheless, I, too, have my schemes for the working people, and they are not hard ones. I am not a gory tyrant, if I am not a hot-headed enthusiast. I believe in removing all obstacles to the improvement of the people, of helping them on in every effort they make in a right direction, of furthering their education so far as it is well. I do *not* believe in helping them to rely on external aid instead of on their own efforts in achieving their ends, nor to look for freedom in a change of social arrangements, instead of in a change of conduct. I do *not* believe in overthrowing instead of perfecting society's natural arrangements, in making the people's energy superfluous, their virtue of a low standard, their subsistence sure. To cultivate the best that is in them, and help it to rise superior and conquer external difficulties is to make a finer nation of men than Nigel Grey is striving for. The fiction of the present day, with its Socialistic tendencies, is for ever harping on one theme: the impression it serves to convey to the mind is the hardship of toil. 'Pity the working classes for their daily labour!' is the cry. Why, it is not only the lower classes that have to labour. Labour belongs to all ranks. Labour is honourable! Work is no hardship. Life would be insufferably monotonous without it. Don't waste your pity on the working man for that. He is a far happier creature with his daily toil than he would be without it."

Constance glanced at George as he said these words, with their heroic ring. All he had said might be true, but – Did it come well from George? Would others recognise the truth or weight of this statement just made while George and such as he remained in the upper ranks? Would they not perceive, rather, in the words a terrible injustice? Work is no disgrace, no hardship! Assuredly not. But the man who says these words should scarcely be so untrammelled by the daily round. Labour is honourable! Ay, but the system is not honourable, which keeps many of those who labour working early and late, poorly fed, and with only a week or a fortnight's holiday in the year, and allows those who do not labour to dawdle through the London season, take frequent trips to the Continent and spend the autumn in the Highlands – lily-handed, admirably dressed, and living on the fat of the land.

They walked on in silence for a little way, then Constance said:

"George, you did not give me a good or honest definition of a Socialist's aims just now, when I asked you. They cannot be all bad and greedy, like you make them out."

George laughed.

"Well, then, I will give you their own definition of their aims in their own words. Only, an' you love me, Constance, drop the subject, for you will never make a Socialist of me if you talk till Doomsday."

"I am not one myself, remember."

"No; and I should think Tom might stand as the awful example for our family. What the Socialists are working for is the owning of the means of production by the community and the means of consumption by individuals. There, *verbatim*.[38]

"Well, that seems reasonable, doesn't it?"

"Now, Constance –"

"But just one question."

"Not one. See, there is Cope going up the drive. Run on and see what he wants, and I'll go round to the house by another way and get the skates."

[6 February 1897]
Chapter VII.

"Good afternoon, Miss Compton," Mr. Cope said, as she came up. "I have brought you the children's songs to practice over. You remember you kindly promised to devote Thursday evenings to teaching them at the schools."

"Oh, yes," said Constance, smiling; "I had not forgotten."

She took the bundle of leaflets from him, and began turning them over.

Mr. Cope, finding his hands no longer encumbered, placed them together in his favourite position, gently parting the fingers at intervals and bringing them together again, which movement was the only sign that he was not at prayer. This action, with his extremely ecclesiastical face, made the resemblance to a saint in a stained window striking. He was looking at the distant view of the pond and its skaters with a benign smile, partly closed eyes, and his head slightly on one side.

"Do you skate, Mr. Cope?" asked Constance.

"Sometimes – a little," said Mr. Cope, diffidently, as though owning to a weakness.

His voice was not as the voice of other men, the pronunciation appeared carefully studied, the tones proceeded from some point at the back of the throat.

"You said the same when I asked you if you played whist,[39] and yet you can always beat my father, who is considered a good player. Come in and see him. My cousin Beatrice is here. I am sure she would be pleased to see you."

"Ah!" Mr. Cope opened his eyes and looked rather disappointed as he murmured something about it being late and he must hurry back for the evensong. "I merely intended to leave the leaflets at the door," he said. "I am sorry I have not time to go in – yes, very sorry."

"I will walk with you to the gate. I wonder if you can guess," Constance continued, "what happened to me on this very spot a few weeks ago."

"I cannot imagine."

"Why, I was attacked by a Socialist – a thorough-going, red-hot Socialist, who gave me his views, and told me his opinion of me. Fancy that for a peaceful Conservative like myself!"

She was working her way up gradually to draw out Mr. Cope upon the subject. A desire to hear his views had come over her. Nigel's subsequent conduct had not undermined the effect of his words, their power and reason still remained.

It is well for us sometimes that the preacher need not always practice what he preaches ere the words take effect. There is something in certain individuals which outweighs their surface failings, weaknesses, shortcomings; you feel that beneath them there is an undercurrent which will never fail, fall short, or disappoint.

Mr. Cope smiled – laughed a little.

"What a terrible situation you have depicted! And what did you do?"

"I listened to it all. I was really interested; a little longer and I might have been converted. I am anxious to hear more on the subjects. Now honestly, Mr. Cope, do you not think there is something very Christian in the Socialist theory?"

Mr. Cope partially closed his eyes again.

"I cannot say I do, Miss Compton. I do not believe in laws making Christians of people; I believe in reformation of character."

This fact was indisputable.

"Well, as do I," said Constance. Then she added, undauntedly, "But laws can make it easy or otherwise for people to do right."

"Undoubtedly," said Mr. Cope, with a sigh, recalling the various times his bishop had pulled him up for extreme practices.[40]

"And we want laws to make it easy," said Constance, warming up. "I cannot help thinking myself that Christ preached Socialism."

"Possibly He did preach some of their ideas, but where the rub[41] comes in is that Socialists don't preach Christ."

Constance was silent a minute. Had she spoken she might have said: What is preaching Christ? Does Socialism not preach him? "The unknown God, whom ye ignorantly worship. Him declare I unto you."[42] Not in individual form does the Lord Jesus come to us to-day, but in each member of our great humanity. Work for these, He says, and you work for Me. Reform and purify your laws, sweep away old abuses, so much nearer do you bring My kingdom. He comes as He said He should, as the least of his brethren. He pants for country air in close back streets and alleys, while the *élite* of the land roll by in their carriages: there is often an empty seat, but not for Him. He languishes in poor, badly built, ill-drained houses. He stretches out His hands to us from the doors of the hospitals not large enough to accommodate Him, so that in pain and sickness He is turned away. He pleads with the man of many acres for a chance in life, a portion of the world's surface for his own. He cries out to the man of riches and culture to bring some beauty and refinement into His sordid surroundings. He is crucified afresh when such diseases as typhoid, cholera, and diphtheria break out amongst us. "Humanity is the Son of God,"[43] but we heed Him not.

But when she did speak it was merely to say:

"What does make Christians of people?"

The clergyman opened his eyes.

"Surely you can find an answer to that question in the Baptismal Service."[44]

"No, no. I am not talking of the members of the Church of England. I am thinking of all God's world outside this little church of ours. There are thousands and thousands who know nothing of the Baptismal Service, wouldn't have time to read it over, or think of it, or understand it, if you pointed it out to them. What is to reach them all? How is one to get at them?"

"Don't you think the church's priests are doing their best, often in the face of privation and dire discouragement?" asked the clergyman, gently.

"Yes, but the harvest is great and the labourers are few. Besides, if the church alone were going to do the work, it ought to have done it more effectually by this time."

"I think your Socialist friend talked to some purpose," remarked the clergyman, looking at Constance with surprise. "To be good is to be happy, Miss Compton; there is no getting over that fact, and you must see yourself that prosperity and plenty does not always mean happiness and peace. I know many poor and humble homes where the faces are bright and the occupants cheerful and contented."

"But how about poor girls who have to sew week days and Sundays for their employers? What time have they to think about religion or practice it? Nothing but laws can make things better for them, or make it possible for them to be good. I have been told," said Constance, very gravely, "that it is girls like myself, women in my position, who help to keep them sewing there, by buying their work at the lowest cost, and never raising a finger to help them. That is a grave accusation – it makes one think."

"Your Socialist friend again?" queried the clergyman, smiling. "Oh, there is much, very much, doubtless, that wants setting right."

Constance looked straight up at him. For a moment the latent power in the girlish face flashed on the surface.

"Are you doing it – I mean, is the church doing it? 'Thy kingdom come'[45] we pray; but to many I see that that kingdom cannot come."

Mr. Cope pulled out his watch. He was not at a loss for an argument, but it really was growing close upon the hour when he must be back.

"We will continue this discussion another day," he said pleasantly. "In the meantime, you must not forget that there is a Head of the church who is working behind our efforts; you must not leave Him out and rely only on man."

"I had not forgotten Him,"[46] said Constance.

Nigel's feelings were not enviable when Miss Compton passed him with that unseeing gaze. He had had reason to feel offended with her, he thought: but, man like, it had never struck him that Miss Compton had her side of the question, and had had good reason to be offended with him. To do him justice, Nigel had an idea that Constance considered him so far below her in the social scale that his doings one way or another would affect her very little. But they had affected her, he was thinking; he was a good deal surprised, more than a little sorry.

He thought about Constance Compton for fully ten minutes, even to the exclusion of his cherished scheme. And, again, at a meeting of the union that evening he answered once totally at random, for Constance's face had risen before him, not with that cool, unrecognising glance, but peeping, rosy, childlike, and laughing, from the fur hood, as when she had said, "I am the Christmas fairy!" He walked back to the draughty room in Sheridan Street plunged in despair. So kind an action (he could see it now), and he had repaid it like a churl! What an idiot he was! He had insulted a lady, for a slight was an insult.

It was lonely in the old house those days without Hilda, doubly lonely that night. The child had rebelled against coming back to town, and Mrs. Linden had put in a plea for her to remain.

"Now do 'ee, sir," she had said; she was always very respectful to Nigel. "Do 'ee leave her here, Mr. Nigel, sir. We've growed used to the little one, Linden and me. Don't 'ee go a-taking her back to them nasty smoky streets. Leave her here, and you can come down o' Saturdays; it'll be a change for yer."

So Hilda had stayed on.

Nigel Grey found plenty to do in town in the beginning of the New Year apart from his regular employment. He did not forget to call in and see Nelly Graham. He had looked in upon her once or twice since that day two months before, when he had artfully arranged for Susie to pay back the borrowed money. Nelly seemed much as usual, perhaps she was getting a trifle thinner, or, as Nigel expressed it, "rather down in the mouth."[47] Work was slack; she had not been able to get through it quickly enough for the firm that had employed her, so they had cast her off, and for some time she had been dependent on any work she could pick up for herself. Occasionally she had gone out to do a day's cleaning, but the work was too heavy for her except now and again. She looked brighter after talking to Nigel for a while.

"And, Nigel," she said, "I've got on famously this winter as regards firing, so far, for a girl as I lent some money to last year has paid it back."

"Oh, that's good," said Nigel. "I've no doubt it came in handy."

His eyes met hers calmly; he congratulated himself upon his powers as an actor.

When he called in at Nelly's a few weeks after, she seemed rather diffident. He thought her changed somehow, shy, but with a certain brightness and glow about her that he never remembered having seen before. She appeared to take more interest than of old in his doings, asked of her own accord after Mr. Ross, and talked of their plans as if she were really interested in them, which she was not, as Nigel knew. Poor narrow-minded little Nell.

As he left the house he happened to note the date of the month – he had occasion to remember it some time later, Nelly had a snowdrop in a glass.

"See!" she had said to him. "Allie Blunt gave it to me. Isn't it early? February is the month for them, and February doesn't begin till to-morrow."

"What a girl you are for flowers!" Nigel had responded. "Every time I've been of late I've seen those everlasting old hips and haws on the table that I gave you ages ago. I'm glad something has come to take their place."

Nelly smiled and was silent. She did not tell Nigel that nothing could take their place, that they were lying now amongst her poor treasures wrapped up in tissue paper, in a drawer in that very room, sacred berries, because his hands – hands which had tenderly helped her over life's stony road – had touched them.

[13 February 1897]
Chapter VIII.

Brierley Heath[48] was a wide, undulating tract of land. It was here Nigel found himself on Easter Monday. He had run down to Brierley to make arrangements with Mrs. Linden to fetch Hilda away on the following Saturday, with a promise that she should come again, later on, when the hot summer days set in. Having settled that matter, he set out for a walk across the heath before returning to town. It was a breezy day, the wind blew in great, soft gusts; overhead were masses of white and blue; the rooks cawed in a pleasant, lazy fashion amongst the tall elms scattered here and there.

Suddenly in the distance he caught sight of Constance Compton. She was coming swiftly along, holding her hat for the wind was treacherous. It had blown a vivid colour into her cheeks; her eyes were dancing in their clear outlook upon life. An inspiration seized Nigel. As she approached he went up to her.

"Miss Compton," he said, "I am inclined to think I made a fool of myself over a very kind action of yours last Christmas. I suppose you won't accept an apology, or – will you? You know I was not educated in your school;[49] had I been, things might have been different. I might have known how to have acted like a gentleman under all circumstances."

"Oh, don't think of it again," she said, quickly. "I dare say you were right from your own point of view; only," she paused a moment, and then said, with perfect artlessness, "I *should* like to know why you were offended."

"I suppose I wanted to be treated as an equal, Miss Compton. I did not want gratuitous gifts which seemed to me to savour of patronage.[50] Men like myself, whose work takes them amongst many classes, get upstart notions, and then they prove how little worthy they are to be treated as an equal."

"Patronage!" said Constance, with a quick flush. "How could you have thought of such a thing? I looked upon little Hilda simply as a sick child to whom I might give a little pleasure. I never patronise," added the girl, with quiet dignity; "it is not my way. Please say no more about it; it has all been a mistake." She looked round in search of another topic. "Is it not lovely out here to-day?"

"Yes, indeed. Just imagine what it must be to me," said Nigel. "I have been trying to think that I was glad my constant visits to Brierley were nearly over (Hilda goes back to town this week), but I can't, though they have run away with a lot of time. One seems to live again on a morning like this."

"Do you think the change has done your sister good?"

"Yes, I am sure of it."

"Are you on your way to the station?"

"Well, yes – a rather rambling way. I came up here for a blow. You are going to Brierley, I suppose?"

"Yes; I am on my way back from Wareminster."

"May I walk a little way with you?"

"Certainly," said Constance, in her easy, pleasant way.

As they walked on in silence for a minute, Constance gave a humorous side glance at her companion.

"More Socialists?" she inquired. "Another theory to propound?"

Nigel laughed.

"Of course," he said. "I am a monomaniac,[51] you know."

"Of that I am quite aware. Well, tell me your latest thoughts on the subject. I am patience itself, but you know the saying:

A woman convinced against her will.
Clings to the same opinion still.[52]

"Do you really want my latest thoughts? I believe you are secretly laughing at me."

"Oh, no. I never laugh at anything that is earnest. The most I should do would be to sigh."

"Because the great consummation seems so far off, of course."

"No, because –" Here Constance remembered that she was the squire's daughter, and Nigel a mechanic, and that, therefore, levity was unsuitable between them, so she pulled herself up. "I am waiting," she said.

"Well, look round at this country, Miss Compton." They were standing side by side looking over the far, softly wooded slopes, where villages nestled in hollows, church spires rose amongst the trees, and white farmhouses dotted the undulating fields. "Isn't this England of ours pre-eminently a farming country? With such a land as this, what do we want with so much imported farm produce? Now, if once land were nationalised and reverted to the people to hold in trust for the nation our peasants could produce their own poultry, fruit, eggs, and vegetables and the people might be saved from drink and pauperism. Just in proportion as occupying ownership prevails, drunkenness and poverty die out. You may see it constantly; it is so in various parts of England. Switzerland has an ideal land system,[53] and in no country in Europe, as you know, is there less pauperism, more widely spread comfort. If such a system succeeds so well there, and also in different parts of France, Germany, Norway, etc. why should it not in England?"

"It would be a great future," Constance said, "if it could come, and bring with it all for which you hope. A future to live for and strive for – to throw your life into your efforts to attain!"

"Yes," said Nigel, solemnly, "a great, great future."

"How would you start?"

"Well, of course, the first thing is to strike at monopolies. Men cannot be free while privileges are given into the hands of a special class – public lands, coal mines, and so on. They shut men out from opportunities of work, they take from the employed much of their earnings, they depress trade, and create want in the midst of plenty. It was perfectly true, what was said at one of our meetings a short time ago, that if Moses had smitten the rock to produce water for the thirsty Israelites[54] these days, some speculator would have piped the well and sold the water at a penny a glass. Surely coal, the natural product of the land, should be as free to the people as water."

"I have heard that monopolies increase the wealth of a nation."

"Nay, for the wealth flows into a few hands only. What we want is a wider distribution of wealth. 'The right use of wealth is to develop a complete human life.'"[55]

There was silence a minute, then Constance remarked:

"You think it is a pity man cannot do them of his own freewill? He is a selfish animal, and cannot understand until he feels himself, Miss Compton. Yes, it does seem strange. We can start workhouses, but not people's playgrounds; infirmaries, but not libraries. We can rail against the Government, but we cannot each individually deny ourselves needless luxuries – the carriage, the horse, the wine – the expense of which might go to brighten the barrenness of other lives. We can fling charity at the poor, and pauperise them, but we cannot go down and work with them, the only work which is of much avail."

"Work with them," repeated Constance, doubtfully. "To a great many people that would not be easy."

"I mean by that, working as friend with friend, instead of throwing gifts to them from a distance. There are little things that everyone can do to raise them from the squalor of their surroundings and give them food for purer thoughts. Now, if you want to see the influence of flowers, you should go down into a close city court, and see how some poor blossom is cherished, how hard hands grow gentle with they change the water, and eyes and voice soften when they look at it or speak of it. If I go through the back streets with a flower in my button-hole – well, it's not there long; a dozen little grimy hands are stretched out for it. In the parks and square gardens sit the children of the wealthy, stringing daisies into chains; they play with them for an hour or two, and tired of them, drop them in the streets, maybe, on their way home; then a ragged urchin comes along and picks them up. That is an example of the dealings of the rich with the poor. So slip the generations away! But the children of the rich might have been taught to gather their daisies with a purpose, and the hands that are trained to give with thoughtful sympathy when they are small shall become the hands of the neighbourly, the kindly, the active citizen by-and-by."

Nigel paused, and Constance looked up at the strong, powerful face. She was beginning to understand why this man's friends thought so much of him, how it was that he held the people spellbound in the Socialist lecture-rooms, why

Brierley and all Wareminster and different portions of the East-end were ringing with the name of Nigel Grey.

"How carefully you have thought out little ways and means," she said.

"No; they have forced themselves upon me. Do you mean in this matter of giving flowers? Every day in going to my work in the North, I pass houses the windows of which are ablaze with them, then gradually I get to streets without a spot of brightness. But there are other things, a chat once in a while, not too interlarded with texts and stock sayings about contentment, something rather which shall expand the mind a little and bring them thoughts from another source – thoughts which the good and wise have held from old time to the present. It sets my heart beating when I think what could be accomplished if people went further, and the rich lady, we will say, could put aside an afternoon now and again to entertain her poorer sisters and brothers at her own house. They have much to learn from each other; the gain would not be only on the side of the lowly. There are histories waiting to be written, Miss Compton, of the patient nobility of lives lived out in dark tenement houses, of help extended amidst straitened circumstances, which put our greatest efforts to shame."

"I fear we are a terribly selfish people, many of us," said Constance, with an unsteady little laugh.

"What a pity it is," she said, a moment later, in her direct, unself-conscious way, "that you Socialists are such a reckless, lawless set – so many of you, that is."

Nigel gave her a quizzical glance.

"I suppose some of us are rather a rough lot, but we fight against great odds, and that sometimes makes men desperate."

He was interrupted by a cry of delight from Constance. She had forgotten the great question of nations, and was now on her knees picking violets.[56]

"And here's another, and here's another," she was saying. "Look, are they not large? Do you see any more anywhere about?"

It just crossed Nigel's mind for a moment, as one of the strange freaks of fate, that this girl, one of the class so antagonistic to him, should have been thrown across his path and that on this bright spring morning he and she together should be looking for violets on the Brierley Heath, as if life had no more serious questions at issue. They walked on a little distance towards the village together, but the conversation had dropped its serious tone.

"What are you going to do with our violets?" Nigel asked, after a while.

"I am going to take them home and put them with the other we have. Oh," she paused, "you get so few flowers in town compared to us – will you have them?"

She held them out, and Nigel took them.

"Thank you," he said, with a singular gravity.

"You cannot carry them in your hand," Constance remarked, her ready smile rippling over her face again. "That would look too innocent for a Socialist lecturer. I don't fancy they do things of that sort as a rule. Fasten them in your coat."

They had reached the entrance to the village, and Nigel came to a standstill.

"Good-bye, Miss Compton," he said. "Here we part."

"Good-bye," returned Constance. "By the bye, next month I shall be in your part of the world. I am going up to town."

She made the statement carelessly, in a default of anything better to say.

Nigel shook his head with a smile.

"Nay; half a world will lie between us," he said.

His tone had a faint touch of sadness in it. But it might have been sorrow for the whole system that brought it there; nothing more. He turned as he spoke, raised his hat, and walked away.

Constance watched him for a second – a curious man, who had put himself on her level, and would have friendship or nothing from her!

Nigel plunged into his work when he reached home, and forgot the morning on the heath, forgot the gentle eyes of Constance Compton. Nay, did he not denounce her class with unusual zeal that night at Fraternity Hall? The feeling of friendship for his companion of the morning remained, but the transitory sentiment was gone. The violets were still in his button-hole at the meeting, where he had placed them that morning, but they were drooping when he reached home, beyond the power of water to revive. So he tossed them through the window into the yard, and fell asleep to dream of the Free Education Hall.

[20 February 1897]

Chapter IX.

Beneath the trees in St. James Park a young man and girl were sitting one evening towards the end of June. The young man was tall and slender, and immaculately dressed in a light suit; he had bright blue eyes. The girl beside him had not bright blue eyes; it would be waste of time to describe their colour, for their expression was what caught and held the fancy. They were kindly eyes, far-searching eyes which looked as though they might see beyond the little weaknesses and disagreeables, and ungainlinesses that lie atop poor human nature, to something sterling and true beneath – that which God shall look to find in all of us when the judgment question shall be asked – not, What were you? but, What did you try to be, and what were life's odds against you? They were eyes that were learning (they were too young to have learnt) to make allowance, to overlook, remembering the path of life is rough and human hearts are sore beset. The owner of these eyes wore a quaintly made gown of some white woollen material looped with silken cords here and there, a simple shady hat, and a bunch of lilies of the valley[57] at her throat. The only colour about her was the rose of her cheeks.

"Then there must be someone else," the young man was saying.

It was Sir George.

The girl (Constance Compton) shook her head.

"It cannot be," George said, doubtfully, "that you do not approve of cousins marrying?"

The laughter-loving face beside him broke into a smile.

"Let us say it is that, dear George. It isn't, you know; but we will pretend it is – we will pretend so!"

"Then that is disposed of; and if there is no one else, and you say you like me, why will you not have me, Constance?"

Why not? A good match, surely, from a worldly point of view. How many would have eagerly grasped it! How many would have triumphed could they have brought supercilious Sir George Cumberland-West to their feet. But, Constance? She started up and walked a few steps over the green sward. Very nice, doubtless, to marry a wealthy young baronet; and possible M.P.! Very nice to live at Westbury House and be Lady Cumberland-West; but – would the life that Sir George had to offer be the life she had dreamed of sometimes of late? Would it be that ideal life which should lead through clouds and sunshine, love and labour to a well-earned home of rest at last? Was she fitted for the commonplace, conventional round of one of England's fine ladies – she who had caught a glimpse of a fuller life? Now that she had realised what it might be made – its infinite possibilities, its high purpose – could she tread the hum-drum path of ordinary existence by the side of that quiet, irreproachably gentleman-like being, George Cumberland-West?

She came back to the spot where he was still sitting.

"George, I cannot," she said.

Sir George had not shifted his position since his cousin left him. He was leaning forward drawing patterns with his cane in the gravel. He did not look happy, but those three words uttered by his cousin added no extra shadow to his face. He seemed to have accepted his doom beforehand.

Sir George was undoubtedly fond of Constance, though with her gradually developing democratic tendencies she was perhaps hardly the wife one would have expected him to choose. But George was not a man who had any great opinion of a woman's theories. He would listen with a smile to Constance on the rare occasions when she gave her view of things; she was not likely to affect the issue of national affairs much in his opinion. And there was something in her quick, active ways which appealed to his rather languid nature. In spite of the snubs he had freely dealt out to her in early days, there had existed a sort of *camaraderie* between himself the bright little girl. He was not so sentimental or so much in love as to believe that if Constance refused him he would never marry but he was wondering just then whether he would ever find a second Constance. She was a woman now, but she had not disappointed the promise of her youth. As he looked at her for a moment, Constance the full-grown girl vanished, and he saw instead a leaf-strewn avenue and a large-eyed, little maiden, Constance the child, running forward to welcome him and offer him a share in her fun, her sweets, or her toys. The years had drifted them far apart now; he could see that plainly, but for that moment of time his heart went back across the track where once it had danced forth with her in that early dawn of life. Then he brought himself sharply back again to the present.

"I was a fool to have tried my chance," he said; "and yet – we have always been friends. You know all the worst of me as well as all the best, Constance. What is it that stands between?"

He looked at her with straightforward eyes.

"Nothing, George, except that we are not suited."

"Oh, that is so played out," said Sir George, irritably. "Why don't you say at once that I am a great deal too good for you, and that you will always be a sister to me?"

"Well, you *are* a nice person to go a-courting," returned Constance.

Sir George went on unheeding.

"I cannot marry a girl whose tastes are precisely the same as mine. Lively couple we should be! We should clash every two minutes."

He poked the gravel moodily with his cane.

"But seriously, George, we are not at all fitted for one another. Six months hence you will thank me in your heart for having said 'No' this evening. I believe I am getting democratic or something in my old age," she remarked, vaguely. "I don't look at things in the way I once did."

"Never mind," said George, stoutly. "We will translate Karl Marx's 'Capital' together, and study the Socialist Encyclical Letter.[58]

Constance laughed, not very happily, at this pleasantry on Sir George's part.

"It would be no good," she said; "you would only win me over in a half hearted sort of way to your own views. You always had the upper hand of me, you know. Oh, George, don't think I am talking platitudes when I say you have done me a great honour, which I do not deserve, and can never accept. London is full of girls prettier, wiser, and better than I, who – will love you better, and be more worthy of you and all you offer!"

"Come, let us go home," said Sir George, rising slowly.

* * *

It was about this time the same evening that a young man walking along the old Brompton Road stopped suddenly, and then retraced his steps. It was Nigel Grey. Something, one of those chance thoughts that flash across the brain, coming from no one knows where, had made him think of Nelly Graham. He had actually forgotten her in the press of work during the last few months. Then it was that he remembered the date of his last visit to her, five months before. His conscience felt anything but easy as he traversed the familiar streets lying between Brompton and Hammersmith. He would look in at her that evening instead of going to see a friend.

Sarah opened the door and admitted him. It struck Nigel that she had a singularly unpleasant and forbidding look. He walked up the stairs and into Nelly's room, with a preliminary tap at the door. Nelly was sitting at the foot of the bed. Nigel could not remember ever having seen her unoccupied before. Her hands were clasped on her lap, and extended in a manner that indicated extreme dejection; her eyes had dark marks beneath them; her cheeks were sunken. There was no flower this time in the tumbler on the table; the room was close, stifling though the window was open. Nigel went up to her.

"Why, Nell?" he said. "Why, Nell?"

The girl raised her eyes, but scarcely answered him. The old look of pleasure at his presence was absent.

"Out of work, Nelly?"

"No, Nigel."

"Ill?"

"N-no."

"Things going wrong with Emma and Jem?"

"Everything just as usual there, Nigel, thanks."

Nigel's conscience smote him, when he remembered that it was fully five months since he had looked in at Emma's either. An uneasy feeling was upon him. He sat dangling his hat between his hands.

"Don't bear malice against a fellow, Nelly. I've been awfully busy."

Nelly looked up and smiled. There was no reproach in her look, only that extreme patience.

"You will soon be a fine gentleman, Nigel, and then you will forget all about us."

"A gentleman!" said Nigel, with sudden energy. "Not if it is to teach me to forget."

"I thought you had forgotten."

Again, that pricking of Nigel's conscience.

"It was only for a time, Nelly. I have been very busy, but when I remembered about you I came round instantly."

"Yes."

The cold apathy had come over the girl again.

Nigel looked round the room. To his eyes it appeared more comfortless than ever.

"I wish I could do something for you, Nell," he said, but Nelly only shook her head.

It seemed impossible to keep conversation up that evening.

"What sort of girl is that Sarah overhead?" he asked, presently.

"A good sort of girl, Nigel, I think – at least, she is kind to me."

"She seemed to me rather a rough specimen."

"Oh, I daresay her manners ain't anything extra," said Nelly, with the faintest little sneer. "She's not been in the way of learning good manners."

"I meant that she had rather a surly look, Nell; that's all."

Nelly made no response; it was impossible to keep the conversation up. Nigel rose.

"No time these days to come round and see Hilda?" he asked. "She's going down into the country again soon for a visit, where she went last winter. But she's at home now, and she'd like to see you."

"Give her my love, Nigel. No, I'm afraid I haven't time to go round just at present."

Nigel went to the door, then turned.

"Nelly, you're not vexed because I've not been to see you oftener?" he asked.

"Oh, no, Nigel; oh, no." Nelly had risen, and as she spoke the colour came rushing to her face. She looked beautiful at that moment. "It's – it's only that I haven't been well; I've been lying down; I didn't feel like seeing anyone," she said, hurriedly.

"Oh, that's all right; because you and I are old friends, Nelly, and mustn't quarrel. I'll be bound," he added, with a poor sort of humour, "that Tom Blunt doesn't treat you like I've done."

Getting no sort of answer, he moved towards the door again.

"And get that ridiculous notion out of your head, Nell, about my being a gentleman and forgetting folks, and so on. That isn't my aim; you know. If ever I am a *gentleman*, as you call it, it will because I hope to do greater things for my people. And," he added, solemnly, "may Fate deal with me as I deal with them. Good-bye, Nell."

"Good-bye, Nigel. Thanks for coming."

Again he encountered that unpleasant young woman, Sarah; this time on the stairs. She had evidently been listening to every word that had been said, and did not even seem to care to disguise the fact. As Nigel passed, she gave him a worse scowl than ever. "I hope she felt edified by my remarks concerning her," observed Nigel, mentally, with some feeling of satisfaction, when he got outside.

[27 February 1897]

Chapter IX. Continued.

Nigel did not forget Nelly Graham again, but some how after that visit whenever he called she seemed to be out. Once he met Sarah in the street; he knew her by her red hair and lowering look. One of his quick good impulses come to him after he had passed her – those flashes of feeling which redeemed his whole character, too apt to sink into the mere desire to be a leader of men. In these sudden impulses, wherein lay the true man, though as yet undeveloped, Nigel could put self away. He turned back, and with a few rapid strides overtook Sarah.

"How is Miss Graham?" he asked, abruptly.

"She's as usual," Sarah answered, shortly.

"Look here," said Nigel, "she tells me you are a friend of hers. Well, I am a friend, too. Last time I saw her – a couple of months ago – I was shocked at the change in her. She won't let me help her – she is too proud; but" – he drew a sovereign from his pocket – "couldn't you lay this out on a few things for yourself – thing that'll be nourishing and good for her – and ask her to share them with you? It's the only way to help her."

Sarah drew back.

"No," she said harshly. "I can't take your money. I'd have to eat part of the things myself, and they'd choke me."

She was pushing past him, but he stopped her. Nelly's patient, little, worn face was in his mind to the exclusion of all else.

"It's such a little thing," he said, almost humbly, "and I ask it as a favour. *Can't* you take it and lay out part now and part later on, and give the things to Nell? Tell her you've had a box from the country or something."

"A box from the country," Sarah laughed loudly. "That's so likely. Who'd ever send me a box of anything? Who ever gave me a helping hand all my life through? Well," after a moment's pause, "give me the money, I'll see what I can do. I'm not to say it's from you?"

"Certainly not."

"No, I suppose not," said Sarah, with her unpleasant laugh, and she passed on.

After that Nigel did not call round at Poplar Street for some time. He had faith in Sarah's honesty, if his fancy was not taken with her manners. Nelly evidently wished to avoid him these days, so having partially satisfied his conscience by looking after her bodily comfort he determined to thrust himself no more upon her for a time.

Things were going with a swing with Nigel Grey that summer. Like a wise man, he had not neglected his employment at the engine works for his political schemes. He had lately been promoted again. This time it was a very decided step up the ladder. The firm had offered to take him as junior partner; he had always stood high in the estimation of the heads of the firm. He had worked steadily there since he was a lad of thirteen, and his abilities and conscientiousness were fully recognised.

Since the morning on the heath, Constance and Nigel had met not infrequently. Now it would be for a few steps along the village street on one of his trips to Brierley to see Hilda, or, again, their paths might lie in the same direction going to or from the station. Once, in Kensington High Street, she had beckoned to him from a carriage, where she sat alone waiting outside a shop door. She had asked him about the opening of the hall which was shortly to take place, and Nigel had tendered her a half hesitating yet eager invitation. They were learning to take an interest in each other's lives, these two.

"Oh, I should like to go very much," said Constance; she looked pleased at the idea. "Lady Drayton, with whom I am staying, would be delighted to go with me, I have no doubt. She is always interested in helpful schemes. I will look Tom Wilton up – I have not seen him for some time – and ask him to escort us."

Nigel began to tell her about his rise at the works. It was his first glimpse of Constance in the great upper world. She wore a spray of yellow roses at her bosom; the arrangement of her hair and hat bespoke the latest fashion. Nigel was not oblivious to the crest upon the carriage door.

The busy world of London passed unheeded. An old blind man with a board and a tray of boot laces groped his way past them; a tired little flower-girl kept ceaselessly offering her wares to the passers-by; a faded woman in a rusty shawl and bonnet, with a weary, despairing look, hurried on her way. The stream of carriages rolled past; Constance bowed to an ample dowager seated in one, with a supercilious pug beside her.

Constance also had been looking critically at her companion. The last six months had carried him fairly into that mysterious region where men may, if they choose, claim the title of "gentleman." Whatever his upbringing, he had left it behind; whatever his friends and surroundings, he had overtopped them. He stood before her, partner in a large firm, a clever, good-looking man, his every movement suggestive of power and capability, perfectly at ease, careful in the details of his dress, with no more sign of having risen about him than many who throng our city drawing-rooms and have sprung from less than he. And yet the fact remained he was still the son of Lord Allerton's steward.[59]

"Do you think," she asked, suddenly, and somewhat irrelevantly, "you could ever turn London into an ideal city? It would be a hard task."

Nigel looked round him at Constance's words, up and down the sunny street, as though pondering for a moment, then faced her again with a half smile.

"Shall I turn prophet and tell you what I see of the London of the future?"

Constance nodded.

"First, I see a city from which all the slums, rookeries,[60] and poor streets are done away. The old historic landmarks remain, but the children of poverty and vice that often dwelt around them are seen no more. They are shipped away and settled where fields of arable land await them: perhaps here, perhaps across the seas."

"But don't you think perhaps we make too much of the poverty and misery of the poor? I have heard so. Don't you think they may enjoy life in their own way as much as we do?"

Constance spoke earnestly. The words were not a salve to her conscience, but the result of statements she had often heard, and some thought on her own part.

At those old, old words, so often uttered by the rich in respect to the poor, Nigel's thoughts went back for one second to a scene he had witnessed the night before, where in a dark, ill-ventilated room in a tenement house, a widow was dying by inches of cancer of the throat – disease terrible to endure even with the most luxurious surroundings – her only means of support coming from the wages of her son, a youth of eighteen, who worked at the docks and was in a confirmed consumption. He would drag himself home from his work at night, halting every few steps for breath; probably of the two the mother would last longer. But when he spoke he only said:

"Do you know what their own way of enjoying life is, Miss Compton? I think you would like to give them a better way, if ever you saw them on holidays, in their special public gardens or music halls – saw their idea of fun – heard their jokes."

"Well, perhaps. Go on with your city, though."

"Oh, yes, my city," Nigel smiled and resumed. "I see recreation grounds, gymnasiums, libraries, universities, public baths, all provided by the State; heat, electricity, and light conveyed through the streets, by the State also. The streets themselves lined with trees and flowers. In the West-end, as well as in the East, the levelling power should also come; for the riches that sensualise men and give them leisure for idle thoughts, which tend to unworthy actions, should be swept away – must be, if the world is ever to be bright and pure. (Some of the society journals bear a very favourable comparison with *The Police News*.[61]) Every man should give his best to the nation or at least something, for what the nation gives him. I no longer see delicate and consumptive girls going to and fro to their work, in rain or shine, day by day or sewing in close, ill-ventilated rooms; or some poor creature from the upper strata of society, who clings to the remnants of past artificiality and greatness, trudging round footsore and be-draggled, to give French or music lessons, struggling to keep herself, and also lay by a little for that fast-coming time when the eye is dim and the hand nerveless, and only charity or starvation lies ahead. Nor do I see old men and women, after braving the storms of half a century, facing the loneliness of the workhouse at last. I see old age, even elderly age, safely and securely provided for: thieves and criminals – a class who spring from the inequality of riches – gradually lessening, soon eliminated, and man improving as he must do when he lives in the midst of refined surroundings, mixes with his fellows, and learns to co-operate in society. I see science progressing, genius and capabilities recognised, inventors rewarded; men with time and clear, unharassed brains to search out life's problems, mysticisms, and contradictions. In short, I see a life where there is hope and opportunity for all."

"Ah," said Constance, a little sadly, "I see it is an ideal city you have sketched. Such a city is not for us, and here."

"Why?"

As she did not answer, he repeated the monosyllable, then added:

"Let me tell you. It is because you have been taught a theory which has no foundation, that sorrow is the heritage of every human child, and that resignation is a virtue. It may be for the toiler oppressed for generations, and unable to grasp the true meaning of life; but for you and me, with money, brains, and capabilities, facing the world's needs, it is a *vice*. Such a city is possible, for *us* and here."

Just then Lady Drayton issued from a shop door and come up to the carriage. So the interview ended, and Nigel took his leave.

As the easy figure, with the shoulders thrown back and the head held resolutely high, disappeared into the crowd a stray verse came into her head:

> Ah well! the world is very discreet,
> There are plenty who pause and wait,
> But here was a man who set his feet
> Sometimes in advance of fate.
> Never rode to the wrongs redressing
> A worthier paladin,
> Shall he not hear the blessing,
> Good and faithful, enter in?[62]

Poor Nigel! We have seen his weaknesses and his failings. Perhaps he was not so worthy a paladin as innocent Constance thought. She even might have had her doubts had she heard his hot denunciations occasionally at Fraternity Hall and the branch lecture rooms. But thus we dream our dreams and think our thoughts of one another, and stretch out our hands, unseen in the darkness, to our ideals, through the mysteries and perplexities and cross ways of life.

A few minutes later and the chance meeting was apparently forgotten. They had turned into the Row,[63] where the wind caught Constance's hair and the sun turned it to vibrating threads of brown-gold. And one or two admirers of the past season rode up pleased at a chance to win a smile from pretty Miss Compton's eyes again. And Lady Drayton, in spite of her philanthropic tendencies, was murmuring in the intervals interesting items concerning a new gown she had been ordering.

[6 March 1897]
Chapter XI.

On Thursday evening Nigel called round at Poplar Street on his way home from the works. It was long since he had been there; he hardly knew what impulse led his foot in that direction that particular day. The landlady's slipshod daughter opened the door. As soon as she saw Nigel on the step, she gave vent to the abrupt announcement:

'Nelly Graham's gone."

"Gone?" echoed Nigel.

"Gone since yesterday morning."

"Left for good?"

"Oh, no her things are here."

"Did she say nothing to anyone – not even to that girl on the top floor – where she was going?"

"Not a word."

The door was shut in Nigel's face. He could not spare time to stay longer.

He walked on, puzzled and troubled: but poor Nelly was not to occupy his thoughts long, not even that was granted her; though, to do him justice, he thought of her many times between then and the opening of the hall a couple of hours later.

The hall, which was situated in B— Street, was a comfortable, well-ventilated room of a good size. It was just before the opening commenced that Lady Drayton, accompanied by Tom Wilton and Constance, entered, the first and last mentioned seating themselves near the door, Tom making his way up near the platform to join some kindred spirits there. Nigel was on the platform, looking his best that evening. There were plenty of things to be seen to, and he was passing hither and thither, but his eyes were upon that trio when the door opened to admit them – Lady Dalton first, with her sleepy, smiling face, colossal proportions, and flowing skirts making Constance in the background look even more girlish than usual in her simple dress with the pure white flowers in her bodice – Tom, with his erect mane, bringing up the rear. For the last fifteen minutes Nigel had been asking himself, would she come after all? When he saw her his heart gave a pound, then stopped short for a beat or two, startled at its own audacity, for – but he would not think to-night, he dared not think. He sat quietly in his seat, his eyes upon the ground, till Mr. Ross rose to give the opening address.

He spoke on his favourite theme – Co-operation; especially on what it had done in the work before them in providing better means of education, promoting culture, and raising the literary taste. All pioneers, he said, should remember to be constructive, not merely destructive, not to tear down faster than they can substitute something better. He bade them work on in hope, and take for their watchword the Biblical phrase, "And they helped everyone his neighbour, and everyone said to his brother, Be of good cheer."[64]

There were several speeches and music before the evening closed. Nigel said a few words. He spoke a little about the hall, and what they hoped to do there. Then he touched on the work of educating and raising the masses in its wide sense. He was one of the people himself, he said; therefore well fitted to speak for them. He had been, and was at the present time, a working man; he wished that to be understood. He hoped to be one all his life; he was there to-night as their representative; he knew their lives and needs. *He* had had a chance, though, which many other working men had not had, namely, parents who had been able to keep him from the overwork and poor living many had to contend with, who had provided him with books and leisure for study, from whose daily conversation, when he was quite a little fellow, he had gathered food for high and earnest thought. But these things were but chances in which Fortune had favoured him; he was there to-night to plead that others might have a chance, too – to show how sorely they needed it.

During the singing at the close of the evening, Nigel made his way down the room to Constance Compton. "Well?" he said, interrogatively. She was sitting at the end of the row, and he stood beside her; he had forgotten to greet her, but she did not notice the omission.

"So, that is Mr. Ross?" she whispered, with a little side motion of her head towards where he was sitting on the platform.

"Yes, that is he."

"I liked his speech – yours too," she added, smiling. She was definitely interested, her eyes looked big and shining. "Tell me," she said, "what did that young man in front mean? I heard the one next him say, just after Mr. Ross had finished his speech, 'Ross is awfully in love with human nature, isn't he?' and the other said, 'Yes, when it's not too respectable.'"

Nigel laughed a little.

"Mr. Ross has a weakness for helping people; he likes to pick someone up who is down – to help to make a success out of a life which is on its way to become a failure. Some people are given that way, Miss Compton."

"It is a nice way," said Constance, thoughtfully. "It is the sort of thing which makes a life worth looking at – worth living, too, I should imagine."

"Do you still think us a lawless set, Miss Compton? Are you still wondering where our religion is? Or do you see the outcome here?"

Constance smiled, but only replied with a slight shake of the head.

"What, is this not enough?"

"Not quite."

They were silent a minute, then she gave him a side glance, with a gleam of fun in her eyes.

"I heard some rather high praise of you just now," she said.

"The youth in front again?" queried Nigel. "We really ought to have him on the platform."

"Yes, the youth in front. Shall I tell you what he said?"

"Certainly; everyone likes praise."

He had no wish to hear what the boy had said of him, except in so far as it must pass Constance Compton's lips to come to him.

"He said," Constance hesitated, evidently doubtful whether to repeat it, then she went on. "He said, 'That Grey, who is speaking, is what I call a practical reformer now; it isn't all stump oratory[65] with him. He is one of the few who are willing to do what they can when they cannot do what they would.'"

"Oh," said Nigel, with a quick flush and the uncomfortable feeling of a man who has received a compliment; he tried to turn it off with a laugh. "It would be worth while trying to cultivate our friend's acquaintance." A moment later he added, in a lower voice: "He little knows me. Do you recollect my once telling you that there is always more we ought to do? In no case am I more painfully conscious of that than in my own."

Constance did not speak again; she sat bending slightly forward, her profile turned towards Nigel. His glance fell upon it, the clear-cut features, the rise and fall of the lashes. At this supreme hour, for which he had worked and striven for a couple of years, he was thinking of nothing else but a girl's face. Constance's white silk gloves had slipped from her lap to the floor; he stooped and picked them up, and then still held them, instead of placing them upon her lap again. A terrible reaction was stealing over him – a heart-sickness which numbed all his faculties; it seemed to come to him with the scent of the white heliotrope[66] in Constance Compton's dress.

It may be the last time – the last time, his heart was saying, that you and I are side by side together – that you and I face life with one common feeling at heart. In the years to come another will stand where I am standing to-night, and hold your gloves and fan at concert and opera, in the great fashionable world which will sweep you away again, out of my sight. For ever divided, you and I, who might have worked together for a lifetime. Even to breathe my love would be an insult to you, Constance Compton, and you can never be mine!

The singing was ended; the people began to file out. Nigel stooped and laid the gloves upon his companion's knee, and Constance introduced him to her voluminous chaperone, Lady Drayton, who seemed to consider him the lion of the evening, and had much to say to him, till he fetched Mr. Ross down from the platform and in turn presented him.

They all stood in a group talking for a few minutes. Good Lady Drayton, keeping a firm hold upon Mr. Ross, was questioning him concerning the institute, from which she verged off, presently into an account of one of the first soup kitchens started by her aunt, and which she purported to have been upon the same principle.⁶⁷ Tom Wilton has come up, and stood, an attentive listener, twirling his cap in his hands. Constance and Nigel stood side by side, both silent and apparently engrossed in Lady Drayton's chatter. Presently the former spoke.

"Is it not time we were going, Lady Drayton? It is getting late and Tom is waiting."

She said the words a little wearily, as though the evening's entertainment had palled upon her. Nigel glanced at her, but read nothing in her face to account for the change of tone. As Lady Drayton began to envelop herself in her wraps, he turned towards her.

"We have tired you out with our prosy speeches," he said, gently.

"Oh, no," the girl answered, "I have enjoyed myself, and have been much interested; indeed I have."

As she spoke she gave him a swift glance, and their eyes met. There was nothing particular to be made out of those two glances, and yet they might have puzzled a bystander given to analysing such things. Neither could have said what was passing in the other's brain; they were too much the man and woman of the world to show that, and yet each read in the other pair of eyes something of that unwritten, unspoken, scarcely realised pathos of life, which comes and goes, and is a part of life, and yet is nameless, because it is too dim and intangible to be put into words.

They said good-bye, and Lady Drayton and Constance moved away, Tom Wilton piloting them through the group of people at the door.

She was gone! But a spray of the heliotrope had fallen to the ground. Nigel stooped and picked it up. He was not used to white heliotrope in his busy city life; his work did not lead him much into the land of flowers. It seemed like some odorous hothouse blossom, breathing to him the difference that lay between the wearer and himself. He placed it between the leaves of his pocket-book, with a grim smile at the irony of fate, the queer freaks of fortune, as he did so. Then he made his way up to the platform and bade his comrades good-night as though in a dream.

Outside, the stars were sparkling in the deep blue of the sky; nothing moved or shadowed their serene beauty, let the hearts of earth's storm-tossed children beat never so wildly; though the wreck of the world lay beneath them, they would still shine on. Nigel walked swiftly along under their cold light, with his own bright star of hope dim within. He reached the house in Sheridan Street and let himself in with a latch-key, passing straight to his own room. How soothing an aspect familiar scenes will wear in moments of great anguish! The draughty old room, with the trellis shadow of the apple branches lying on the floor, and the flecks of moonlight here and there, seemed to stretch out its arms to Nigel as a mother to her wandering son. Come back to me, it said. Let the great world of pomp and fashion sweep by, carrying with it whom it will. Come back to the old starting place to-night!

[13 March 1897]
Chapter XI. Continued.

He stood in the moonlight trying to wrestle with himself and rally. It was only his own life that was wrecked, he kept saying; the great tangled network of other human lives was still there to work for – the iron wheels still ground them down. Who was he to cry like a child for what fate chose to withhold? It had not withheld much from him in the past compared to its dealings with many; now his turn had come. One life, but one amongst the myriads, like one of yonder stars that shoot across the sky, fall, and pass beyond our ken. So would it be with him; his life would add its tiny spark of light to the rest, then pass to its appointed place in the great infinity, and a hundred years hence what would it matter, the heart-break and the pain tonight?

Would it be any consolation to him to have known that Constance, after leaving the hall in B— Street, had gone home to her own room in Lancaster Gate, and had sat for a whole long hour looking out at the gold-spangled sky and thinking how strangely paths cross and re-cross in life? And how people are thrown together only to be swept apart. And in every one of these partings each carried away something of the other's life – perhaps a sunny remembrance, perhaps an unrealised influence, some pleasant thoughts, a few scraps of information; and in return may be tendered the heart's devotion, a lifetime's fidelity, nights of tears and days of yearning, and the lingering of some old name in our prayers as the years roll on. In truth, a strange debtor and creditor account!

Chapter XII.

The world stands still for no man's grief. Work and Duty – life's solemn sentinels – with outstretched arms stand ever beside us. "This is the way, walk ye in it"[68] they say, and no man can wholly disregard them. Thus it came to pass that on the evening of the next day, on his way home from the works, Nigel found himself upon the doorstep of 10 Poplar Street. The door stood ajar, so he did not knock but walked upstairs and tapped at Sarah's door. He had to pass Nelly's room on the way, but some instinct told him that she was not back. Sarah's door swung open to Nigel's tap, and the girl herself appeared in the doorway. Her eyes were swollen with crying, her red hair was tossed and tumbled; she was huddled up in a shawl, for the room was fireless; on the table amid a heap of littered scraps of material a tallow dip[69] guttered in the faint draught from the door.

"Come in," said Sarah; she spoke as though she had been expecting him – "Come in, I've a few words to say to *you*."

Nigel stepped doubtfully over the threshold. The girl's manner puzzled him; a dread presentiment was upon him.

"Have you heard anything of Ellen Graham?" he asked, anxiously.

"Heard of Nelly? answered Sarah, with a hoarse laugh. "Oh, yes, I've heard of Nelly. You may hear of her, too, if you like to go round to Guy's 'Orspital,[70] where her dead body lies."

"What?" Nigel caught his breath quickly. "Nelly – Nelly dead?"

"Yes," said Sarah, raising her voice. "Dead, dead! can't you hear me? You murderer!" she hissed.

Nigel looked across at her with heavy eyes, his breath seemed to be going again, the room swam.

"What do you mean?" he asked, slowly.

"Nelly's drowned herself; they found her dead body last night. What were *you* doing last night? They tell me you are working for the people; they stick your name up on posters as the friend of the working classes – much you care for them! Didn't Nelly belong to that class? Didn't she need your help as much as any of them? And you brought her to this! Oh, I know what your fine-sounding speeches mean. They're to bring you fame, they are; they're to help you to be a gentleman – that's all you care for, though a dozen Nellies fling themselves to their death."

The girl's grief and passion made her tragic; they made her eloquent. Hard and coarse though she was, all that was best in her was uppermost just then.

Nigel sank into a chair; he could not have stood another second.

"What have I done," he asked, "that you should speak so of me?"

"What have you done?" Sarah laughed again. Hateful laugh. Nigel could have put his hands up to his ears to shut out the sound. "You're not blind. When gentlemen like you go paying attention to poor girls who've hardly a friend in the world, you must know what'll follow. Nelly loved you – she loved you, poor little creature. Maybe she thought you cared a little for her in return. She'd reason to think so, for you were round time and again last winter afore you got tired of her, and gave up coming. Nelly had a hard, hard life. Maybe she had been looking forward to a time when you would take her away from her work and her struggle. Maybe," added Sarah, contemptuously, "'twas simply yerself she cared for. I s'pose some girls might care for you, though you're not my sort."

She looked him over with cold, critical eyes.

"Tom Blunt says you'll be in Parlyment one of these fine days a-making the laws. Oh, yes, you're climbing up to be a gentleman – but it's over Nelly's dead body, mind."

As Nigel sat stunned and speechless, Sarah continued:

"You sent her money, too."

"You told her about that, then?"

"The money you gave me? Not I. I'm talking of that money last winter – the fifteen shillings you pretended came from Sue."

Nigel glanced up.

"How did she find out Sue didn't send it?" he asked, but without a gleam of interest in the monotony of his voice.

"'Cos Sue herself turned up at last, and paid part of what she'd borrowed back, and she said as how she'd never sent that note. Nelly told me all about it."

"Why should she think I'd sent it?"

"She knew it. Nelly was very, very lonely; she's hardly a friend in the world but you. Besides she knew, and I knew – we remembered after – as how we'd been talking of Susie and the money the night you come to see her. Nell thought you was Alice Blunt at the time, and she knew all about it, so it didn't matter her hearing. Now, I should like to know what Nelly was to make out of that action of yours. Was she to imagine as anyone who cared nothing for her would go to that trouble?"

Nigel roused himself and said, with sudden anger;

"You know I've not neglected Nelly – never. I've been round to see her; I've given you money for her. Come, you can't deny I've tried in every way I could to provide her with small comforts. It was difficult enough, for Nelly was proud, and would accept help from no one; but I did my best."

"There are some things," said Sarah, "as money can't buy."

The words fell on the dreary room with an extreme pathos, and silence followed them. Presently Sarah spoke again.

"I don't say as you'd any call to give her anything. You 'adn't, in the first place; but, having once took her up, what right had you to cast her aside?"

"I never did."

"You let her see, and plainly, the last year, a-falling off with your visits and one thing or another, as she was nothing to you. Whatever you may have meant yourself, you didn't lead her to believe that last winter when you came round so often, and sent her money and all."

"I would have done as much for anyone," said Nigel, sorrowfully, "who was as lonely and poor as Nell."

Poor Nelly. He walked to the window and looked out. Through the rain and the mist the gas lamps gleamed a dull yellow at intervals down the quiet, rain-swept street. There were a few passers-by, hurrying along under dripping umbrellas, making their way as fast as they could to some little spot of light in the great city which they called "home."

Nigel turned drearily back to Sarah again. The girl shrank away as he approached; she made no effort to hide her feeling of repugnance. Nigel shivered.

"I think you have made a mistake," he said. "Nelly liked me just as I liked her – as a friend. It was some other reason which took her to – her death. She was ill, overworked – there are a hundred reasons, God help us! for any working girl in her position taking that desperate step."

The stony horror in Nigel's face touched even Sarah's heart a little. She began to think that perhaps he was not quite so blameable, after all. She came a step nearer, and said, more gently, but still harshly enough:

"D'ye think I couldn't tell in a thousand little ways as Nelly thought a deal of you? If I'd wanted anything to set me straight on that point I found it yesterday. Look here," she turned to the table with its litter of needlework. "I went into Nelly's room yesterday morning to see if I couldn't finish the work she had in hand for her, for I knew she'd be behind-hand with the payment if it weren't done. I couldn't see it at first anywhere, but after a while I found it in the bottom drawer. And as I took it out this fell out from the folds. See, d'ye know it? I knew it. I remember Nelly telling me how you gave it her last autumn – how you brought it back from the country in your coat."

It was the shrivelled spray of hips and haws. Nigel stood looking down upon it. There are faded leaves in every life – the lowliest, the most prosaic – faded sprays of dead hopes, possibilities never realised. It is a terrible thing to be bound up with those dead leaves of other lives, to be the influence, however unconsciously, which withered them, instead of sunning them till they expanded into full perfection. As he stood there, with the sound of the rain, and the soughing of the wind against the window, his memory went back with a rush to that fateful day at Brierley. He saw again the soft sunshine lying on the level fields, the dry leaves cracked at his feet. Was it yesterday or a lifetime ago that he had stood beneath the shadow of the "old Manorial Hall," and talked to the squire's daughter? Ah, that fateful day! He might have learnt perchance to love Nelly – Nelly, so pretty, so patient, so *brave*, until life laid its hand too heavily upon her – had it not been for that fateful day.

"I wish," he said, slowly and unsteadily, "that I had gone down under the water instead of Nelly. I wish to heaven *I* had the courage to pitch myself off the Thames Embankment."[71]

But Sarah did not hear. She had gone down on her knees, and with her head on the table was sobbing noisily:

"I loved Nelly, I did. She was my only friend, and she is gone!"

With a great sob in his throat, Nigel found his way somehow down the stairs and out into the street – into the cruel, ceaseless, business world of London, which cared nothing for one more dropped out of its ranks. He could never again lift up his head, he thought; his work had failed, he was a traitor to the cause. He had brought sorrow unutterable, sorrow and death, upon the people – the people he had meant to give his life for. And his heart, that heart which had throbbed for years in unison with their joys and troubles, had passed out of his keeping, and gone over to the enemy, the class he had once vowed to fight to the death. "You are climbing up to be a gentleman," Sarah's voice had said; "but it'll be over Nelly's dead body, mind!" So he walked on, half blinded with a restless conscience and an aching heart, hearing at every stop the swish, swish of the black waters which had sounded in poor Nelly's ears before she faced the solution to that enigma men call Life, which lies beyond Death's silence.

* * *

It is not only the lower world which Death shadows with his presence. At that hour, when Nigel was making his way from Poplar Street to his home, Constance Compton was steaming along in the down express to Brierley. People talked with bated breath in the village; at the Hall the blinds were down, and the great house wrapped in gloom, for Squire Compton lay dead – stricken down by neuralgia of the heart![72]

[20 March 1897]

Chapter XIII.

Spring had come again, sunshine lay abroad on the land. The six months which had passed since Nigel's interview in Poplar Street had brought their changes. Nigel was about to leave England. It was but a poor heart at the best he had brought to his work all the foregoing winter, and one day in a talk with Mr. Ross he wound up by saying, "I believe I want a thorough change. How would it be to chuck up everything and go out to the colonies?" He said the words as though he were half joking, though in reality he was in dead earnest, and awaiting in anxiety his leader's answer.

To his surprise, Mr. Ross replied, "If it were only your political work you were giving up here, I should say, a good thing, Grey; you are eminently fitted for the colonies; and though we should miss you immeasurably here, yet we should know that wherever you were, you would be doing good work, and I think that perhaps your enthusiasm in it would come back with change of scene and air, and in a country where life goes with a quicker swing than in old England."

Nigel looked up quickly.

"You have noticed, then, have you, that my heart has not been quite in my work of late?"

"Yes, Grey, I have," said Mr. Ross, kindly.

"I've had two pretty sharp blows," Nigel said in a low voice. "One I shall get over some day, I have no doubt, though it smarts at present; the other I can never entirely get over."

He was alluding in the first instance to his hopeless passion for Constance Compton which had so suddenly asserted itself that evening at the C— Street Institute; in the latter part of his sentence he was referring to the tragic end of poor Nelly.

"But," continued Mr. Ross, "with regard to your going abroad there is more to be considered than your political schemes – there is your post at the work. I am not sure that a man has a right to deliberately throw away everything he has attained by years of steady honest work; beside you are not a very young man to start life afresh."

"Oh, as to that, we are thinking of sending out a branch firm to Melbourne; I could go as superintendent, doubtless. I have been talking, as well as thinking the matter over. A brother of mine is out there; it might not be a bad thing to go. Of course, it is not so brilliant a prospect as staying on here, but may I not 'do what I will with mine own'[73] in this case," he quoted with a half laugh.

"Could you not go just to inaugurate the firm for a twelvemonth or so?"

Nigel made a little gesture of the hands: "If I go, I go for life," he said. After a moment he added, "You don't think it would be deserting my post to leave England."

"No, Grey," returned Mr. Ross, "you are an Englishman – no fact can alter that; therefore the world is yours to brave and conquer. You can never be deserting England, while you are fighting the battle for justice and freedom."

So Nigel was going to face life in Australia. Somehow, prompted by a sudden impulse one idle afternoon, he found himself in the train rushing at full speed towards Brierley. Having once taken his ticket for that station he had never ceased regretting the fact, and was still fretting at his stupidity when he alighted.

It was a sunny spring day, like the days a year ago, when he had walked that stretch of road so often. He strolled through the neat little station with its broad flower beds, bordered by cockle shells, and stocked with red and white daisies and sea pinks, out upon the highway, wondering why he had come, and thinking how pitiably weak he was. At the turn of the road he caught a glimpse of the heath, and straightway his mind went back to the April morning when he had strolled across it with *her* – the never-to-be forgotten morning of his life! He despised himself for that momentary burst of sentiment, and turning his head resolutely away from the heath, he buried his hands deep in his pockets and walked swiftly along, the May-wind tossing the stray curls of his hair under the fore-and-aft cap[74] he wore. It was towards Mrs. Linden's cottage he was making his way, with a view to telling her of his future plans and bidding her goodbye.

As he had to catch an early train, he did not stay long at Mrs. Linden's. When he reached the garden, on his way out, he stood for a moment looking round – trying, maybe, to fix the pleasant English picture in his mind, to be recalled in the years to come.

The cottage, as has been stated, was situated about a mile from the village, in a lonely spot near a small wood; the heath skirted it on one side. One figure only was visible on the heath that afternoon, as Nigel looked across it – a girl in black; her back was towards him. He never knew what possessed him – he was full of erratic impulses that day. He started off at a quick run after that slight figure, groaning in spirit at the sound of his own flying footsteps. Was it for this that he had held so tight a hand over himself for months? But he did not slacken his pace. Infinite pain for the sake of infinite pleasure should be his once again; yea, though the pleasure should be his but for a moment, and the pain should last for years – perchance in the scales they would strike a balance. So he reached her side at last; not perhaps quite as a lover should reach the side of his mistress, but decidedly out of breath, flushed with the exertion, and holding his tweed cap in his hand.

"I could not resist coming to wish you good-bye, Miss Compton," he said. "I am going away to Australia, and I came to say good-bye to old friends in the village."

"What! Mr. Grey?" Constance stopped short, and faced him with the colour tingling in her cheeks. "How you startled me! I have not seen you for so long. I am glad to see you, though."

She held out her hand. As Nigel took it the thought struck him that it was the first time she had ever offered it to him.

"You are in mourning, Miss Compton," he said, glancing at the black dress with its crape trimmings. He noticed that she was paler than of old, now that her flush had subsided, and her eyes had lost their dancing light.

"My father," she said, "he died last November. Had you not heard?"

"No," returned Nigel, rather wonderingly. "I suppose it was because I was so wrapped up in trouble of my own in the early part of the winter that I gave but little attention to the outer world beyond my ordinary work. I have not been down to Brierley since last summer; and Tom Wilton, as you know, has been away in Germany all the winter. I am very sorry," he added gently.

"You say you have been in trouble?"

Nigel made a gesture of assent, but did not answer. Constance glanced at the handsome mouth with its firm repression, the forehead with its troubled pucker between the brows.

"I, too," said Constance, "am saying good-bye to old scenes for a time, or shall be shortly. Here, across this heath, my father used to hold my hand in the long-ago years, when we went out together searching for the first spring flowers. When the path was rough, he would lift me on his shoulder and carry me. Sad how seldom the hands that guide us over life's first rough places are beside us when we need them in the later years, or at life's close."

They were passing under the spreading boughs of a large elm, where the rooks were sleepily cawing overhead; Constance stopped and rested one hand upon the gnarled old trunk for a minute, and they both stood and looked around as they had done a year ago. At that time Nigel had been pointing out the advantages England offered as a farming country. Now their minds were far from thinking of the ultimate good of the nation: they were engrossed with the sadness and apparent failure of individual life. For it all comes back to this at last – the individual life.

Individual life – mysterious problem! – behind which, through which, works the great Will, beneficent, but unchangeable – the Law of which all other laws are but symbols – the Life, in which is our life, both universal and individual. It is only in moments of high tension that we fully realise that something – higher and stronger than man's endeavour – which is throbbing all around us, which has been silently working from the first darkness and chaos through the little lives of men; shaping out of their strivings and aspirations, their failures and mistakes, their joys and sorrows, the fulfilment of a noble, blessed purpose, of which we cannot see the end to-day. Not in so many words did the thought come to Nigel and Constance, that soft spring day on the uplands; but they realised it, as we all have at times, as they watched the train curving through the fields below, the upward sloping meadows by the river, where the cows stood idly chewing, the green dips and hollows where white cottages nestled, with their pleasant gardens stocked with homely flowers and herbs, now breaking into colour and perfume from which straggling lanes led to farm or cottage, with hedges white with privet and hawthorn, and long festoons of convolvuli and honeysuckle. There were touches of gold where the gorse grew here on the heath about them; gold again where portions of last year's ricks stood about in the surrounding fields, shifting lights and shades in the distance, over the sweet odorous country redolent of fresh springing life, cloud shadows moving over the misty line of the low Berkshire hills. A blue sky flecked with soft white clouds stretched above the windy sweeps and fragrant valleys. On the left below them rose the grey tower of Brierley church, beneath which sleep those whose warfare is ended – simple village lives, dull or clever, eager or indifferent, impatient, gentle, troubled – a handful of the countless millions created to evolve the great eternal plan.

Nigel looked at his companion. In her black dress, with her shadowy eyes gazing over the far country, what a contrast she offered, he thought, to the girl, who replete with life and colour, and in the height of fashion, had chatted conventionally to him in Kensington High Street six or seven months before. He was more at home with this sorrowful Constance; he knew on what ground to meet her; they were on the same level at last.

> For the whole world is knit in ties
> Of common brotherhood in pain[75]

She looked young, and fair, and simple, framed in that most meet setting for innocent girlhood; a quiet, English landscape. She would be walking here over this breezy heath in the years to come, when her eyes should have lost the sorrow of to-day and retained only a tender sympathy. He could fancy her the idol of some man's hearth, cheering him on his way up the rugged hill of life, folding the hands of little children beside their cot at nightfall. It seemed to Nigel, at that moment, as though he were putting everything from him, turning his back on all he loved, going away into oblivion. Well, that was right! What had he said in Nell's room? "May fate deal with me as I deal with my people." And his was the hand that had sent Nell to her death!

When he spoke he gave no trace of the heartbreak within. So much has civilisation done for us. There was only a certain gravity of tone.

"So many changes since we walked together here a year ago, Miss Compton."

"So many changes," Constance echoed.

"You are saying good-bye to Brierley, you say?"

"Yes. Next week there is to be a double wedding at Westerbury. My cousin George is to be married to Lady Grace Allerton and his sister to our recent vicar, Mr. Cope. When that piece of excitement is over I am going abroad with Lady Drayton, and the hall is to be closed for a time."

"Indeed!" said Nigel.

They were both walking on again now. Suddenly he asked,

"Do you ever think of our conversation, when last we trod this path together?"

"Yes, sometimes. It is deeper – more worth thinking of than a great deal of the fashionable chatter I have had to join in since."

[27 March 1897]

Chapter XIII. Continued.

"Do you ever talk fashionable chatter?" Nigel asked with a slight smile.

"Oh, yes, I have to. The world does not give us a chance to be earnest; and yet we all want to be."

"I, too, think of it sometimes. I suppose you thought me a very lawless fellow; you hinted as much. Perhaps, in some ways, we have both modified our views since then. Perhaps you see more clearly," there was the slightest tremor in the grave voice, "that some amongst us – lawless and fanatical though we might seem – are yet striking a blow, though perhaps unconsciously, for Him for whom the Christians fought of old; that out of the squalor and the misery of a great city some amongst us, maybe, are building up a religion that shall stand long after the types and shadows of form and ceremony are swept away.

There was a sort of patient, solemn intonation in Nigel's voice which Constance did not remember ever having heard there before. He looked at her with tired, troubled eyes, which yet retained their old bravery and unflinching purpose.

"The great Leader taught His followers to pray that His Kingdom might come on earth as it is in heaven," he went on. "No one can walk through the streets of our cities or the lanes of our villages without feeling that the Kingdom is very far off in spite of nineteen hundred years of Christendom; but if busy brains are rousing up to think and give their best; if men are no longer on their knees, but in the forefront of the battle; if patient hands are carrying out practical work, may they not be making of life itself a religion? of toil a prayer?

For what is it they are working for? Do you not see in it – I often do – a dim foreshadowing of the New Jerusalem coming here on earth? when pain shall be mitigated, when sickness shall be relieved, when want shall be banished, and many, many tears now falling be wiped away."

There was a quick catch in the girl's breath. She did not answer for a whole minute. They walked on in silence. She could not argue; there was no longer any need for argument. They seemed, in mental attitude, these two, to have reached a level plain, and to be standing together and looking at a fair and far-off vision – the land of Beulah[76] – beyond the distant hills. Whether they would ever reach it, who could tell? But the way along which they had to press was bleak and rugged. Whose hands – would there be any? – outstretched to help and steady along the pathway to that distant ideal? Had Constance spoken at that moment, she might have broken down in tears, as she used to do long ago, stumbling in the twilight over the heath on her way homewards, and scratching her child hands with the brambles. She was unstrung, and lonely, and depressed. Presently she pushed her troubled thoughts away, and tried to speak practically as she asked, "Are you going to take Hilda to Australia?"

"No; she will stay behind with my aunt; at any rate till I have made a home for her. You would scarcely know the child these days, Miss Compton, she is getting so big and strong. The doctors think she will quite outgrow her weakness in time."

"I am so glad. But will she not miss you terribly?"

"She gets on very well with my aunt, and she can build castles of the time when she will come out to keep house for me. She is a visionary little woman."

"You will marry," said Constance, lightly.

"I think not."

"Have you given up your share in the Engine Works?"

"No. But we want to establish a branch at Melbourne, and I have volunteered to go out to superintend it. The senior partners have been doing their best to dissuade me, but – I want a change," he finished abruptly.

Chapter XIV.

Presently Nigel stopped, and held out his hand. "I shall not be down at Brierley again before I start, Miss Compton, so I must wish you good-bye now," he said.

Constance did not give her hand in return. She was looking down at a little sprig she had plucked from a bush when passing, and which she was now pulling rapidly to pieces.

"You are in a great hurry to say good-bye," she said. "Do you bid farewell as rapidly and carelessly to all your friends? You will never see any of them again for years, some, perhaps, never more in life."

There came a swift moisture to Nigel's eyes; he thrust the hand she had not taken deep into his pocket, and caught his underlip sharply for a second, between his teeth.

"True!" he answered in a low voice. "You and I, for instance, are never likely to cross each other's paths again. Strange fate that threw us two together! Have you ever read "Progress and Poverty?"[77] No, I suppose not. I have been thinking of a sentence at the wind-up: 'But they who fight with Ormuzd, though they may not know each other – sometime – somewhere – shall the muster roll be called.'"

"Then you still intend to fight for Ormuzd?" she asked, looking up, "you will not give up your political work when you have left England?"

"No, I shall go on with it; though I can't say I haven't lost heart in it to a certain extent. But I have made it my life, you see – at least my life would be a failure without it, and life is a responsibility for which we all have to render an account someday, I imagine. Anyway, I am not reckless, or bold enough to care to hand mine over as so many wasted years at the last."

"Why do you want to run away to Australia and leave your London work?"

"Because –," Nigel paused and looked at his companion; the spirit of the heath and the spring day was upon him; his breath came quicker. "I have made a muddle of my life, and I want to begin afresh over there."

"What has gone wrong? Tell me, will you not?"

An irresistible impulse came over Nigel to unburden his heart before he left her forever. There was no hope for him, but at least she would be merciful – sympathetic. He could bear *her* sympathy – no one else's. He was ever a man of impulse; he came a step nearer.

"I will tell you," he said. "I was fool enough to set my affection on some one infinitely above me, not only in worldly position, but in goodness and beauty – someone, who, for aught I know, may have given her heart away long before ever she met me, but who in any case would give no more thought to me than she might to a fly who brushed her cheek in passing."

Constance dropped her sprig of privet to the ground and stooped to pick it up.

"Don't you think it is better to go away, and begin life anew without telling her?"

"Perhaps."

"Ah, but tell me."

Constance hesitated a moment, then without looking up, she quoted:

> He either fears his fate too much,
> Or his deserts are small,
> Who dares not put it to the touch
> To lose or venture all?[78]

"Then you think I had better try my chance?"

"Nay, don't appeal to me. The verse came into my head, so I said it," said Constance, flushing rose red, even to her broad, white forehead and curly hair.

"But remember," Nigel went on, unheeding her explanation, "I have but a moderate income this girl owns an estate and a fortune. It was not my dream to marry such a wife as that. I have always meant to choose one who could have helped me on the uphill journey, braving the changes of fortune with me, till we reached the end together. And she probably never contemplated such a thing as having for her suitor anyone who is not in the ranks to which she belongs. Would that not make a difference?"

"I think not. It should make no difference to you, if you believe in the Socialist motto, 'What has thou that thou didst not receive?' It is not to her praise or blame that she has riches."

"The she is far above me in social standing; or at any rate by birth."

"But you belong to a class which does not recognise social standing, but believes in universal brotherhood."

"Oh, Constance Compton!" Nigel cried, "we are fencing with each other, and neither is deceiving the other one little bit. You know who the 'someone' is, who stole my heart from me; now tell me – for you only can tell me is there any chance for me?"

But Constance did not tell him – at least not in words. She bent her head a little lower for a moment over the unfortunate sprig of privet, plucked its last leaf from it, dropped it to the ground, then suddenly, shyly raised her eyes, those clear, calm eyes which sanctioned no disguise, no coquetry, no double meanings. Words were not needed, for Nigel read his answer there.

So they wended their way homewards through the sunset light. Of course Nigel missed his train, but there are times in a man's life when such an occurrence may pass unheeded. After trouble, misgivings, and the shadow of death, happiness had come to them. Too often between us and our heart's desire a great gulf is fixed: it may be the solemn stream of death, or it may be one of those bitter and impassable seas of human life, with no bridge across and salt with tears; but these two, so far, had grasped the fruition of their hopes. The strange, inexplicable currents of existence, which still lie beyond our comprehension and control, had drifted them together, to become part of one another's life forever, to learn to give and take in a noble brotherhood of service, to stand side by side in the ranks where the recruits are gathering daily, glad to endure the battle's heat, if by so doing they may fight the world's sin and sorrow; and if their faces were somewhat grave for those of new-born lovers, at least they were full of the one and only hope that makes life worth the living – that good part which shall never be taken away.

Ella Jeffries, 'A Shop Girl' (1898)

Chapter I.

Half-way though the evening service, and in the course of reading out the notices the minister had reached the following: "I should like to acknowledge these subscriptions to the renovation fund: Mr. Cardigan, twenty guineas; Mr. Jones, two guineas" – going on to enumerate the other sums. Mr. Cardigan and others who had given largely looked smugly satisfied with themselves or hypocritically humble or shamefaced and annoyed, according to their natures, whilst those who had not given at all fumed over the execrable taste of the Rev. Mr. Doucely in pandering to the self-conceit of the big subscribers.

A number of the congregation, however, simply let the notices pass in at one ear and out at the other, whilst they thought of other things. Among these was Miss Brown, one of the "young ladies" at Mr. Cardigan's shop. She was of the type of shop-girl one sees in hundreds in large towns – pretty and fragile and tastefully dressed, with fair, fluffy hair and all too transparent skin. It was a sweet young face, but the eyes were tired and wistful-looking, even when the mouth smiled as she whispered something to her companion – a healthier, studier-looking girl, also a shop assistant.

The sermon began, and she turned her face towards the preacher, but one could see she was not taking in much of the address. It is as easy to look at the preacher as at anything else, although one's thoughts are elsewhere; besides, it looked better.

"There are times," said the speaker, "in your life when you do not know which way to take. Pray about it, my friends – my young friends who are perhaps just beginning life – and you will be directed."

At least two pairs of eyes, hitherto dreamy, suddenly focussed on the preacher's face, and flashed out with an earnestness too keen as to be almost painful as they drank in his words. One pair belonged to Mr. Cardigan's assistant and the other to young Parkins in the oil shop up the street. But the minister wandered off again into hackneyed texts and anecdotes and platitudes, and the light died down again in the two pairs of eyes.

The young man from the oil shop was just behind her as they went into the vestibule, and his face twitched as he noticed how the light from the gas jet seemed to shine right through her white face.

"Poor little thing, how tired she looks! But it wouldn't be right for me to say anything until –. If he would only give me a rise I –"

"Good evening, Miss Brown," he said, solemnly raising his hat, as he went down the steps, for he was a very conscientious young man.

"Good evening, Mr. Parkins," she said, primly and decorously, in exactly the same voice in which she said good-night to the old church officer.

Chapter II.

"Nothing more to-day, Mrs. Cairns? What do you think of this new line in curtains?"

Then Mr. Cardigan made himself agreeable, inquired after his customer's family, and talked on local matters generally, while Miss Brown sent the customer's money running along the counter to the cashier's desk and made up the parcel.

"You are closing at eight now, I see," said the customer.

"Yes, on three days a week. The Shopkeeper's Association unanimously agreed upon that at our last meeting. Shop assistants have a fine time of it now compared to the days when I was an improver. Well, good afternoon, Mrs. Cairns."

The affable smile had left his face when he came back to the counter. It was nearly tea-time and there were no customers in the shop for the moment.

"Miss Brown!" he said, sharply.

She was rolling up some ribbon in a listless, half-hearted fashion, and started when he spoke.

"Yes, sir."

"I wish you would make an effort to be a little brighter and more agreeable with customers. I don't mean that you are uncivil, but you look so uninterested in your work. Ladies like one to take an intelligent interest in what they are buying – in matching colours and that sort of thing. Then you go about in such a dead-and-alive, half hearted fashion. I don't know what young people are coming to. Now, look at me. I am always brisk, ain't I? never see me moping, do you?"

"No, sir. I am very sorry, I – I –"

"All right, my girl. Just you brisk up a bit. Jump about smarter, you know. It's smiling faces we want here. You are in good enough health, I suppose?"

"Ye-yes, sir."

"Very well, then. Let me see an improvement in your manner before the end of the week or I am afraid I shall have to git someone else in your place. There's plenty, you know, only too glad to git a chance of coming to a business where the assistants are so well looked after. I do my dooty towards my young ladies and young men, and I expect as they will do same by me."

And he hurried off, for his brougham[1] was waiting at the door.

She stood just where he left her with eyes impassive and expressionless fixed on the ribbon she was sorting.

"Miss Brown's been getting a wigging. Poor girl, how bad she's been looking all day! There's the tea-bell! I say! do look at Miss Brown. She's fainting, I do declare – poor old girl!"

They took her down to the dining room, and with the help of cold water and smelling-salts she "came to" in a few minutes.

"Have your tea now, dear. It'll do you good," said one of the other girls. "Don't you think you'd better go home?"

"No, no; I'll be all right after I've had a rest. Don't say anything to the governor. You know how waxy he is when anybody has to go home ill."

"Yes, it's best not, if you can help it," said the other, dubiously. "One can do that once too often. Well, I must go; the shop's full. But don't you come up for half an hour. I'll tell Mr. Walker if he asks.

Miss Brown went upstairs in half an hour. Seven o'clock struck, eight, nine, ten, and even the brightest and smartest of the girls began to look exhausted and washed out. They had ceased smiling and chatting and taking forced interest in the purchases of the workmen's wives who were still straggling into the shop at half-past ten; for if shops did not close until half-past twelve there would still be tardy customers.

At last the door-gate was shut, and there came the welcome music of iron shutters being drawn up in the street. The long, weary Saturday was over, and for a day the slaves were free to rest their tired bodies and aching heads.

Edith Brown's face looked almost ghastly under the incandescent light as she left the shop: there were dark rings below her eyes and that strained, tired look about them that is the effect of utter exhaustion. A man was walking up and down in front of the shop. He wore a light covert coat and spats.[2] His moustache was black and his chin bluish.[3] His face was rather bloated; he was too fat for so young a man, and his eyes spoke of nothing but meat and drink.

He threw away his cigar-end as she came out, and she greeted him with a listless "Good evening."

"Hulloa, dear," he said, jovially. "Why, how tired it looks! Have my arm! No? All right!"

He walked along beside her, looking down into the white little face with a beerily affectionate expression in his heavy eyes. She seemed to take his presence as a matter of course, but made no attempt to converse with him.

"Why don't you speak to a fellow, Ede, when he comes to meet you?"

"I don't want you to come and meet me, as I've told you before. I wish you'd leave me alone to-night – I've such an awful headache."

"And no wonder. Look here, Ede. What's the good of bein' so stubborn? Here you are slaving there till you're dead-beat, as well as losing your looks. Now, here am I – well off. The trade's been a good spec.[4] for me. I could keep you like a lady; you could keep your servant, have your droring-room and nothing much to do, and what more do you want? Now, I say, be a sensible girl and think it over. Chuck up old Cardigan and marry me."

She began to cry, and, taking this as a hopeful sign, he bent closer to her, and tried to get his arm round her waist. She was now sobbing bitterly, but she jerked away from his arm with a movement of disgust as a whiff of brandy and stale tobacco was breathed across her face. He went on eagerly, however.

"You say you don't fancy me, but that don't matter – I'll make up for both. Come on, Ede – say yes."

She had suddenly stopped crying, and was looking straight in front of her with a set, hard face.

"You say you don't mind. Very well. I'll marry you whenever you like."

* * *

She went heavily upstairs to her room. The girl with whom she shared it sat at the fire in her petticoat: she had taken off her black skirt to put fresh binding on it. As the door opened she lifted a little coffee-pot on to the fire.

"Well, Ede! Why, what have you been crying about?"

"My head's bad."

"Poor child! I've made you some more coffee. It'll boil up in a minute."

The girl sat down, and, taking off her muddy shoes, she sat limp and utterly done, while the other poured out her coffee.

"Ag," she said, putting down her cup, "I can't hold up no longer. I knew the guv'nor would grumble sooner or later, and he did on Monday. Said he'd have to give me the sack[5] if I don't brisk up. I get worse every day. I fainted again 's evenin', and I'm sure I'll faint before the customers some day. That would look so bad I'd *have* to go."

"Yes; it *would* look bad for him, and no mistake, and him such a good, charitable, chuchgoin' man."

"Oh, he ain't worse than any of the others, but I don't s'pose it'll ever be any better."

"A young fellow in our shop was telling me that some places have a sort of shop assistant's trade union like the workmen, to try and get eight hours or something. We'd jolly soon get notice to quit if *we* belonged to anything of the sort here. I was awfully strong when I first went to business, but, you know, I've felt it telling on me lately, though mine isn't so bad as yours, being the confectionery business. I *do* get a chance of sitting down now and then."

"Well, do you know, I feel sometimes as if I could scream out, I get so tired. Someone wrote in the papers about seats behind the counter, but it did no good except for the guv'nor to ask us if we'd been complaining. My head always starts about four now, till I don't know how to bear it. I *can't* go on no longer, so I'm going to marry him," she said, in a hopeless, mechanical voice.

"Edie! him – Joe Corbett? Why, you always said you hated him – a great beast! Dear, you can't do that," and the other girl's honest, kind face looked troubled and anxious.

"There's nothing else for me to do. I've no home, like some of the girls. I think I'd marry anyone just now, jest so as I could have one good long rest."

"But he *is* such a bad man, and then he's a publican. Don't you remember what you and me once said – that we would never marry anyone who wasn't a Christian, after that sermon Mr. Doucely –"

"It's easy for Mr. Doucely to preach. *He* doesn't know what it means to stand all day in a shop till you feel as if your legs were going to break and you can hardly stand, and knowing that you may get the sack any moment, because your head's so bad you can't look sprightly, if it was to be cut off. You know, Ag, I've tried to live straight and do the right, but I must give it up. I know it's a wicked thing to marry a man I hate, but what am I to do? Prayin'? It seems to me that prayin' is only for rich folk as don't want anything very much. My head's in a maze, but I must go through with it now. Don't speak of it more than you can, Aggie, dear. It only makes it worse for me."

The other girl was silent for a few minutes as she put away the supper things, then she blurted out, desperately, her back turned:

"Ede, I never dared say so before, you're so touchy, but are you sure – dear, don't be cross – but, do you know, I often wondered if there was nothing between you and young Parkins. I often think – I can't tell why – that he likes you, and –" She had turned round, and read what she expected in her chum's face. "Oh, Edie!"

"Ag, don't say anything more," said the other, in a harsh voice. "*He* doesn't care one bit about me, or he would have spoken, of course, and neither do I." Then she broke down. "Aggie, I'm a liar. I do care. He's the only one I have ever cared for." The she said, fiercely: "Promise me, on your oath, you will never say a word – promise! I should die of shame if I thought anyone knew."

* * *

Eighteen months later.

Joe Corbett was a favourite at the club. He was on the platform singing a rollicking comic song, the men at the tables below thumping in chorus. The steward came into the smoke-clouded room, and at the end of the song handed a note to the singer. It had been hastily scribbled by the doctor.

"Damn!" he said, reading: "'Your wife has had a relapse. Come home at once.'"

"Joe Corbett is sorry as 'e can't give 'is hencore," announced the chairman, "as 'e 'as bin called away. But Mr. Chowles will now favour with 'Billy 'e fell down the drain.'"

* * *

His wife was dead when Joe Corbett got home, and fortunately for itself and the world, the poor, puny little child died next day. Poor Edie had a long rest at last.

And whose fault was it that a girl happened to choose the trade of shop assistant as a means of livelihood, that her health was ruined through long hours and perpetual standing and unhealthy surroundings, that she lost faith in Christ and Christianity, and that she was driven to commit sin (for a loveless marriage is sin)?

Nobody's fault? economic conditions? will of God? environment? survival of the fittest? So say the trustees – those who hold the wealth and the intellect of the country in trust for their little brothers and sisters.

And one day there will be a reckoning.

Colonel Bradbury, 'Guilty – But Drunk' (1899)

Many years ago, while the State of Georgia[1] was still in its infancy, an eccentric creature named Brown was one of its circuit judges.[2] He was a man of considerable ability, of inflexible integrity, and much beloved and respected by all the legal profession; but he had one common fault. His social qualities would lead him, despite his judgement, into frequent excesses. In travelling the circuit, it was his almost invariable habit, the night before opening the court, to get "comfortably corned,"[3] by means of appliance common upon such occasions. If he couldn't succeed while operating by himself, the members of the bar would generally turn in and help him.

It was in the spring of the year: taking his wife – a model of a woman in her way – in the old-fashioned but strong "carry-all,"[4] he journeyed some forty miles, and reached a village where "court"[5] was to be opened the next day. It was along in the evening of Sunday that he arrived at the place, and took up his quarters with a relation of his "better half,"[6] by whom the presence of an official dignitary was considered a singular honour. After supper, Judge Brown strolled over to the only tavern in the town, where he found many old friends, called to the place, like himself, on important professional business, and who were very glad to meet him.

"Gentlemen," said the Judge, "'tis quite a long time since we have enjoyed a glass together – let us take a drink all round. Of course, Sterritt (addressing the landlord), you have better liquor than you had the last time we were here? – the stuff you had then was not fit to give a dog!"

Sterritt, who had charge of the house, pretended that everything was right, and so they went to work. It is unnecessary to enlarge upon a drinking bout in a country tavern – it will quite answer our purpose to state that somewhere in the region of midnight the judge wended his very devious[7] way towards his temporary home. About the time he was leaving, however, some younger barristers, fond of a "practical,"[8] and not much afraid of the bench, transferred all the silver spoons of Sterritt to the judge's coat pocket.

It was eight o'clock on Monday morning that the judge rose. Having indulged in the process of ablution, and partaken of a cheerful and refreshing breakfast, he went to his room to prepare himself for the duties of the day.

"Well, Polly," said he to his wife, "I feel much better than I expected after that frolic of last night."

"Ah, judge!" said she, reproachfully, "you are getting too old – you ought to leave off that business."

"Ah, Polly. What's the use of talking?"

It was at this precise instant of time that the judge, having put on his overcoat, was proceeding, according to his usual custom, to give his wife a parting kiss, when he happened, in thrusting his hand into his pocket, to lay hold of Sterritt's spoons. He jerked them out. With an expression of horror almost indescribable, he exclaimed:

"My! Polly!"

"What on earth's the matter, judge?"

"Just look at these spoons"!

"Dear me, where d'ye get them?"

"Get them? Don't you see the initials on them?" – extending them towards her – "I stole them!"

"Stole them, judge?"

"Yes, stole them!"

"My dear husband, it can't be possible! – from whom?"

"From Sterritt, over there; his name is on them."

"Good heavens! how could it happen?"

"I know very well, Polly – I was very drunk when I came home, wasn't I?"

"Why, judge, you know your old habit when you get among those lawyers."

"But was I very drunk?"

"Yes, you were."

"Was I *remarkably* drunk when I got home, Mrs. Brown?"

"Yes judge, drunk as an owl, and forty times as stupid."

"I thought so," said the judge, dropping into a chair in extreme despondency. "I knew it would come to that at last. I have always thought that something bad would happen to me – that I should do something very wrong – kill somebody in a moment of passion perhaps – but I never imagined that I could be mean enough to be guilty of deliberate larceny."

"But there may be some mistake, judge."

"No mistake, Polly. I know very well how it all came about. That fellow, Sterritt, keeps the meanest sort of liquor and always did – liquor mean enough to make a man do any sort of a mean thing. I have always said it was mean enough to make a man steal, and now I have a practical illustration of the fact," and the poor old man burst into tears.

"Don't be a child," said his wife, wiping away the tears. "Go like a man over to Sterritt, tell him it was a little bit of a frolic. Pass it off as a joke – go and open court, and nobody will ever think of it again."

A little of the soothing system operated upon the judge as such things usually do. His extreme mortification was finally subdued, and over to Sterritt's he went with a tolerable face. Of course, he had but little difficulty in settling with him – for, aside from the fact that the judge's integrity was unquestionable, he had an inkling of the joke that had been played. The judge took his seat in court; but it was observed that he was sad and melancholy, and that his mind frequently wandered from the business before him. There was a lack of the sense and intelligence that usually characterised his proceedings.

Several days passed away, and the business of the court was drawing towards a close, when one morning a rough-looking sort of a customer was arraigned on a charge of stealing. After the clerk had read the indictment to him, he put the question:

"Guilty, or not guilty?"

"Guilty – but drunk," answered the prisoner.

"What's that plea?" exclaimed the judge, who was half dozing on the bench.

"He pleads guilty, but says he was drunk," replied the clerk.

"What's the charge against the man?"

"He is indicted for grand larceny."

"What's the case?"

"May it please your honour," said the prosecuting attorney, "the man is regularly indicted for stealing a large sum from the Columbus Hotel."

"He is, eh? and he pleads –"

"He pleads guilty – but drunk."

The judge was now fully aroused.

"Guilty – but drunk! That is a most extraordinary plea. Young man, you are certain you were drunk?"

"Yes, sir."

"Where did you get your liquor?"

"At Sterritts."

"Did you get none anywhere else?"

"Not a drop, sir."

"You got drunk on his liquor, and afterwards stole his money?"

"Yes, sir."

"Mr. Prosecutor," said the judge, "do me the favour to enter a *nolle prosequi*⁹ in that man's case. That liquor of Sterritt's is mean enough to make a man do anything dirty. I got drunk on it the other day myself, and stole all of Sterritt's spoons. Release the prisoner, Mr. Sheriff; I adjourn the court."

LABOUR PROPHET

Elihu, 'Nobody's Business', *Labour Prophet*, September 1892, p. 69.

The *Labour Prophet* (1895–8; 1899–1901) was the official periodical of the Labour Church. It was edited by the Labour Church founder John Trevor (1855–1930) throughout its first publication run, apart from a brief period in 1897 when it was edited by Reginald A. Beckett (n.d.). Priced at one penny, it was published monthly in Manchester and London between September 1895 and September 1898. It was revived as the *Labour Church Record*, a free quarterly, between January 1899 and October 1901 and was edited by Charles Allen Clarke (1863–1935). For Clarke's full biographical details, see the *Bolton Trotter* headnote in Volume 1, pp. 1–2.

The *Labour Prophet* occasionally carried contributions from Robert Blatchford and Keir Hardie and some fiction, including a short story by trade unionist Ben Tillett (1860–1943). Elihu is the pseudonym for Samuel Washington (n.d.), author of books such as *Whose Dog Art Thou? An Argument for a Labour Party* (1892) and *A Nation of Slaves* (n.d.). He published articles and stories in *Justice* and the *Workman's Times* as well as in the *Labour Prophet*.

Elihu, 'Nobody's Business' (1892)

Upon a heap of straw, in a bare garret, a man lay dying. It was in the heart of one of the richest cities in England. Within a stone's throw of where he lay in that last dread struggle the merchants' exchange was thronged with busy traffic, and huge wealth flowed in an unmeasured stream; and this man was dying – of hunger. Whilst they bought and sold there, making an increased babel of sound, he lay in silence yonder. His glazing eyes, moving wearily over the mouldering walls of the den in which he lay, lighted for a moment upon the window in the roof, and upon the glimpse of blue sky that showed through the broken panes. A sudden gleam of recollection passed over his sunken face, and he lifted a hand towards the light, but it fell back again upon the straw. His eyes closed, and a faint smile passed over this feature, and he lay in perfect stillness. Was he dead? No, not dead yet; but he was dying. Upon one side of him, unseen, knelt Death, gazing on him with dread, sightless sockets, with grizzly, unseen hand choking his breath. Upon the other side knelt Hunger, weird and gaunt, with cruel, sunken eyes, crueller than death. And there, unseen of mortal eye, whilst the blue sky lay overhead, and the noise of children at play, and the busy hum and rattle of a city's traffic floated up from the streets below, these two dealt with him after their kind; and there was no hand reached out to save him.

There was a merchant on 'Change as this man lay dying who, in one stroke of business, made a thousand pounds, and went home and thanked God, and was glad, for his wife and children's sake, that things prospered with him. But he knew nought of the man who lay dying of hunger within a stone's throw of him as he buttoned up his pocket book;[1] did not know that Hunger and Death were staring in grim silence so in to the face of a fellow-man.

Ten thousand men and women passed to and fro on that day, near where the man lay dying of hunger, but none turned aside down the narrow court, nor mounted the dark stairway that led to his garret. It was no business of theirs; they had each their own affairs to look after. They did not know the silent tragedy that was being enacted so near them; it was nobody's business to know. He had had money once, and friends and wife and children, but his wife and children were dead, and his money gone through a stroke of misfortune that beggared him, and in his old age he was cast helpless upon the world; but that was nobody's business. He struggled hard for a time to maintain himself, but who would employ an old man when young ones offered? The sickness came, and misery, and abject want; but, of course, that was nobody's business, and now he lies dying, and it is nobody's business yet. And nobody knows; it is nobody's business to know.

He lies yet perfectly still. His eyes remain closed. The faint smile has not died away from about his mouth. He is dreaming of his childhood. He sees the old homestead, the trees, the river, the high hills stretching away height beyond height until they merge and melt into the blue sky. See! His lips move. He "babbles o' green fields."[2] It will soon be over.

A quiet shudder passes through his frame, and with a sigh the soul is freed of its burden. The grinding, heartsick misery is past now and forgotten. Death loosens his hold of the man's throat, and Hunger glares no longer on him; they had "business" with him, but it is done now; and silent and unseen they pass on their way and leave him lying there; and with fixed glassy stare he lies stark and rigid, unwept, unpitied, unhelped, unknown. As a man might have died in the midst of some lonely and uninhabited desert, so has he died in the midst of a city full of people.

No man saw it; but in the broad daylight an angel came down from God and passed over the city – over the thronging streets, over the factories and churches, and houses and shops, and, entering the garret where the man lay dying, the angel, too, knelt beside him. But Hunger and Death were not afraid of the angel, for they were also God's messengers. The angel watched and waited, and when their work was done he bore upward the spirit they had freed from its weary bondage and stood with him at the foot of God's throne; and God wiped away all the tears from his eyes.

And God said, "It is a great city from whence thou art come; are there many that dwell therein that serve me and keep my commandments?"

And the man bowed his head in the presence of God's glory, and answered Him, and said, "Yes, Lord; and they have built many temples in Thy name."

And God said, "I have given them much possessions and great riches in that city, and yet thou hast died of hunger and want."

And he answered, "Yea, Lord; for I was solitary and alone, and where so many strive together I could find no footing, because that I was stricken with age and infirmity, and none had compassion on me."

When he had spoken it was so, that there was suddenly a great silence in heaven for a space, and the songs of the unnumbered multitudes were hushed.

And God said, "What hearest thou?"

And he answered and said, "I hear the cry of them that are oppressed, and of them that suffer hunger and want, and that are in bitterness, rising up from all the land."

And God said, "Even so, for their cry cometh up before me continually. This people build temples in my name, and worship me with their lips, but their hearts are far from me. I have opened wide mine hands for nought, and poured out riches upon this nation, so that there has been none like unto them until now in all the earth, and lo, they strive greedily together as men that have not enough; and they that lay hold my riches say, 'Lo, it is all ours; it is we that have made it; and as to these multitudes they are not truly our brethren. God has created them poor to labour for us.' And they blindly seek every man in his own gain and are heedless of one another, even as the beasts that perish."

SOCIAL DEMOCRAT

Anon., 'Rent of Ability', *Social Democrat*, August 1898, pp. 253–6.

Anon., 'A Life for a Life', *Social Democrat*, April 1900, pp. 126–8.

The *Social Democrat* (1897–1913), subtitled *A Monthly Socialist Review*, was first issued in January 1897 and was printed and published by the SDF's Twentieth Century Press. Priced initially at 2*d*., the periodical was expanded to sixty-four pages and the price raised to 6*d*. in 1903, then reduced to 3*d*. in 1908. It was edited by *Justice* editor Harry Quelch, who also contributed articles and fiction. The periodical had a more pronounced internationalist perspective than most other British socialist periodicals. Contributors included Edward Aveling (1849–98), Eleanor Marx Aveling (1855–98) and R. B. Cunninghame Graham (1852–1936).

The *Social Democrat* regularly published short stories, and Jack Mitchell has traced many of the anonymous stories back to Harry Quelch: 'They never bear his name, but one can establish authorship through comparison with texts collected in a volume published in tribute to Quelch (*Literary Remains*) ... There is circumstantial evidence that several of the unsigned or pseudonymous pieces in both the *Social Democrat* and *Justice* which cannot be traced back to *Literary Remains* are also by Quelch'.[1] Both of the stories included in this volume were authored by Quelch and are reprinted in *Literary Remains*. Henry (Harry) Quelch was the son of a Berkshire blacksmith who began work at the age of ten and moved to London aged fourteen. He edited *Justice* from 1886, when Hyndman handed him editorial control, until 1889, when he worked to organize a London dockworkers' union. He returned to the editorial chair in 1891 and continued to edit *Justice* as well as the *Social Democrat* until ill health forced him to retire in 1913.

Notes
1. Mitchell, 'Tendencies in Narrative Fiction', pp. 67–8.

Anon., 'Rent of Ability' (1898)

"That's all I have to say, Smith. I won't have a discontented fellow like you about the place. You upset the other men, too, and so I must make an example of you, and you must leave."

"But I have never said I was discontented with my place, or the work, or you, Mr. Swanage; and I don't see, as long as I do my work properly, why you should want to turn me off."

"Didn't I hear you yesterday morning, standing on a stool or something, at the corner of Bell Street, with a mob of riff-raff round you, saying that you had come to preach the gospel of discontent? A pretty preacher, could only make other people as discontented as yourself, and that if you could only make other people as discontented as you were there would very soon be an alteration in the condition of the working people?"

"Yes, I know I said that; but I was expressing discontent with the present system, and not with you or my employment."

"And what's wrong with the present system, I'd like to know?"

"What's wrong with it! The question is what's right with it. A system which compels the great mass of the people to an existence of life-long slavery in which they only get a bare pittance to live upon, while the class which owns the means of existence lives in riotous luxury on their labour, is surely one with which no right-minded man should be content."

"Come, come, I don't want to hear any more of that silly socialistic rot. If you can spout it at street corners you are not going to spout it here. The mass of the people compelled to slave, indeed! Who compels them? They need not work unless they like. That's what I say to you; you needn't work unless you like, and as you don't like you can just clear out."

"I never said I didn't like work; and as for not needing to work if we don't like, there's no such freedom. We must work or starve. But I don't object to that. What I complain of is that we should be compelled to work for a mere existence, so as to be able to go on working; while the bulk of what we earn goes to those who don't work at all."

"I won't listen to such silly outrageous nonsense, I tell you. You get what you earn; if you don't, go somewhere else and see what more you'll get."

"If I get what I earn, and all of us work for you get what we earn, where does your profit come from?"

"My profit? I don't make any profit out of you! What I get is what I earn. When you or any other man earns as much as I do he will get as much as I do."

"Well, you get, I suppose, about ten times as much as any man in the place; do you mean to say that you earn as much as any ten men here?"

"Certainly, if a man gets more it proves that he earns more; higher remuneration is but the return for superior ability."

"Well, I never thought you had ten times the ability of any one of the men you employ; indeed, so far as the work here goes you haven't got the ability of one. If it wasn't for Wilkins, your manager, who does know something about the business, you couldn't go on at all. But you fancy your profit, which other people earn for you, is due to your own ability. Every man gets what he earns, and those who get large incomes do so because of their superior ability, you say. I suppose, then, that young Marchmont, who is known to be a hopeless imbecile, but who has an income of ten thousand a year, possesses ten times your ability?"

"Go!" exclaimed Mr. Swanage, in a towering rage, rising and pointing to the door of the office, "what do you mean by talking to me in that fashion? Go to the foreman and get your money and leave at once."

Smith turned on his heel and went out.

George Smith had been employed for some years at Swanage and Co.'s engineering works. The speciality of the firm was the construction of motors for light machinery and vessels. George had taken a great interest in his work and had frequently suggested small improvements in construction which had been of advantage to his employer. Just now he was engaged upon working out an idea for an entirely new kind of motor, which, if it could be proved to be workable, would effect a great conservation of energy and an enormous saving in the cost of production. He had intended to offer his invention to his employer, once he could demonstrate its practicability. But a workman proposes and the employer disposes. George Smith was a sincere and active Socialist; the intelligence which made him a good, useful, and clever workman also directed his attention to social questions, and, in spite of his individualistic prejudices, he was forced to recognise the soundness of Socialist theories. Active in body as well as mind, he no sooner became convinced of the truth of Socialism than he felt it to be his duty to endeavour to convince others, and thus whatever time he could spare from his work and his experiments he devoted to the propaganda of the principles he had accepted. Thus it came about that he was addressing an open-air meeting in a Western suburb one Sunday morning, and his employer, coming out of church, was inexpressibly shocked to discover one of his "hands" holding for the to a small crowd of "riff-raff" – as Mr. Swanage invariably styled the working class – on the evils of capitalism, the crimes of capitalists, and the necessity for a Social Revolution. This unexpected interview at the street corner led to another interview, as detailed above, on the following day in Mr. Swanage's office. Smith had never assailed his employer personally, and had never considered him as more than a creature of the system in which he lived and for which he was no more responsible than others, and he thought it rather hard that he should be thrown out of work simply for daring to have opinions of his own. However now he was out of work he must make the best of it and look out for another job. But he found that while looking for a job was not difficult, it was very wearisome, for jobs were not easy to be found. After wasting a couple of weeks seeking in vain for employment he thought of his projected new motor. He interviewed the heads of several engineering firms on the matter, but none of them were inclined to have anything to do with it. He felt certain, however, that it would turn out a great success if only he could get it taken up. At last he determined, if he could only raise sufficient money to make a start, to work the invention himself. With some difficulty he managed to raise among sympathisers, the principal being a Socialist friend named Adamson, a sufficient sum to make a beginning. The amount was not nearly sufficient to ensure the success of the undertaking, but he struggled on against all obstacles and difficulties until he succeeded in putting the Smith-Adamson motor on the market. From that time his success was assured, the motor was proved to be the most useful and economical that had ever been produced, and George Smith found himself at the end of a few years at the head of a thriving and growing business.

* * *

"Wilkins," said Mr. Swanage to his manager, "I have gone carefully through the whole accounts and I find that we are hopelessly insolvent. We have been steadily going back ever since that Smith-Anderson motor came out, and there is no doubt it is that which has beaten us. I have gone on hoping that we should be able to recover lost ground, but it is no use. We are beaten absolutely; there is nothing for it but to call our creditors together and see what terms we can make with them."

The meeting of creditors was held, and Swanage and Co. went into liquidation. The losses on the business for some years past had been ruinous, and there was nothing for it but to sell off everything.

Meanwhile the tremendous success of the Smith-Adamson motor had necessitated a considerable extension of premises, and when the sale of Swanage and Co.'s plant and stock took place George Smith was the principle purchaser, and he also took over the premises. Most of the workmen employed by Swanage and Co. were retained in the employment of the new firm, and Smith was very glad to re-engage the manager Wilkins, whose knowledge and experience would, he knew, be very useful in the business.

Business went on briskly in the new works, and, twelve months after the liquidation of the firm, almost everybody but the creditors had forgotten that Swanage and Co. ever existed. It was about nine o'clock in the forenoon when there came a timid knock at the door of the manager's office, and, in response to a sharp "come in," a somewhat seedy-looking elderly individual entered. He was wearing threadbare, rusty black clothes, and a tall hat which had evidently seen better days. He removed his hat from his head as he timidly addressed the manager.

"I have called, Mr. Wilkins," he said, "to know if you had any opening here for my services. I have not been fortunate enough to find employment elsewhere, or I should not have troubled you, as you may imagine I do so with some reluctance."

Wilkins, who had listened with some impatience to this speech, replied shortly, and almost without looking up from his desk, that they had no vacancy for anybody just then.

"But surely you can find me something," said his visitor. "You know who I am, don't you, Mr. Wilkins?"

"Oh, yes, I know who you are. Your name is Swanage, late of the firm of Swanage and Co.; but I don't see what I can do for you. If you were a mechanic I might find you a light job, but you see you don't know anything about the practical part of the work."

"But couldn't you give me something to do in the office?"

"There is nothing that I could set you at which scores of other and younger men couldn't do better. You were never very good at accounts, and I find an office boy as useful as you could possibly be here. There is really nothing you can do. You see, it was one thing when you were master here; no doubt you estimated your own services pretty highly; but, really, you are of no use to us."

Swanage turned to go, with a downcast look on his face, when just as he opened the door another man stepped in and he found himself face to face with George Smith. For a moment both were embarrassed, but George was the first to recover himself. Grasping the hand of his old employer, he exclaimed, "Good morning, Mr. Swanage, this is an unexpected pleasure. Come into my room."

He led him into an inner office, the very place in which their last interview had taken place.

"Now," he said, after handing his visitor a seat, "what can I have the pleasure of doing for you, Mr. Swanage?"

"I called to see if I could get any employment here. I am terribly hard up, and would be willing to do anything that I could, but Wilkins assured me there was no opening."

"No, I am afraid we have nothing much in your line, but with your superior ability you should have no difficulty in finding employment.

"Ah, but you seem to have displayed the superior ability now, and so I have been driven to the wall."

"I don't think it's a question of superior ability at all, Mr. Swanage. We are all dependent on one another. I could never have brought out the Smith-Adamson motor but for the discoveries and inventions of other men, and the knowledge I was able to acquire while in your employment. If I had not taken this particular principle and adapted to practical purposes, someone else would have done so sooner or later. And I am quite sure that sooner or later the Smith-Adamson motor will be rendered obsolete by some further development. Those of us who have these things in our hands only exploit them for our own profit. There is no great ability required to do that; but I am looking forward to the time when no one shall have this power, but when all inventions and discoveries will be for the benefit of all."

"Do you mean to say that you are still a Socialist?"

"Of course! Why not? Circumstances may alter cases, but a change of circumstances does not change a man from a Socialist into an anti-Socialist. I know the present system is wrong, and shall do my best to overthrow it, although I personally have been fairly successful. But this is rather beside the question. The point just now is what are you going to do?"

"Well, frankly, unless you can give me employment, I shall have to go to the workhouse."

"What! In spite of your superior ability?"

"Oh, don't say any more about that. I see it is much more a question of circumstance and of opportunity than of anything else."

"Well, what do you think of doing?"

"I can think of nothing. Can't you give me something to do?"

"Well, as a matter of fact, there is so little that you can do of any use. However, I cannot treat you as you would have treated me. Had I come to you in a similar case you would have given me an order for the workhouse and thought it a most generous thing to do. But we working people are set of soft-hearted fools, so I will just pay you the same wages per week as you were paying me, and you can just come here and potter about, or stay away – just as it suits you. Only don't forget that these wages are due to the work of other people, and are not due, any more than the profits you used to get, to your superior ability."

Anon., 'A Life for a Life' (1900)

"Go on, lads; give it to the beggars; exterminate the vermin," shouted young Symons, a subaltern of the Blankshires, as the order "Fix bayonets, charge!" rang out, and the now sadly thinned ranks once more pressed forward up the deadly slope. Hardly had he uttered the words than he fell forward on his face, as a fresh burst of leaden hail from the heights before them staggered the advancing British.

All day long the fight had raged. The attempted surprise of the strongly fortified Boer[1] position in the early morning had failed. Hour after hour the British artillery had shelled the heights, its fire sullenly replied to at intervals by the enemy's guns. Slowly the attacking infantry had been pushed forward under such cover as the inequalities of the ground afforded, many a man falling under the hail of bullets which steadily poured down upon them. Now they had got to within charging distance, and the day was closing in. Maddened with thirst and weariness, frenzied with hate and the lust for blood, they struggled up the slope, the leaden hail beating down upon them, men dropping at every step. Time and again they staggered and hesitated; again and again they rallied and pressed on; shouts, orders, curses, the groans and cries of falling men and the commands and imprecations of officers mingled in horrible confusion as again and again the ranks were swept by the withering fire from above. In vain they rallied, in vain the officers cursed and swore and begged and implored and threatened. The task was impossible. The wavering line broke and fell back before the withering fire, men falling here and there as they retreated down the slope. The attack was over.

It was nearly dark now and Corporal Scott, as he limped along with a bullet in his leg and another in his shoulder, felt, as he heard the occasional "spat" of a bullet as it struck the ground, that he didn't much care if one put an end to him there and then. Presently he heard a low moan, and turning in the direction from whence the sound proceeded, he came across Lieutenant Symons.

"Can I do anything for you, sir?" asked Scott.

"Give me water," feebly murmured the officer, pointing to Scott's water bottle. The other shook his head. The bottle had been emptied hours before.

"I'm afraid I couldn't carry you, sir, even if you could get on my back," he said.

"It's no use," the other replied. "I'm afraid I'm about done for. Anyhow, I couldn't get on your back."

"You mustn't give up, sir, and I can't go and leave you here." said Scott. "Where are you hurt?"

"It's gone right through me, I think," said the other. "I've tried to get up and crawl back. But I can't."

Scott knelt down by the officer and undid his tunic. He found that he was badly hurt and had bled freely. He bound him up as well as he could. It was getting cold and the rain was beginning to fall, its patter on the ground being occasionally broken by the more emphatic "spat" of a bullet. Scott gathered a few of the smaller boulders which were scattered about, and formed a sort of rampart for the wounded officer, and caught some of the raindrops, with which he moistened his parched lips, and then lay down by him and took him in his arms to protect him from the biting cold. Hour after hour they lay there; occasionally in the distance Scott saw the will-o'-the-wisp glimmer of the lanterns of the bearer parties as they sought over the field for the wounded, but none ever came near them. Occasionally Scott dozed, only to awakened by the patter of the rain. It was dawn before they were found and taken into camp.

* * *

Serious as Lieutenant Symons' wound had been, he was first out of hospital. The cold and exposure of the night had caused inflammation in Scott's wounded limb, and as soon as he could leave the hospital he was invalided home.

Before leaving the hospital Symons visited his subordinate's bedside. "Goodbye, Scott," said he, "I am off to the front again to have another shot at the beggars. I owe it to you that I am alive now. It may be that we shall never meet any more, but if I come through all right don't forget to come to me if ever you should want a friend.

* * *

A colliery village in the north of England in the dusk of a November day. A dull, leaden sky, from which a cold, almost imperceptible drizzle was falling. Near the pit-head, and in front of the manager's house, a detachment of the Blankshire regiment was drawn up; the men in their dark grey great-coats, looking sinister and threatening in the gathering gloom. Further down the lane leading from the house, and facing the soldiers, was a crowd of people – colliers and their womenfolk – neither noisy nor demonstrative, but angry and menacing.

The great lock-out of miners had been in progress some two months; both sides were angry and obdurate. Distress and hunger were rife among the colliers and their families, and the men were becoming exasperated, but the masters refused to concede a single point. There had been some incipient rioting at several places; at one of the mines near the village of Wingstone the engine-house and timber-stacks had been set fire to; and the owners and the magistrates were fearful of worse disorders. They had, therefore requisitioned military protection, and a detachment of the Blankshires, under the command of Captain Symons, had been sent to protect this particular colliery, whose manager the colliers had expressed their intention of interviewing, as he held an official position in the masters' association. The interview was refused, the manager alleging that he feared violence. As the hours slowly passed the colliers, held at bay by the soldiers, grew more angry and menacing. As the evening drew on the crowd increased in numbers.

Captain Symons, withdrawn from the social gaieties of the county town, voted the whole business a "beastly bore," and muttered deep curses, under his breath, on the colliers, the lock-out, and all connected therewith.

The silence, broken only by the scarcely perceptible drip of the rain, and the low murmur of the crowd, was ominous. The air seemed charged with the pent-up elements of coming storm.

On horseback, by the side of Captain Symons, was the local magistrate, one of the most unpopular colliery owners in the district. Turning to the officer, he said a few words in a low voice at which the other nodded, then, urging his horse a few paces towards the crowd, who on their side pressed towards him, he shouted, as he waved a paper in his hand: "I have stood this long enough. I am now going to read the Riot Act, and if you don't immediately disperse I shall order the troops to fire."

He rapidly read over a few sentences from the paper he held in his hand and then wheeled his horse and resumed his place by the side of the officer.

How much or how little of what had taken place was understood by the crowd is problematical, but, as the magistrate turned his horse, a stone, flung by someone in the rear of the crowd, struck him in the side. At the same instant a tall man in the front stepped forward and raised his hand, as if about to speak.

"Did you see that?" shouted the magistrate to the officer. "You must disperse this crowd or there will be mischief."

The captain turned to his men with a sharp word of command. There was an ominous rattle as the rifles were brought to the "present." "Fire low," said the officer, "we must teach these cattle a lesson." "Here, what the devil are you up to?" he shouted to the man nearest him, snatching the rifle from his hand. "Do you think you are rook-shooting?" A volley rang out as the officer levelled the piece at the tall man, who had his back towards him and was facing the crowd, whom he appeared to urging to disperse. As the volley sounded the man swung round and fell forward on his face, his arms outstretched, the blood gushing from his mouth. Several others had fallen too, but he the crowd did not move.

For a moment there was silence. Then a shower of stones rattled round and upon the soldiers. Then another sharp order, and then another volley and another. The crowd broke and fled. "Fix bayonets," cried the officer, " and clear the street." With bayonets fixed the men advanced at the charge, but the crowd scattered and ran in all directions, leaving several of their number on the ground, some of whom were killed and others too seriously hurt to get away.

"That's my buck," remarked the officer, as he passed the man whom he had shot, and turning him over with his foot, so that he caught a glimpse of his face. Something in the features seemed familiar to him, and for a moment there came to his mind the memory of a cold wet night on the South African veldt, but only for a moment, as she shrugged his shoulders and passed on.

* * *

"Who was that tall fellow who was shot? Do you know?" asked Captain Symons of the magistrate, as they were dining together that evening. "He seemed to be a ringleader, and a regular fire-brand, I should imagine."

"He was something of a leader;" answered the magistrate, "but I don't think he was much of a fire-brand. He had the reputation of being one of the coolest and most moderate among them. He had been a soldier, I believe. Oh, only a common solider, I mean," he added, as he noticed a curious look in the other's eyes, "but he had a fairly good character, and had seen service in South Africa. His name was Scott."

The captain relapsed into silence. He had paid his debt.

TEDDY ASHTON'S JOURNAL/NORTHERN WEEKLY AND TEDDY ASHTON'S JOURNAL

Ben Adhem, 'Blood on the Cheap Trip', *Teddy Ashton's Journal: A Gradely Paper for Gradely Folk*, 29 May 1896, p. 12.

Teddy Ashton, 'Bill Spriggs an Patsy Filligan o'er Winter Hill. Likewise Bet', *Teddy Ashton's Journal: A Gradely Paper for Gradely Folk*, 26 September 1896, p. 147; 2 October 1896, p. 157.

James Haslam, 'Murdered by Money', *Teddy Ashton's Journal: A Gradely Paper for Gradely Folk*, 17 April 1897, pp. 378–9.

Teddy Ashton, 'Greensauce Sketches. Georgie's Fust Day in t' Factory', *Teddy Ashton's Journal: A Gradely Paper for Gradely Folk*, 11 December 1897, p. 237.

Teddy Ashton, 'Th' Kock-Krow Club an' th' War. Darin Decision to Form a Kock-Krow Volunteer Corps to Batter th' Boers', *Teddy Ashton's Northern Weekly*, 25 November 1899, p. 445.

Fred Plant, 'The Absent-Minded Beggar', *Teddy Ashton's Northern Weekly*, 11 August 1900, p. 6.

Teddy Ashton's Journal: A Gradely Paper for Gradely Folk (1896–1908) was first issued on 22 May 1896 in Bolton by owner, editor and chief writer Charles Allen Clarke. (Biographical details for Clarke may be found in the *Bolton Trotter* headnote in Volume 1, pp. 1–2.) In March 1898 he changed the title to *Northern Weekly and Teddy Ashton's Journal* in order to attract sales from outside the Bolton area. The title was shortened to *Teddy Ashton's Northern Weekly* in May 1899. It was published, respectively, in Bolton, Manchester and Blackpool, selling for a halfpenny.

Clarke wrote much of the paper himself under a series of pseudonyms, including 'Ben Adhem' and the famous 'Teddy Ashton'. The paper carried a great deal of fiction and poetry, serializing Clarke's long fictions such as *Lancashire Lads and Lasses* (1896), *A Daughter of the Factory* (1898) and *Slaves of Shuttle and Spindle* (1899), as well as serial and short fiction by regular authors Arthur

Laycock (n.d.), James Haslam (1869–1937) and Fred Plant (n.d.). Haslam was the son of a handloom weaver, and he became a journalist after his early working years as a little piecer in a cotton mill. He lost this employment when, along with Allen Clarke and J. R. Clynes (1869–1949), he attempted to form the Lancashire Cotton Piecers' Association. After the failure of the union, Clarke employed him on his early socialist paper the *Labour Light*, and he became a regular contributor to Clarke's *Teddy Ashton's Journal/Northern Weekly*, the *Clarion* and the *Labour Leader* as well as to non-socialist papers such as the *Liverpool Weekly Post* and the *Manchester Guardian*. He was the author of short stories as well as the serial 'The Mill on the Moor' (1898–9), which was published in bound form under the title *The Handloom Weaver's Daughter* (1904). He went on to help form the National Union of Journalists and was editor of the union's periodical, the *Journalist*, as well as managing the journalism and publication section of the Co-operative Wholesale Society periodical. Plant was a prolific contributor of short stories to Clarke's *Teddy Ashton* periodical and the author of serials 'The Ladder of Life (1897–8) and 'Tamsie: A Tale of a Hatting Town' (1899). No further information for him has been identified.

Ben Adhem, 'Blood on the Cheap Trip' (1896)

Early on a certain sunny Whit-Friday[1] morning, the cheap trip trains[2] were shooting westward with sound and smoke through a dark stone tunnel, built under busy streets, on the railway that linked with iron the chimney portion of Lancashire to the far-off healthy sea.

Over this tunnel was a road, bound on either side with walls about six feet high. A lower wall four feet high, enclosing private land, ran down from the bridge on either side, north and south. Up this low wall children could climb, and thence to the arch of the tunnel, from which, if not careful, they might fall to the metals below. But this thing was no concern of the railway company; they had built their own wall sufficiently high for general safety, and had nothing to do with private property-owners and their dangerous stinting, for cheapness sake, in the matter of walls.

As was only natural, children did scale the walls, easily getting on the very centre of the bridge, and from this perch watching with shaking delight the roaring trains whizz out of the tunnel with flame and fume. Often the faces of the children were quite blackened with the sudden upward puffs of smoke.

On this Whit-Friday morning a boy of eight, with his sister of five and a baby a few months old, came to the bridge.

"Let's get on the wall an' watch the trains, Jane," said the lad.

"I've got the baby, Joe," said Jane. She had often been on the wall before, on occasions when she had not been burdened with the baby.

"We can manage it all right," said Joe, seeing a spice of adventure in the position. "I'll help you with the baby."

Jane did not need much persuasion, though she was timid on account of her little living charge. Yet, she longed to watch the trains speed away. She had never been on a railway journey in her life, and the only joy she could take in the cheap excursions was to watch the packed trains speed away and away, till lost round the distant curve up the valley, and wonder, in innocent envy, what that glorious sea was like to which the thousands of lucky trippers were going for a merry holiday. Jane had no shoes, no stockings, no hat; her frock was ragged; she was not clean. Her brother's trousers were old and torn, his shirt was all remnants; he had no shoes nor stockings, either, and he was far less clean than his sister; while the baby was dirtier than both put together. But all this disgrace was nobody's business but their parents', and they, an idle, careless couple, were less fit to take care of themselves than their neglected children. On this particular morning they sat drinking together at the "Blue Pig;" they would end this holiday as they had ended so many others, by having a nasty connubial fight in the street, resulting in one, or both, being locked up. But this sort of civilisation we have always with us,[3] and, in a free country, it is nobody's business but those concerned.

Joe and Jane and the baby got on the bridge. Jane went first, and Joe handed the baby to her. She reached the middle of the bridge with difficulty, but once seated there, with the child in her arms, felt all right. Then Joe lay on his chest beside her, with his head far out in the air, looking down towards the mouth of the tunnel.

They had not been there a minute before the great clanking, hurrying noise of a coming train was heard, and all at once out roared a locomotive, with a long string of carriages.

"Isn't it bonny?" said Jane. "The baby likes it, too, I think. Oh, Joe! I do wish we was on that train. I wonder where it's goin'."

"Blackpool, very likely," said Joe. "All the holiday trains goes there. It's a spiffing place; water there a hundred times bigger than Jinkins's factory lodge."[4]

"Never!" said Jane.

"'Tis so," said Joe; "an' sands with no slutch[5] on 'em, where the children can play, an' dig it up with spades."

"An' the bobbies[6] not drive 'em away?" asked Jane, incredulous.

"They daren't drive 'em away, there. In fact, I never heard of there bein' any bobbies at all there."

"Oh, it *must* be a nice place!" exclaimed Jane. "But how do you know all that's true, Joe?"

"Tom Rylan told me, an' he's been for half-a-day. An' there's ships there, real ships a-sailin', an' donkeys to ride on, an' no factories, an' no smoke, an' no work, an' everybody's jolly an' does nothin' but spend their money like kings an' queens."

"Oh, how I wish we was there, Joe, an' the baby, too. Perhaps the baby wouldn't cough all night if he was there."

"I guess he wouldn't. I never heard of anybody coughin' there. There's nothin' but good fun there, an' nothin' that nobody doesn't like."

"I wonder if we'll ever go there, Joe. I'd be satisfied if we only went for five minutes – just to see it all once – only a little once."

A she spoke the poor girl looked yearningly out the west, where the land looked so bright, and the sky so blue, and a tear came into her eyes.

"Hurroo! There's another train comin'!" yelled Joe.

In his excitement he accidentally gave Jane a push. She screamed and fell forward, clutching at the stonework in vain. She dropped on the first carriage of the train, head first, and was hurled bleeding to one side of the railway track.

She was dead. The baby was killed, too.

But the cheap trip train sped merrily on to the beautiful sea – with a child's blood on it.

Teddy Ashton, 'Bill Spriggs an Patsy Filligan o'er Winter Hill. Likewise Bet' (1896)

[26 September 1896]

I went o'er to Blackpool on a day-trip to fot' Bill Spriggs back. I fun him havin a camel-ride on t' sands wi Mayor Card'll and six teawn councillors, just after some roarin adventures on t' Big Wheel; but that tale yo shall have later on.

"Come off that bloomin camel, Bill," says I, "an horry back to Trotterteawn wi me: for there's desperate fun gooin on, an it's thy duty, as a Tum Fowter to be in it?"

"What's up this time?" axed Bill.

So I towd him abeaut Winter Hill, an heaw Colonel Ainsworth an his happy men were trying to stop gradely folk fro' gooin across t' moors.[1]

"That'll never do," said Bill. "Th' public mun have reaum for their honest feet. I'll come an willin. A wed chap fears noather police nor prison."

Well, Mayor Card'll and t' six councillors tried to persuade Bill to stop wheer he were; but he wouldn't be coaxed.

"Neow, neow," says Bill, "duty fust, Blackpool second."

Then Mayor Card'll an t' six councillors pood their pocket handketchers eaut an wept – wi one eye on t' November elections. While they were wipin their noble een Bill an me slipt away, an were soon on eaur road back to Totterteaun[2] as fast as the L. & Y.[3] could carry us: which is abeaut as swift as Tommy Piggy's courtin, what's been walkin a girl eaut ten year neaw, and seeams no ner t' weddin yet.

As t' train flew alung at a wonderful snail-gallop I towd Bill th' history o' t' Winter Hill affair; heaw Colonel Ainsworth claimed t' road as his, an heaw t' public said it were a public road an allus had been; an heaw Colonel Ainsworth put a gate up an a sign, an heaw a creawd o' folk t' other Sunday upset that gate and scattered that sign to t' four winds of heaven an t' thirty-nine winds o' Winter Hill, an heaw Colonel Ainsworth were gooin t' prosecute t' ringleaders; an heaw t' public said they'd have their road, an t' Winter Hill road too, an' wouldn't be done eawt of a footpath by Colonel Ainsworth or any other mon, or wife an chaplain noather.

"This'll never do," said Bill. "I've run up that road mony a time, to get away fro' eaur Bet's rowlin-pin; an is one o' my best roads of escape fro' matrimony to be snitched off me i' this landlord fashion? Never! I'll stick up for my reets if I dee for it as lung as I live!"

"Goo lad! Bill," said I, "theau't a gradely good patriot."

"Neaw look here, Teddy," said Bill, "durn't be cawin me no names. A bit o' friendly chaff's aw reet, but there's such a thing as gooin to far, as Muggy Rinkle said when he seet off for Moses Gate and geet in a hexpress train fust stop Salford,[4] an as Colonel Ainsworth said when he put his bloomin gate up. Durn't caw me that name no mooar, Teddy."

"But it's a compliment," said I.

"Aw reet," said Bill, "say no mooar."

We geet in Trotterteawn by dinner-time or theer-abeauts.

"We mun hunt up Patsy Filligan," said Bill. "He mun have his feet i' this job."

"He's been ill," said I.

"I know," said Bill, "but he'll be weel enoof for this merry game. Patsy's only ill when there's hard wark knockin abeaut."

We fun Patsy readin Smiles' "Self-Help,"[5] which a kind friend had lent him. He'd axed this friend for t' loan of hauve-a-creaun,[6] but t' friend had said Smiles' "Self-Help" would be mooar serviceable.

Patsy chucked "Self-Help" in t' coal-hole, an greeted us wi sweet smiles.

"Look here Patsy," said Bill, "we're gooin t' do summat for eaur fellow-men this afternoon. There's a road wants makin o'er Winter Hill. Thee an me's just geet t' feet t' do it wi. Joe Shufflebottom's been an tried, but though he manages to put his toes in a lot o' things, his sole's not big enoof for this job. He's left a mark on Winter Hill wheer he's walked, but he's no feet for makin a public highway, has he hek as like![7] So thee an me ull do it, Patsy! Put on they biggest shoon an come alung!"

Patsy jumped up an skriked, "Filliloo! boys! Is it agen the landlords ye're goin? Then I'm one of ye – nay I'm a dozen of ye! If it's anythin agen a landlord, I'm in it! My great shoes, Bridget: the pair wid the howlin hobnails! – the pair that'll do for either dancin on a landlord or his land!"

"Let's have a bit o' dinner fust," said Bill.

"Where's the belabourin Betsy?" asked Patsy.

"Left her at Blackpool," said Bill.

"Doesn't she know you've come?" asked Patsy.

"Neow," said Bill, wi a grin, "it doesn't do to let wives know too much neawadays."

After dinin on red-herrins an coffee we seet off for Winter Hill: takkin t' tram up Halliwell Road. We'd a job to get Patsy's shoon in t' tram: an once we thowt he'd ha't' poo 'em off, an have 'em sent after us on a lurry; but at last we managed to squeeze 'em through t' doorhole after rubbin 'em weel wi a peaun o' tallow candles.

We geet off t' tram at th' Ainsworth Arms an walked bouldly up Halliwell Road. When we reiched t' top we had five minutes rest an a smook. Then Patsy tightened his shoe-laces an we seet off again.

"There's nobody abeaut," said Bill, "we han it aw to eaursels. It's bonny up here, isn't it? It's a dal shame that anybody should try to keep t' folk off this pleasant stretch o' moor. Is a mon to have noather freish air nor nice walks because he's poor? What reet's any one mon to aw this, I'd like to know? Owd Ainsworth will have a job to get through t' needle's eye o' Scripter[8] wi aw this on his back, weren't he? No one mon owt to have mooar land than he con look after with his own honds. Come on Patsy, bring them little feet forrud, and we'll soon make a road."

We went on past t' place wheer t' gate an sign had been pood deaun; but met nobody. Then we looked behind an seed two fellows comin after us. We sit deaun an waited on em.

"Yo're trespassin," said one on em, as soon as they geet up to us.

"So are yo," said Bill, "be off wi yo whum."

"We're Mestur Ainsworth's men," said t' chap.

"I'm sure yo're noan God Awmighty's men," said I, "if looks is owt to goo by."

Th' chaps stared, an said it were no use fawin eaut.

"It would be a bad job for yo if yo did," said Patsy glancing deaun at this feet.

Th' men looked at Patsy's shoon an fair dithered. Then one of em went on to say wi a wink, that they geet three bob a day to come an tak t' names o' trespassers, an they were farmers, but this were a better job, an they hoped t' bother would last a lung while, an they'd tak it as a favour if Bill and Patsy would give em their names, just to show they were doin summat for their money.

Bill an Patsy lowfed. "We're happy to oblige yo," said Bill.

"Yo can have our names wid pleasure," said Patsy. "It'll do your master good to see 'em. Out wid your book an write 'em down."

"Will you write 'em deawn for us?" said one o' t' chaps, pooin' eaut a penny note book.

"Why?" said Patsy.

"Because noather of us two con read or write."

Well, at this confession we aw lowfed till we freetent a million grouse away.

"That's rich," said I, "gettin three bob a day to tak names, an corn't write! I think yo'd better tell yore gaffer that it would look better on him to spend his brass i' education an noan i' blockin footpaths up. Heawever, bring yore book here."

They gan me t' book an I wrote down Bill Spriggs, M.P., Patsy Filligan, gent, and Teddy Ashton, author.

"Neaw give yore mestur them names," said I, "an watch him oppen his een when he sees 'em. Good afternoon."

An on we went; an I sung t' following song I'd made for th' occasion, Bill and Patsy jeinin in t' chorus wi aw their din.

WILL YO COME O' SUNDAY MORNIN?

Will yo come o' Sunday mornin
For a walk o'er Winter Hill?
Ten thousand went last Sunday
But there's room for thousands still!
O the moors are rare an bonny,
An the heather's sweet an fine,
An the road across the hill tops
Is the public's – yours an mine.

Chorus – So come o' Sunday mornin
For a walk o'er Winter Hill,
Ten thousand went last Sunday,
But there's room for thousands still.

Oh shame upon the landlord
That would thrutch us up in town!
Against such Christless conduct
We will put our feet firm down!
Ay, we'll put our feet down strongly,
Until we've clearly showed
Twenty thousand feet each Sunday
Can soon mark out a road!

Must poor folk stroll in cinders
While the rich cop all the green?
Is England but the landlord's
Who locks up each pretty scene?
If they only could, these tyrants
Would enclose the road to heaven!
So let us up an fight 'em
Even seventy times an seven!

So come o' Sunday mornin
For a walk o'er Winter Hill,
Ten thousand went last Sunday
But there's room for thousands still.

"Is aw that eaut o' thy own yead, Teddy?" asked Bill.

"Ay," I said, "eaut o' my own yead an t' dictionary."

"I durn't think Ainsworth's a bad soart," said Bill. "I darsay if us three went an talked to him –"

"We'll consider it," said I.

We geet deawn to Wright's Arms, an were busy at t' pump, when we yerd a greight din on t' moor. Lookin reaund we seed a chap that looked like Col. Ainsworth's chaplain – fleein as if for his life. Then aw at once a woman coom i' seet, chasin him. Hoo had a rowlin-pin in her hond. It were Bed Spriggs i' search of her husband.

(*Th' rest next week.*)

[3 October 1896]

Bill an Patsy crept eaut o' their hidin-places an watched Bet chase t' parson-lookin chap.

"By gum!" said Bill, "eaur Bet's on t' job too, Patsy. If hoo gies that fellow just one whack wi t' rowlin-pin he'll feel that he's been wed twenty year, by gow, will he!"

"She's a-doin it beautiful," said Patsy. "Notice the elegant trotters she has for runnin, Bill. Let us go to her. Ye needn't fear the missis to-day, Bill; for all appearances point to the happy circumstance that she is on our side. I believe she has come to help us an not to oppose us."

"I think Patsy's reet for once," said I.

Th' mon as Bet were after were neaw hauve-a-mile away, an Bet gan up t' pursuit. Hoo hadn't wind enoof.

Bill an Patsy an me went up to Bet.

"I compliment ye, Mrs. Spriggs," said Patsy.

"I'll talk to thee in a bit," said Bet, then to Bill, "What are ta doin up here?"

"We coom a making a highway," said Bill, "public duty."

"Mooar like public-heause duty," said Bet. "Owt for an excuse for a gallivant an a spree. Makin a highway, eh? Such characters as thee an t' company theau keeps con make nowt but a low way, I'm certain."

At this peint up coom t' two men that had tan Bill's name, an Patsy's an mine.

"They'n took Bill's name," said I to Bet.

"Han they," said Bet, "then they'd better gie it him back an be sharp abeaut it."

"I think so too, Bet," said I. "For it's t' name he gan thee when he wed thee; an if they tan it an keep it, wheer will theau be?"

"Noan much wuss off," said Bet, "for he gan me nowt *but* his name when I wed him. Heawever –"

"We want yore name missus," said one o' t' chaps to Bet.

"Oh, done yo?" said Bet. "Wheer will ta have it, eh? In t' yerhole or across t' jaw? Tak thy feaw face whoam an keep it theer for th' health o' thy country. It's enoof to gie one t' diarrhoea."

"I want yore name," said t' chap. "Yo've no reet here."

"Who says so," demanded Bet.

"Colonel Ainsworth."

"Fot him here, an I'll talk to him," said Bet. "Theau't noan havin may name. Hastn't ta geet one o' thy own? What done they caw thee on thy own hearthstone? Bug-peawder, wha? Goo an dreawn thysel an do a good turn to thy wife an family if theau has one. Be off neaw, while theau't safe," an Bet pood her rowlin-pin eaut.

"Why, it's Bet Spriggs!" gasped booath o' t' men at once, an seet off runnin like Owd Ned's racin-dugs. They never stopped till they geet to Rivinton Pike.

"Well Bet," said I, "Come on, an I'll trate thee. Theau't a brick."

"Aw reet, Teddy," said Bet, "Come on, Bill. Thee an me agrees for once, so's heaw; theau't in t' reet on it to come across t' moors. I durn't see why anybody should want to stop us. Yo seed that chap as I were after wi t' rowlin-pin? Let's get sit deawn, an I'll tell yo aw abeaut it; it's a rare tale. Come on, Bill. I'll let thee off to-day, seein as theau's shown a bit o' pluck."

"He put a bowd front on," said I. "Has to forgeet that do, Bill?"

Bill grinned.

"Oh, but I've summat to settle wi him yet," said Bet. "Abeaut that big wheel at Blackpool. But we'll let it stond o'er for to-day. Come on Teddy.

James Haslam, 'Murdered by Money' (1897)

It was the close of an ideal spring afternoon. The air was sweet with the scent of early flowers and its balmy influence cheered the hearts of those who remained out of doors to inhale it. The grassy bands leading from Brigson's mill were daintily decorated with plots of white and crimson daisies and the rugged coltsfoot, with here and there a chaste-looking cowslip nodding its golden-yellow head to the workpeople that passed to and from the mill.

The air, too, was melodious with the lusty notes of birds, new arrivals of spring, some of them, which sought rest and habitation in the small clusters of woodland abounding in this semi-rural vicinity.

As these subtle songsters strove to sweeten the early evening hours with their instinctive music – some with their earliest gushes of melody since their flight from the sunny south, the men and women and the boys and girls came scuttering out of Brigson's mill, almost before the engine had stopped.

A genial April breeze kissed their oily faces and stripped their clothing of loose cotton fibres as they hurried home to tea.

"Yon's Matilda Pryde in a mighty sweat," said Sally Oakes.

"To be sure," responded Polly Dobson, "hoo'll ha for t' meet t' young Mestur to-neet, happen."

"H'm," jocularly ventured another of Matilda's workmates. "Pryde allus goes before a faw."

The other females laughed, and Betsy Bibby lauded the witty observer with, "Goo lad, Mary; thy feyther ull ne'er dee while theau lives. Theau'rt too sharp. If theau doesn't mind theau'll o'ertak thyself."

Lies and evil stories spread with rapidity anent the wooing of Matilda by "t' young Mestur," and many ill-foreboding epithets were heaped upon her pretty, innocent head.

"Hoo's a giddy bit," blurted her workmates whenever she passed them either in the mill or out of doors.

The fact of the matter was, Matilda had been seen with "t' young Mestur," Mr. Harold Brigson, and the gossips of the mill and the neighbourhood looked upon it as a very ill-omen indeed.

There was something tenderly-sweet in the physical proportions of Matilda Pryde; something in her charming facial looks and bewitching shape that had won her more admirers than young Harold Brigson. Her gentle features, sportive and spiritual-looking, her bright brown eyes and luxurious black hair, and her shapely figure, had attracted the eyes of young men of various stations and professions in life, many who could not understand why such a chaste human flower should be stunted and deprived of its fragrance and beauty by the defiling atmosphere of a modern card-room,[1] – as the fragile fibres of cotton are ripped and distorted by the forked "beaters" of the scotching machine.

The young Master's association with her was regarded suspiciously by most of the people who had seen them together, but his attachment to Matilda was kept strictly secret from his relations and friends.

To Matilda, her life seemed to be entering into new glories. She was by no means offensively haughty. True, she carried herself erect – too erect, many of the other factory females thought in their jealousy, and it was opined that her fine, lithe figure would some day be brought to the gutter with a woeful fall.

Fancies sweet and new crowded her brain and she heard nothing or knew nothing of the ill forebodings of her factory acquaintances. She lived and moved and sang in a world of new delight and love, so seemingly far and far away from her cottage lowliness and poverty. So long as she believed – and what maiden so sweet and favoured, could not? – in the sincerity of her plutocratic lover, she perceived increased love and riches before her and the present hours of her life were sweet with those fancies, ideal and poetic, which are common in most youthful minds under the delectable influence of Cupid.

She sang the day away at the mill; labour seemed light indeed under the winsome wings of love. Her voice as melodious in tone, as her face was in playful smiles, could be well heard above the "hurr-ing" din of the "flies"[2] that whizzed round and round on the frames at which she worked.

"That's a bonny ring, Tilly," said Mary Morrison, the morning following the afternoon described at the beginning of this story, as she helped Matilda to "doff".[3]

"H'm!" replied Matilda, delightfully, and the gem emitted a brilliant ray of its gold and its rich stones upon the shining steel flies as she swiftly darted her deft, delicate hands in and out among the spindles and roving.[4]

"Did ta get it fro t' young Mestur?"

Matilda always spoke confidently to Mary Morrison, and the latter was much older of the two.

"H'm!" hummed Matilda, blushing. "Harold gave it t' me."

"Hadn't theau better be careful wi him, Tilly?"

"Why, Mary?"

"Why, theau 't young yet, and has getten a lot to find eaut."

"Getten a lot to find eaut!" Something seemed to flash into the mind of Matilda which checked for the nonce, her flowing jubilant love-spirits. Mary Morrison observed the effect and quietly went on "Owder fooaks than us, say, Matilda, as young Harold's just like his fayther were, when he were young. They sen as Nellie Brantwood as works in t' watch-heause is his child and that her mother as used to be a slubber-tenter[5] deed in t' warkheause."

"Deed in' warkheause!" whispered Matilda, showing signs of sudden pain, which she tried to relieve with a long drawn sigh.

What had affected charming, merry Matilda so deeply! Was it the mere conversation of Mary Morrison, or some other force, spiritual, Providential, or psychological – call it what you will – that had been sent to warn the unmindful maiden of the rocks ahead?

Whatever it was it can only be said that such warnings are nearly always too vague to be convincing.

It was true that Harold Brigson had been playing the part of double dealer – with Matilda Pryde on one hand and with a rich lady acquaintance on the other. It was true, however, that he loved Matilda. It was also true that his intentions towards her were honourable, and that he was determined to marry "bonny Tilly," as she was often appellated, if other obstacles to the union could be conveniently removed.

The differences of birth, education, and opulence between him and Matilda had not yet interfered with his fervent feelings towards her, but the circumstances, friends, and relations to which these privileges had introduced young Harold, placed him in an awkward position.

What must he do? What could he do! – here was the bane of his life.

* * *

Nearly five months passed over. Seated in a luxuriously-furnished room of his father's palatial residence, overlooking a pretty verdant landscape, young Harold meditated deeply upon is peculiar situation. As the day faded into night and a full harvest moon raised itself above the tops of the trees and the hills adjoining, his father quietly entered the room.

The usual family greetings were exchanged, and after the evening papers had been curtly scanned over, Mr. Arthur Brigson – Harold's father – seemed to prepare himself for a serious conference with his son. Whether by some unconscious process of telepathy the son anticipated the intentions of his father, cannot be said, but such was the case.

"Well, Harold," broke in the father, "I – I've been thinking over your engagement with Miss Amelia Crewdson."

Harold's features gave an unpleasant twitch.

The father continued, "I've been think – thinking of drawing up an agreement with you, and settling a yearly sum upon you, now that the marriage is arranged; and –

"Yes, father," interrupted Harold a little convulsively, and turning his eyes towards the windows on the western side of the room, he looked across the open fields where the moon was prettily spreading her fairy rays, and where, in half-an-hour's time, he was under promise to meet his pretty Matilda.

He had expected this topic of conversation from his father for months, though he could not bring his mind to a definite mode of action respecting his connections with poor, plain Matilda, and the jewelled Miss Amelia Crewdson.

His relationship with Miss Crewdson was not of his willing choosing – it was the old story – riches – position – and loveless conventionality. All sorts of wild ideas had flitted through the fickle convolutions of his brain concerning the matter, but never any notions of a lasting or decisive character. To yield to the wishes of his father, his friends and Miss Amelia Crewdson meant dishonouring his sweet expectant Tilly, and meant perhaps bringing the life of another honest working woman to a disgraceful end – death in a mill lodge or suicide by hanging.

Harold had pondered and pondered – the soul at times getting the better of the flesh and *vice versa*.

At an advanced stage of the conversation, the father said, "'Willowwood,' the house purchased for you will be ready in a month hence, so that it will be necessary to have the marriage immediately."

Harold stammered, spoke evasively and showed signs of painful irritation.

The father suspected that the conversation was not at all cheering or tasteful to his son in whom he took great pride, but the reason was far beyond his subtle guessing.

"What's the matter?" curtly came from the interested parent.

"Hadn't we – we better *drop* the matter, father?" asked Harold, tottering as he tried to raise himself from his easy chair.

"What's this mean?" demanded the more-than-ever interested parent, in sterner tones.

"It means – it means –" shuffled Harold, looking on the ground.

"It means what?" broke in the father impatiently.

Harold raised his eyes, set them firmly on those of his father, and in a feverish frame of mind continued, "It means that I am, in my word of honour, bound to another woman."

"To whom?" gasped the father, as he raised his stunted figure and placed his left hand flatly on his flabby cerebellum.[6]

"To Miss Matilda Pryde, of –"

"Miss Matilda Pryde. Who can she be?"

"A Jack-frame tenter[7] at our No. 1 mill."

"The devil she is!" spluttered Mr. Arthur Brigson. "This affair must be stopped – at once – now – oh Harold! – after all my care, thought and money!"

"It – must – not be stopped!" muttered young Harold in deep and measured tones. "It can't be stopped now – honourably!"

"What!" screamed the exasperated parent; "Come to that – my God! –" and he suddenly fell with a groan into his chair.

Mr. Brigson had truly divined the position of his son.

"Can it be the same sinful feeling," he asked himself, that led me into lustful error and racked my mind with evil anticipations when my ways were young and unbridled; the same feelings that have whipped me bitterly since for my wantonness of the flesh and my faithlessness to the woman who trusted me – too much – and worshipped me?"

Well, it wasn't exactly a similar disposition; perhaps better educational advantages had given it a more altruistic tone in the son, and perhaps it was qualified with a little more conscientiousness inherited from some other member of the family pedigree. The soul-aches would probably be more painful on the part of the son, for his animality was not so predominating, over the spiritual and conscientious, as in the case of the father.

A click of the door and in rushed Mrs. Brigson, tremblingly and breathlessly inquiring the matter.

Harold left his father moaning and sighing in the chair and he stepped in an agitated manner towards one of the windows admitting the light of the moon, whilst the servants awaited the events with anxious curiosity.

Mr. Brigson assured his wife that there was nothing to be alarmed about, and Harold left the room and the house, and hastened towards the rural spot where Matilda had arranged to meet him, during which, Miss Amelia Crewdson was making her way through an adjacent avenue of trees towards the residence of the Brigsons.

It was an idyllic evening. Harvesters singing and laughing as they returned from the fields, nodded to Harold as he sped on his errand of love.

True to her promise, Tilly was waiting, and as she greeted him with a smile of love, the thought of taking wicked advantage of her trustfulness and simplicity gave a painful shock to his agitated mind.

The more the situation approached a climax, the more wavering young Harold seemed to become. Whether to act heroically or villainously, caused him hours and hours of worry. The part of the villain would have been the better one, perhaps for material advantages.

His father and mother, with the assistance of Miss Amelia Crewdson, came to the old stereotyped conclusion – a three month's tour on the continent, to be accompanied by Miss Amelia. This they were confident, would bring the problem to an agreeable solution.

Harold received the mandate from his father with extreme indifference, and resolved within his mind to do no such thing. Had it been arranged to go on the Continent alone, he might have yielded, but he held Miss Crewdson in great dislike. She was not a creature of beautiful proportions, nor was she the type of woman suitable to the temperaments of the man she sought.

"Don't whip too severely, father!" Harold pleaded one morning.

"The lash cannot cut too deeply one way, my son," answered the father.

"And that way I presume is against Miss Matilda –"

"Miss Matilda!" repeated the father in injured and half-sneering tones, "Don't pollute this room with that name again, Harold! Good morning!"

"Good morning," replied the son; then under his breath, "and good-bye!"

Argument has little or no effect on young Harold; he was too young for that yet. He regarded all persuasions to cast Matilda Pryde aside as contrary to his honour. In time as the whims of youth left him, he might have submitted to the circumstances that were the curse of his relationship with Miss Amelia Crewdson. For the present, however, that was impossible.

* * *

The night previous to the morning on which Harold Brigson was to have departed for the Continent, "Fairfield," his home, was the rendezvous of many of his friends, who had come to present him with their good wishes during his brief absence from home.

But the night wore on and no Harold appeared. As the scene of animation and festivity became one of alarm and fear, Harold Brigson might have been seen stealthily entering No. 1 of Brigson's Mills, for what purpose only he and God could have known, at the time. Also half-a-mile away from the town, surrounded by darkness, the silent stars of the night, and big-limbed trees that swayed and moaned in the breeze, was Matilda Pryde, waiting and waiting, and growing afraid, chilly and disappointed.

"Oh, have the worst fears come true?" Tilly asked herself, "Am I deserted at last and disgraced? Is this the beginning of my endless sorrow?"

The Brigsons at Fairfield, and their friends, waited and waited too, until the hours of early morning, and Matilda Pryde, after returning home wept herself to sleep on an impoverished bed, and awoke with bitter feelings gnawing at her heart.

She went to her work at six o'clock in the morning in a paroxysm of sickness, and on reaching the mill door, she was met by Mary Morrison.

"Has ta heard, Tilly?" asked Mary excitedly.

"Heard what!" asked Tilly alarmed.

"T' young Mestur's shot hissel in t' scutchin[8] room!"

"He – what!" reeling backwards Matilda Pryde fell senseless on the mill steps.

"Is it true abeaut him botherin wi Tilly Pryde, I wonder?" asked Sally Oakes of Betsy Bibby in another part of the mill.

"True enoof, as anybody con see," was the reply; "what a terrible pity!"

So far as young Harold Brigson was concerned, however, the problem which had been the bane of his life, was settled; but the release of his soul was the beginning of Matilda Pryde's great sorrow.

Teddy Ashton, 'Greensauce Sketches. Georgie's Fust Day in t' Factory' (1897)

Yo'n been towd heaw Georgie Greensauce left Marton to goo warkin at a factory at Gilnow, an heaw he landed at his mother's cousin's husband's, Mestur Scrowlband, mill manager, who decided to make Georgie into th' odd mon at t' factory, as he were fit for nowt else.

* * *

Th' next morning, after breakfast, Mr. Scrowlband took Georgie to t' factory; an while they were on t' road – it were only abeaut five minutes' walk – he said, "After to-day theau'll ha to start thy wark afore breakfast – at six o'clock, not hauve-past eight."

"Durn't make no alterations on my acceaunt," returned Georgie. "Hauve-past eight's good enoof for me. I durn't believe i' warkin on t' wrung side o' my breakfast, nor on t' reet side noather, – if I con help it.

"I'this world, Georgie, we corn't please eaursels, but han for t' do as we must," said Scrowlband.

"Tell me summat as I durn't know," said Georgie.

"Theau'll ha t' mind what theau't doin i' t' factory, Georgie. There's whizzing wheels that'll trap thy fingers, and snaky straps that'll snatch thee up by t' yure o' t' yeard,[1] if theau't not as careful as an owd maid with her first wooer."

"An which is t' safest part o' t' factory?"

"Th' eautside," answered Scrowlband.

"Yo talk sense sometimes," said Georgie. "An what's yore job i' t' factory?"

"I'm t' manager," replied Scrowlband. "I walk abeaut an see that everythin's gooin on aw reet."

"Couldn't yo let me ha that job?" axed Georgie.

Scrowlband lowfed. "Theau't noan clever enoof for it," he said.

"Yo're cleverer than me, then?' axed Georgie.

"I should think I am," said Scrowlband.

"An yet yo'n geet wed?" said Georgie.

Scrowlband lowfed again. "That were in my green young days," he said.

"Should I tell yore wife that?" said Georgie.

"I'll gie thee a bat in t' yerhole if theau talks o' sich a thing," said Scrowlband.

"So yo're cleverer than me," said Georgie. "I shouldn't ha thowt it. An yo're a manager an ha nowt to do but walk abeaut an watch other folk wark because o' yore uncommon cleverness. There's summat wrung i' this do. For my opinion, I think as them that's noan clever should ha t' promenading jobs, while t' clever uns should be put to do t' clever wark; for, as yo say'n, it taks a sharp mon to mug among machinery, while any foo con walk abeaut wi a dickey[2] on."

Scrowlband smiled, but he didn't attempt to upset Georgie's argument. He said, "Well, theau mun be cautious, Georgie, that's aw; an theau'll ha' t' minders an piecers an t' wenches in t' cardreaum and weivin shed.[3] An there's another thing. Theau's never to tell nobody that theau't a relation o' mine, or my wife's rather; an if anybody should ax thee if theau't owt akin to me, theau munt say neow."

"I'll tak good care to do that," said Georgie, "for my own sake. Though I am a foo', I have my feelins."

Scrowlband thowt o' lowfin, but changed his mind, which put a quare an comic look on his face. They'd neaw reached t' factory, and went through t' watch-heause into t' wareheause. Scrowlband cawd one o' t' packers – a young chap named Charlie Webster – to him, an said, "Charlie, tak this youth and show him aw through t' mill. Show him everythin, and explain aw as theau con. He's comin to be th' odd mon here, and his name's Georgie Greensauce."

"Aw reet," said Charlie. "Come on," an he beckoned Georgie to follow him; while aw t' rest o' t' packers grinned merrily at Georgie's clownish appearance an remarkable yure. "We'll goo in t' cardreaum fust," said Charlie.

"Anywheer ull suit me," said Georgie, "so lung as I like it. But let me tell thee one thing. I'm no relation o' t' manager's."

Charlie looked puzzled, and then brasted eaut lowfin at this information. "I should think not," he said.

"Well, there's nowt to lowf abeaut," said Georgie. "I were only tellin thee. An durn't disremember it, or theau'll get me i' trouble, happen. I'm no relation o' t' manager's."

They went an looked at t' scutchers and jack-frames; an' multitude of wheels an straps, an t' dreadful din, amazed an freetent Georgie.

"Let's ge eaut o'this hobble-hole,"[4] he said. "I'm one o' them that likes a quiet life. I never could abide neise o' no soart."

"Theau'll ha' t' get used to it," said Charlie. "Besides doesn't ta know t' reason o' aw this uproar?"

"There con be no reason for it," said Georgie.

"But there is. Aw this din's made o' purpose to prevent t' wenches and women talkin to one another at their wark. Theau knows what females are; an con guess what a clatter o' tongues there's be i' this cardreaum if t' neise o' t' machinery didn't make talk impossible."

"I should never ha' thowt o' that," said Georgie. "It's noan a bad idea; for I darsay t' gabble o' so many females as there is here would be awful if we could only yer it."

"It would that an aw. So theau sees that aw this rattlin an roarin's really a mercy."

"Ay, though it's like cutting a mon's yead off to cure t' yeadwarch,"[5] said Georgie.

"But this din's nowt," said Charlie. "Wait till we getten i' t' weivin shade. Theau corn't yer neise for din theer."

Aw t' cardreaum lasses stared at Georgie an giggled one to another, and Charlie pood foo's faces an made aw soarts of mockin meemaws behind Georgie's back, till aw t' room were in a ticklin titter; an then they met one o' t' carders, an Charlie said, "This is Georgie Greensauce, eaur new loblorry,[6] an I'm showin him through.

"Ay," said Georgie to t' carder, "an think on this mestur, that I'm no relation o' t' managers."

Th' carder lowfed and wondered what the hek kind o' chump they'd getten in t' factory neaw. Then Charlie took Georgie throught' five spinnin reaums, an they met th' o'erlooker, an Georgie said to him, "Think on I'm no relatin o' t' manager's," an he said t' same thing to such o' t' minders as they seed at their wheel-ends; an they went back, deawn t' factory steps, through watchheause, an across t' yard to t' weivin shade, where Georgie impressively an conscientiously towd aw t' tacklers an several o' t' weivers that he were "no relation o' t' manager's," an repeated this statement so often to everybody that Charlie begun to wonder whether he were gradely reet[7] or not.

Indeed, lung before dinner-time it were a bye-word aw o'er t' place that Georgie were "no relation o' t' manager's," but luckily Scrowlband hadn't yet yerd on it.

But before t' factory stopped for baggin time[8] one o' th' o'erlookers went to Scrowlband and said, "There's been rare sport gooin on t-day."

"What o'er?" axed Scrowlband, wi a suspicious fear o' t' truth in his mind.

"That new odd mon," an th' o'erlooker chuckled. "He's been aw o'er t' factory tellin everybody that he were no relation o' yores."

"Th' dal foo'!"[9] roared Scrowlband. "Were thyere ever such an idiot allowed a meauth afore?"

Scrowlband went whum and awaited George's arrival. He coom in smiling. "Some o' t' spinners has been treatin me to a gill an –" he begun, when Scrowlband interrupted him so furiously that Georgie started quaking, an wisely kept near t' door.

"What the thunderin hek has ta been doin to-day?" bellowed t' manager. "Theau's been tellin everybody theau were no relation o' mine, an makin another lowfin-stock on me."

"I did that to please yo," said Georgie, humbly. "I thowt if I went reaund to everybody an towd 'em in t' beginning as I were no relation o' yores that it would prevent mistakes i' t' future."

"Mistakes i' t' future!" yelled Scrowlband. "I could purr thee back to Marton when I think o' what theau's done to-day. It were a monstrous mistake theau were ever born. I marvel what thy mother were thinkin abeaut."

"Yo, very likely," said Georgie, wheerat Scrowlband foamed an run at Georgie wi uplifted fist; but his wife copt howd of his arm and pood him back.

"Let t' lad a-be," hoo said. "He'll mend i' time."

"Mend!" said Scrowlband, despairingly, "there's no mendin for that sort but endin. This come o' listenin to thee."

Heawever, Scrowlband rapidly cooled; he were aw feigherworks; a big sharp flust,[10] then his temper were o'er. But he said, "Well, I'll try him for a week or two, an see heaw he goes on, but if he makes any mooar lowfin-stocks o' me I'll pack him straight back to Marton wi t' picture o' my boot-toe weel painted in his hide i' black an blue. An as it is, he murn't stop wi us. He mun have lodgin's fun somwheer else."

"I'll find him a place to-morn," said Mrs. Scrowlband. "Owd Widow Martin ull be glad of a lodger. Get thy tay, an do give o'er scowlin', do! Draw they cheer up, Georgie, an try to be a sensible lad for t' future."

"I'll be my best," said Georgie, "but I'm feart that this isn't t' best soart of a world for bein sensible in. There's too many foo's to interfere wi a chap.

Teddy Ashton, 'Th' Kock-Krow Club an' th' War. Darin Decision to Form a Kock-Krow Volunteer Corps to Batter th' Boers' (1899)

Bill Spriggs coom to me in a rare flutter t' other day.

"Teddy," said he, "I'm a patriot. I'm a 'Rule Britannia' chap. I'm a 'God save the Queen' felly. I'm a Hinglishmon."

"Nobody never said theau weren't," said I.

"An' they'd better not," said Bill, emphatically. "Caw a special meetin o' t' Kock-Krow Club. At once. To neet. This very neet."

"What for?" I axed.

"Th' Kock-Krow Club mun do its duty in this here war. England's attacked. Owd Kruger's feightin us, wi fifty theausand Boers at his back. Therefore we mun let Britannia know that th' Kock-Krow may be relied upon. We mun stond by t' Union Jack. We mun put eaur shoulders to th' Empire. We mun protect th' Queen. We mun do a little bit for Owd England. Just run reaund t'Fowt and tell eaur members there's bin a special 'War an Patriotic' meetin to-neet. Tell 'em if they durn't turn up I'll purr their ribs in wi my own feet. Also tallygraph to th' Owdham, Wigan, Rachda,[1] Bury, Preston, Liverpool, Bradford, Huddersfield, London, and everywhere-else branches to send their dellygates on by express train. For we mun have a good do to-neet. We mun let th' Boers see that Tum Fowt's determined to stond by Owd England – we mun show Owd Kruger that if he lays a finger on Britannia Tum Fowt will tak a run purr at him, wi aw its clugs, an punce him off his bloomin skeleton. So hurry up, Teddy. An write some poethry for to-neet if theau con – some poethry wi whiskey in it, that'll stir th' soul of every mon that hears it to t' roots of his yead. Off wi thee and do as I've towd thee."

There were nowt for it but to obey. A secretary's beaund to do as his President orders him.

So I did as I were towd, an did it so weel that th' owd "Dug an Kennel," neaw cawd "Kock-Krow Hotel," were packed in every part by eight o'clock at th' neet, th' time o' th' meetin. Kock-Krow dellygates had turned up fro aw parts of England, an were arriving aw t' time th' meetin lasted. Ruchut Roughyet fro

Owdham, Papper Tummy fro Bury, Siah Guster fro Wigan, Gillibra fro Chorley, an dozens mooar, were aw theer, excited and enthusiastic.

"By gow!" said Tommy Dod, "if owd Kruger could only see this noble an fierce meetin he'd want his breeches washin to-morn."

Bill Spriggs were in t' cheer, of course, an amid a greit clappin of honds an stampin o' feet, an brandishin o' pint pots, he geet up to open th' proceedins.

"Fellow Kock-y-Kaily Krowers," said Bill, "we're met heer to-neet for a greit purpose, a glorious purpose. (Cheers.) We're met here to show eaur loyalty to t' Queen an eaur pratoism[2] to eaur country, on which th' sun never sets, because we'n made special arrangements wi Providence to that effect. We're met here to stond by eaur grasy[3] Queen. (Loud applause, an singin o' "God save the Queen.") We're met here to show that Tum Fowt is true to Britannia in this here crisis. (Cheers.) We're met here to chuck defiance at owd Kruger (groans) and to tell him to his ugly owd face that if he'll only come to Tum Fowt any mon of us is ready to tackle him, fair up an square, clugs an aw in. (Wild clamour an excitement for ten minutes. "By Gow!" said Siah Guster, "I'll feight th' old badger any day, an i' my stockin feet."[4]) "We're met here," continued Bill, "to do eaur duty to eaur good owd country. Shall we be behind like a ceaw's tail? (Cries of "We'll be no ceaw's tails, will we hek as like!") "Australia's sendin a regiment to t' Transvaal, (cheers), Canidy's[5] sendin a regiment to t' Transvaal, (cheers) Indy's sendin a regiment to t' Transvaal, (cheers), every British colony's sendin a regiment to t' Transvaal, (cheers), an I ax shall Tum Fowt be left behind? (Cries o' "Never!") Well then, let Tum Fowt send a regiment o' volunteers to t' Transvaal! (Cheers.) Us Kock-Krow chaps all make terrific feighters; we're aw wed, (sighs); we'n faced matrimony, so war ull be nowt new to us (hurrah!); it'll be nobbut a little change for us. So let's sen a Kock-Krow regiment to th' Transvaal, to th' seat o' war, an we'll make th' Boers shiver i' their breeches. (Tremendous enthusiasm an cheers.) I neaw caw upon eaur noble an poetic secretary, Teddy Ashton, to read us some verses he's written for th' occasion, an though I durn't want to praise Teddy to his face, I'll bet that eaur Tum Fowt poet can turn eaut as good poethry as any mon – poet laureate or anybody else, – poethry that'll make a mon jump up, that'll stir his inside up, and that'll freeten t' Boers eaut o' their wits. I've greit pleasure in cawin on Teddy to read us his poethry" (loud cheers, an singin of 'For he's a jolly good fellow.')

When t' cheerin had quietened down I geet up an read t' following: –

LANCASHIRE'S SOULDIER LADDIES

Fro factory teawn an moorside breawn
Come Lancashire's souldier ladies,
As bould an hot as kilted Scot,
Or th' Fusilier Paddies;
So here's a cheer for th' Lanky[6] lads,
For they're aw theer, is th' Lanky lads;
Owd England would be nowhere, if it weren't for th' gradely Lanky lads.

Stupid owd Kru, silly owd foo,
At England has been slappin,
But he wouldn't ha done if he'd only known
What Lancashire were at scrappin –
For they'll wallop him thick will t' Lanky lads,
They'll make him sick, will t' Lanky lads,
An settle him quick – will t' rollickin, gradely Lanky lads.

Eaur colonies may send men to t' fray;
We give 'em hearty welcome,
But when t' Boers feel eaur Lanky steel
They'll think that here has hell come; –
They'll make 'em dance, will eaur Lanky lads,
They'll ha no chance wi eaur Lanky Lads,
They'll purr 'em to France, and Germany, eaur gradely Lanky lads.

There were vast cheerin an sheautin when I'd finished my verses, an Bill Spriggs jumped up, waving his arms, and sheauted, "Deawn wi yore names, them what's jeinin th' Kock-Krow Regiment."

There were fifty names deawn i' no time, an Bill Spriggs were made captain o' t' lot, while Tommy Dod yelled eaut that he'd stond th' expenses o' t' rifles an uniforms eaut of his own pocket.

It were decided to have a grey uniform, wi green facin's, an a cock crowin, in red, on t' breast o' t' tunic.

Then I wrote t' following letter, which were posted straight away to Lord Salisbury an Joe Chamberlain:[7] –

"Dear Mestur Salisbury and Chamberalin, – Yore humble servant is authorised by a large public meetin to tell yo that Tum Fowt is forming a Kock-Krow regiment, which will be on its road to embark at Liverpool soon after yo get this letter. Pleease tell t' Queen that Tum Fowt will stond by her. We know yo weren't refuse eaur offer, so that's why we're takkin it as accepted, an eaur regiment o' Tum Fowt volunteers is settin off as soon as it con. We're payin aw eaur own expenses, assisted by Mestur Tommy Dod, as loyal a little chap – retired pork butcher, an used to slaughter – as ever breathed th' breath of heaven. This might be a hint to Her Majesty to knight Mestur Dod th' next time hoo's distributin honours. For Tommy's a worthy man, and deserves it. Yo might tallygraf to t' Transvaal, so that Kruger will hear of it, that a Tum Fowt regiment's on his track. We think he'll give in beaut further feightin as soon as he hears that news. We hope so – in th' interests of peace, of course, – Yores gradely, on behalf of Tum Fowt,

"His mark **X** Bill Spriggs.

"Teddy Ashton, Sec."

Fred Plant, 'The Absent-Minded Beggar' (1900)

Westchester was *en fete*.[1]

The local reservists and a few who had volunteered out were about to have the usual "send-off."

The road leading to the station was thronged with a dense, cheering crowd, who had rushed from their hives and warrens to cheer the "noble few" on to victory – perhaps death.

Above the hubbub of the multitude the approaching strains of a band was heard.

"Here they come!"

The crowd, impelled by a mystic influence of enthusiasm, swerved right and left and onward.

In a somewhat sheltered corner near the entrance to the station, a girl, barely out of her teens, stood with her hands gripping the rusty railings and her pale face turned in the direction of the approaching band.

Her brown eyes were opened to their fullest and the breath came and left her parted lips in sharp, irregular gasps.

Her dress, which was of a tawdry-finery description, had become unfastened at the neck, disclosing a thin silver chain and the top portion of a small locket.

The crowd around the gates of the station became one mass of struggling humanity. Suddenly something in the form of a man wormed itself free and succeeded in gaining the sheltered spot wherein stood the girl.

"Hello, Liz!"

The girl turned quickly and, as she saw the ragged old man, her brow wrinkled.

"Who expected to see you here?" he went on. "Didn't know you'd heard, an' there's no getting to see you just lately."

"Shut up!"

"That's a nice way to speak to your ole dad, anyway."

"I tell you to shut up. I'm in no humour for talking to you just now, and you wouldn't be if you knew what I do."

"Oh, then you've heard, have you?"

"Heard what?"

"About Bill – your brother Bill."

Liz started.

"What about Bill?"

"There, I thought you didn't know! Bill's going out to help to pull Kruger's whiskers – going to do a bit for his Queen out in South Africa."[2]

"Has he got tired of doing a bit for her at the oakum job,[3] then?"

"That's sisterly, that is. You oughter feel proud of Bill. What's it matter what he's been now he's willing to do a bit for his country? He's a bloomin hero, is Bill, and'll do his whack with the best of 'em. See! Can you see the red jackets? Ah, his nibs, the Mayor, is making a speech from the balcony yonder ... But you haven't told me yet. If it isn't Bill you've come to see off, who is it?"

"Lieutenant Bancroft."

The girl's father gave a low whistle.

"You don't mean to say that old Squire Bancroft's lad is – is your mash?"[4]

"And has been for six months," said Liz. "Who do you think gave me the money to get you out of quod[5] with?"

Then her lips tightened and she partly turned away.

"Well, I am surprised," said the father. "He's leaving you all right, eh?"

"He wanted to do, but I wouldn't take anything. He's going to marry me when he comes back from the war. I'm going to go back to the shirt making and wait till he does come back. That means you needn't hang about me any longer for money. When me and Len are married I'll see you don't go hungry, bad as you've been to me."

"Marry you! Oh, oh"!

"Yes. What are you laughing about? Marry me? Yes! He told me only – only yesterday."

"And you believed him?"

"Why shouldn't I? Didn't they want him to marry that rich Miss Hurlingham? And didn't he refuse to do because of me?"

"He'd tell you that, of course, but he never introduced you to his father and mother, did he?"

"Well, and if he didn't, he will do when the time comes – he said so."

The dissipated parent laughed and said Liz was a "silly jay."

The next moment the crowd in front of the gates parted right and left before the line of mounted police and the honoured handful of red jackets hove in sight. Foremost amongst them was Lieutenant Bancroft, a tall, fair-haired young fellow of stalwart build.

As Liz beheld him a soft wailing sound left her lips. But the sound stopped short in a muffled gasp as she saw, walking at Bancroft's side, with her gloved hand upon his sleeve – Miss Helen Hurlingham. Her face was up-turned to his in pride and she was whispering something, which caused him to pat her cheek in playful remonstrance.

Liz dashed her hand across her eyes and forced herself through the human wall in front. Her mantle had fallen from her shoulders in the struggle and her mass of dark hair hung in long wavy braids down each side of her face. The band blared and thousands of voices sang "God Save the Queen." All at once the Lieutenant became aware that someone – a woman – had placed herself directly in his path.

It was Liz.

One brief glance he gave then his face clouded.

"Len?"

"Kindly allow us to pass, my good girl," said Lieutenant Bancroft. And as a blue-coated officer swept Liz aside the gallant Lieutenant whispered to his lady-love, "We can excuse many things at a time like this – even to people of that class addressing one by one's pet name."

Like one in a dream Liz was carried along the platform of the station.

And as she stood with her white face uplifted, to catch one tender look from her false lover, a hand was placed on her shoulder.

"Wot, oh! Liz! Haven't you got a word to say to your brother before he goes away?"

On the footboard of the train Lieutenant Bancroft had stooped and kissed Miss Hurlingham upon the lips and then upon the third finger of her left hand. The next moment he had entered the train as though the parting had been too much for him.

"Yes, Bill," whispered Liz. "I have something to say to you. I want you to do something for me out in Africa. I want you to kill Lieutenant Bancroft! But for him I should have gone right – as the old mother told me to do ... He promised me last night that I should be his wife when he comes home. I should have been his wife before he went away – you understand! ... And today he doesn't know me!"

"Can't do it, Liz; it ain't in the regulations; and Bancroft ain't a miser with his money. Buck up; you'll be all right. We're off for a slice o' South Africa, and it'll be shared out when we get back."

* * *

The train steamed out of the station. The multitude went back to their hives and warrens. But next morning a girl's bedraggled body rocked with the river and upon the still white breast nestled a locket, one of the things Lieutenant Bancroft had "left behind him" – a locket, containing his photograph.

WORKMAN'S TIMES

Anon., 'Sunshine and Shadow', *Workman's Times*, 22 October 1892, p. 2.

'Citizen', 'The Blackleg', *Workman's Times*, Chapter I, 12 August 1893, p. 1; Chapter II, 19 August 1893, p. 1; Chapter III, 26 August 1893, p. 1; Chapters IV and V, 2 September 1893, p. 1; Chapter VI, 9 September 1893, p. 4; Chapter VII, 16 September 1893, p. 4; Chapter VIII, 23 September 1893, p. 1; Chapter IX, 30 September 1893, p. 1; [Chapter X], 7 October 1893, p. 5; Chapters XI and XII, 14 October 1893, p. 1; Chapter XIII, 21 October 1893, p. 4; Chapter XV, 28 October 1893, p. 4; Chapter XVI, 4 November 1893, p. 3; Chapter XVI, 11 November 1893, p. 4; Chapter XVII, 18 November 1893, p. 4; Chapter XVIII, 25 November 1893, p. 4; Chapters XIX and XX, 2 December 1893, p. 1; Chapter XXI, 9 December 1893, p. 1; Chapter XXI, 16 December 1893, p. 1; Chapter XXII, 23 December 1893, p. 1; Chapter XXIII, 30 December 1893, p. 1.[1]

Martin Fair, 'Nan: A New Year's Eve Story', *Workman's Times*, 30 December 1893, p. 4.

Dan Baxter, 'A Terrible Crime', *Workman's Times*, 30 December 1893, p. 2.

The *Workman's Times* (1890–4), first published on 29 August 1890, was owned by John Andrew (n.d.) and edited by Joseph Burgess. This weekly periodical was priced at one penny and published first at Huddersfield, then London and finally Manchester, before ceasing publication on 17 March 1894. It also briefly published local editions for Birmingham, Hull, Tyneside, Teeside, Sheffield, Staffordshire and the Midlands. The periodical was used by Burgess to organize the foundation of the ILP, but despite this Keir Hardie refused to adopt the periodical as the party's official organ and instead used his own *Labour Leader*. The *Workman's Times* suffered from competition from both the *Labour Leader* and Robert Blatchford's popular *Clarion*, despite including contributions from socialists such as Hardie, John Trevor of the Labour Church, Katherine St John Conway and Robert Blatchford.

Of the four authors included in the selection for this volume, the anonymous author has not been identified, and no biographical details have been found for

Martin Fair. Full biographical details for 'Citizen' are given in the headnote for the *Clarion* in this volume on p. 3; Dan Baxter's details are given in the headnote for *Justice*, also in this volume on p. 48.

Notes

1. The chapter numbering across the serialization of 'The Blackleg' was not always continuous: following the publication of Chapter XV in the 28 October issue, there is no Chapter XIV, and the next two chapters in the issues for 4 and 11 November are both numbered XVI. This repetition may have signified the continuation of a single chapter, but as there is a distinct break between Goodman and Garnish's conversation in the 4 November issue and the narrative voice that opens the issue of 11 November, it may be assumed that this was a mistake in the writing or printing process. Similarly, the chapters for 9 and 16 December are both numbered XXI, despite a clear break in focus and chronology between these chapters. Furthermore, the instalment for the 7 October issue, Chapter X in the series, was published without a chapter number. It is clearly a coherent chapter, and the omission is likely to be a printing error.

Anon., 'Sunshine and Shadow' (1892)

"The glamour of th' impassioned South
About her beauty lies;
A mellow cheek, a scarlet mouth,
And Dark, beseeching eyes.

"My old belief in truth and trust
She brings back sometimes yet;
Ah! You are smiling? Well, you must!
You never knew Arlette."[1]

"Do look at Arlette Alvard! I declare, the child reminds me of nothing else in this world so much as a bright-winged butterfly. Like it, she has lived only in the sunshine, and I do believe that the cold frosts of adversity or sorrow would kill her just as easily. Arlette was made for the sunshine of life, God bless her! not its shadows."

Thus spoke the kind, sweet-voiced matron of Madame St. Aubrey's Seminary to one of the teachers, who stood with her at a window watching the final departure of a bevy of fair "girl graduates" of that time-honoured institution.

And she smiled through a mist of tears as she waved her handkerchief again in answer to Arlette's last salute, and then the carriage whirled away toward the great arched gateway of the drive, and the "bright-winged butterfly" was taking her first unfettered flight into the wide world beyond.

"Good-bye, Arlette, good-bye! Give our love to Lilias, and tell her we should all like to be her bridesmaids," called one and another of the envious girls who had still a year or two of boarding school life before them.

And Arlette sent back a gay retort to each and every one, though there were tears in the laughing voice and a mist in the great, soft, gipsy-dark eyes as they dwelt with a last lingering look on the dear old seminary.

But sadness could not long enchain her thoughts, especially when the immediate future held so much to interest them.

For was she not going to spend a gay two months with Lilias Minden, her dear old school friend, who had graduated two whole years ago? And at the close of those two months was she not going to realise the very desire of her heart – to be the brilliant "maid of honour" at the marriage of her darling, lovely Lilias?

With such a fascinating prospect as that in view Arlette soon forgot her parting tears.

Her old school-fellow received her with open arms.

"So you, too, have left school for ever?" said Miss Minden, presently, with a touch of sadness, as it seemed. "Don't you regret it just a little bit, Arlette?

"Regret it? No, indeed," retorted the emancipated schoolgirl with a bright, silvery laugh. "Of course I was sorry to part with all the girls – and teachers too, for that matter – for I like them every one. But with such glorious times ahead – Oh, Lilias, how could I regret it?"

And her great black eyes glowed like two brilliant stars.

"Just think of being out in the big, gay world as free as the air at last; think of the balls, and theatres, and travelling, and – Oh, a long time from this you know" – with a laugh and a quick-rising blush – "a lover and a wedding of my own, perhaps. And – Why, goodness gracious! Lilias" – with a look of intense wonder as she saw a strange, unaccountable shadow sweep across her friend's fair face – "you don't regret that your school days are over, do you?"

"Nonsense! Of course I don't, you goose," laughed Lilias, with an instant change of look and manner. "Haven't I enjoyed all those gaieties which you are just anticipating? And isn't my own marriage with the best fellow in the world only a few weeks distant? What a fanciful child you are."

"You will not have the pleasure of seeing Vernon for several days yet," she added, smiling, "as a business matter has called him away from town. So you will have to curb your impatient curiosity, and put up with my poor society as a substitute until he comes."

"I'll try to make that do," laughed Arlette, gaily. "And now I just want a bunch of roses to make myself presentable for tea. And, oh, what lovely roses you have got, Lilias!" she cried eagerly, as she glanced through the open window. "I'll just run down into the grounds and get an armful."

And she was out of the house in a moment, flying down the gravel walk to the wilderness of roses beyond the lawn, a happy light in her dark eyes and a song on her scarlet lips, as she flitted from one rose bush to another, like the "bright-winged butterfly" to which the matron had likened her.

All at once some slight noise drew her attention, and looking up quickly, she saw – leaning against the low stone wall which ran below the terrace with his arms crossed carelessly on its tops, and his eyes following her every movement with smiling admiration – the handsomest young man Arlette had ever seen.

She had no idea who he was; but she saw, as he gracefully lifted his had, that his light-brown hair fell in little wavy ripples away from a proud, bold brow; that his eyes the bluest, surely, that ever were created, and that the smile which lighted up all his frank, handsome face was simply irresistible.

And so all those half-formed dreams, which had hitherto floated vaguely about in her girlish mind, suddenly crystallised about this fascinating stranger and all in a moment Arlette's heart thrilled with the consciousness that it had met its king.

Not that Arlette really understood that she had fallen in love; but she felt as if it were all a delightful dream when her handsome hero vaulted lightly over the low wall, and with a graceful apology, to her that he was about to call at the house, and begged to assist her in carrying the roses.

"When I heard you singing" he explained, "I thought at first it was Miss Lilias, or I should not have stopped there as I did. I am a friend of hers, you know," he added, with a smile.

So they walked back to the house together, he rambling from one topic to another in his easy, amusing fashion; and she saying little, but listening with a shy, half-dreamy air that was infinitely charming.

In the hall they met Lilias, who stopped short, with a look of astonishment.

"Vernon," she exclaimed, giving the young man her hand, with a welcoming smile, though the expression of her fair face scarcely changed. "Why, what a surprise. You were not detained in the city, then, as you expected. And you and Arlette have already become acquainted, I see," she added, laughingly.

"I found this young lady among the roses, where, it would seem, she naturally belongs. But, as for being acquainted –"

And he gave his fair *fiancée* and expressive glance which brought about a formal introduction instantly.

Poor Arlette! her heart had almost ceased beating when she heard that first exclamation of surprise from Lilias, as they entered the hall.

She felt the warm blood ebbing from her cheeks as she turned aside, listening, as in a dream, to the greeting between the two affianced lovers.

So this man was Vernon Hildreth – Lilias' future husband?

Arlette could not have told you why it was, but she knew that, all in one brief moment, life had changed for her, and it could never be the same again.

It was a struggle which had to be constantly renewed, for no day passed thereafter in which she and Vernon Hildreth did not meet.

Sometimes she trembled under a glance from those blue eyes of his, which seemed to flash to her inmost heart a secret that she dared not think of.

Could it be that he loved her – loved her instead of Lilias?

Arlette bowed her beautiful dusk face upon her hands, and wept passionate tears of shame and anguish.

"Oh, if Lilias would only quarrel with me, or do something, so that I could leave her," she sobbed, like a passionate child. "Why doesn't she see it all? Oh, I must go away; I cannot bear it!"

"Arlette!" said a low, husky voice close beside her.

She started up with a stifled cry, but Vernon Hildreth took her arm, and gently drew her down again upon the garden seat from which she had risen.

"Arlette, I understand your trouble, darling; do you think you suffer alone?" he asked, his strong voice choking. "Oh, Arlette, my lovely Southern flower, don't you know how I love you? My God, how hard it is to bear!"

"You are a coward, Vernon Hildeth!" cried the girl, proudly shaking off the clasp of his hand upon her arm. "You – almost the husband of my friend –"

"Arlette, Arlette! you must not despise me," he broke in, passionately. "Could I help loving you when I found you there among the roses? Could I help it when I saw you every day after that, and your sweet eyes sometimes spoke to me to innocently the language of your heart? But have no fears, Arlette. I will never be disloyal to Lilias – never again," he went on, with a kind of bitter pathos in his voice. "My heart would have its way this once, or break; but you can trust me hereafter, little one. It is hard to think that we met too late, but – Oh, forgive me, darling. I shall atone bitterly enough for this one sweet moment."

And catching her suddenly to his heart, he pressed a dozen impassioned kisses on the lovely scarlet lips that would have scorned him so, and as suddenly releasing her, went swiftly away from her side, leaving his heart for ever in her keeping.

Before she slept that night Arlette spoke to Lilias of her wish to be released from her promised attendance at the marriage.

Lilias raised her lovely blue eyes with a look of intensest wonder.

"Why, what are you thinking of, Arlette?" she asked, reproachfully. "I will never forgive you if you desert me know."

And Arlette, the proudest, the palest, and the loveliest of maids, stood beside her friend at the altar, and listened calmly to the vows which changed the sunshine of her own life to shadows.

* * *

"Arlette, you will not refuse to love me now?" pleaded Vernon Hildreth three years later. "It was her wish – her last wish, darling. And – the strangest thing of all is that poor Lilias died of a broken heart."

"A broken heart!" exclaimed Arlette, her rich, dusk cheeks and scarlet lips growing pale. "Then you allowed her to guess –"

"No, not for one instant," he interrupted earnestly. "But – she confessed to me just before she died, Arlette, that her heart had passed from my keeping to another's long before our wedding-day. Someone she had met in her travels abroad. And it was honour alone that made her give her hand to me. Oh, Arlette, could we only have known."

And the strong man bowed his head upon his hands.

"Fate has willed it so," answered Arlette, softly. "Oh, Vernon, what a strange blending of sunshine and shadow all our lives have been."

'Citizen', 'The Blackleg' (1893)

[12 August 1893]

Chapter I.

It was a grand majority!

There had been municipal elections in the town and Mr. Crushem, of the respectable and influential firm of Crushem and Grindem, was the Liberal candidate. There were also other candidates – two of them – one a Tory of the old school, and also respectable, strictly within the meaning of the act; the other a Labour candidate, an ex-employee of the firm of Crushem, Grindem and Co., and not respectable, strictly within the meaning of the act.

Besides, the successful candidate, the senior member of the eminently respectable and influential firm of Crushem and Grindem, was a Home Ruler, in favour of justice to Ireland; so likewise was the Labour candidate a Home Ruler and an Irishman.

But, of course, not being respectable, he didn't count.

Thus, the grand majority.

The senior member of the firm was not what you might call a self-made man, but his father before him was, and what the senior member now enjoyed in worldly goods was claimed to have been made by his father.

I say *claimed* advisedly, and without prejudice. Previous to the election Mr. Crushem had not been known in local circles and had not made his mark in local politics.

But what he had omitted in the local Council Chamber he made up for in the local hospital, and there, at least, there were unmistakable marks of his commercial fitness in the number of cripples recruited from his firm.

Some of the cripples formed the grand majority, being free and independent electors and Home Rulers in favour of justice to Ireland.

Of course the grand majority of 400 were not all cripples, because some were in the workhouse and had *no votes* or things, except two who had gone to the workhouse after the sitting of the Revision Court[1] and were still on the register.

For these two the senior member sent his carriage, and in return for the master's kindness they voted for him.

Which was as it should be, of course.

Mr. Crushem was essentially a religious, God-fearing man, strictly within the meaning of the act. So much so, that he had gone to the expense of building a corrugated iron chapel, with a tinpot bell on the gable end, which religiously every Sunday morning, at 10.15 a.m. prompt, commenced a creaking, clanging, horrible discord, the creaking of the rusty old frame and the grunts of the equally rusty old bellringer almost equalising the clatter of the rusty old tongue inside the demoralised pan-mug dignified by the name of bell, which ceased with a strange and welcome abruptness the moment the foot of Mr. Crushem crunched the cinders on the floor. The congregation were also some of the grand majority, and composed entirely of the more or less respectable portion of Messrs. Crushem and Grindem's employees at the docks, dubbed by the irreverent and disrespectful employees of the firm as "the tin chapel gang," who were always sure of a full week.[2]

Of course, such opinions as those entertained by the irreverent were not respectable, and were therefore looked upon with disfavour by Mr. Crushem, who never lost an opportunity of preaching on the enormity of the sin of disobedience to their superiors, and the parable of "Be ye content in the position in which God has placed ye."[3]

Amongst the irreverent employees there were those who contended that they were not in that position, and, who as those who composed the minority votes of 180 cast for the labour candidate at the election, declared that a just and merciful God, in whose sight all men are equal, brought Crushem into the world naked as well as themselves. Whereas, they and their wives and children were still almost in that position, that they had built up the fortune of Crushem, Grindem, and Co., wherewith he was able to procure carriages and horses, meat and wine, and purple and fine linen.[4]

Needless to say, such expressions were shocking to the moral, commercially-trained, Christian mind of Crushem, who, with a truly Christian spirit, determined to show those miserable sinners the error of their ways, as the sequel of this story will prove.

Among the more irreverent portion of the employees was one John Goodman, whose father before him and himself had served a lifetime in the service of the firm.

The old man and his wife had ended their days in the workhouse, while John was yet in his teens. Now John was married, and until he began to entertain such extreme opinions, was a member of the constant gang.

And as it is from the commencement of John's irreverence that our story dates, and I wish my readers to bear in mind, had John not commenced to be disrespectful and irreverent, this story would not have commenced at all – that I venture to offer an excuse for a rather descriptive, but none the less necessary opening.

And so, the first scene of the drama is laid in the vicinity of some arches, on a bleak, cold, cheerless January morning in the year 1889 at 6 o'clock a.m.

Notwithstanding the fact that the hiring does not commence until 6.15, for fully an hour previous, the fitful splutter of the one solitary asthmatic gas lamp would disclose to a close observer groups of men endeavouring to shelter from the piercing wind and sleet, behind the numerous pillars, while in through the gate a continual stream of shivering, scanty clad humanity was wending its way to be swallowed up under the arches in the same mysterious manner.

In one of these gangs was John Goodman, and five or six of his mates, who had just arrived at the door of the policeman's hut in one of the abutments of the massive granite dock gate.

The policeman standing in the door, from which could be seen within a cheerful roaring coal fire, greets John, as an old acquaintance, with a cheery "Good mornin', Jack; fine weather for your business!"

"Mornin', Bob," says Jack, "Aye, lad, the weather's purty tough; but we can stand the weather if the business is as plentiful. Have you noticed has the boss arrived yet?"

"Not yet, my lad," says the policeman. "Won't you step inside till the cab comes? You look wet through already. Not in good trim to face a day like this. Where's your oilskins?"[5]

"No, thank you," answered Jack. "Your fire will only make me nesh[6] for the rest of the day. As for my oilskins – well, they've gone the way of all my togs to keep the bums[7] out."

"I'm sorry to hear that, old man," said the policeman. "I allers thought you were strict T.T.[8] When did you break?"

"I'm much obliged for your sympathy, mate, but I'm still strict T.T., and I haven't broke at all, only spoken my mind to the boss, and voted at the election for the Labour candidate."

"H'm, bad policy that, Jack, for a working man, especially you as had such a good job once. Take my advice, lad, and chuck it. It's not a paying game," said the policeman.

"Sorry I can't oblige yer, mate," said Jack. "You're quite right about the paying part of the business, but I'm goin to see it out for all that."

"Aye, well, you know your business best, my lad," said the policeman. "Hullo, here comes the boss's cab. You'd better hurry up and secure a front place at the arches, as I heard him say last night to the foreman as how he'd only start two hatches with deal in if the weather was wet, and there's as many poor, half-starved devils passed through here since five o'clock as would man all the ships in the port," and with a cheery "good luck to you," the bobby shut himself and the blazing fire in from the blinding sleet, and the serried, struggling, half-starved mass of humanity fighting and tearing the few rags off each other's back, in their eagerness to look piteously and abjectly into the face of the man and beg for the privilege to work wherewith they might live on the crumbs that fell from his table, provided for with their labour.

The bobby was right. The hiring was over, and out of the three thousand men that presented themselves only thirty were employed, and, strange to say, Jack Goodman one of the thirty.

"I wonder what struck old Hoppy to put Jack on this morning," said Chris Kennedy, a white-haired, weather-beaten old veteran, one of the few remaining connecting links of the old time crab-hand winch[9] days.

"Maybe he's a Townie," suggested Tom Rogers.

"The devil a fear in him," said Christie, "and if he was there's not that much love 'atween them, for ever since Jack shook the false teeth out iv Hoppy, he hates Jack as the devil hates holy water."

"That's so," said another, "and if ye noticed, mates, there wur none of the tin-pot chapel gang out this morning, and take my word for it if it clears up 'tween now and dinner you'll see every mother's son of 'em out, and Jack and his gang broke to make room for them."

"I wonder what ould Hoppy's got his knife inter Jack for so deep," said one of the crowd, "he used to be the first man on before Hoppy got promoted."

"Well, min," said Christie, "that's a long story, too long to tell here, wid de wind wislin through our rags, and as I'm acquainted wid de hist'ry and have no inclination to face de ould Dutch[10] and childre' and take de bit o' tommy[11] from dem, little enough for themselves. I votes as how we goes and bites de lug in de cocoa room man fur pints o' cocoa till Saturday on spec,[12] and I'll tell ye all about it."

This humane proposition was unanimously agreed to, though some doubts were expressed as to its success, as the cocoa man's slate bore mute but eloquent evidence of previous good intentions not yet redeemed, but Christie's eloquence proved equal to the occasion, and having comfortably settled themselves behind their pints of hot water dignified by the name of cocoa, Christie commenced his narrative.

"Well, boys," said he, as he took a sip of the "scaldy,"[13] "they say it's uncharitable to look a gift horse in de mouth, but s'elp me iv this stuff doesn't beat Banagher,[14] and as yez know he bet de devil."

"Aye," said Barney Bropby, "but he hasn't beat the devil's father, and that's Crushem, Grindem and Co."

"What's that got to do with bloomin' cocoa?" said another.

"Everything to do with it," said Barney, "don't you know that Crushem, Grindem and Co., are the biggest shareholders and directors of the company who run these houses?"

"That's so, Barney," said Christie, "and what's more, these places wur started under de cloak iv philanthropy, to give us a square meal at a fair price. They said as how they didn't want any profits, and now they're a-paying 15 per cent. and if you notice when Crushem sends us supper money, it's allers close on eleven o'clock when we can go nowhere else but inter his own cocoa rooms, and all the subs come back to him in dividends. But let's get on wid de story."

"I don't suppose as how anyiv ye, but ould Barney there, knows as how one time Jack's wife, who's well up in book larnin,[15] was a governess in Crushem's house, when Hoppy, after he got the hurt that has given him de limp, was made timekeeper, and a kind of bob-lolly-boy[16] round de garden and stables, when nothin' else was a-doin'."

"Aye, and a cheeky whelp he was," said Barney, "when he got his stripes."

"Well then, boys," said Christie, "yer must know as how Jack, who is a fine-built chap, and well larned, too, for a docker's son, as, God rest ould Billy Goodman's soul, may be thanked for that, as he kept the young 'un to school till he wur over fifteen, intending him for a schoolmaster iv he'd a lived. But, as yer know, boys, when he died, Jack had to take on de support iv de family as wur left orphans; and, though heavily handicapped, he managed to keep at his book larnin.

"Well, by all accounts, Jack, on account of his smartness, was med kind of under timekeeper before Hoppy came to work fur de firm, and being much about de boss's house, made acquaintance wid his present missus, and they at once fell to-courtin'.[17]

"Jack was allers a straight, upright chap, and never wur guilty iv a mean action – as you know, boys, none iv us wur ever robbed iv our time before Hoppy got promotion.

"But when Hoppy did get promoted, you all know how he used to work us on till half-past the hour fur knockin' off, and told Jack not to book us anything extra, and now Jack refused and booked us full time.

"Well, along o' this, Hoppy began a-casting sheep's eyes at Jack's gal up at the house, and the gal, she ups and tells Jack how he's a-persecutin iv her.

"So one day Jack loses his temper in the shed when de boss is present, and who has been primed by Hoppy for some time again Jack until de boss gets prejudiced.

"So this day Hoppy makes a narsty, sneering remark about Jack and his gal, when Jack goes for him, and picks him up, and shakes him till his false teeth drop out, and all de boys laughs.

"Of course the boss disrates Jack, who leaves in a huff, and Hoppy gets his place, and still persecutes de gal, who leaves her place and marries Jack, who now earns his livin' wid a hook instead iv a pen,[18] and he's just as good a man with one as the other, as ye all know, mates.

"And that there's de secret of Hoppy's dislike to Jack. How he come to put him on this mornin' I don't know. He's got a reason for it, never fear. He's one iv those e're chaps who does nothing for nobody without receiving summat back."

"Aye, mates," said Barney, "another thing Christie forgot to tell you, and that is, before Hoppy got to be boss there was no rushing and shoutin' at the men, no "tin chapel gang," and very few accidents. Now the ship is manned by chaps as lives in houses owned by Hoppy, and who enter all their family in Hoppy's books, as he collects for a burial society, and never a day passes but what someone leaves in the ambulance for the hospital opposite."

"Hush! Listen!" said Christie, as the rumbling of wheels, and the shrill burr-r-r of the ambulance whistle to clear the road is heard. "Here comes another victim, and I'll lay ten to one its from the men who were put on this mornin'. Let's go out and see."

When they get outside, the ambulance is drawn up before the hospital door, and the men are lifting out a crushed, bleeding form. Christie presses forward to see, and reels back and staggers as if struck when he sees the features of the victim.

He clutches Barney, and turns to him with a face as white as the form on the stretcher, exclaiming "My God! Barney, mate, it's Jack;" and sinking down on the steps, mutters, "Oh! the – murderin' thief. He had a reason for puttin' him on."

[19 August 1893]

Chapter II.

There were two passengers in the ambulance the second one being a youth about 16 years old, with his left arm horribly mangled and his face crushed out of semblance of his former self.

It happened thus:

When Jack Gooodman reached the ship at twenty minutes to seven – the starting time being seven o'clock – the first job given to him by Hoppy was to reeve off a fall (rope for hoisting cargo) in the empty gin on the main hatch spars.[19]

In order to do this it was necessary either to lower the span,[20] or hoist a man up to the span. It was too much trouble to slack off the span, and so Jack, having made a bowline[21] in the rope, and sitting in it with the end of the rope he was to reeve in his hand, gave the signal to the youth in charge of the fall to hoist away, and be careful.

He in turn looked round for the lad turning on the steam, and told him to "go ahead the winch." The steam was turned on, but before Jack was half way up the span, the boy at the winch was called away by Hoppy, and the shaky old valve of the shaky old winch took charge by turning itself on at its own sweet will much to the alarm of the boy in charge of the fall, which, owing to the wet rope on a dry and heated drum, was beginning to singe, to the danger of Jack, suspended between heaven and the ship's deck.

The youth, seeing no-one at the valve, reached over with is left hand to ease it, when –

His jacket was caught in the unguarded cogs of the winch, dragging him in among the machinery, crunching the clothes and bones of his poor body into one unshapable mass. In his endeavour to save himself he lets go the rope, and down comes Jack with a sickening thud on the half-covered hatches, which alone saved him from being dashed to pieces 30 feet below.

I shall now ask my readers to come with me inside the hospital, which will entail a further descriptive inquiry into its surroundings and associations. The most striking and prominent feature of the institution is the porter, who rules the inmates and visitors with a rod of iron – so to speak that is to say, if the inmate or visitor is not fortunate enough to have a rod of silver to counteract the aforesaid rod of iron.

The porter is not one of the tin chapel gang; but is one of the grand majority.

Thus his position of head porter, because Mr. Crushem is a member of the Hospital Committee, and when the annual balance sheet of the hospital is published Mr. Crushem's name appears as a subscriber for a large sum.

It never entered the mind of the grand majority that if they returned Labour candidates there would be less cripples and less necessity for hospitals and impudent, well-fed, callous hospital porters and things.

Such an idea had entered the mind of the irreverent, who, were endeavouring to found a trades union and drive the trade out of the port, &c., &c., when there would be no use for such glorious humane institutions as hospitals, and strange to say such ideas were also entertained by no less a person than the house surgeon of the hospital, who was now examining the two patients, and asking questions of Christie, who after a herculean struggle with the fat rod of iron porter, had forced his way into the ward where his friend lay.

"Luk id here, dochter," said Christie, pointing to the porter, who looked as if he was going to explode from supressed wrath, "iv yez don't take that mis-shapen cork-fender out o' mi sight, yez'll have three cases instead of two on yer hands."

"Hush! speak easy, my lad," said Doctor Smythe. "Is he a friend of yours?"

"He is, sir," said Christie.

"H'm, very well, now, be calm, and you can stay here with him for a while," and turning to the porter he said, "It's all right, Bolger. Let him stay a while."

"Can't do that, sir," spluttered Bolger, "it's against the rules, and I'll report it to the chairman of committee."

"Very well, Bolger," said Dr. Smythe, "make your report, and by the way," as Bolger with a grunt of dissatisfaction turned to go, "I want you to let me know when Mr. Crushem arrives, as I also have a report to make to him, that these two accidents make a total of 11 from his firm during the month, and" – with emphasis – "mind you don't forget, Bolger, or I may perhaps add to my report a few items which have lately come to my knowledge which may perhaps necessitate a change in your department."

"Holy smoke, dochter, but yez hit him hard that time," said Christie. "But what's your opinion o' poor Jack? Will he pull through?"

"Can't say yet, my lad," answered the doctor, "he's badly hurt. A very bad fracture of the skull, which would have proved fatal immediately with a man of less robust constitution; but he's evidently a man who has not abused himself, and the chances are that he may pull through with great care. Is he married?"

"Aye, that he is, sir, to one o' the dacentest craturs that ever wore an apron, an' it's a' most a pity she wears one, as she's as good a man as Jack."

"Very well, now," said the doctor, "you'd better go, my lad, and break the news to her gently. Don't alarm her unnecessarily. Just tell her to come down here, and while you are away I'll make arrangements for her to stop to-night until the danger is over, and if he lives to-night he will pull through nicely. As for the youngster, I'm afraid his case is hopeless, and I don't know but what he'll be better off out of this grinding, crushing, competitive world than to be forced to stay in it a helpless cripple to suffer a more cruel death of starvation, as I believe he is the orphan of a man who lost his life in the same trade."

"That's so, dochter," said Chris. "God bless yer, sir; but yer one o' the right sort. I'll be off and break the news to Jack's gal as gently as I can, though pon mi sowl I dun no how I'm a goin to manage it; but," giving himself a shake and buttoning up his old rags with an air of determination, "here goes in de name of God, and may he grant de poor chap a longer lease of life to carry out his wish iv dooin something to make de life iv a docker more aisy and secure than it is at present. Good day, dochter, and God's blessin be wid yer."

"Good day, my lad," said Doctor Smythe, "and may your wishes be realised, for heaven knows it's wanting."

So while Christie is away on his gruesome errand I take the opportunity of introducing my readers to the doctor.

Doctor Alexander Smythe was the son of a true blue Tory father, proud of his family history and antecedents, who always "voted at their party's call, and never thought of thinking for themselves at all," and who looked upon any deviation from the blatant Jingoism of his forefathers as rank treason to the honour of his family and his gracious queen.[22]

His position in the commercial world as a prosperous stockbroker, or, more strictly speaking, a gambler in the products of other men's labour, had enabled him to give his son Alexander a liberal education, with the result that Alexander had graduated at Oxford successfully in every respect, and had chose surgery as a profession, in which he was rapidly attaining a prominent position.

Alexander had also graduated in political thought; but alas! for the hopes of his father (who looked forward to the time when his son would take up the Parliamentary history of the family denied to him), Alexander had contracted a vicious and inexcusable habit of thinking for himself.

It came about this: –

The 'Varsity in the young days of Alexander's father was a close corporation strictly monopolised by sons of the privileged classes, who blindly followed their equally blind tutors along the darkened path of political economy, accepting the law of supply and demand as fulcrum and lever of our social system.

But "it came to pass"[23] that there was a slight difference in the elements constituting the 'Varsity of Alexander's own days; a sprinkling of the sons of the common people had by some mysterious means gained admission and fought their way to the front, and having no expectations, devoted more time to study and less to the Jew money lenders that at one time infested the neighbourhood.[24]

The opinions entertained by the new element were something akin to the opinions held by the irreverent employers of Crushem, Grindem, and Co., only couched in more grammatical language, and covered with the respectability of the university, although to a great extent they were even yet looked upon with grave suspicion by the jog-trot-you-cannot-be-too careful members of the community.

But, in spite of every obstacle, Socialism had taken hold, and left its mark, and was being unconsciously and daily preached by men like Doctor Alexander Smythe, who would nevertheless blush to be called a Socialist, and while to-day Dr. Smythe is putting the theory into practice in his profession, his one time colleagues are thundering it from the platform, and pulpit, and board schools, and even the doctor himself is no longer afraid of the title, the avowal of which has brought about a decided coolness between him and his one crown, one queen, one Parliament, Church and State father, whom he has lately mortally offended by accepting the position as honorary medical adviser to a common, vulgar Trades Society, and by taking sides with the local Labour party on the question of sanitary reform, and against the personal interest of the jerry-building town councillor. The doctor's socialism was infectious and to his credit be it said, he took good care to spread his advocacy of the people's rights, and so well had he proved his case by eloquent argument that his sister had given up a life of luxury to minister to the wants of the victims of our competitive system that filled the hospitals, and so it is she he consults with, standing alongside the beds of the two recent additions to the monument of England's commercial greatness.

It is her hand that cools the fevered brow of Jack Goodman, as he slowly returns for a brief interval to a consciousness of his position, and looks vacantly into the strange face bending over him. It is her gentle hands and voice that persuade him to "keep quiet now like a good fellow," when in a dreamy state he makes a feeble but unsuccessful effort to rise, and answers his almost incoherent question as to his whereabouts. And gently soothes him when the situation is made plain to him, as he falls back with a groan, exclaiming "Oh! my poor, poor lass, whatever will she do?"

And while Jack lapses again into merciful unconsciousness, and the widowed mother kneels sobbing bitterly over the mangled body of her only son, for which the last spark of his life is slowly flickering, the shrill bur-r-r of the ambulance whistle is again heard above the noise of the traffic outside, and the doctor and nurse are called away to the receiving room to attend another victim from another eminently respectable firm represented by another eminently respectable member of the Hospital committee, whose voice will be heard above the loudest at the close of the service on Sunday, in the Parish Church, joining in the refrain: –

> Praise God from whom all blessings flow.
> Praise Him ye creatures here below.
> Amen!!![25]

[26 August 1893]

Chapter III.

There was an awful row in Manchester-street, Shanty Town, where Jack Goodman and his family resided, not from choice, but necessity, and as Christie entered the street a curious spectacle presented itself to his view.

Half way up the street the steps leading down to the cellars beneath the pavement with their one narrow dark apartment, into which a ray of sunlight never strayed, the doors leading to the first floor of the houses above them again were filled with females of all ages and sizes and conditions, gesticulating and urging on the half-dozen combatants, who – with power to add to their number – were filling the air with horrible imprecations.

At the door of the branch police station in the street, surrounded by an awe-struck crowd of barefooted, ragged, unkempt urchins, stood a representative of the law, looking on with an amused smile, and occasionally blowing his whistle as a warning, which, however, had not the slightest effect.

"What's de matter, boss?" said Christie, as he came up to the policeman.

"Oh, its only the usual Monday afternoon exchange of courtesies between the women," answered the officer. "They won't do any harm; they're simply blowing off the foam of the beer they've consumed on money raised on the bundles subscribed among them, and the cause of the present row is simply because Mrs. Brady over there, whom you see tying up her hair in preparation for a fight that won't come off with Mrs. Carson, who, after helping to consume the price of Mrs. Brady's bundle, has ungratefully refused to return the compliment by also subscribing to keep up the fun. And what makes the sin more grievous in the eyes of Mrs. Carson and her allies is, as you may perceive, two or three of them have come provided with their husbands' breakfast cans in anticipation of the feast."

"But, by the way, Christie, what brings you up in these diggings? Attracted by the fun, I suppose?"

"God help us! No, sir," said Christie, "I don't see anything funny in such degradation as this. I takes a drop – sometimes too much – on account iv bein' a martyr to de bowel complaint, but let me tell yer, boss, this is 'most enough till make me swear off, in spite iv de docther's orders."

"Aye, I've noticed, Christie, you've been under the doctor's orders a good many times lately," said the policeman, with the slightest suspicion of a smile.

"Rather a desperate complaint yours, Christie, my lad and must require desperate remedies, I've no doubt. Still I don't mind advising you as a friend if your doctor orders you go into other people's houses and smash King Billy's portrait,[26] that the cure is likely to turnout worse than the disease," and to hide the smile gradually extending over his countenance the limb of the law turned with military precision on his heel, and entered the bridewell[27] to answer the ring of the telephone leaving Christie to run the gauntlet of the groups of women standing discussing the merits of the respective combatants in the dispute.

Arrived at the door of Jack's residence a little higher up the street, Christie's timid knock was answered by Jack's sister, a remarkably handsome girl of twenty years, whose face for evidence of grief, and whose eyes, dim with tears, told Christie that the ill news had preceded him.

"Oh, Christie!" said the girl between her sobs, "I'm so glad you've come! Have you heard about poor Jack?"

"Hush! Don't cry, mi poor lass; iv coorse I have. Sure, isn't it that brings me here to break the news till yer, which I'm afraid will break d heart iv de poor cratur inside. How does she take it?"

"She is not inside, Christie," said Kate Goodman. "She was gone to the hospital before I came in answer to a message sent by her to the shop where I'm employed, and when I arrived home I found Dan Curley, who had brought the news, here waiting for me."

"Oh! then bad luck till his ugly mug!" said Christie; "it's just the kind o' work that suits such a dirty bird of ill-omen. Is he inside now?"

Kate held up her finger warningly, and nodded her head.

"Then I'll not come in, mi lass, for a sight iv him id be sure to bring on my enemy, de bowel complaint. De dirty schemer! So good day, Kitty, mi lass, and may de Lord assist yez in yer trial and tribulation."

"Oh, don't go, Christie," said Kate, catching him by the coat as he was moving away. "Do come in and stop until Mary comes back, because you know" – lowering her voice to a whisper – "I'm not so fond of Mr. Curley's company no more than you are. I don't want to stop here alone with him, and I can't leave the house for the sake of the children, so come in to oblige me, there's a dear old fellow."

"Right yez are, mi lass; that puts a new feature on the job," said Christie, as he entered and sat down in the kitchen, acknowledging the presence of Dan Curley with a surly nod.

The salutation was not acknowledged by Curley, but as he leaned forward to get a light for his pipe from the fire his white, gleaming teeth clicked sharply together, and a sinister look overspread his features, boding ill for those who opposed his wishes.

A first acquaintance of Dan Curley would entirely contradict Christie's assertion as to his ugliness. On the contrary, in his ordinary mood Dan Curley was what might be considered a good-looking man of medium height, with well proportioned limbs and body of an athlete, surmounted by a finely-shaped head, bearing a plentiful crop of bushy, light-coloured hair, and a close-trimmed pointed beard and moustache, which served to hide the thin lips of a large and cruel-looking mouth, which, on further acquaintance, entirely marred his appearance. This feature, together with a habit of bringing his well-preserved, gleaming white teeth together when engaged in discussion with an opponent, conveyed to the reader of character the impression that behind the calm, smiling exterior lay the vindictive spirit of the sneaking wolf, controlled only until an opportunity presented itself of preying upon his fellows for personal gratification.

His history previous to his association with the docks was shrouded in mystery, and vague rumours were afloat as to his birthplace, some locating it in America, others in France, also of his associations with certain political incidents in which lives were sacrificed, and which on reaching his ears he took no trouble to dispel, contenting himself with a penetrating look from his wolfish-looking eyes, and an enormous click of his gleaming white teeth for an answer. This and the absence of all fingers but two on his left hand, which it was whispered were blown off by an charge of dynamite, gave him an air of importance among his mates that he was not slow in taking advantage of.

He was no one of the tin chapel gang. In fact, his religious faith was as great a mystery as his birthplace, though to a few of his confidential friends he as much as confessed himself to be an atheist.

Nor yet was he one of the grand majority because he had no vote.[28] But, as a set-off for his disenfranchisement, he was possessed of a fluent tongue, which he used in the interest of the Liberal candidate, Mr. Crushem, and for which he was secretly rewarded.

Between Hoppy and Dan Curley there existed a secret compact of long standing to work in different directions for the same object, namely personal gain and gratification of animal desires, and to achieve these objects and still retain the favour of Messrs. Crushem and Grindem it became necessary that Hoppy should assume the role of tyrant, while Dan Curley should act the part of jackal by apparently agreeing with the grievances of the men and reporting progress to Hoppy, who used the information received by leaving the discontented ones on the stand to wear the shoes off their feet looking for a job until such times as they, to use his pet expression, came to their senses.

Thus was the wicked discontent of the wicked dock labourer, who would drive the trade from the port, &c. &c., crushed in the bud – as it very properly should be, of course.

Another bond of sympathy between Hoppy and Curley was the animal passions of both men, and in more than one instance had the honour of a man's home and name been bartered for a constant job.

At present the affections of both gentlemen were bestowed, but not appreciated, on Jack Goodman's house, and while the inmates were as yet unconscious of their foul intentions these lustful, crawling things were endeavouring to slowly weave their web around them, which accounts for Curley's presence in Goodman's house on the day of the accident.

"Sad business, this accident of Jack Christie's,"[29] said the suave voice of Curley.

"H'm, yis, 'tis," said Christie; 'but I dunno as how yer sympathy 'll help 'im much."

"Oh, Christie!" replied Kate, "don't say that. I'm sure Mr. Curley was very kind and sympathetic, and acted with great regard for our feelings; and I'm sure I shall never forget his kind offer, knowing our unfortunate position to financially assist us in our trouble, and which while fully recognising the generous spirit in which it was offered, we felt our duty to refuse."

"Well, Miss Kitty," remarked Christie, standing up and putting on his cap, screwing the lid tightly on his pipe, and ramming it and his two arms up to the elbows into his breeches pocket. "I'm a hignorant man, but I've heddication enough to know as how I've no manner o' right ter be uncivil to yer visitors in yer own house; so by yer leave, missie, I'll toddle off back to de hospital and see if I can get news o' Jack, and if anything 'll bring him round again it'll be the news that you've refused assistance from Dan Curley."

"Come, come, friend Christie," said Curley with an ominous click of the teeth, as Kate made a movement to prevent Christie going, "you're rather severe on an old mate. In what way have I offended you?"

"Yer no mate o' mine, Dan Curley," said Christie, "and yez haven't offended me. Yer knows a trick worth two o' that, Curley. But I knows them as yer have offended in a manner as I'm not a goin' to shock this inercent gal bi mentioning; and what's more, yer knows as how I knows it."

"Very well, Mr. Kennedy," replied Curley, with another ominous click of the gleaming teeth, "I have not the slightest wish to interfere with the friendly relations that exist between Miss Kate and such an old friend of the family who takes such a lively interest in their affairs and such an important liberty with their guests, and as Miss Kate, with charming taste, which I am sorry I cannot appreciate, allows such impertinence to go unchecked, I take the liberty of relieving you of my presence," and with an evil scowl to Christie, which changed almost on the instant that he turned to bow, hat in hand, in mock deference to Kate, he opened the door leading to the lobby and walked into the street.

"Thank goodness he's gone," said Kate, with a sigh of relief as the door closed after him. "I was on pins and needles until you came in, but I'm afraid you've made a life-long enemy of Mr. Curley."

"Yer needn't be the slightest bit afraid o' that, Missie. Why, bless yer art I'd sooner have the illwill nor the goodwill iv a skunk like yon any time. A chap allers knows how ter deal wi' an enemy when he declares hissel like yon chap has done, better nor yer can when under cover iv friendship they tries to stab yer in de back. I've often felt inclined to tell yon sneaking cur and his bosom friend Hoppy what I thought about them," and sitting down again and taking out his pipe and knocking it in the heel of his fist to clear the vent, he struck a match and exclaimed between puffs, resembling in sound the noise made by the clapper of a flywheel pump[30] –

"I've many a time – smack – thought as how I'd – smack – feel better in 'aven – smack – it out wi' 'em both – smack – an so I do, but I'll never feel properly satisfied till I have a proper good go at Hoppy for to-day's doin's."

"Why, surely, Christie," said Kate, every vestige of colour leaving her face, as she grasped the table to steady herself. "You don't think Mr. Screwem, or 'Hoppy,' as you call him, had any hand in injuring poor Jack. My God! it is too horrible. Why, Mr. Curley told me how it happened; he said it was an accident."

"Well, Missie," replied Christie, meditatively, "I'm not a-going to say as how he had, neither am I a-going to say as how he hadn't. But I can't help mi thoughts, and they is as how Hoppy's never put Jack on for nigh on ter four years, and whatever show he got in de firm was only when de master, Mr, Crushem, himself put de men on. Neither can I forget how Hoppy has it in for Jack on account ov de missis, and 'cos Jack walloped him before all de hands in de shed, and from what I heard on de road up from de youngster who was driving de winch, and who was broke (discharged) at dinner time, I'm inclined ter think as how there wur summat else beside accident."

"Come, Christie, old friend," said Kate, as with an effort she recovered herself and placed her hand on his shoulder, "it's not like you to harbour bad thoughts against any one, and I'm sure you must be mistaken, because I heard Jack the other day telling Mary how the master stopped his cab in the street when he saw Jack idle, and asked him why he didn't shape to the stand, and when he told him that he thought it was no use, he almost commanded him to attend and he would give Mr. Screwem instructions to put him on and give him back his constant number."[31]

"Yes, lass, I heard all about it. I also knew as how Jack, iv he'd only hissel to think on, would sooner starve nor accept it, but," pointing to the cradle containing the latest addition to the family of three children, "it's these he's thinking on night, noon, and morning, more'n anyone else."

And in corroboration of Christie's assertion the back door is pushed in, and a little curly-headed girl of three years toddles into the kitchen, with her two little fists rubbing her eyes and exclaiming between the sobs that threaten to burst her little heart, that Ma'ye Pwice has tolded her 'bout her daddy bein' tooked in de yospital, an was goin' to be put in de bewwie hole.[32]

[2 September 1893]

Chapter IV.

Mr. Crushem was in an exceedingly bad temper. Scarce had he arrived at his office at ten that morning when he was rudely interrupted in his perusal of the morning paper by a request to grant an interview to the mother of the boy Johnson, who had succumbed to his injuries, and now lay awaiting interment. The widowed and now childless mother had foolishly appealed to the master to grant her the means to put the poor boy decently under the ground.

The master had curtly referred her to the Poor-law Authorities,[33] and severely condemned the false pride of the common people, and their foolish objections to take advantage of these institutions. And the widowed and childless woman had writhed under the lash of censure, bowed low before the great man, and retired in all humility to face the bitter March wind and the blinding sleet, that saturated her scanty raiment, and oozed through her string-bound apologies for boots, as she plodded wearily along to her miserable abode, now more desolate than ever.

Mr. Crushem, with a grunt of indignation, had again settled himself before a roaring fire in his comfortable office chair, smoothed his morning paper, and recommenced the perusal of the yearly reports of the British Workman's Philanthropic High Dividend Society and the local tramway company, in both of which he had a large interest, when –

The door was again opened, admitting a cold draft from the outer office, causing a slight suspicion of a swear word to escape the lips of Mr. Crushem, as he confronted the clerk, who timidly informed him "that John Goodman was waiting outside to see him."

"Tell him I'm engaged," roared Mr. Crushem, "and shut that door after you quick," as the clerk in his fright was retiring, leaving the door open after him, and which was answered by a sharp rap on the door, causing it to swing open to the full extent, revealing the form of Jack Goodman in the doorway, supporting himself with the stick that had forced the door open, his head and face still covered in ghastly bandages.

"Asking your pardon, sir," said Jack, as Mr. Crushem stared speechless with indignation at the audacious intruder upon his sacred privacy. "My business won't detain you long. And what is more important to me, it will not admit of delay."

The terrible wreck of the former man, the ghastly appearance had its effect upon Crushem, who, after closing the door himself, motioned to Jack to take the chair he had vacated.

"No thank you, sir, what I've got to say can be said standing."

"I've been terribly injured in your employ, owing to the culpable, if not criminal, neglect of your foreman. I've been six weeks in the hospital, my wife has been forced to pawn our clothes and sell some of the furniture to feed the children and keep out the bailiffs. And now I've come straight from the hospital, against the wish of the doctor, to ask you, what are you going to do about it?"

"Well, my man, your unbecoming rude behaviour is not likely to advance your cause, which I can only excuse on the ground of your misfortune, and for which I am very sorry. But tell me, what do you expect to do?"

"Well, sir," replied Jack, "I don't want to be rude or unbecoming. And I hope my seeming want of courtesy – simply owing to my fear of not being allowed to see you – will not interfere with your granting me that compensation for injury which the law would allow me, were I to appeal to it."[34]

"H'm! so you've come to talk law, have you, my good fellow?" said Crushem with a sneer. "If that's your point, the law is open to you, and this interview – might I say forced interview? – is at an end, and," walking to the door and opening it, "I must wish you good morning and good luck to you with your law."

"Stop, sir," replied Jack, as he closed the door and put his back against it. "I didn't come here to badger you, nor am I going to be badgered.[35] My object was to give you an opportunity of doing a fair thing and avoiding an action at law, which, in the interest of those dependent upon me, I should feel bound to take if you refused to listen to reason."

"My good fellow," said Crushem, as he rested his foot on the chair Jack had vacated and stroked his beard complacently, "it is yourself who are unreasonable, both in want of due respect to your superiors and in your ignorance of the law you claim as your protection. How long have you been laid up?"

"Six weeks yesterday, sir, and as for due respect to –"

"Ah! Well, we'll dispense with that item, if you please," and ringing the bell on the desk, Mr. Crushem told the clerk who answered it to bring the copy of the Employers' Liability Act[36] from the outer office.

"Now, then, my good fellow, I know you can read,"[37] said Crushem. "Just cast your eye over this clause, and you will find according to the Act that you have shut yourself entirely out from the benefits of the Act by neglecting to enter action within six weeks after your accident."

Such indeed was the case, which completely staggered poor Jack, and for a moment the copy of the Act and the desk, which he grasped for support, and Crushem, and the ink bottles, and blotting pads, were mixed in an indistinguishable heap before his eyes, as he almost reeled from the shock. But recovering himself with an effort, he turned to Crushem and replied –

"Yes, sir, the game's yours, and you're entitled to the stakes, just as I am entitled to my opinion, I suppose, to tell you that this game has been played with loaded dice, and I am entirely at your mercy, from which my experience teaches me there is not much to expect, so by your leave I'll bid you good morning," and he staggered towards the door and turned the handle.

"Stay, my good fellow," said Crushem, as he in turn closed the door and stood with his back against it, "there you wrong me. Now I'm willing in consideration of your once good conduct (which I regret to say has fallen off lately, since you began to entertain your revolutionary ideas) to allow you to go back to work, and find you an easy job, such as winch driving, at 1s. 6d. a day less than you were heretofore receiving, until you are entirely recovered."

Jack's first impulse was to hurl the insinuation as to his character, and the humiliating offer back into the smiling hypocritical face of Crushem, but the thought of the home stripped of old associations, and the knowledge of the bare table, and necessities of life for the little ones, restrained him, and without answering a word he opened the door leading to the outer office, and almost groped his way out into the blinding sleet, leaving Mr. Crushem free to study the stock and dividend reports in the columns of his daily paper.

Jack's arrival at home caused quite a sensation in the household, as he had given no intimation of his intention to leave the hospital.

In fact, he had intended to go straight back there from Crushem's office, but the longing to see the "chicks" was too much for him, and so he finds himself in his favourite chair, which alone had escaped confiscation, with a chick on each knee, and his wife delighted at having him home again, busying herself in attending to the wants of his inner man.

"Now children," said she, "don't annoy poor dad. Jack, dear, do put them down, and rest yourself. I'm sure you'll knock yourself up again after the trying day you've had," and peering anxiously into his face with her hand on his shoulder, "Are you sure you've done right in coming out a day like this." With an affectionate caress, "Not but what I'm downright glad to have my poor illused husband home again."

"God bless you, lass; don't bother about me. It's done me more good than all the doctoring to be among you once again, and the prattle of the chicks, instead of tiring me, has strengthened me in my resolve to stay here now that I've come, and to accept the offer of Crushem for the time being, humiliating as it is."

And in answer to his wife's question as to what offer he referred to, he acquainted her of his visit to Crushem and the result, and of his decision to accept it as the only alternative to starvation.

"My dear lad, let us be thankful to Almighty God that you're spared to us," said his wife. "I suppose you've heard of poor little Johnson's death?"

"Yes, my lass. I saw him carried away to the deadhouse[38] to await the sitting of the picked coroner's jury, who will, after a discussion of a few minutes, pass a verdict of accidental death, when it was nothing else than murder. I saw the poor lone mother this morning coming from the employer's office, her few poor rags clinging to her skin with the wet, and her teeth chattering with cold and hunger. She told me the master had referred her to the poorhouse. The poor lad will be buried in a nameless grave, and the mother in all probability will shortly follow him. And oh! my lass, may God forgive me, but in my bitterness I almost refused to believe in the existence of a God that would allow such a state of things to exist."

"Can nothing be done for the poor creature? Hush Jack! Don't speak like that. It pains me to hear you. Christie's been here a while ago, and he says he's going to give all he earns to the widow this week. Aye! poor Christie's good at promising that kind of thing, but, with all his generosity, it never comes off, because, God help him, his own claims all he earns."

"God help us all, my lass. We're a miserable, weak, ignorant, selfish lot of creatures, bound to the chariot wheels of a few greedy exploiters, who are building up gigantic fortunes on our graves and broken bones."

"Jack, dear, don't! I don't like to hear you talking like that. Besides, you know, you needn't excite yourself. I know you're quite right, dear; but then you can't remedy it yourself, and if you make the attempt, the very first to condemn you are the people in whose interest you are working."

"Aye, I know that lass; but it's not their fault. It's the fault of the ignorance with which they are surrounded that makes them crush the life out of each other in their mad, mistaken race for a bare existence. But if God gives me strength, and pulls me through this, I promise to do one man's part, regardless of the consequences, to dispel the ignorance that is slowly crushing out our lives to build up fortunes for our exploiters.

Chapter V.

It was a very satisfactory dividend. The directors of "Rattle-his-bones and Co.'s funeral establishment" had met and declared a dividend of 35 per cent., and "great was the rejoicing thereof."[39]

Alderman Fatpurse, the chairman, congratulated the shareholders on the very pleasing facts represented by the balance sheet, and hoped they would one and all live long to enjoy their profits. He himself had received several applications from men of money to sell his shares, but he knew a good thing when he saw one, and he meant to stick to his shares, which he considered were a greater source of revenue to him, in proportion, than was his business. – (Here, hear, from Councillor Gull the Public.)

Alderman Fatpurse was a ship's provision broker and a prominent Liberal. Councillor Gull the Public was a Tory and a shipowner.[40]

Alderman Grindem, in returning a vote of thanks to their excellent chairman, referred to his kindly, genial spirit, and hoped he would long be spared to them to guide the destinies of the company, whose dividend was very welcome during the present depressed state of trade. He hoped he would be excused if he just touched upon in passing, a rumour that had reached him from a source he could depend upon, that the dock labourers were allowing themselves to be led away by a paid agitator to form a union.

"These creatures were the pests of society, and wherever they appeared there was sure to be a disruption of trade. In his opinion the law should step in and stop these men, who were living on the hard-earned coppers of the working men, and driving trade out of the country. – (Loud and continued applause.) The trail of these pests was covered with disastrous strikes. He sincerely hoped the men would not be foolishly led away, and he wanted them to know – he hoped the press present would make a note of it – that in case any dispute arose they had plenty of men in the agricultural districts working for 12s. anxious to take their place." – (Loud cheers.)

Of course the press took a note of it, and the placards of the following day's issues bore this startling statement: –

EXPECTED GREAT STRIKE OF DOCK LABOURERS.
STATEMENT BY MR. ALDERMAN GRINDEM.
EMPLOYERS PREPARING FOR THE STRUGGLE.

And in a special leader of a column and a half the *Daily Blatherskite* endeavoured to prove that black was white, and white was no colour at all; and the pulpit thundered forth, from behind £5000 a year, strong denunciation of paid agitators.

[9 September 1893]
Chapter VI.

There had been a heated debate in Mr. Smythe, senior's household at the breakfast table, and Mr. Smythe, senior, was exceedingly wroth. It came about thus:

The previous day Mr. Smythe, senior, had met Mr. Grindem, shipowner, and Alderman Fatpurse on the exchange,[41] where a serious disarrangement of Mr. Smythe's business had occurred, owing to the refusal of the dock labourers to discharge Mr. Smythe's cargo out of Mr. Grindem's ship onto Alderman Fatpurse's waggon, causing wailing and gnashing of teeth. Alderman Fatpurse, who had bought some of the cargo from Mr. Smythe, claimed compensation for delay and loss of business from Smythe, who referred him to Alderman Grindem, shipowner who in turn referred them both to the devil, accompanied by a threat to starve the lazy hounds into submission.

On Smythe's arrival at home the same evening he was shocked to find on the table in his son's room, where he had gone to seek him, a handbill announcing a meeting of the Labour party, at eight p.m. that evening, with Dr. Smythe in the chair, and a book entitled "The evils of Competition," open at chapter V., which commenced as follows: –

What an inhuman, unnatural, horrible thing is our present competitive system, that allows one man to gamble and grow rich on the products of other men's labour? What a sinful waste of energy is our system of distribution, when we see dozens of shops in one street engaged in the distribution of commodities, whose well-stocked windows and gaudy fronts but serve to hide the poverty and hunger of the slum workers whose labour has created all these things, and whose children are dying for the want of them, but which are beyond their reach according to the so-called law of supply and demand.

Such language was, to the carefully-trained mind of Smythe, senior, rank blasphemy, and such was the effect upon him that, closing the book with a bang, he threw it at the bookcase on the opposite side of the room, smashing the glass door to atoms, thus attracting the attention of the occupants of the next room, his daughter and a Mr. Garnish, a friend of the doctor's, who had called to see him, who hurried in to learn the cause of the disturbance.

"Why, pa," inquired the young lady, as the old gent in his rage was tearing the handbill into a thousand pieces, "what in the name of goodness is the matter?"

"The matter is, Miss, that there are traitors in the camp, and that I have been nursing vipers in my bosom in the shape of one of my own flesh and blood, who is disgracing the history, the unblemished history of our family, by his outrageous ideas of the rights of property, and equal distribution of wealth, and his vulgar association with navvies and hod carriers."

"Oh! father, how can you talk like that about Alex., one of the best and kindest of brothers, and the most obedient sons that ever lived."

"How can I talk? How can I blame, Miss," spluttered Mr. Smythe, senior. "Is it not time to talk when I find my son, whom I have reared in luxury, and provided with a respectable and honourable profession, going headlong to the devil, and if I mistake not," going over and taking a book out of the girl's hand, "dragging you along with him."

"There you are again," he roared, after having examined the title, and flinging the book on the table, "Morris's minimum wage, another d—n Socialist robber! Nice books for a young lady in your position! What's anybody's wage got to do with you, I'd like to know? Haven't you got wages enough? Isn't there other books to read of a character more becoming girls like you, instead of stuffing your head with rubbish like that, breathing dynamite, barricades, and disloyalty to our gracious Queen in every sentence?"

"I'm sure, sir," said Mr. Garnish, "if you would only read William Morris[42] carefully you would form a different opinion of him. There is not the slightest evidence of anything of the character you mention in his writings, but simply the quiet earnestness of a true man who is endeavouring to do something to relieve the present inequality of the producers of wealth."

"Well, I'm sure, sir," answered Smythe, senior, "that I've no inclination to read your friend Morris at all, and I'm just as earnest as he is about what you call the present inequality of the producers of wealth. The present condition is good enough for me, and it will have to serve those who belong to me, and what's more, I'm not going to have you, sir, coming here to stuff their heads with such fal-lals as this," picking up another book and glancing at the title page. "The land for the people. Faugh! I'd like to know what they would do with the land if they had it tomorrow, if it were not for the men of brains who find money and work for them?"

"And now, let me tell you, miss, I don't want you to be spending your time in this fashion any longer and when that scamp of a brother of yours comes home from his navvies' meeting tell him I want to see him in the morning before I leave for business," and with his hands clasped behind him and his head bent, Mr. Smythe, senior, stamped out of the room without deigning to notice or bid good evening to Mr. Garnish.

"Your respected father seems considerably out of sorts this evening," said Garnish, after an awkward pause. "I pity Alex if he's in no better humour in the morning."

"You mustn't mind father's humours, Mr. Garnish," replied Miss Smythe, "and you need have no fear of the interview between him and Alex. Father will have time between now and morning to consider, and by breakfast time the edge will be off his temper, because he knows from experience he always gets the worst of an argument with Alex on these questions, though I must confess he has never behaved as he has done this evening. I declare he frightened me. I hope," with a sigh, "Alex won't lose his temper about the wreck of his library."

"I sincerely hope not, Miss Lucy," answered Garnish, "and I am truly sorry that I – as the language of your father seems to convey – have been the unconscious cause of any unpleasantness between the members of your family, and" walking into the lobby followed by Lucy and taking his hat from the rack, "I cannot but accept – until your father unsays the language he used towards me to-night – as a hint that my visits here must be discontinued."

"Now, Mr. Garnish, it is you who are losing your temper," said Lucy. "I think I can promise you that to-night's episode will not interfere with your visits. Besides, for Alex's sake, I am sure you will think no more of father's hasty words. Think how Alex would miss you."

And as the eyes of those two kindred spirits looked into each other's for a brief moment, and those of the girl were suddenly attracted by the pattern of the carpet, and her hand trembled in the clasp of her companion, a faint suspicion crossed the mind of Mr. Garnish that he would be missed by more than one member of the Smythe household.

As surmised by Lucy, a night's sleep combined with a secret fear that he would come off second best in the argument, had considerably smoothed the ruffled temper of Smythe senior, who greeted his son at the breakfast table with his accustomed nod, and was answered by the doctor, who had been forewarned by Lucy, with a cheery, "Good morning, sir. Anything fresh?"

"Humph! No, sir; everything's stale" – with a jab at the ham – "as stale as your companions of last night, sir;" and to cover his nervousness at making the attack he passed his still full cup over to Lucy to be replenished.

"I'm afraid you're out of sorts this morning, sir," answered the doctor, with a faint suspicion of a smile; "liver out of order;" and not heeding a warning kick under the table from Lucy, "shall I prescribe for you?"

"Confound your prescriptions, sir; I'm in no humour for jokes. If you could make out a prescription for these friends of yours from disturbing the trade of the port you would confer a lasting benefit to the community."

"Beg pardon, sir," replied the doctor, "if I offended you, but I am prepared with a prescription even for the disease you refer to, and what is more, my friends of last night are willing to act upon it, but I grieve to say that your friends refuse to swallow the dose."

"Humph! yes, I know your dose. I had a taste of it yesterday, and I don't like it; it's poison, sir. The taste I had of it yesterday is likely to cost me over £100. I don't want any more of it, so you can save it for your friends, who will swallow any kind of pill you may think fit to offer them, with a sugared coating on it."

"I'm sure I'm very sorry, sir, for your loss, but I am also at a loss to know in what way my dose is connected with it. Will you explain?"

"Alick, dear," said Lucy, "let father finish his coffee, so that I can give him a fresh cup before it gets cold."

"Thank you, my dear," replied Smythe senior, now considerably mollified by Lucy's attention. "Well, sir, the explanation is that the fellows whom you so prominently identified yourself with last night had earlier in the day refused to discharge a portion of a cargo that I had bought and sold again to Alderman Fatpurse, and which, in consequence, will now be left on my hands with a falling market."

"What was the cause of their refusal?" inquired the doctor.

"Well, I didn't take the trouble to inquire," replied Smythe senior; "that was the shipowner's business, not mine."

"Was it not your business to get the cargo out?"

"Yes, of course."

"Then, sir, don't you think it was your business also to inquire into the cause of delay and endeavour to remedy it?"

"Well, now I come to think, I did hear it was because some men were employed who were not members of the union, and who were complained of by the members of the union as being incompetent, and because they were asked to work on stages rigged by these men complained about."

"Don't you think, sir, that was a perfectly sound cause of their refusal?"

"No, sir, I don't think it was. In my opinion, it was only an excuse to force Mr. Grindem to submit to their terms, to employ none but union men, and (with indignation) I think it is monstrous that an employer should be interfered with in employing whom he thinks fit."

"Very well, admitting that, sir, don't you also think it is monstrous to interfere with men working only for those employers that they think fit?'

"Of course it is; but then nobody forces them – they need not work for those employers if they don't like."

"Are you quite sure about that, sir? Is it not dire necessity that forces them to work whereby they may live? Let us place ourselves in these poor chaps' places – which God forbid, sir, should ever come to pass – but let us suppose, for argument, that we were reduced to physical labour to earn the barest necessities of life, and that all employers were allowed to exact their own terms, as in a great many cases they are to-day. Suppose those terms were such, as they also are to-day, entailing danger to life and limb, and the only alternative for those who refused to accept those risks was starvation for self and family. Don't you think, sir, that such conditions are unfair, which force men to sell their manhood by taking another man's job under horrible conditions, and at less than a living wage? and don't you think the men are justified in forcing the employer who will not recognise this to recognise that the men who create his wealth must be considered?"

"Yes, yes, my boy; but are the men not considered? Does not the employer pay them what they earn?"

"No, sir, he does not pay them what they earn. He pays them a wage only, and as little wage as he possibly can. If he paid them what they earn, the employer himself would only be in receipt of what he earns as a mental worker, to which he is entitled, but no more. As it is, if he employs 100 men, he gets his own share as a mental worker, and so much from the products of every one of the 100 physical workers in addition; and the more he can screw out of each man the more he gets for himself, and the less the 100 men who produce it."

"And to which he is legally entitled, my boy, so long as he is able to buy his labour cheap,' said Smythe, sen., rising from the table, and good humouredly offering his son a cigar from a morocco, silver-bound cigar-case.

"Aye, sir," said the doctor, also rising and accepting the cigar. "Now, sir, we are getting within the scope of my dose; if you admit the right of the employer to buy his labour cheap, you must also admit the right of the men to sell it dear, which can only be done through combination."

"Of course I do, my boy. I never questioned that right; but I do certainly question the right of the men to interfere with him getting cheap labour."

"But don't you see, sir, the source of cheap labour is that there are hundreds of thousands of men who have no market for their labour, and others who from the same cause spoken of the other day by Alderman Grindem, are also at the mercy of employers who buy cheap labour because the men, of necessity, are forced to sell their labour cheap or starve, and are induced by the offer of employers like Mr. Grindem to take the places of men in the towns for a little more than the wage they are receiving and considerably less than Grindem is paying his men.

"So you see, sir, the worker is not free to sell his labour to the best advantage and is forced to accept any conditions offered to him by the employers, who is free to exact a maximum day's labour for a minimum day's wage."

"Aye! there is certainly something in what you say, my lad. There's too many people in the country. That is what's the matter; it's emigration we want," replied Smythe senior.

"There you are wrong again, sir," said the doctor. "There are not too many people in the country, but there are too many idlers in the country, and if every man was allowed to work that wants to work, and every man made to work that wants to live, there would be no strikes because there would be no blacklegs, and so no low wages and no twelve accidents and deaths in one day in one neighbourhood, and no paupers' graves and widows and orphans living on the rates."[43]

"Aye, my boy," said Smythe, 'yours is a pretty picture and I must confess you're not a bad artist, but how do you propose to find work for all the people?"

"Well, sir, that's the part of my dose which I don't expect you to swallow in a gulp, and besides I notice" – looking through the window in the direction of the signal box – "your train is signalled and I am due at the hospital. We will repeat the dose some other time."

"Very well, my lad," said the old gentleman, shaking hands with his son, "you always do get the best of me in these arguments. But, seriously, you'll please me much if you can see your way to discontinue preaching this doctrine to ignorant men. You'll only make them discontented with their lot in life."

"Yes, sir, but it is because they are ignorant that they are discontented, and are likely to do more harm in their blind discontented ignorance than if they were educated, which we are endeavouring to bring about."

"Come, father," said Lucy, appearing at the door with his hat and gloves, "you'll miss your train if you don't hurry."

"Thanks my dear," said her father as he took them, and as he stooped to give his usual salute, he whispered rather shamefacedly "does Alick know about the bookcase?"

"No pa," said the girl, "he has not been in the room."

"Ah!" with a sigh of relief. "Then get it fixed before he comes home, like a good girl. I'm sorry I lost my temper. And, by the bye, Lucy," as she turned to go, "you must apologise to Garnish if he happens to call, for my rudeness last night. Good morning. What! has Alick gone?"

Two hours after, from some mysterious cause, Mr. Garnish called for the apology.

And great was the apology thereof!

[16 September 1893]

Chapter VII.

There were great rejoicings in the Crushem Mansion.

For be it known Mr. Crushem had been returned by another large majority as a member of the board of the guardians of the poor(?),[44] and had also been notified of his appointment to the magisterial bench, and while all the juvenile Crushems were having high jinks in the Crushem Mansion in honour of the occasion, Mr. and Mrs. Crushem were being entertained at the political club.

"Gentlemen," said Alderman Fatpurse, rising on his short legs, displaying a white bow-windowed waistcoat and a heavy gold chain and seal above the edge of the table, and a gorgeous expanse of shirt front with blazing diamond studs, "it is my esteemed privilege to be entrusted with the toast of the evening, the health and prosperity of our worthy friend and colleague and his good lady, Mr. and Mrs. Crushem. It is hardly necessary for me to comment upon the many good qualities of our guests. Suffice to say that Mr. Councillor Crushem will worthily fill the duties imposed upon him by recently conferred honours, as he has done in other capacities in the council chamber. As a man of very extensive business capabilities, he has unselfishly used those capabilities in the interest of the public in his capacity of chairman of the watch and hospital committees. In the latter case in particular Mr. Crushem has given ample evidence of his generous nature by supplying horses and carts to convey the holly bushes so generously granted by the Lord of the Manor to decorate the walls of the hospital, thereby gladdening the hearts of the unfortunate inmates on Christmas-day who have been crippled in – er – that is to say – er who have been – er as it were – hem – who have been unfortunately injured at the docks. Therefore, ladies and gentlemen, knowing as we do the many excellent qualities of Councillor Crushem and his good lady, we congratulate them both on the recent honours conferred, and hope they may long be spared to enjoy them."

Alderman Fatpurse's proposal, which was listened to in dead silence especially that referring to the hospital, was seconded by the Rev. Mr. Crawthumper, of the Established Church,[45] who said that he most heartily joined in the congratulations, and corroborated from personal knowledge the existence of Mr. and Mrs. Crushem's many good qualities. Mr. Crushem was not a member of his congregation, nor yet did he agree with him politically, but there was one trait in his character that stood out prominently above all political and denominational considerations with which they of mixed political opinions could all heartily agree, and that was his persistent and courageous opposition to the lawless, violent spirits who were endeavouring, by their false teachings, to drive the trade out of the country. – (Hear, hear.) Mr. Crushem, as a large employer of these ungrateful men, for whom he found employment to save them from the workhouse, had before given evidence of his fitness to deal with them, and if he had seemed severe, he was only so in kindness to the large majority of the poor dupes who were being led away by leaders for mercenary motives. – (Hear, hear.) They were, he believed, now threatened with another upheaval of dock labourers, and he sincerely hoped Mr. Crushem would again exercise those qualities that on a previous occasion had proved so effective. He was also sorry to see ministers of his own denomination pandering to these demagogues and agitators by allowing their churches to be used to make working men discontented with their position in which God had placed them – (hear, hear.) – and which, he had no hesitation in saying, made it harder for him to keep his flock in that meek and lowly spirit which fitted all of us for a glorious hereafter. – (Loud and continued applause.)

The allusions of the speakers to Mrs. Crushem had a curious effect on that good lady, and the expression on her refined and somewhat pallid countenance could not, even by the most vivid imagination, be construed into gratification.

On the contrary, with the exception of occasional signs of weariness, and she lay back in her chair betraying contempt for the sentiments uttered, there was a general expression of indifference in her looks and conduct not quite in keeping with respectable etiquette.

And the reason was Mrs. Crushem's eldest daughter Lilian was a bosom friend of Lucy Smythe's, and accompanied her on some of her charitable expeditions. Lilian and her mother had met her on the same day bent on a mission of mercy, and Lilian had persuaded her mother to cancel her shopping expedition and accompany her to the house of her pensioner, Mrs. Brophy, the poor old widow of a deceased employee of the firm of Crushem, Grindem, and Co.

And after traversing many dark and noisome streets they arrived at Mrs. Bophy's residence in a hole in the wall between two rows of warehouses (where the court of ten houses with three storeys each and a family in every storey, and one tap in the middle of the court and one w.c. close to the tap for the convenience of the whole colony) they found the colony gathered round the steps leading to Mrs. Brophy's apartment, a cellar beneath the pavement, muttering prayers that God might rest the poor crathur's sowl, an' giv her a crown o' glory for all her sufferins, and they were sure the crathur was better off.

And so she was. A deal better off being stiff and dead on a filthy, reeking mattress in the corner of her dark, cheerless, miserable hovel than to live conscious of her inhuman surroundings. And with this scene still fresh in her memory, Mrs. Crushem's kindly Christian nature, which, like some pure spirit, seemed to have unconsciously strayed among the fallen ones, revolted against her present surroundings, though too weak to carry her revolt any further than her own recollections.

When Mr. Crushem rose to speak and return thanks on his own and her behalf she half rose in her seat to utter a protest, but the protest came from an entirely unexpected quarter in the shape of a telegraph messenger.

Mr. Crushem has only got as far as "Mr. Chairman, ladies and gentlemen," when he appeared, and insisted on delivering it personally according to instructions to Mr. Crushem, and which entirely changed the tenor of Mr. Crushem's carefully prepared and paid for speech, and the substitution of the following:

"I am truly sorry, ladies and gentlemen, that something has occurred necessitating my immediate presence at the docks. You will regret to learn that the nature of the case is that it is the bursting of the cloud spoken about by our rev. friend, Mr. Crawthumper, and that the men have been duped into knocking off, which, if not rectified at once, will not only cause considerable loss to myself, but to the shipowner, by delaying the ship one tide.

"Under the circumstances I must beg of you to excuse me for a short time, and to accept my sincere thanks and appreciation of your great kindness. I hope to be able to return to fulfil my duties as your honourable guest, leaving in the meantime my good lady in your care until I return."

Mr. Crushem did not return that night.

When he arrived at the docks he found the ship deserted, and every hatch stopped, with stages half unrigged, trucks kecked up with loads still resting on the lips of the trucks, and falls hanging idly from gins, on spars and booms.[46]

Hoppy, warned by the rattle of cab wheels, was at the main hatch gangway to meet him, and in reply to his question, "What is all the bother about?" explained that when the clock in the tower was on the stroke of five Jack Goodman, who was driving a winch at the after hatch, turned off the steam and walked ashore. When he saw the winch stopped he went to inquire the reason, and was told by the men over the hatch, who were putting on their coats, that it was knocking off time, and as there were no orders to work on their day was up.

"Never mind that infernal rigmarole," irritably replied Crushem; "tell me how it comes that the ship is stopped, when I ordered a fresh lot of men out at six to work the first half night."

"That's easy told, sir," said Hoppy. "The men came to the gate, but no further, because Jack Goodman met them, and told them not to go to work because I refused to book the men in the main hatch an hour extra for working on till twenty-five minutes past five."

"So it's that ungrateful scoundrel, Goodman, that we have to thank for this," said Crushem between his closed teeth, "but," turning sharply to Hoppy, "why in the name of common sense did you allow the ship to be stopped, and the shed full of cargo, and the ship advertised for passengers to leave on the morning's tide? Confound your bungling, why didn't you keep the men at the discharging ship? A nice mess you've made of it."

"Beg pardon, sir, that's exactly what I did."

"Well," eagerly enquired Crushem, "and they –"

"They were also got at by Goodman, and refused to stay."

"Damn his cheek," roared Crushem, so far forgetting his religious profession as to indulge in a cuss word. "But in the name of heaven, how did he influence them all?"

"Well, sir, I was telling when you stopped me," pertinently replied Hoppy, "as I was saying, Goodman, after he stopped the men that were ordered out, went to the discharging book shortly after six and told the men what had happened. I was intending to knock them off at twenty-five past, and book them to six, according to custom, but at ten minutes past six they all came down here and demanded to know if they were going to be working another half hour for the boss for nothing."

"Well, and what did you tell them?" "Well, sir, I told them that they could start here at the loading ship, and work all night, when Goodman jumped up on a case of goods and made a speech to them about the meanness of taking other men's jobs, and accused you of stopping half-a-crown out of his wages last week for the cab that took him to the hospital when he was hurt."

"The infernal scoundrel," muttered Crushem, "but were there no police about?"

"Not until after they had gone to hold a meeting in the Cocoa Rooms, so Dan Curley said, who went with him, and who has since come back and told me all that transpired."

"Ah, so Curley in in it too, is he?" said Crushem, with an ominous frown.

"Yes, sir; he's in it because he can't help himself. Everybody seems to be in it; the whole line o' docks seems to be gone mad about this new union," and handing him a handbill to read, "That's the kind of talk they indulge in."

The handbill that Hoppy placed in the hands of Mr. Crushem read as follows: –

Comrades all and fellow-workmen, – For the second time in the history of the town an attempt is to be made by a body of earnest men to change the unjust conditions at present prevailing among dock labourers.

For some years past never a day has gone over without some of our fellow-creatures and comrades being carried away to the hospital, while the presiding genius of that institution is the one man responsible in his ungodly greed for gain for the most of the cripples who go there and the corpses that come out of it.

In your present unprotected position, with every man's hand raised against his fellow, and the horrible conditions of your labour, you don't know but that your turn may come next.

This we can remedy by combination, but not without. We, therefore, appeal to you to attend the meeting to be held on Tuesday next to hear addresses from prominent Labour leaders on the necessity for combination.

Unity is strength.

By order of the Committee.

And this was the reason Mr. Crushem didn't return to the banquet.

[23 September 1893]

Chapter VIII.

The large ramshackle building with a corrugated iron roof dignified by the name of cocoa worm[47] in a by street leading up from the docks was packed almost to suffocation with dockers, every available position being taken advantage of.

The tables groaned, not beneath the necessaries of life, but beneath life without the necessities, even the counter, over which, under ordinary circumstances, certain mysterious and awful concoctions known as two's of pie, and one o' scaldy, were dispensed by a bar-maid with an eternal smut on her, and her assistant, an individual with a blue flannel shirt rolled up above his elbows, displaying a pair of brawny arms covered with hair, and a greasy paper collar round his neck, (a kind of cross between a coal heaver and a ship's scullery man) was now packed with dockers to the danger of the two dilapidated tea and coffee urns placed at each end.

Jack Goodman had been unanimously elected chairman, and, strange to say, Dan Curley had, without dissent, been elected secretary, *pro tem*.[48]

There were those among the audience, Jack Goodman included, who felt inclined to utter a protest, but were debarred for want of any positive evidence to support it, and in the interest of the harmony of the meeting it passed without question.

But there were a few who, without any positive proof of his unworthiness, mistrusted him, and determined to keep their eye on him.

The case of Dan Curley's election was his ready tact and glib tongue, and being possessed of a keen perception and knowledge that first impressions are generally the best while they last, had voluntarily undertaken to get a list of the men's names with a view of joining the union, and then in a covert speech of half an hour, in which the pent-up feelings of the ignorant men were cunningly appealed to, had succeeded in gaining their confidence.

He was followed by Jack Goodman, whose practical suggestions to take things quietly, systematically, and constitutionally were listened to with marked impatience by some of the more daring spirits, who had been roused by Curley's appeal.

"Look here, mates," said Jack, rising from his seat, and giving the table a thump which vibrated through the building, "there's not a man in this room but what knows me and has worked with me. I see some here who have helped to nurse me when a kid. – (Cries of "Hear, hear," and 'That's so, Jack, my lad.") The majority of you have shared all vicissitudes of life with me from childhood to manhood. – (Hear, hear, and loud cheers.) We've shared the same bench at school, and the same lessons when the teacher's back was turned. – (Laughter.) We've sagged school[49] together, shared our water bites when bathing, bunced[50] our marbles and buttons – (Loud laughter) – and have walloped and been walloped by each other with that philosophic spirit that characterises boyhood." – (Loud and prolonged laughter and cheers.)

"Very well. Now I want to ask you chaps have any of you ever known me to shirk a baffling match or a fight? – (No, never!) Have any of you ever known me when captain of the school bafflers to ask the rank and file to do anything that I wouldn't do myself? – (No, by G—d! That's so, Jack!)

"Well, now, mates, we've passed together through the preliminaries of boyhood, which fit us to fight the battle of life as men, and now that the stern realities of life are before us, and we have entered on the battle, in which you have chosen me to lead, all I ask for is a renewal and exchange of that same confidence in each other that helped us to win our battles as lads. Are you willing to extend it? – (Cries of "Yes," "Yes," and loud and prolonged cheering in which the barmaid with the eternal smut and the cross between a coal-heaver and scullery joined heartily).

In fact, young Tom Conlan, who out of pure charity had his arm round the barmaid's waist to save her from being thrutched[51] off the counter, declared that she added an extra smut in endeavouring to wipe away with her apron evidence of her emotion caused by Jack's speech.

But, under the circumstances, of course, Tom's evidence cannot be accepted as impartial.

"Well, now, mates," continued Jack, after the affect of his appeal had passed away, "we've convinced Mr. Curley of our confidence in each other, and now all that remains for me to do is to convince him – (here he turned and looked Curley straight in the face), – if necessary, of the honesty of our intentions, and the courage and intelligence to carry them out to a logical conclusion.

"There's no one more than myself who recognises the justification of physical force[52] and the very evident capabilities of Mr. Curley. But while I don't for a moment question the honesty of Mr. Curley, I do question very much the success of the plans he proposes, viz., opposition to the law of the land." – (Murmurs of dissent, and cries of "To hell with the law," during which Curley made an attempt to speak, but was interrupted by Jack, who continued.)

"Now, mates, let's go at this thing in a business-like fashion, and not like a bull at a china shop.

"I don't agree with the law any more than you do, but it's there all the same, and in the possession of and worked by the employer against you. The employer makes the law, and administers it for his own benefit; and the worst part of the whole business is that we have put the employers in a position to do it." – (Cries of "Hear, hear," and "No, no.") "Let me ask the gentleman who cries "No, no," were they not the votes of dock labourers and other workers which returned Mr. Crushem to the Town Council, and gave him the charge of the police?" – ("Yes," and cheers).

"Was it not on that account that he was chosen as J.P.[53] by those who administer the laws made in Parliament by employers who are sent there by workmen? – (Hear, hear, and loud cheers.) And has he not the power, as a justice of the peace, to send for your army and navy (supported by your contributions) to enforce the law with bullets and cold steel when the policeman's batons have failed?" – ("That's so, Jack; more power till yer elbow, me lad.")

"And last, but not least, have you not returned him, only last week, as a member of the Board of Guardians, with power to refuse your wives and children relief from your own funds, while you are either shot or locked up in prison for breaking the laws?"

"Well then, mates! you've all of you got a little bit o' commonsense. Use it to some purpose. This sort o' thing exists all through the land of the brave and the free, that you are so fond of laying back your ears and roaring about at election times. You can alter all this, not with bullets, but with votes. At present the employers have all the bullets. – (Curley: "Capture the bullets, and wrap the ideas round them;" and cries of "Hear, hear," and "That's so, Curley.")

"Aye!" continued Jack, "that's a beautiful idea; but it lacks one very important thing. You've first got to provide the bullets – (loud laughter) – and what's more, when the bullets reach the destination the ideas you wrap round them fall on barren ground and bear no fruit. – (Loud applause.)

"No, mates; at present the odds are all against us, and our only remedy is legal combination. First, to join the union to protect ourselves from the present unjust laws that press so heavily upon us. Secondly, to refuse to be bamboozled by employers of labour, who range themselves under the banner of either political party to suit their own selfish end, and keep us split up in different political and religious factions.

"Unity is strength. As an example of this, you have only to look at the employers, how they unite in the lobby of the House of Commons and Town Councils, where they sink the religious and make-believe political opinions, to defeat any measure for your benefit.

"Therein, mates, lies your power. Unite in trades unions to protect yourselves from the present unjust law while it exists, and unite your votes to change the bad laws into good ones. The only way, mates, is to change the law, and the only way to change the law is to change the men who in their own selfish interest have made it."

The applause at the conclusion of Jack's speech was supplemented by the audience standing on the forms and waving their caps, with three cheers for the National Union.

So great was the extra pressure caused by the enthusiasm on the limited space that young Conlan was forced to extend his charity to the barmaid, which may perhaps account for the appearance of a smut mark on Conlan's left cheek, after the subsidence of the excitement, and of which an explanation was vigorously demanded, by the cross between a coal hewer and scullery man.

What an ungrateful old world this is. And how one's best intentions are liable to be misunderstood. We can't be too careful.

The most remarkable feature of the meeting which seemed to have escaped the notice of everyone but Jack was the lack of enthusiasm on the part of Curley.

During the whole course of Jack's logical speech Curley never raised his head (except by covert side glances in Jack's direction) from the note book in which he was making notes, the only outward sign of his inward thoughts being the peculiar click of the gleaming teeth in the midst of the applause, and which Jack declared months afterwards used to send a cold shiver down his spine and which was intensified by a few extra clicks on the appearance of Mr. Garnish, who was greeted with cheers and cries of "Ganway there, boys, for Mr. Garnish and speech."

To which Mr. Garnish replied by briefly stating that while not being acquainted with the merits and details of this particular dispute, he nevertheless fully recognised the necessity for combination, owing to the unjust conditions prevailing in connection with dock labour.

For instance, the loss of a whole night's rest for eightpence when ordered out in the middle of the night on spec.[54]

The systematic filching of the men's time by mustering to start work half an hour before the legitimate time for starting in the morning, fifteen minutes at dinner hour, and twenty-five minutes in the evening. The rigging of stages etcetera for ballast jobs for which the men were not paid, and the unguarded machinery, employment of boys for long hours at dangerous jobs, with men's lives depending upon them, and the use of rotten and imperfect plant, which filled the hospital with cripples and the poorhouse with widows and orphans.

"As I came along to this meeting," said Mr. Garnish, "I witnessed a remarkable instance of the inhuman inequalities of our unsocial commercial system.

"In one direction came the ambulance (with the speed of a bird on the wing) bearing the crushed and bleeding form of a dock labourer, and a little further on, in the opposite direction, came the handsome family brougham of the employer, with its high-stepping bays and silver harness and pampered menials before and behind, bearing inside the employer and portion of his family returning from a banquet, with a broad expanse of shirt front sparking with gems, and rings on the fingers of every member of the family, representing in value a king's ransom."

Cries of "Shame" and "We know him," during which another smut was added to the charms of the barmaid, another reassuring hug from Tom Conlan's protecting arm, and another vow of vengeance registered by the coal-heaving scullery man.

"My advice to you men, that now you have plucked courage to make a start to free yourselves from the horrible slavish trammels of ungodly commercialism, is to appoint your officers and a committee of management, in whom you can place implicit confidence, for, mind you, men, this is a big job you've undertaken, and requires men possessed of moral and physical courage mayhap to guide it, together with a certain amount, more or less, individual sacrifice on the part of each. And the man who is not prepared to make these sacrifices had better stand aside now, at once, and not retard the movement by allowing the weakness or cowardice, inherent in slavish natures and born of ignorance, to interfere with success."

The result of Mr. Garnish's advice was the selection of a committee of fifteen to meet nightly while the dispute lasted and to act as stewards for looking after the contributions of all those who had given in their names when they received the wages due to them on Saturday.

A vote of thanks, three rousing cheers and a promise of future patronage was given to the proprietor of the cocoa rooms which forced a blush through the smut on the barmaid's cheek, was followed by an exodus of the audience into the street, where a remarkable coincidence presented itself.

Coming in one direction was the ambulance returning from its mission of mercy, and in the other direction, coming from the docks, was Mr. Crushem, in a hired hansom, his arms folded over his low-breasted evening dress waistcoat and his hat tilted over his eyes, nursing his wrath on his way home, from which he had only a few short hours before emerged in the plenitude of his pomp and power.

"Blessed are the meek and lowly, for they shall find peace."[55]

Mr. Crushem, T.C., J.P., and L.G., had found the pieces.

[30 September 1893]
Chapter IX.

After the audience had dispersed, the committee stayed behind to arrange a plan of campaign and future meetings.

Mr. Garnish, as treasurer, advanced a sum to be refunded out of contributions to carry on the work. "He that advances money to a strike fund lendeth to the Lord, and shall receive his reward hereafter."[56]

Mr. Garnish and Goodman were both in favour of meeting the employer to endeavour to avoid a prolonged dispute, but, strange to say, Curley was entirely opposed to any conciliatory methods.

A few of the more daring spirits supported Curley – in perfect good faith – and a vote was demanded, which resulted in conciliatory methods being adopted, the minority loyally falling in with the wish of the majority, and Curley was instructed to write to the employers and arrange a meeting between them and the men's representatives.

After the committee had dispersed Goodman, Mr. Garnish, and Curley stood at the corner of the street before separating to discuss the situation, during which Curley appeared particularly anxious to get away, in order to attend to the correspondence, and on that plea bid Goodman and Garnish good night.

"Wait a minute, Curley," said Goodman, "your way is mine, and I'll leave you at home."

"Let him go," said Garnish, sotto voce, "if he is in a hurry, and walk a little of the way with me, I want to talk to you privately, and you can get the last car[57] back."

"Not to-night, Mr. Garnish," replied Goodman, as Curley walked slowly away along the street. "I'll come down and see you to-morrow, and I'm particularly anxious to see Curley home to-night, for reasons that I can't explain to you just now, but," with a grip of Mr. Garnish's hand which conveyed a world of meaning, "I'll give you my reasons another time."

And when the two men separated on their way to their respective homes, they carried with them a feeling of mutual distrust against Curley.

When Goodman turned round to seek for Curley after bidding Mr. Garnish good-night, Curley was no longer visible, but when he reached the corner of the next street the striking of a match in the gateway of a timber yard on the opposite side of the street attracted his attention, followed by a flame from a piece of paper that Curley held in his hand lighting his pipe, and in the illumination thus caused Goodman saw a second figure stealing away in the darkness under the shadow of the deal wall, with a gait and a back very much like Hoppy's.

On the impulse of the moment Goodman was about to make sure that his suspicion was right by rushing after the retreating figure for the purpose of identification, but on second thoughts he saw that this would only rouse Curley's suspicion and make himself ridiculous were his suspicion unfounded.

So he contented himself by asking "who's that just left you, Curley?"

"Haven't the slightest idea, Goodman. Some chap who was lighting his pipe here, and wanting a smoke myself I asked him for alight, and as it was only the match between us, I utilised this bit o' paper" – holding the flaming loosely folded paper towards Goodman, with the words, "want a light, old man," which Jack did not seem to have heard, for Jack's eyes were almost glued to the margin of the paper towards which the flame was slowly creeping, illuminating the follow portion of words and figures, which were ever after written on Jack's brain in letters of fire: –
—phone No
   —graphic address
      —hem Mudport.

Jack Goodman, during the remainder of the journey towards Curley's house, past which he had to go to reach his own, was much pre-occupied, and various questions of Curley's as to future line of action remained unanswered.

For Jack remembered vividly giving Curley a box of matches, which was not returned, to light the gas at the lower end of the cocoa room. And he reasoned thus: – If Curley still had that box of matches – and he had every reason to believe he had – why should he use a bit of paper to light his pipe?

Of course he knew that he occasionally himself, when he wanted a light, had cadged matches for the whole day, forgetting that he at the same time had a full box in his pocket, and therefore that was not very peculiar.

But there were them significant half-burnt words on the remaining unconsumed portion of the paper, and the halting gait and the familiar back that disappeared in the darkness as he overtook Curley.

Were these purely curious coincidences, or phantoms of his imagination born of mistrust of Curley, and did they justify him taking him by the throat, as he felt inclined to do, and forcing an answer form him.

Instinctively Goodman half stopped and turned on his heel to go back to the gateway to secure the remnant of burnt paper. But he remembered that Curley had crushed it out in the heel of his fist, and that he was now stuffing it into the bowl of his pipe, and watching his movements covertly, as they paused opposite Curley's lodgings.

Goodman's better reason prevailed, and after bidding Curley a curt good night he wended his way homeward, not to sleep, but dream troubled, terrible dreams of a seething, struggling mass of helpless humanity within four enclosed walls, fighting, screeching, and tearing the few rags off each other's backs in their endeavours to get through a narrow door into a purer atmosphere, guarded by Crushem, Grindem and Co. with loaded pistols, while all round the tops of the walls danced countless figures of Curleys and Hoppys armed with long poles tipped with cruel spikes, hurling back again into the human cauldron those who had been fortunate and daring enough to climb to the top.

Curley's slumber was not similarly disturbed, simply because Curley did not slumber.

On the contrary he was never more wide awake. For shortly after Jack and he had parted, the solitary guardian of the peace, waiting under the gas lamp lower down for the sound of the sergeant's footstep, noticed the door of Curley's house slowly opening, and drawing back into the shadow he awaited developments.

Slowly and cautiously, wider and yet more wide the door opened, and in the aperture appeared Curley's figurehead and gleaming teeth, which clicked with evident satisfaction as he imagined the coast clear.

His body followed his head and he stood on the doorstep turning up the collar of an immense coat, and turning down the brim of a felt wideawake[58] over his eyes.

This performance being completed, he cautiously pulled the door to after him without a sound, satisfied himself that he had not forgotten his latch-key to readmit himself, stepped out on to the sidewalk, and set out lightly and briskly up the street in the direction of Villadom.[59]

The policeman – like all average painstaking policemen with an eye to promotion – began to get curious, and hastily explaining the nature of the case to the sergeant, who had just come along, he started the trail.

Unconscious that he was followed, Curley walked briskly along, and, emerging from slumdom, crossed the rubicon[60] that divides the common people who create wealth from those who enjoy it.

The rubicon was a long, well-kept avenue of stately trees, in whose shadows, far back from the road, were built the handsome edifices of the kings of commerce.

At the gate of one of these Curley paused and struck a match, which sounded with clear distinctness in the dead silence of the night and caused the policeman to slip the lanyard of this truncheon round his wrist, and see to the unscrewing of his darbies[61] so as to have them ready in case of emergency.

Curley having satisfied himself of the name to the surprise and disgust of the policeman – who had looked forward at least to a sergeantship and glory in the local press for the clever and courageous capture of a notorious burglar – Curley walked boldly up to the front door, rang the bell, which was answered by a page who looked as if he was thinking of dispensing for the night with his buttons, and after a slight delay, the notorious burglar disappeared within the spacious doorway.

And the disgusted and disappointed policeman wended his way back to the slums, cursing his luck.

[7 October 1893]

The interior of the Crushem mansion was a household to be possessed of an artistic taste, the sight to behold, proving some members of the one pleasing feature of its surroundings, but which nevertheless stood out conspicuously an inhuman contrast to the hovels of those who had contributed to build and beautify the houses of Crushem.

Mr. Crushem, shortly after his elevation to the magisterial bench, had been interviewed by a representative of the *Daily Blatherskite*, which devoted two columns to a description of the interior.

A few weeks previous to this the same representative of the same *Daily Blatherskite* paid a visit to the slums, wherein dwelt the dockers employed by Crushem, and the first thing that struck the eye of the visitor on that occasion was something like a half cwt[62] of mortar, or an occasional loose brick, that the jerry builder had, in his hurry forgotten to tie up.

The *Blatherskite* man on this occasion saw no dreams of blue and gold, but –

He saw plenty of blue mould, not in any way resembling a dream, but hard, stern realities.

He had written a very descriptive account of his visit, for publication, but –

It was suddenly discovered that a great many of these houses were the property of Mr. Crushem. More of them the property of Hoppy, his foreman, and the rest of the property of Crushem's esteemed friend, and worthy Alderman Fatpurse, and that each and all of them were friends of the *Daily Blatherskite*.

Of course, these things make a difference. Consequently that article never appeared.

Thus the hopes of a budding and aspiring journalist were crushed in the bud. 'Twas ever thus!

Strange to say, this was the very question that was being discussed in the drawing-room into which Curley was ushered by the yawning Buttons, where the editor of the *Daily Blatherskite*, Crushem and Hoppy were seated, with a decanter between them, glasses half-filled with rare old port (Crushem being a temperance leader, never took anything stronger than port[63]), and smoking choice havanas[64] from a box that lay open on the table.

"Take a seat, Curley," said Crushem, motioning to a vacant chair, upholstered in purple plush,[65] and placing the decanter and cigars before him. "Help yourself, my man. You received my note, I suppose?"

"Yes, sir, I received it all right, and took the liberty of lighting my pipe with it for fear of it falling into other hands, as owing to the position I'm in one can't be too careful."

"Quite right, my man," chimed in the *Daily Blatherskite*. "Burnt documents, like dead men tell no tales."

"Let me see, you attended the – er – meeting of the men to-night, did you not?" asked Crushem, carefully flicking the ash of his cigar into a silver plate on the table.

"Yes, sir, I did," stolidly answered Curley.

"H'm, and what might I inquire was the – er – purport and outcome of the – er – meeting?"

"Yes, sir," cautiously replied Curley. "You may enquire and receive an answer conditionally that I am also allowed to enquire and receive a satisfactory answer as to the outcome so far as I am concerned of the information at my disposal."

"Come, come, Curley," said Hoppy, "you need have no fear of the consequences, and you can trust the master to treat you generously if you serve his interest in this matter." – ("Hear, hear" from the *Daily Blatherskite*.)

"Quite so, sir," replied Curley. "I don't for a moment question any of you gentlemen's good intentions, but good intentions are not a marketable commodity, but this being a case of supply and demand, where the demand is considerably more than equal to the supply and the marketable value enhanced by the scarcity, it becomes a monopoly in my hands, owing to the entire absence of competition, which places me, sir, in the sound commercial position of demanding my own terms, and which (with a click of the gleaming teeth) without any reflection upon the present company, who are not purchasers, I prefer to sell my wares to the purchaser direct, and without the intervention of a third party."

"Now look you here, Curley, my lad," said Hoppy, starting up, and in his excitement bringing his fist down on the table with a thump, thereby upsetting the *Daily Blatherskite*'s glass, and which, by the *Daily Blatherskite*, in a manner peculiar to journalists, was immediately replenished. "Don't you try on any of your side with me, because it won't do, and what's more, you know it won't; d'ye hear? How much would your commodity be worth if the men got to know of your presence here to-night, I'd like to know?"

"Don't you see, my fine fellow, this is a case of 'will you walk into my parlour said the spider to the fly,' and you're in the parlour now, as well up as you think yourself."

"Not at all, my dear sir; don't excite yourself," coolly replied Curley, with two or three sharp clicks in succession. "You simply over-estimate your own cleverness, and I have always been of the opinion that you are a very over-estimated man. You don't suppose I have come here without considering both the risk and the gain of coming, do you? If so, allow me to tell you that I feel quite safe and easy about myself, and my safety lies in the commercial principles that prevents you gentlemen from doing anything that does not pay or return a dividend. The course you suggest would not pay, and (with another click) I feel quite safe on that account; besides, I have told you nothing yet, and you can't be too careful."

"The gentleman is quite right," said the *Daily Blatherskite* (who had slipped a piece of paper under the table to Mr. Crushem, with the following sentence written upon it: 'Humour him; we will leave the room, and you can tell us when he has gone, and, besides, there's the photograph.') "so with your permission I would suggest that we leave you together," and, turning to Hoppy, "Come, sir, I'll walk home with you, it is past twelve, there are no conveyances. Luckily, our way lies in the same direction. Good night, my dear Crushem, and let your motto be, 'Be just, and fear not.'"[66] And taking Hoppy by the arm, he conducted him out of the room, leaving Crushem and Curley together.

"Now, Mr. Curley," said Crushem, as the door closed behind the retreating forms of Hoppy and the *Blatherskite* editor, "let us get to business. You have certain information to give, for which I suppose you want your price. Might I enquire the figure?"

"Yes, sir," replied Curley, "and as the bargain will include not only present but future information on the same subject, and, if I might be allowed to say it, advice as to how to checkmate Goodman and his crowd, together with the risk I am running, I should think" – and here the teeth clicked again – "the price will be a modest one indeed if it runs into three figures."

"H'm," grunted Crushem; "how am I to judge of its value?"

"Well, sir, it does run a bit like buying a pig in a poke.[67] But how am I to judge your honesty?"

"Ha! h'm. I don't think," said Crushem, laying back in his chair and ramming his hands up to the elbows in his pockets, and jingling the loose coins in his pockets, "I don't think I would lay too much stress on that word if I were you," and as Curley looked over Crushem's shoulder in the direction of a draped statue of Justice he fancied he detected a sneer on the chiselled features.

"Oh, all right, sir," said Curley, rising as if to move towards the door. "If you won't stump up there's an end of the matter."

"Come, come, my man," remonstrated Crushem, "don't be so deuced hasty. Sit down, and have another cigar," and taking a handful out of the box, "here, take these, and put them in your pocket; and just to show you that I trust you here" – taking out his pocket-book and selecting a five pound note – "here's something on account as guarantee of good faith."

"Thanks, sir, I prefer cash,[68] if it's all the same to you. Them things are not in my line, and might cause inquiries to be made, and it would be awkward for me to explain."

"Oh, very well; here you are," said Crushem, throwing five sovereigns on the table at which Curley's eyes glistened and his teeth clicked: "Now, then, what about this meeting?"

"Well, sir," replied Curley, as he pocketed the coin, "they've decided to form a union. I'm appointed secretary *pro tem*. A chap's coming here from a distance to give them a hand, and a committee is appointed to draw up rules to submit to the employers, and I need hardly tell you they mean business, and that you'll have a job to get men in the morning to man the ship."

"Yes, curse them," muttered Crushem. "I have already experienced difficulty in that direction. There's over three hundred pounds gone by their action to-day, but," bringing his clenched fist down on the table, "I'll be even with them yet, and if I don't make some of the ungrateful scoundrels that I've clothed and fed rue this before many months are over, I'm not Mr. Crushem J.P."

"You'll have to hurry up, sir," said Curley, "or they'll get ahead of you, as others have given notice of their intention to join. This is going to be a bigger job than the last attempt at forming a union, which I believe died out on account of the weak energy, intelligence, and pluck, and from what I know of the men in this movement there's plenty of all three commodities this time."

"Ah! I see, Curley, you know more than I thought you did," said Crushem. "Now, what course would you suggest? Mind, if you prove yourself a valuable ally, you'll find me a generous one."

"Well, sir, seeing that I'm in the know and occupying a responsible position and am trusted by a great number of the men, it will be necessary for me, in order to retain that confidence, to abuse you publicly every time I get the chance."

"Oh, yes, of course, I see that," said Crushem. "Abuse me to your heart's content, and to keep up the delusion I suppose I must return the compliment, eh?"

"Well, I'm not so concerned about that, sir, but this thing must be crushed in the bud if you intend to retain your present position, and I should again venture to offer you advice, to get a supply of men from outside as quickly as possible. I'll undertake to manage that, if you like, and when that is accomplished we must at once issue a bogus notice, as if it emanated from the strike committee, ordering a general strike.

"And as they have no funds, are not yet sufficiently organised, the men will stop work, their places we can fill up with imported men, the thing will fizzle out in a week, the leaders will be discredited, and you, the masters, can demand your own terms."

"Splendid! Capital! Curley, my man, you're a treasure. Allow me to express my admiration of your foresight, and if you stick to me in this business you'll not be sorry for it. And now I must bid you good night, and I will expect you tomorrow evening at the same time, when I will ask you to repeat your opinions in the presence of a few more gentleman, who will also pay you well for them," and, opening the door leading to the hall, he called out, "James, see Mr. Curley to the bottom of the garden the back way."

As the door of the room closed behind Curley the door of a large clock standing opposite to him in the hallway flew open, and a sepulchral voice gave forth the small wee hours, "Cuckoo, cuckoo."

[14 October 1893]

Chapter XI.

Doctor Smythe had an interesting patient in the person of the eldest Miss Crushem.

It happened thus: – Miss Crushem had been to visit one of her old pensioners in a cellar in the slums. The steps leading down to the rabbit burrow wherein the family of five persons starved and slept was coated with ice, and Miss Crushem had slipped from the top to the bottom, striking her pretty head against the jam of the door, and the hospital being close by (hospitals are always close by the slums), she was conveyed there, and carefully attended – oh, so carefully attended to – by Doctor Smythe, who, after taking a wonderful long time, and using a wonderful lot of bandages, had her conveyed home to the Crushem mansion, and was now attending her professionally. And judging from the frequency of his visits, the case would appear to be very serious indeed.

Still there did not appear to be anything very seriously the matter with Miss Crushem on this occasion of the doctor's third visit on the afternoon of this particular day nearly three weeks after the accident. And it has been suggested by some that the broad piece of sticking plaster, conspicuous among the raven locks, covered a multitude of sins. In fact, had anyone been anxious enough to watch the doctor's movements while dressing his patient's wounds, they would probably have noticed his moustache in closer proximity to that sticking plaster than his hands.

Lately, however, even the sticking plaster was neglected, and the patient's pulse seemed to have travelled up to her chin. For it was here that the doctor laid his left hand, while his moustache attended to a locality considerably below the sticking plaster, while the owner of the chin would look straight down her nose and blush up to the sticking plaster.

"Well," said the doctor, after the usual professional salute, "and how is my patient this morning? And what does she think of her medical adviser?"

"Your patient is very well, sir," replied the girl, "and she thinks her professional medical adviser is a professional humbug. Don't you think we are doing very wrong, Alick, by this deceit?"

"My dear girl, make your mind easy on that point; all's fair in love and politics. And besides, my bill for professional attendance will more than compensate your father for what you are pleased to call deceit. Besides," taking a book from her hand, and glancing at the title, "Looking Backwards,"[69] "I'm very much afraid I shall again have to take up my professional duties if you indulge in so much Bellamy."

"Oh, Alick, dear," exclaimed the patient, "don't include abstention from Bellamy in your horrid prescription. He is a darling. If you do, sir (with mock seriousness), I shall certainly discard the sticking plaster, and then your professional duties will end."

"H'm! that certainly would be a Roland for my Oliver[70] with a vengeance. But, all the same, I shall be fearfully jealous of Bellamy, if you allow him to occupy all your thoughts to the entire exclusion of your attentive medical adviser."

"You silly boy; you know there is no danger in that direction. In fact, sir, if you only knew it, Bellamy only serves to enhance your position."

"H'm! then on more mature consideration," replied the Doctor, inspecting the sticking plaster with his moustache, "Bellamy may stay, and I'm awfully obliged to him. But seriously, my dear girl, this must be my last professional visit," of course with the accent on the professional.

"Then, I suppose, sir, the next consideration is your fee?"

"Ye-es; you are right; and, to be candid with you, I'm afraid I shall have some difficulty getting it," replied the Doctor.

"Why, is it so very large," asked the girl.

"I'm afraid it is, dear, larger than your father will be prepared to give. Can't you guess what it is, dear?" said the Doctor, as he sought for her pulse at the back of her neck, while he seated himself on the arm of the chair. "It is your own sweet self I am going to ask for. Have I your permission?"

"Alick, dear, you know you have; but don't you think you are putting me rather cheap? Am I not worth more than three weeks' medical fees?"

"My dear girl, of course you are. Don't be too severe on me. You're worth all the world to me, and may I never get another patient if I don't beard the lion in his den this very moment and ask him for my fee." And, rising from his position on the chair arm, he walked towards the door, when he was arrested by the voice of his patient shyly asking, "Alick, dear, won't you look at the sticking plaster? Just for luck before you go."

It took fully five minutes to arrange that sticking plaster.

Chapter XII.

There was again great activity in Mudpuddle-street. But for a different cause than on the previous occasion.

The same women lined the steps of the cellars, and doors, and room windows, and talked and shouted across to their neighbours in the opposite windows. But, strange to say, there was an entire absence of the black can, while the female heroes of a hundred fights about bundles now sympathised with each other in their general misfortune.

The whole of the street was owned by Crushem, and his tenants, mostly his employees, were, owing to bad times, somewhat in arrears with their rent.

It happened thus: – When Crushem was nominated for the Town Council, his agent and rent collectors connected with his extensive slum property were instructed not to collect any rents, but to confine their duties to solicit the votes of the *free* and *independent*[71] electors living in Crushem's property in favour of Mr. Crushem's candidature. And the wives of the "free and independents," with a fortnight's rent to the good, brought all the influence of their nature to bear upon the spouse of their bosom to vote for the landlord, who was unanimously voted a dacent gintleman in favour of justice to Ould Ireland.

There had been many attempts since the election by Crushem's agents to gather in the arrears, but they had, owing to slack times, not been very successful.

This Monday morning Crushem's agent had notified all tenants in arrears to pay up within a certain period.

Mrs. Maloney, the wife of one of the men on strike, was the first to receive the notice, and had communicated the alarming fact to her subtenants[72] upstairs. As the agent went up one side of the street the women congregated to meet him as he came down on the other side, and their demeanour gave promise of a very vigorous interview on his way back.

On reaching the line of battle, Mrs. Maloney opened fire with – "Luck id here, mistha, what d'ye mane by this?" holding out the notice at the end of a brawny arm worthy of a blacksmith.

"The meaning is, my dear madam," said the collector, in a suave voice and trembling limbs as he surveyed the crowd of angry women, "the reason is, my dear ladies, that the landlord wants his rent, and I, as his servant, am instructed to get it."

"Why, bad luck till his ugly carcass. Didn't we get our husbands to vote for him and more betoken, you lantern-jawed, misshapen piece of humanity? Didn't you tell us that you wouldn't collect any rents for a fortnight, and, besides, how can we pay rent when he's sacked our husbands?"

"My dear madam," replied the agent, as his knees knocked together and his few remaining teeth chattered in his gums, "you are in error. Mr. Crushem is only too anxious to give your husbands work, but they refuse to work, and as these homes belong to Mr. Crushem, he very naturally objects to allow them to occupy them when they won't work to pay the rent."

"Yes, bad luck to you and him, you slippery thief of the world!" shouted Mrs. Maloney. "Yez wants to make scabs of our men for your own dirty purpose, and you can just go back to your tinker of a master and tell him that the wimen will fight their husband's battles as they fought his last November, and that the wimen that put him into the Council will put him out when his turn comes."

"Tell him our men refuse to be blacklegs, and that we refuse to leave the homes that we've paid for three times over."[73]

(Good girl, Molly! Your sowl to glory! from the crowd.)

"And now," said Mrs. Maloney, gathering her skirts round her, and stepping on one side, "will you ladies kindly make way for the gintleman to leave the neighbourhood as quick as he can; and I'll be obliged till ye, ladies, if ye'll show him the way."

This advice was eagerly acted upon, and as Crushem's agent passed through the lane of angry women folk he left mementoes of his visit in the shape of a damaged three-decker,[74] a soiled paper collar, and a few handfuls of wiry hair which some of his numerous and vigorous admirers expressed their intention of preserving in lockets to poison the rats, and a humane policeman from the station lower down conducted him to a more congenial neighbourhood.

Scarce had the excitement of Crushem's agent's visit subsided than another exciting incident occurred in the shape of a fever van, which came slowly down the street from the direction of the fever hospital.[75] This was the fifth visit that Mudpuddle-street had received from this gruesome institution; still every time it appeared the neighbours gazed awestruck to watch its progress.

And the van drew up in front of the door of poor old Tom Burrows, who had served a lifetime in Crushem's service, to be carried away to that institution from which few ever return, the eyes of the watchers were wet with tears, and exclamations were heard, "God be good to us; it'll be our turn next, and what, in God's name will become of the poor childer?"

[21 October 1893]

Chapter XIII.

At the monthly meeting of the Bumbledom Town Council, it was proposed by Councillor Crushem, seconded by Alderman Fatpurse: –

That in view of the very threatening attitude of these dock labourers, calculated to create a very serious breach of the peace, that we request the authorities to draft extra police into the district, and also that we petition the magistrates to request the Home Secretary to place a number of troops at our disposal for the protection of property.[76]

Alderman Fatpurse said: – "It was with feelings of considerable regret – in fact, with very mixed feelings indeed – that he rose to second the resolution, because he had a great and lasting respect for the labouring community, who were the staple commodity of the trade and commerce of the port, and of which they were justly proud. – (Hear, hear.) He was sorry to have to appear in antagonism to the working men, but he felt sure that in the end they would see that it was for their good to – er – (Mr. Garnish: "To be shot.") No, he sincerely hoped there would be no necessity to shoot, as he was sure the very presence of an armed force would prevent disorder, and allow those sterling, level-headed men who were anxious to return to their work to do so unmolested. He, for one, knew hundreds of them who were willing to do so if protection were afforded them. And knowing this he would be failing in his duty as a representative man if he refused to give them assistance. Moreover, with a proper escort, he was prepared to head these men and march them down to the docks the following morning." – (Loud applause.), during which Mr. Garnish had risen in his place, and, after having succeeded in catching the Mayor's eye, replied as follows: –

"Mr. Mayor and gentlemen" – with the accent on the gentlemen – "I scarcely know whether to be angry or amused at the speeches of the two gentlemen who have spoken on the resolution, because both the ludicrous and tragic elements prevail to a very large extent. Up to the present I have had a certain amount of respect and admiration for the business capabilities of these gentlemen and I am yet charitably enough disposed towards them to think that they are as yet unconscious of the position this resolution will place them in. And like my estimable friend – with the accent on the estimable – I feel, though returned on the same ticket and by the same constituency as the proposer, that I would be failing in my duty also as a public man if I did not endeavour to ask these two gentlemen to see themselves as others see them."

There was dead silence during the delivery of this audacious speech – you could feel it – and the heavy gold chain and locket resting on the broad and expansive bosom of the Mayor was visibly agitated.

"In the first place," said Councillor Garnish, "the resolution speaks of the threatening attitude of the men – (Hear, hear.) The gentleman who says "Hear, hear" must be possessed of a very vivid imagination. I have been among them – (Hear, hear.) Yes, and I'm proud of my acquaintances – (shame), – and as yet I have nothing to be ashamed of, but intend to assist the men in their legal and perfectly peaceful combination to secure better conditions of life. (Dead silence.) Now then! Let us see upon whose shoulders rests the shame. The resolution requests an addition to the police force. And the persons who will have to charge the police force, who are they? (Dead silence.) Are they not the very men who employ the dock labourers who, in the opinion of the police authorities, are calculated to create a breach of the peace?"

On this occasion the silence was broken by his Worship, who, after a hurried consultation with the Town Clerk, rose with a firm gasp on his gold mounted ivory mallet to call Mr. Garnish to order.

"Might I ask, Mr. Mayor," said Mr. Garnish, "upon what grounds you base your ruling?"

"On the grounds of personal reflections upon members of this Council that are simply disgraceful, sir," replied his Worship. And the gold chain was again very visibly agitated, and there was loud applause.

"Can your Worship deny that what I state is true?" asked Mr. Garnish. (Dead silence.) "I see there is no denial. That being the case I am bound, with all due respect to your worship's opinion, to complete my case. Therefore, there being no signs of a breach of the peace, I challenge the right of this Council to spend the people's money to send for police and soldiers, which would only tend to create a breach of the peace where none at present exists, especially when the mover and seconder of the resolution themselves are the magisterial authority to whom we shall have to appeal. And I respectfully ask the town clerk through your worship to define under what Act the Council is empowered to deal with the question of supplying troops and police?"

This request of Councillor Garnish caused great commotion, and quite an army of supernumeraries were occupied during the lull in fortifying the town clerk (who received 10s. per hour) with legal evidence, and who, after a considerable lapse of time, during which he had conferred with the proposer and seconder, delivered judgment in a pompous tone as follows: –

"Pursuant to Vic. —, cap. —, sub. sec. —. The powers to secure additional forces for protection of the public peace are vested in the justices of the peace in the locality." But laying down the Act he added, "There is nothing to prevent this Council, as custodians of the public weal, from recommending the authorities to do so." – (Loud and continued applause.)

"Then, Mr. Mayor," said Mr. Garnish, "as one of the aforesaid custodians, I feel it my duty to present a minority report to the public, that this Council, composed of magistrates, are petitioning themselves to spend the ratepayers' money to send for soldiers to shoot the ratepayers."

The resolution was carried with only one dissentient.

* * *

It was rather unfortunate for Doctor Smythe that he should have chosen this particular day to ask for his fee, for Mr. Crushem had only just returned from the Council meeting and sat nursing wrath, when the doctor solicited an audience, and it suddenly occurred to him that the Doctor was a friend of Mr. Garnish, and he had also a faint suspicion of the relations existing between his daughter and the Doctor, elements which perhaps might be used to his advantage, and if not, then he would make short work of the whole business, pay him his fee, and forbid him the house, thus his revenge.

The audience was granted.

"Well, Doctor," said Crushem, as he pushed the cigar box across the table, "to what do I owe the honour of your visit? I may tell you at once that I'm not in much of a humour to receive visitors, and especially a visitor whose bosom friend has grossly and publicly insulted me during the last hour."

"I'm sorry to hear, sir," replied the Doctor, "that any friend of mine should have so transgressed. May I ask to whom you refer?"

"Why to that conceited ass Garnish, who actually accused me in a full Council meeting to-day of being personally interested in moving a resolution for troops to be sent here to prevent a riot and destruction of property by the men, whom he is encouraging to rebel against their masters. And by the way, I hear you are also mixed up in this business, and even your silly old fool of a father has lately got his head full of Labour bureaus and boards of arbitration. 'Pon my soul, sir! I don't know what the country is coming to with such confounded disloyal socialistic notions."

"I'm sorry to hear, sir, that you entertain such a poor opinion of me and my friends. I don't mix my opinions as easy as I do my medicines. The object of my visit to-day was to ask a very great favour from you, but as you don't seem in the frame of mind just now to grant it, and as I have no wish to risk a refusal, I'll postpone it to a more convenient occasion," and the doctor stood up to depart.

"Come, come, my boy," said Crushem, in a more modified tone, seeing that he had gone a little too far. "You know me long enough, I'm sure, to take offence at my abruptness. Your old dad only laughs at it which generally has the effect of making me laugh too and putting me in a better temper, and as you know I've been severely tried of late."

"Now as it happens I fancy I can guess the favour you are going to ask. You can't blind me with your sticking plaster and formidable case of instruments, you sly dog. Now I happen to have a favour to ask you, and as exchange is no robbery suppose we exchange."

"My dear sir, nothing would delight me more, I'm sure," replied the doctor, grasping the hand held out to him, and which, owing to its clammy nature, caused a shudder to run through him, "and if it is in my power to grant it, you may consider it done. What is the nature of it?"

"Well, my lad – it is within your power, and, to come to the point, it is that you shall go to the next meeting of the men, use your influence to get them to come back to their work, and leave their union, which is only being built up to pay a lot of lazy, loafing agitators. Tell them if they persist in their present conduct, that there are hundreds waiting to take their places, and police to protect them, that are willing to come back but we will not have any of the sneaking scoundrels who led the revolt back at any price. Do this, as I know you can, if you like, and consider the request you were about to ask granted."

"And what, sir, if I refuse," sternly asked the doctor.

"H'm. Ah! Well," muttered Crushem, noticing the cloud about to burst. "In that case – er – you could – er – hardly expect to – but surely you will not throw away your only chance of winning your fair lady?"

"From what I know of my fair lady, the sweetest and fairest lady, to me, at all events, in the world, I should lose my only chance of winning her were I to accept her father's conditions, who, strange to say, seems to be as ignorant of his daughter's constitution as he is of social questions. So –"

"You refuse then," roared Crushem.

"I do, most positively refuse!" replied the doctor, "and were you not her father, and in your own house, my refusal would assume more vigorous proportions."

"Then, Sir Jakanapes," said Crushem, going over to the door and opening it, "our interview is at an end, and as your honour did not inconvenience you in making love to my daughter under the cloak of medical adviser, let your bill be presented through the post and I will settle it by cheque. For once the door of this house closes upon you you never re-enter it while I'm master here, and d—, but I'll commence to be master from this, out," and slamming the door after the doctor's retreating figure he threw himself into his chair, muttering "Confound him for a cheeky young cub. I'll put a stop to his love-making."

The doctor had fully made up his mind to depart without seeing his patient but as he was getting his hat from the stand in the hall a reproachful voice from behind whispered, "Is the doctor forgetting his prescription? What if the patient has a relapse?" Then noting his look of distress, "Oh! Alick, dear, have you failed?"

"Yes, my love, failed with the father because I refused to surrender my manhood to his greed for gain," and he related the interview, "but may I hope that my action commends itself to the daughter?"

The daughter's answer was very suggestive of more sticking plaster.

[28 October 1893]

Chapter XV.

A special committee meeting was being held in Jack Goodman's kitchen to discuss the situation and receive the secretary and delegate's report. Curley the secretary, had not arrived, and in his absence Jack Goodman, as president, gave a condensed statement.

"The membership up to date numbered 10,000, all fully paid up, and every day hundreds more were being added.

"Up to the present only one firm – Crushem's – had been affected, and as their policy was 'defence, not defiance' they had no wish to cause trouble elsewhere, and if Crushem would only listen to reason the dispute would be settled tomorrow.

"The rules had been drawn up and submitted to the employers, and pending a reply he warned every member to be guided by the officials they had chosen to fight their battle, as he had every reason to believe an attempt would be made by Crushem to secure assistance from other employers to lock out their men in order to break up and discredit their combination. Therefore let no man act without official notice, as one false step might land them into difficulties. – (Hear, hear.)

"It had come to his knowledge that blacklegs were being imported from other towns by Crushem, and pickets were at present watching the railway station to endeavour to persuade these unfortunate, misguided men to return from whence they came."

"Let's chuck 'em in the dock, boys," said a committee man.

"No, no, lads," replied Goodman; "don't you do anything so foolish; don't you lay a hand on 'em at all. That would only be playing into the hands of the enemy, and you will be tried for intimidation by magistrates who are your employers, and you know from experience what the result would be."

"That's so, Jack, mi lad," said several.

"It's no use," continued Goodman, "blaming the blacklegs, though God knows I've no love for them; but many of the poor devils who will be coming here are driven by starving wives and children to sell their manhood. And you who are husbands and fathers know what an effect the plaintive cries of our helpless little ones for food has upon the beings responsible for their existence.

"So, lads, while we condemn the system which forces them to do this, let us set ourselves to change the system instead of abusing its victims."

While Jack was speaking a considerable commotion was heard outside in the street, a rush of hurrying feet, angry voices and shrill whistles, which one of the committee put down to the ambulance, and to satisfy his curiosity went to the door to ascertain, when –

No sooner had the door opened than a wild, hunted-looking man sprang past him into the lobby, slammed the door to, and, before the committeeman could recover himself, shot home the bolts, and then stood wiping the blood from his face which oozed from an ugly would over his left eye, that gave his pallid features a ghastly look under the feeble flicker of the gas lamp that shone through the fanlight over the street door.

The noise brought all hands out into the lobby, and as an explanation became necessary the intruder was conducted into the kitchen to give an account of himself.

This, under ordinary circumstances, and from a physical point of view the intruder seemed very capable of doing, for though the few remaining rags that the mob had left upon him hung rather loosely on his spare frame he looked a dangerous customer to tackle, and his fearless and defiant attitude as he stood erect, awaiting the pleasure of his audience commanded their respect.

Jack Goodman was about to question him when the knocker on the front door was attacked with force sufficient to wrench it from its socket, and the voices of an angry multitude demanded immediate admission.

"That's Curley's voice outside, lads," said Goodman. "Go and open the door Christie, and let him in; perhaps he may throw some light on the subject." And turning to the intruder – "here, my lad; take a seat here behind me near the fire, don't you be afraid" – as the intruder hesitated – "nobody'll hurt you while you're here." "Thanks mate," said the intruder. "I'm not afraid of any man living, but when it comes to have to tackle a crowd like them outside, a chap's bound to go to the wall," and as the outer door opened to admit not only Curley, but a dozen others, and the sound of a scuffle was heard in the lobby, the blood began to ooze from the ghastly cut on the forehead afresh.[77]

When the uproar had calmed down, Curley and a few of his friends were admitted into the kitchen, and Curley opened the discussion by denouncing the stranger as a scab who had just arrived by train from the country, to take the men's place who were on strike, and he demanded his immediate delivery into their hands to teach him a lesson as a warning to others.

The very mention of the word scab was sufficient to prejudice the minds of the majority of the committee, who immediately joined Curley in his demand, and things began to look ugly for the stranger.

"Now my lads," said Goodman, "don't be too hasty in condemning a poor devil unheard. The greatest criminal has the right to be heard in his own defence, and while I've no wish to doubt our comrades here, I think we should allow this poor chap a hearing."

"That's so Jack my lad," said Christie and a few others, "fair play is bonny play, let's give him a chance to square his yards if he can."

"Mates," said Curley with the usual click of his teeth, "you hear what your leader says: believe the word of a scab whom your leader is harbouring before the word of your comrades. I tell you mates I saw this skunk get off the train along with the rest of the scallawags; the pickets here are my witnesses with whose assistance we managed to cut a few of them off from the main body. The other skunks gave us their promise to go back to where they came from, but his chap here actually defied us, and severely handled two of our mates in the bargain, and now here's your leader taking his part and harbouring such vermin."

During Curley's speech the stranger had coolly taken a pipe from the hob and lit it at the fire, and was now calmly listening to Curley's tornado of abuse, the only outward sign of his inward feeling being the quick succession of puffs at the pipe and the volumes of smoke issuing from between his lips, while Jack Goodman, with an ugly look on his face sternly confronted Curley.

"Look here, Dan," said he, "if it wasn't for the job we have on hand, and the fact that your are in my house – a fact that you haven't the good manners to recognise – I should ram your lies down your throat. As it is, I shall expect you to unsay them words and apologise at once," and he made a step towards Curley, with his hands clenched.

"Let the skunk deny it if he can," sulkily replied Curley, a question which was re-echoed by the majority of the men, who began to look with suspicion upon Goodman, a fact that was taken advantage of by Curley, and which he followed up by saying, "The infernal scab has left two of our mates for dead lads. Let's have satisfaction out of him."

Things were looking ugly for the stranger, who by this time stood up with the tongs in his hand, while the blood from the ugly-looking wound flowed faster.

"Look here, mates," said Jack; "have any of your ever known me to do a dirty trick?"

Faint murmurs of "No lad, we haven't," and "we hopes as you'll not spoil your reputation," said another.

"I'll take care of that, never fear, Ned; and my reputation for fair play is at stake if I allow a bully like Dan Curley to incite you, lads, to injure a defenceless man; and an Englishman's reputation for hospitality is at stake also, if I were to allow any man who seeks the protection of my roof to be abused while it shelters him."

"What d'ye mean by calling me a bully?" asked Curley, advancing to the middle of the floor. "I tell you, lads, I speak the truth about this skunk here; he's a scab, imported her to take the bread out of your mouth. I know the place he came from."

"Mates," said the stranger, "that last sentence of Mr. Curley's is nearer the truth than anything he has yet said;" and stepping into the middle of the floor in front of Curley, "Mr. Curley does know the place I came from, and what's more, there's the suspicion, mates, in my mind that he was one of the recruiting agents to fetch us here."

This astounding statement caused every eye to be turned upon Curley, who stood as if struck dumb for a moment. But only for a moment, and turning to the men he said, "You can see, chaps, how this thing is worked. This is a clumsy attempt to divert suspicion on to me. It is scarcely necessary for me to say that not one of you believe it."

"Yes, Dan Curley," replied Christie, slipping out into the middle of the floor, "here is one! And I can answer for a couple more that believe it – (cries of "That's so, Christie.) More-be-token, we believe you know something about this," unfolding a sheet of paper, and displaying a poster bearing the following startling announcement:

> To the Duchess of the Port of Mudpuddle
> Fellow workers – The day of your deliverance is at hand, when an opportunity will be given to you to turn the tables on your oppressors and exploiters of your labour. Hundreds are looking to the union everyday. The situation is in your hands. By to-morrow morning not a docker will be outside the union. Then is your time to STRIKE! STRIKE! STRIKE! Strike out like men; be hard; and the victory is yours. HARD CASH is coming from other ports. BY ORDER OF THE COMMITTEE.

[4 November 1893]
Chapter XVI.

The strike poster had done its work not wisely, but too well.[78]

The following morning scarcely a man presented himself on the stands for employment.

A hurried meeting had been held at the dock gates, and Goodman had advised the men to go back to their work in every firm but Crushem's until further orders.

It was no use. The slumbering spirit of discontent with their surroundings had been aroused in the breasts of the multitude, and the memory of past injustices added fuel to the flame which had been smouldering, only awaiting the hand to stir up the embers. A general strike was the order of the day, and, notwithstanding Goodman's repudiation of the forged poster, the *Daily Blatherskite*, with the characteristic loftiness and heavy humour of all *Daily Blatherskites*, devoted a full page of morning and evening issues placing – strictly within the meaning of the act – the responsibility entirely upon the shoulders of Goodman, and, with characteristic charity, refused to publish a contradiction.

Thus is the *Blatherskite* press, whose dividends and salaried slaves are contributed to by the people – used against the people who create the salaries and dividends. Selah!

And the text of the High Priest of Mudpuddle on the following Sunday morning was: – "Saul was out looking for his father's asses, and lo! he hath found them!"

"What miserable hounds these hireling scribes are," said Mr. Garnish, as he stood reading a copy of the *Blatherskite*, after the meeting, "and the worst features of their infernal system is that even their victims feed the source of their own misfortune.

"See yonder; that's the third car load of special editions of their infamous lies that had been disposed of by the ragged, bare-footed children of the dockers, and see how the dockers themselves eagerly buy them out the moment they arrive. Nay, even I myself, who loath and despise the infernal rag, am forced to contribute out of pure perversity to learn what this organ of the British public has to say about the question. It's a funny old world, Goodman. I wonder what it's all about?"

"God alone knows, sir," replied Goodman, "and sometimes I even question even if he knows; and if he does, how that just, merciful, and all powerful divinity they used to tell us about in Sunday school in whose sight all men are equal allows such monstrous, inhuman inequality to exist?"

"Come, come, my lad! you must not talk like that, you know; its not respectable," said Mr. Garnish. "Always remember that whatever happens under our good old cast iron commercial system is the will of God, but which I am very much afraid does not include the Labour agitator who interferes with the law of supply and demand.

"Now, sir, you're chaffing me, and though I'm not in much of a humour, with this great responsibility thrust upon me against my wish, I cannot but see with you the tragic humour, so to speak, of our lop-sided system.

"I used to think one time that everything that happened was the will of God. My poor old mother made use of the same expression when my poor old dad was carried home a cripple from Crushem's employ. I've stood by the bedside of the youngsters he left behind, and seen their little lives crushed out by starvation and disease brought about by the law of supply and demand, and insanitary laws made by jerry-building town councillors. I held the poor old mother's form in my arms when, twelve months after, she breathed her last, her poor old spirit broken in her unequal fight with the same cursed law. But I've never heard any babbling about visions of angels and bright hereafters that the parish magazines tell us soothe the last moments of the poor; and, strange to say, somehow or other, the parable of the rich man, the camel, and the eye of a needle does not present itself to me in the same light as it used to do. It seems to me that there are such a lot of fellows willing to take their chance in the next world, and prefer being rich in this.

"Then, again, about this law of supply and demand? It's funny how inconsistent its advocates are about themselves. For instance, take the discussion of the council at the last meeting, when a large sum was granted for the purchase of a picture, for which there was no demand, and the refusal of the same Council to grant money to open out works for the unemployed, and so save the wholesale slaughter of the innocents (children of the unemployed) from starvation, and for which the demand far exceeds supply. And, again, take the monuments erected to the memory of our great generals, whose descendants are in receipt of princely pensions. Is there any demand for monuments? And yet the very natural demand of the poor old heroes who have made England's name famous in the martial history of the world, is far from being supplied, except it be the demand for parish coffins and nameless graves, as a reward for services rendered, in the interest of their own native land.

"And again! I have never heard of there being any particular strong demand for German pauper princes, to be paid princely salaries by the good old mutton-headed, free and independent British elector![79] Yet the supply is unlimited. Why, even their own pet argument as regards the labour market, where they claim that the demand for labour regulates the price, the bottom of their argument is completely knocked out by their own comic economics, for, according to their own professors, the land of this country is capable of supporting twice the present population. And yet if the majority of the present population who produce everything, endeavour to put the theory of the professors into practice, they are condemned by the minority, composed of M.P.'s, Lords, Town Councillors, Guardians of the Poor (what blasphemous hypocrisy), magistrates, and other members of our criminal classes, who produce nothing but workhouses, gaols, and slums, that we are driving the trade out of the country.

"And what I say is, that if the trade of the country is to be built upon the graves and broken bones of the workers, as it is at present, then the sooner it leaves the country the better for the workers.

"There is at least one consolation – the trade can't take the country with it, and I'm sanguine enough to think that the workers, without a foreign trade, could make a better job of the country than the idlers have done with a foreign trade. Anyhow, they couldn't possibly make it any worse."

"Why, my dear Goodman," said Mr. Garnish, "what a terrible revolutionist you are; but seriously, my lad, you have got a big enough job on at present, and although I may tell you candidly there's an ugly look about it, and, as the Yankee puts it, I think it just a leetle too previous, if my assistance is any use to you you can depend upon me to see you through. By the way, I heard you denouncing the strike notice. How do you account for it?"

"Well, sir, as yet I can't exactly account for it, except as an invention of the enemy to cripple us and that we have a traitor in the camp somewhere. We haven't found him out yet, but we're on his track, and old Christie actually accused –"

"Dan Curley, for a dollar!" exclaimed Garnish, interrupting Goodman.

"Yes, sir," replied Goodman; "you've guessed it the first time. Have you any grounds for your suspicion?"

"No-o," replied Garnish, hesitatingly, "that is, no tangible grounds, only a mistrust of the man, coupled what might be simply a coincidence, that I happened to be in the Chief Constable's office the other day in my capacity as a member of the Watch Committee, when the sergeant was giving a report of a suspicious character seen prowling about in the vicinity of Crushem's house after midnight, and whose description tallied with Curley's."

"Do you remember the date, sir?" inquired Goodman, eagerly.

"No, I don't know that I took particular notice of the date; in fact I should have forgotten all about the incident only you happened to mention the fact of a traitor in the camp. Yet stay; now I recollect, the report was given the morning after the meeting in the Cocoa Room, because the meeting of the Council was held the same day."

"Then, by God!" said Goodman, as he stood still and clenched both hands, "there is something in it," and he raised the incident of the half-burnt memorandum to Mr. Garnish, and the shadowy figure of Hoppy disappearing in the darkness.

"The infernal scoundrel," said Garnish, "I believe he is quite capable of it. However, you must act with caution, with such slender evidence, and, above all, don't allow him to think you suspect him. There are more than you watching him, for now I recollect the man in charge – who is a smart detective – on referring to the list, unconsciously gave expression to a grunt of satisfaction when the description was read out. You must tell Christie also to keep his suspicion to himself for the present, and you must endeavour to at once counteract the impression created by the forged notice by bringing about a meeting of masters and men as soon as possible."

"I'm afraid that will be very difficult in their present state of mind, sir," said Goodman. "The mischief is done, and though I condemn the means by which this crime has been brought about, I must admit the conditions prevailing justify the notice. Why, sir, do you know Dr. Smythe tells me that no less than 28 cases have been admitted in the accident ward of the hospital, an institution supported by money stopped out of the wages of Crushem's employees and that they are now busy fitting up the new wing, as they expect to not be able to deal with the number of cases which will occur among the inexperienced men who are coming to take our places. Isn't it horrible, sir?"

"Yes, my lad; it is indeed horrible, and if we don't watch ourselves there's worse to come. I suppose you know that Crushem, the Town Councillor, is going to petition Crushem, the magistrate, to send for soldiers to awe Crushem's employees into submission to Crushem."

"Lord, sir! how you do drive it home to be sure. Yes, I read your protest, and was proud of it. So was the missis. Aye, sir, and if we had a few more men like her (excuse the bull) we would soon have some one there to help you."[80]

"It does make me feel bad, to see the poor gulls going like lambs to the slaughter to put down their cross in the polling booth for the men who, as employers on the one hand are crushing them out of existence, and on the other, as jerry builders are stinking them out with rotten sanitary laws made by jerry builders."

"Hullo," said Mr. Garnish, as he stood in front of a large bill poster's hoarding, where the bill poster was sticking up a large, flaming poster about four foot long. "What's this with Crushem's name on?"

The flaming poster bore the announcement of a public meeting in the Town Hall, under the auspices of the British and Foreign Bible Society, to propagate the claims of the heathen.

Chair to be taken at 8 p.m.,
By Mr. Crushem, T.C., J.P.

[11 November 1893]

Chapter XVI.

Have you, my readers, ever witnessed a procession of men out on strike?

And if you have, did it ever strike you how supremely unconscious the multitudes are of their power? And what a good job for society (strictly within the meaning of the Act) that they are unconscious?

That's just how it struck at least two of the onlookers of the vast procession of the dockers of Mudpuddle, as they marched, 15,000 strong, to the open-air meeting to be addressed by their leaders.

To the student of humanity a procession of locked-out workers is an interesting and pathetic sight.

Interesting because of the varied types of humanity, from the buoyant, youthful, elastic step of youth, ignorant as yet of the responsibilities of family cares, the jogging clog-trot of the more domesticated married animal, equally as ignorant of his responsibilities of citizenship, to the short, quick, but feeble and broken step of the old veteran, who is rapidly graduating for the workhouse, the usual reward offered by our glorious constitution (upon which, &c., &c.) to the worn-out industrial slave in the land of the brave and the free.[81]

"Isn't it wonderful, doctor?" said Mr. Garnish to Doctor Smythe, as the procession filed past, "the amount of enthusiasm those men are capable of creating in such a short time and without any preconceived idea or notice. There was no idea in Goodman's mind of any such display last night."

"Yes, it is indeed wonderful," replied the doctor, "but, unfortunately, it is wasted on the desert air. If we could only manage to persuade them to carry such enthusiasm to the polling booth, what wonders we could achieve. Can you advance any reason for their conduct at election time?"

"A reason, yes," replied Garnish; "but not, I'm sorry to say, an intelligent one. There are various reasons. For instance, ignorance of their power, hereditary pig-headedness, that what was good enough for their fathers is good enough for them. Home Rule for Ireland, integration of the Empire, in which they can't claim a insignificant blade of grass that sprouts from its surface, and inherent snobbishness of centuries, a cursed slavish system, which I'm afraid cannot be changed within the present generation except by such upheavals as this in our present industrial system."

"'Pon my word, Garnish, you seem to be more pleased than otherwise at this strike."

"No, doctor, not exactly pleased, because I know the suffering a struggle of this description entails upon the helpless children, and yet I'm not sorry, because I see the handwriting on the wall of a brighter future, and the Phoenix of political action arising from the ashes of a disastrous defeat, founded upon ignorance."

"Then you think the men will be defeated?"

"Yes, I do. Every thing points in that direction. In the first place the men's combination is only an infant. In the second this is a disorganised attempt, the men leading the leaders instead of the leaders leading the men, thirdly the fight has been forced by the masters, with the object of breaking up the men's organisation, whose funds they know – from enemies within the camp – are limited, and lastly because had they the wealth of the Rothschilds[82] at their back they would ultimately be defeated while the supply of blacklegs is unlimited."

"Yes, I admit, you are right as regards the blacklegs, but do you think the masters will be able to secure sufficient blacklegs to fill the places of 20,000 men?"

"My dear doctor, of course they will, without any difficulty, so long as there are 700,000 starving men to draw upon. Of course I admit that under existing conditions, while working men in their blind political ignorance will persist in voting Liberal and Tory, and contribute to building a Parliament of employers to make laws in the interest of employers, that strikes are the workers' only weapon of defence."

"But so long as there exists this great army of unemployed, the only strike that can be successful is a national strike of all kindred industries, thus exhausting the supply of blacklegs before one-half of the men's places were filled."

"But have there not been cases of strikes in isolated trades where the workers have been successful?"

"Yes, there may have been temporary but not permanent successes. For you must remember that in all those cases the trade unions have gone back to work when victorious with an exhausted exchequer, that it has taken years upon top of years to build up. The masters know this, and also that it will be some years before the workers will make a similar attempt, therefore, knowing this, the masters have them completely at their mercy, and knowing also (because the master from his very position of master is a student of mankind) that after the worker has felt the pinch of starvation and parted with all his little household goods, and the recollection of the sufferings of himself and little ones fresh in his memory, that having gone back to work he will be very reluctant to throw himself idle again."

"And so, after a few short weeks of fancied security, the worker is again threatened with a reduction similar to that which caused the strike – Why? He hadn't the courage nor the heart to refuse, when he knows from painful experience the only alternative is starvation and no funds to back him up."

"Yes, Garnish, I'm afraid what you say is only to true. God help them and all of us, it's truly a cursed system that allows such conditions to exist. Still, I hope the men will win this fight speedily, for if it is prolonged I'm afraid there'll be mischief done. There was an ugly rush made this morning by some of the men as the blacklegs were being conducted to the docks by the police, and – See! Good God! Garnish the head of the procession has stopped at the railway station, and there is a train load of blacklegs going over the bridge. For heaven's sake, man, come along! There's going to be mischief, and for our own men's sake we must prevent it.'

"With all my heart, doctor," replied Garnish, "but I'm afraid you're too late. See! here comes a squad of police with two dockers with their heads broken by policeman's batons, and, I suppose, to-morrow they'll be sentenced to two months' hard for running with their heads against policeman's batons."

Such was the case. When the head of the procession neared the station a train was heard approaching along the line, and the cordon of police drawn up inside the passage leading to the station, suggested to the dockers the expected arrival of blacklegs.

The suspicion speedily received itself into a fact, for as the train slowed up crossing the bride the windows of the carriages were filled with the heads of blacklegs with a desire for geographical knowledge.

They were not kept long in suspense, for your average docker is as keen on the scent of a blackleg as is a bloodhound or Indian on the trail.

For as the heads appeared a mighty shout, extending to a roar, went up from the angry multitude, and language more forcible than polite, accompanied by a shower of stones from the newly-tarmacadamed road, were hurled at the windows of the carriages where the heads appeared. The police having received strict orders from the Watch Committee, of which Mr. Crushem was chairman, to charge the crowd at the slightest sign of disorder, simply carried out their order to the very letter, and, after bludgeoning the crowd, arrested two of their number for allowing themselves to be bludgeoned.

As the prisoners and their escort approached the Doctor and Garnish, a movement among the crowd behind was attributed by the police as an attempt at rescue, resulting in a fresh charge being made by the rear guard, another capture of a docker, who was handcuffed, and literally dragged along by the handcuffs, his limbs trailing over the sharp jagged stones that covered the roadway.

Mr. Garnish, his blood fairly boiling with indignation at the treatment of the men, called the attention of the sergeant in charge to the inhuman act, and was curtly told "to mind how own business."

"I'd have you to know, sir," replied Garnish, "that this is my business."

"Oh! it is, is it?" sneered the policeman. "Then I call upon you, in the Queen's name, to assist us in our joint business in securing these dangerous characters."

[18 November 1893]

Chapter XVII.

The spirit of Crushem was satisfied within him.

He had attended the Police Court that morning, and though out of his turn, had sat on the bench, whilst three of his employees had been sentenced to two months imprisonment for being in the way of the batons of the police whom he (Crushem) had ordered to bludgeon them.

He had also the satisfaction of assisting in sending Garnish's case to the Quarter Sessions, the charge against Garnish being interference with the police in the lawful execution of their duty, and refusing to assist them to prevent an attempt at rescue of a prisoner when called upon in the Queen's name. There was, however, one thing he regretted, and indignantly resented, viz., the interference of the Magistrates' Clerk with the sentence of six months pronounced by Alderman Fatpurse. The Magistrates' Clerk had actually sympathised with the prisoners by pointing out the illegality of the sentence to the magistrates, and some one in court (he believed it was Doctor Smythe) had actually laughed.

Such a state of things was intolerable, and must be seen to at once. He would write a letter to the Magistrates' Clerk remonstrating with him, and ringing the hand-bell on the table, he told the servant who answered it to send his private secretary. The private secretary was a very recent acquisition to the Crushem household.

Dr. Smythe's patient – the eldest Miss Crushem – had before her accident acted in this capacity, but since the Doctor had been forbidden the house, though she had dispensed with the sticking plaster for some time, she showed no inclination to resume her duties, in which he (Crushem) was sorry to see she was encouraged by her mother, on the plea of illness, described by Crushem as moping for the Doctor.

Thus the private secretary, who, though only a few days in office, had proved himself, even to Crushem's satisfaction, eminently fitted for the position. Quiet, unobtrusive, and attentive to his duties, there was still a something about the man which created an impression that however much occupied with a task he was at the same time keenly alive to the smallest detail of his surroundings.

Such was the impression created in Curley's mind on the previous evening when, in company with Hoppy, he had visited the Crushem mansion to report progress. The private secretary was sitting with his back to Curley, busy with the typewriter, when he entered the room, and though he never paused to look round when he entered, and never changed his position, while Curley was in the room, a suspicion prevailed in Curley's mind that the private secretary knew his every movement, and he fancied he detected a familiar expression in the private secretary's back that somehow or other seemed to recall an old acquaintance.

In fact, so unobtrusive was this private secretary that he had entered Crushem's sanctum and stood fully a minute during which he had taken a mental note of everything in the place, including the photograph, and a telegram lying on the table, bearing the following message: –

300 men left by midnight train, more to follow.
CURLEY.

before he almost caused Crushem to jump out of his chair with an abrupt "You sent for me, sir, I believe."

"God bless my heart, yes, Mr. Scrubb. Why! how you startled me," exclaimed Crushem. "I didn't hear you knock."

"Beg pardon, sir, I knocked twice, and as the door was wide open I thought you were aware of my presence; hope I have not disturbed you? But, as you sent for me, and I –"

"Yes, yes, of course, I want you to write a letter for me to Mr. Sharp, the magistrates' clerk, pointing out to him the bad taste he displayed to-day in interfering with the sentence of six months passed upon those riotous scoundrels who interfered with the police who were protecting honest men seeking work, and just convey to him a hint – as I know you can – of the advisability of not interfering in future.

The expression of surprise which for a moment appeared on Mr. Scrubb's features was as quickly replaced by one of stolid indifference as Crushem turned at the door and asked:

"By the way, Mr. Scrubb, what are my engagements for this evening?"

"You are to take the chair at 7.30 at a meeting of the Society for the Prevention of Cruelty to Animals, and are due at the annual banquet of the hospital committee at 9.30. I was just finishing your speech on the inhuman practice of overloading and tight bearing reins when you summoned me."

"H'm! Well! You can finish it and send it on by messenger," said Crushem, as he closed the door behind him.

For a few moments after Crushem had left the room the private secretary stood gazing at the ornamented ceiling, and then with a chuckle he drew the chair up to the desk and sat down with his hands up to his elbows in his pockets gazing at the telegram before him on the table, while a smothered exclamation of "Well I'll be damned," or words to that effect, escaped him.

"So, Mr. Dan Curley, alias Steve Marlow, this (picking up the telegram) is more of your devilment. I thought I recognised your familiar hand in this dirty business when that old chap, Christie, accused you the other night. Now I'm sure of it. H'm, so much the better for my purpose. All's fish that comes to my net, though I'm sorry for the poor chaps you've duped, and I'm afraid I must let you play your dirty game and serve your dirty master (and mine for a time) a little longer, until I can land you fairly.

"You've been a wary old fish to catch, my friend, and fought shy of the most alluring bait; but I fancy you'll not be able to detect the hook beneath me to smuggle myself aboard that train and come here as a blackleg, for, from the description given by the men of the scab recruiting agent, I fancied I was on the right track. Luckily, he didn't seem to recognise me the other night in my ragged condition and long beard. He is less likely to recognise me now, unadorned by any hirsute appendages.

"Ah! It's some satisfaction after years of hardship and persecution, living the life of an outlaw and fugitive from justice for his crime, to find myself so close to clearing my good name, and living a man's life again.

Alas, when I think of it. The long years of imprisonment – of separation from the children and wife that think me dead. Shot while attempting to escape, the papers said. I wonder who they shot? It wasn't me, at all events. Poor Molly, it's hard on you, my lass. Hard to think that the same roof covered us only the other night – so near, and yet so far – and yet I couldn't speak to you.

"God grant me patience to carry this thing through without giving myself away, as I sometimes feel inclined to do by choking the life out of the author of my misfortunes, every time I meet him.

"I must manage it before Crushem discovers the truth about the forged references. Luckily, he has to write to America about them, and, if luck attends me, I should have my job finished before then.

"What a trump Goodman is. I owe him a debt of gratitude which, if an opportunity affords, I shall pay him back; perhaps I may be able to do it in this business – who knows? Stranger things have happened. And now to write Crushem's letter. Bah! What a contemptible hound he is. 'Pon my soul, I feel more like kicking him than serving him."

"Oh, I beg your pardon, sir," said the voice of Miss Crushem, who had entered the room. "I thought pa was here. Can you tell me where I'll find him?"

"Yes, miss," replied the secretary, glancing up from his work sideways at the girl. "He's gone to take the chair at a meeting of the Society for the Prevention of Cruelty to Animals."

"Oh, dear, I'm so sorry," said Miss Crushem, turning to go.

"What for – the animals?" asked the secretary, suddenly wheeling about in his chair.

"No, of course not," nervously answered the girl; and then, as with a sudden consciousness of the sarcasm of the question, asked, "Why should I be sorry for the animals?"

"Oh, I don't know, miss," replied the secretary, guardedly, himself a little confused, as the clear, dark eyes met his own, "except, of course, that anyone would be sorry for animals which were cruelly treated. But" – with decision – I'm afraid, miss, the cruelty is not limited to the four-footed animal species."

"I'm afraid you're right, Mr. Scrubbs," replied the girl with a sigh, while a slight suspicion of a tear appeared in the corner of the luminous eyes, "it was about a case of cruelty to one of the two-footed species that I came to ask pa's assistance, and I'm so sorry I missed him, as the case is so urgent and deserving."

"My dear young lady," remarked the secretary, as he deferentially placed a chair for her, "can I be of any assistance to you? If so, pray command me, for with a knowledge born of bitter experience of the many wants of common suffering humanity, their claims always demand my attention, especially when championed by such an eloquent exponent as yourself."

The out-spoken and flattering speech for the moment created a spirit of resentment in the girl's mind, as being too familiar from one who, comparatively speaking was a stranger and a dependent, but only for a moment, for the girl noticed there was no familiarity in the attitude of the secretary, who stood deferentially awaiting her command with chivalrous respect. And so the angry light died out of the dark eyes, which again grew luminous with pity, as she exclaimed, "Oh, Mr. Scrubb, if only you could assist me, if only you knew how deserving a case this is."

"My dear young lady; I not only can but will, if you will but give me the opportunity," said the secretary. "As for the deserving part, I never yet met a case in my somewhat chequered career (and God alone knows I have met many) that was not deserving, no matter what cause was responsible for its existence, and believe me again, my dear young lady, I shall feel highly honoured by your commission in this matter."

"I believe you, indeed I do," said Miss Crushem, holding out her hand, "and I feel emboldened by your outspoken sympathy in trusting you with this task, which I would willingly impose upon myself were I able to do it. I came here to ask father's assistance, but which I must now confess I was not so sure of receiving, to give me the opportunity of saving the life, if not lives of some of the poor creatures who are the helpless and innocent victims of the present strike. If you'll kindly wait a few moments, or, better still, if you will kindly allow me to write a letter at your desk," – with a little sigh of regret, "It used to be mine before you came, you know – which I will ask you to deliver to a very great friend of mine, who will gladly assist you in this mission of mercy."

And having received the required permission, Miss Crushem sat down to write her first letter to her lover since he last settled the sticking plaster.

And as the private secretary stood over her, arranging the ink and blotting pad the face of Dan Curley, unseen by the occupants of the room, appeared at the window fronting the lawn, and the private secretary still held the telegram in his hand behind his back.

[25 November 1893]

Chapter XVIII.

The three hundred men mentioned in Curley's telegram had arrived.

But they were not marched from the passenger station through the streets as on a previous occasion. A meeting of the railway directors had been held, and on the recommendation of Alderman Fatpurse and Councillor Crushem (both large shareholders) they had decided to run the trains direct inside the dock gates by the loop line used for goods traffic.

Thus was the money of the workers, which builds up railway dividends, used against the workers to defeat their cause.

The shipping companies placed their idle ships at the disposal of the Employer's Association to accommodate the half-starved miserable wretches whom hunger had driven to take the places of the men on strike. And the Dock Company had placed their commodious sheds also at the employers' disposal to accommodate those whom the ships were unable to hold.

Inside the docks a curious sight presented itself to those who had heretofore been used to the stringent regulations strictly enforced by the Dock Company. Previous to the strike anyone found in the possession of pipes or matches was visited with a penalty of the law in the shape of 40s. and costs or a month's imprisonment. In fact, the notices still hung in a prominent position, while all around, sitting on bales of cotton and other inflammable merchandise, sat and stood and sprawled hundreds of blacklegs striking matches, smoking pipes – which were actually distributed by policemen – and drinking beer which was distributed to them by Crushem's foreman in the presence of Crushem, the great temperance advocate, and the conscientious police officer, who before the strike would pounce down like a hawk upon a coal heaver smoking his pipe on a flat out in the middle of the dock, looked on in supreme indifference at the cloud of smoke arising from a hundred pipes in the mouths of the blacklegs.

Of course circumstances alter cases. These were some of both. In fact the blacklegs provided the cases, and demanded that as they were shut out (or rather shut in) from the luxuries of beer and baccy, that such should be provided for them free of cost; and as they were masters of the situation, they were provided by the employers, who complained of the dictatorial tone of the legitimate docker locked out.

They were a curious mixture of humanity, these blacklegs. From the round-shouldered, awkward, long-legged youth of 16, the decrepit premature aged, upon whom starvation had set its mark to the gaunt frame of the once stalwart worker, upon whom the few rags which covered them hung in suggestive looseness, and from the habitual loafer to the broken down respectable clerk or shop walker, who still clung like grim death to old associations in the shape of a very much soiled paper collar and the soleless sharp-toed boot.

The latter pieces of social driftwood were the subject of much comment and rough jokes from their more depraved associates, and such remarks as "Mind you don't catch cold cully i'dout yer collar," and "De boss 'll send de laundry maid round this evenin', sir, to collect yer soiled linen," were often indulged in, while another would volunteer to put a shine on the dilapidated fashionable but soleless uppers with the ship painter's black brush.

Hundreds of these ill-assorted specimens of humanity were huddled together in one corner of the shed, and slept, and eat, and smoked, and spat on each other in narrow bunks rudely built in tiers against the wall, while in the opposite corner the stench arising form the filthy habits of a great number of them could be detected outside the dock walls when the door of the shed was opened to draft them to the various shops to which they were told off.[83]

The incapacity of this motley crew was such that it took ten men to do the work of two ordinary dock labourers, and owing to their awkwardness accidents occurred almost every hour, and the special ward in the hospital kept up by contributions on the men on strike was full to overflowing.

The men locked out worked any hour that the master chose to tell them for 6d. per hour, and all they contended for was a more regular system of employment and less broken time.

And the men locked in were paid 5s. per day, with board, lodgings, bacca, and beer, and only worked when they chose to do so.

On the evening that the private secretary was intrusted with Miss Crushem's note to Dr Smythe the doctor was in the ambulance department when the ambulance was summoned for the sixth time that day, and he determined to accompany the ambulance.

Their destination was the shed where the blacklegs were housed, and the victim on this occasion was the result of a drunken brawl among the blacklegs.

It happened thus. After finishing the day's work at five o'clock a packman had been admitted, by special permission, to dispose of his wares, such as stockings, belts, caps, shirts, and other articles of clothing, and the packman, with an eye to quick sale and large profits, succeeded in smuggling some bottles of "chain lightning" (cheap whiskey) in among his haberdashery.

Needless to say the packman succeeded in doing a roaring trade, and disposed of every article in his pack, "chain lightning" included, and had risen from the bale of cotton he was seated upon very much satisfied with his day's work, when – he suddenly felt a lightness in his starboard pocket, wherein rested the coins of the realm he had taken in exchange for his goods, he discovered himself minus both pocket and money, *the pocket having been cut clean away.*

The packman swore and stamped with all the vehemence of his nature, and when all hands were mustered and searched with no result, sat down and wept copiously, and after he had been conducted outside the dock gates the bad whisky he had dispensed began to take effect, and the rogues fell out about the distribution of his plunder.

Nature's weapons were first indulged in by those directly interested; then the partisans of both sides entered vigorously into the dispute, and for a considerable time the air was full of curses and oaths of all descriptions, and with the disturbance the limited number of the defenders of the public peace were unable to cope.

The military summoned to protect the blacklegs from the violence of the unionists were now summoned to protect the police from the violence of the blacklegs. And when order was once more restored there were candidates for the ambulance who required attention.

But there was something more than the wounded that attracted the doctor's attention in the shape of the fearfully tainted atmosphere of the shed, where the hundreds of men were huddled together, and the presence of disease, the direct outcome of the inhuman, insanitary surroundings, and walking over to Crushem, who had been hastily summoned from the annual banquet of the hospital committee, he called his attention to its existence.

"Mind your own business, sir," roared Crushem, "and leave me to mind mine; which you'll find, Mr. Impertinence, I'm quite capable of doing without any assistance from you. And hark you, sir, your unwarrantable cheek will do you no good, I can tell you, as your conduct of late has given considerable annoyance to all the members of the committee I have just left, who are already talking about your successor."

"This is my business, sir," replied the doctor, "essentially my business, and I would consider myself a disgrace to my profession did I allow such a scandal to pass without comment. And let me tell you now, sir, so that you may convey the intelligence back to the gentlemen of the committee you have just left, that they may make up their puny minds quickly about my successor, and that I refuse most positively to be in any way identified with a committee of gentlemen who feast and make merry over such misery as this."

And turning upon his heel, the doctor left Crushem in a state bordering upon explosion.

[2 December 1893]
Chapter XIX.

When the private secretary turned round after closing the door he had opened for Miss Crushem, he caught sight of Curley's face through the window, but with remarkable presence of mind he did not betray any knowledge of his presence. He went over to the desk and resumed the business, which Miss Crushem's entrance had interrupted, before delivering her message to the doctor.

He had just competed his task and was rising, when a knock at the door was immediately followed by the form of Hoppy carrying the surplus cash left over from the payment of subs to the blacklegs at the Docks. There was no love lost between Hoppy and the private secretary, because Hoppy looked upon the private secretary as an intruder, while the private secretary looked upon Hoppy with amused contempt and so placing the bag containing the money on the table, with an exclamation between a snort and a grunt, Hoppy demanded a receipt from the private secretary for its safe delivery.

"All right, my dear fellow, don't get excited," said Scrubbs, "count it out there on the table smartly, as I'm in a bit of a hurry, and I'll give you a receipt for the amount."

"Do you doubt my word, then?" indignantly asked Hoppy.

"My dear fellow, don't get excited," replied Scrubbs, "just place the matter beyond doubt by counting it," and coolly lighting a cigarette he walked over to the window, drew aside the curtain quickly, thereby catching another glimpse of Curley's figure crouching in the shadow of the wall outside, and, as if unconscious of his presence, the private secretary, after gazing for a moment out of the window, walked over to the fireplace, leaving an uninterrupted view from the outside to the table where Hoppy was piling up the money.

"Here you are, Mr. Secretary," said Hoppy, sneeringly, "perhaps you'll oblige me by checking this. I think you'll find £23 in gold and twenty-seven in silver, making fifty in all."

The sum was found correct by Scrubbs, and a receipt tendered for that amount to Hoppy, who departed with a No. 9 hump;[84] and as Scrubbs replaced the money in the bag, and placed the bag in the safe and locked it, he was conscious of the fact that his every movement was watched by the glaring greedy eyes of Curley.

Chapter XX.

Mr. Crushem had arrived home very tired and ill at ease, at 11 p.m.

Since he had left the house at 6 p.m., many things had happened to vex his spirit, and the various materials which made up the menu at the supper of the hospital lay heavy on his chest.

Never before in the whole course of his life had Crushem been so cornered as at present. Accustomed to have his word unquestioned, his slightest wish obeyed by those whom he considered beneath him, he was now suddenly confronted with the fact that his heretofore obedient slaves were for once his masters, and in the midst of his tribulations the thought would occasionally flash across his mind why his slaves had not exercised this power before.

Not that he agreed with them. Oh, dear no! But here were the stern facts before him, that the combined exercise of the intelligence of slaves is more than equal to the power of their masters, and that the slaves possessed the same faculties for thinking – in a more or less degree – as the masters who had claimed up to now the monopoly of human intelligence, and in Crushem's opinion justly so.

It was then all the more humiliating to find that all along he had been living in a fool's paradise, and even in his own dividend-sodden brain, a slight suspicion was beginning to arise as to which side had the best of the argument.

"Confound that cheeky young hound of a doctor," he muttered, as he filled himself a third glass of port with one hand, and unconsciously fingered the keys of the safe that the private secretary had left on the table. "It's all that impertinent puppy's fault, with his crazy notion of elevating the masses. Still I admire the cheeky young beggar's pluck, and which I suppose is the principle reason my daughter admires the young scamp. H'm, what a pity that old fool of a father of his (who by the way is almost beginning to be as crazy as the son) does not endeavour to utilize the young beggar's brain in business. D—n, but he is a distinct loss to the world of commerce; but with his present opinions a disgrace and an enemy to his class that must not be tolerated. So if he will gang his own gait,[85] and throw in his lot with the mob, he must accept the consequences of his own action. But" – and he thumped the table in his excitement, bringing his hand down on the bunch of keys – "I'll be d—d if he drags one of my flesh and blood with him as long as I live. Hullo! what's this? Why, the keys of the safe, as I live! Now that's the first careless action that Scrubbs has been guilty of since he came. But there, I suppose he has forgotten them, or imagined they would be all right, and may be back for them at any moment. And why shouldn't they be all right? H'm, the question is, is Scrubbs all right himself. His credentials were first-class. Curious fellow, though, all the same. Gives one an impression that he is always on the look-out for something. I think I'll just make sure and see if everything's all right in the safe" – and picking up a note lying on the table – "What's this? H'm! So Hoppy's been here and left the money with Scrubbs, and Scrubbs says he has gone out, and will be back in an hour. Now that's strange. Why should he go out for an hour at this time of night? I must certainly make sure now at once that everything is all right" – and going over to the safe he opened it, gave a sigh of relief as his eye caught sight of the bag, which he lifted out and placed on the table previous to counting it, drew up his chair, gave the fire a fresh poke, filled himself another glass, and having emptied the contents of the bag on the table, commenced to count it.

Meanwhile, outside the window the movements of Crushem were closely watched by Curley, crouched, cat-like, beneath the window-ledge, and as the money tumbled out of the bag on to the table, the upper part of his features appeared above the ledge, and his eye magnified the sum total that Crushem was counting into three times its value.

Early in the evening Curley had visited Goodman's house, for the purpose of interviewing Goodman, but finding no one at home but the children was about to depart, and when going out his foot kicked against Goodman's cotton-hook[86] on the floor of the lobby where the children had been playing with it, and with his inherent selfish nature that existed within him had picked up the hook and stuck it in his belt. He had come straight from Goodman's to Crushem's, and the hook was still in his belt, and the fiendish idea occurred to him that by its means he might kill two birds with one stone, so to speak. What more easy than to quietly push the window open – he knew it was unlatched – because, curiously enough, Scrubbs had unlatched it and forgotten to close it when he left the room, and to creep unawares on Crushem, whose back was turned to him, and more than half stupified with his over-indulgence, to give him a blow behind the ear with the mallet-like end of the hook collar the swag, and decamp, leaving Goodman's hook with Goodman's initials rudely carved on the handle, behind him, thus paying off an old score with Goodman and enriching himself.

The precaution, however, was not necessary, for Crushem having counted the money and found it correct, had, feeling somewhat drowsy, settled himself back in his chair, and was now snoring like a foghorn, with one hand resting on the bag of money on the table.

This gave Curley his opportunity so far as the money was concerned, and so quietly pushing open the window and cautiously closing it after, he quietly approached the slumbering form of Crushem, turning down the gas as he proceeded between him and the window by which he had entered.

When he reached the table he noticed what Crushem's bulky form had otherwise hidden from him, that Crushem's hand rested upon the bag of money. And so in case he should awake during the process of exchange, Curley loosened the hook out of his belt and held it in one hand, while, with the other, he endeavoured to stealthily commence to draw the bag away without disturbing the sleeper.

But Crushem never slept with more than one eye shut, and instinctively woke when Curley touched the bag, when – without more ado – Curley brought down the hook with crushing force on the head of Crushem, who fell to the ground with scarcely a groan. And as Curley went out at the window, the door of the room opened to admit Miss Crushem, who nearly stumbled over the prostrate form of her father.

Chapter XXI.

[9 December 1893]

There was a committee meeting at the rooms of the National Union, with Jack Goodman in the chair. And after the minutes had been read and passed as a true record of the committee signifying in the usual manner, Christie, who had been installed as delegate, was called upon to give his report, and the committee settled itself to hear the event of the evening.

Christie, impressed with the grave responsibility and dignity of his position, had compiled an elaborate report in a formidable-looking book of extraordinary dimensions; and after arming himself with an imposing pair of heavy-bound brass spectacles, glittering in all their pristine vigour, commenced as follows: –

"Wednesday mornin', 6.30 a.m. – Went to the timber corner, med the min put their buttons up.[87] Bad hire. Walked through the carters' dock. Went round the West Injies.[88] Back to office.

"Thursday mornin', 6.30 a.m. – Went to timber corner. Buttons up. Went round the West Injies. Met Tom Curley's wife. Dacent man, Tom. Back to office.

Friday mornin', 6.30 a.m. – usual round.

Saturday mornin', 6.30 a.m. – Went to timber corner. Met Curley. He told me men were still hard. Met a scab, busted him. Ordered away by polis.[89] Went. Back to office."

"Mr. Chair, through you," said Tom Noon, a member of the committee, "I want to know am I in order in asking the delegate a question?"

"Yes, certainly," replied Goodman.

"Well, sir, through you I want to ax him if he got wet walking through the carter's dock? And what kind o' weather he experienced round the West Injies!"

The committee smiled in unison at this sally, an operation which was repeated, when Christie, with offended dignity, looked over his copper-bottomed spectacles, and asked the chairman, if "through him he had come there to be made a cod iv?"

"At this stage, Mr. Chair, through you," said another committee man, "I want to know what the delegate means by usual rounds and where he was when scabs were hired at the Black Sea stand?" – "Hear, hear," from several members of the committee.

"Well, Mr. Chair," answered Christie, "through you I had a touch iv the bowel complaint on this particular mornin'" (roars of laughter, during which Christie again looked down severely over his twenty horse-power spectacles). "And the usual round, Mr, Chair, manes the usual round: what else can in mane, I'd like to know?" And looking round triumphantly – "It shows the limited acquaintance iv some iv yer with the schoolmaster, ye ignoramuses."

The next was the secretary's report of the Strike Fund, which showed a deplorable lack of sympathy on the part of other trades unions; the more respectable skilled artizans' unions being conspicuous by their absence in the contributions sheet; and as Curley read out the replies from the various trade unions and the scanty list of the contributions, just a flicker of a smile was discernable on his features, and his teeth clicked together as he read out a communication from the Local Trades' Council for Goodman to attend to answer charged preferred against him in connection with the "Strike, strike" poster.

"Gentlemen," said Goodman, "you've heard by the contributions sheet how we stand, our own resources almost exhausted, and very little coming in, especially from the quarter from which we most expected assistance. The skilled trades, with plenty of funds at their back, have practically refused to assist us. I suppose we are not respectable enough. You can see the press and the public are down on us, for there is a prevailing impression in the minds of the good, old, fat-headed B.P.[90] that we ought to be content with our present wages of five shillings per day.

"Now, does any man here earn five shillings a day for the week round?"

Cries of "No, nor two, some of us."

"Very well, then, do you know of any one who does?"

"Yes, the tin chapel gang."

"Aye! I admit, lads, there are exceptions, but like angels' visits, they are few and far between; but the fact of such an artificial wage existing is good enough excuse for the prejudiced B.P., who are now howling for our blood on account of the regrettable incident which occurred last night and which they are laying at the door of the men on strike, without the slightest possible evidence to support them. I refer to the outrage on Mr. Crushem, which Doctor Smythe tells me is likely to end seriously, and the robbery from the safe."

"Serve him right! To h—ll with him. Hope the old — finished," exclaimed several voices.

"Now, now! my lads, take it easy," said Goodman, "I'm sure you don't mean that, and on more mature consideration, you'll see as I see now that such expressions condoning such outrageous acts of violence, will do us more harm than good, and I am convinced as I am of my own existence, 'that an enemy hath done this.'[91] Now, lads, with all these obstacles in our path, are you prepared to go on with the fight?"

Cries of "Yes" "Fight to the bitter end," and "Stick out and be hard Jack, my lad, we'll see you through."

"Very well, mates, I'm satisfied, and with our support and confidence, I am prepared to meet all obstacles; and while I can understand the position taken up by an ignorant, selfish British public, I cannot understand the impertinence of the Trades Council communication whose representatives have refused to assist us, and who now demand an explanation from me of something I have never done, but which, without a particle of evidence, they assume that I have. What do you say, boys, shall I answer it?"

Cries of "No, don't, never mind 'em," and "We know who issued the strike poster."

"Gentlemen," said Curley, who, on rising from his seat, was received with cries of "Sit down, Curley," and "Go on, Jem, give 'em all beans," "allow me to say – (a voice: We'll allow you nothing) – "that I don't altogether agree with our chairman" – (a voice: Ye never did.) "Well, I hope you'll allow me to have an opinion, and my opinion is, that if our chairman refuses to meet these charges, the cause will suffer, and not our chairman, and I hold that it is the first duty of a leader to sacrifice his own opinion on any subject in the interests of the main body."

Having uttered these words of wisdom, Curley was about to resume his seat when a commotion was heard at the entrance to the office, followed by the appearance of a squad of police and two or three plain-clothes men.

"Sorry to interrupt your deliberations, gentlemen," said the inspector in charge, "but our duty is imperative, and I'm afraid you'll have to manage without your chairman, as we have most particular and pressing business with him."

At the entrance of the police every man rose to his feet but Curley, who still sat clicking his teeth, with his face as white as a corpse, which suddenly changed colour, when the inspector named his errand, and for a few moments things had an ugly look. The silence which followed the announcement of the inspector was broken by Goodman himself, with the question, "Might I enquire the nature of our business with me, gentlemen?"

"Well, my lad I'm sorry to tell you that the charge against you is attempted murder and robbery, on the person and residence of Mr. Crushem, last night; and I grieve to say that, so far, appearances are against you. It just depends upon yourself, my lad, to account before the magistrates to their satisfaction, for our whereabouts last night. In the meantime, I must warn you that anything said by you now will be used in evidence."

At the mention of his whereabouts on the previous evening, Goodman staggered a little, but, recovering himself, quickly said: –

"Comrades, I need hardly ask you not to believe this ridiculous charge, which I have no doubt I will be able to dispel to the entire satisfaction of the authorities. In my opinion this is only another dodge of the enemy to break up our organisation."

"Hear, hear, Jack, me heartie," shouted the men, "they won't succeed, though."

"Well, I hope not, comrades. Stick together like men, and you're bound to win, whatever becomes of me. Our cause is a just and a righteous one, and not dependent upon any one man. Be men then, my lads, just and righteous men, and you cannot fail. And now, Mr. Inspector, I'm ready to accompany you."

And placing himself between two of the policemen, and motioning back his mates who crowded threateningly round his body guard, Goodman was conducted through the streets, and pointed out by the respectable shop-keeper whom the rumour had reached as a truly desperate character.

[16 December 1893]

Chapter XXI.

As the private secretary left the house by the back to deliver Miss Crushem's message to the doctor, Mr. Crushem entered by the front. The Secretary has a reason for leaving the back way; in fact two reasons. One was not to let his absence be known to the inmates, and the other to come upon Curley unawares. But as he crept cautiously in the shadow of the shrubbery on the lawn, he saw through the window Mr. Crushem enter the room and settle himself in the chair he had just vacated, while the figure of Curley was altogether invisible, and concluding that the arrival of Crushem had been the cause of his disappearance, he hastened to perform the duty allotted to him, but which circumstances eventually prevented him from doing. For, arriving at the doctor's house, a distance of something like two miles form Crushem's, he learnt that the doctor had just left in a hansom with a messenger from the Crushem mansion to request his immediate presence, as Mr. Crushem had been found unconscious on the floor of his study, where he had been brutally attacked, and the safe rifled of its contents.

Something remarkably like an oath escaped the lips of the private secretary, as he turned abruptly away from his informant, Miss Smythe, and hurried away, bitterly reproaching himself for not having made a closer inspection of the grounds before leaving. "The infernal scoundrel," he muttered, "who would have thought he would have ventured so far as to add murder to his list of accomplishments. What steps should I take now I wonder? I didn't intend to pull him up just yet awhile until my plans were more matured, so that, while clearing my own name, I might also at the same time help Goodman. But my friend Curley has by his latest exploit considerably precipitated matters, and so his blood be upon his own head, as the villain on the stage puts it. So I'll just call in at the police offices on my way back and put the bloodhounds of the law on his track." And so, muttering to himself, and stopping occasionally in his walk as some new idea struck him, and which from his chuckle of satisfaction evidently took his fancy, the private secretary made his way to the police station.

But here was another surprise awaited him, and his reception was not quite so satisfactory as he had expected, for as he entered the police station he noticed a quick and simultaneous exchange of glances between two or three plain clothes men, who were just about to depart, while from behind he found himself in the grip of two stalwart men in uniform, who from their presence appeared to have suddenly sprung from the earth.

A terrible fear took possession of the private secretary, and for a moment the place swam before his eyes, during which uniforms and plain clothes and a couple of shivering outcasts of society awaiting their removal to the cells were indiscriminately mixed up. Recovering himself, with an effort which was not lost sight of, but noted by the lynx-eyed officers of the law, he sternly demanded an explanation of their conduct.

"That's the very question I was going to put to you, sir," quietly replied one of the detectives, "but you seem to have the knack of forestalling us – might I say agreeably forestalling us. We were just about to go in search of you when you voluntarily and kindly saved us the trouble by coming yourself, and no sooner do you arrive, than you put the very question uppermost in our mind – an explanation of your presence."

"Well, gentleman," said Scrubbs, "the explanation of my presence here is my wish to give you information which will lead to the discovery of the scoundrel who committed the outrage to-night at the house of my employer, Mr. Crushem, and to put you on the track of the miscreant."

"Oh, yes! we recognise the valuable assistance you've given us, captain, so much that we are loth to part with you, and have provided suitable accommodation for you to say overnight. Just bring the gentleman this way, men, and show him his room, No. 26, the first turning to the right in the corridor. I hope you'll have no cause to complain of damp sheets, sir, we always study the health of our patrons, in this establishment." And with a chuckle, which seemed to be contagious, the officer opened the half-door separating him from the prisoner, who was rather rudely pushed through from behind by his captors.

"One moment gentlemen," said the secretary, "might I ask the nature of the charge against me?"

"Certainly, sir," replied the officer, "the charge against you, founded on purely circumstantial evidence as yet, is that you were the last person seen, and known to have been present, in the house, and in the company of Mr. Crushem, and that shortly after, he was found in the room (which you had a few moments previously left) murderously assaulted with intent to kill, and robbed of a considerable sum of money, which no one but yourself and another knew him to be possessed of."

"Gentlemen," said the secretary, with considerable relief as he heard the charge, "I can understand your suspicion, which at first sight is justifiable, but if you will allow me before conducting me to what you are pleased to facetiously call my apartments, I may be able to clear the fog that at presents clouds your intelligence. As you truly say I was the only person, who within your knowledge knew of the money, and who also within your knowledge was the last person in the room. But gentlemen, with all your astuteness you don't profess a monopoly of the knowledge of mankind, for I am here to tell you there was a third person, who knew of the money being there, and who, if I mistake not, was in the room after I left it." And in as few words as possible the private secretary gave an account of the presence of Curley outside the window, his sudden disappearance as he departed on his message to Doctor Smythe's, and his astonishment at hearing the news when he arrived there, causing him to hasten to the police-station, little thinking of the reception he would be met with, all of which was carefully noted down; and the private secretary was again conducted to his apartment, when Doctor Smythe entered the office, with the hook with which the blow was given, and which had been found. This, together with the Doctor's assurance that he would be responsible for the appearance of the secretary before the magistrates when he would be able to prove an *alibi* in the secretary's favour, had the effect of saving him a night in the police cell. But the most curious feature of the case was, that although the Doctor had taken particular notice of the initials on the handle of the hook, he never for a moment connected them with the name of Jack Goodman.

Not so, however, with the officers of the law. To them the hook was a very important clue, which they lost no time in following up the next day by finding out where the hook was sold, who it was sold to, and the date upon which it was sold. This, together with the fact that Goodman was the leader of the strike, and had more than once publicly expressed his opinion of Crushem, was sufficient evidence to warrant his arrest, the news of which caused great consternation in the minds of his numerous friends, a howl of prejudice by the punch and judies,[92] and a deep and heartfelt sorrow in the breast of the doctor at being the unconscious instrument of this humiliation to a man whom he knew to be innocent, and whom, please God, he would prove to the world to be innocent before many days were over.

The news of Goodman's arrest spread like wild-fire, and had, for a time at least, the effect which Curley intended it should have, of demoralising the men, but only for a time.

For Mr. Garnish, having been consulted by Doctor Smythe, took up the running broken off by Goodman's arrest, and at a mid-day meeting on the day following, had completely dispelled the bad impression created in the men's mind by solemnly assuring them that his innocence would be proved, that he had visited him that morning and had brought a message from him to the effect that if they thought well of it, he (Garnish) should take his place until he regained his liberty, which please God would be soon. Were they content to accept such a poor substitute as himself (cries of "Yes, yes," and "More power till ye Councillor, we'll have you in Parliament yet.") "Very well, my lads, if you are content to accept me, though conscious of my inability to take your leader's place. I'll do my best under the circumstances (cheers). I heard a chap in the crowd say something about sending me to Parliament ("hear, hear, so we will"). Well now, if you're in earnest, I'll make a bargain with you. I'll agree to accept the honour conditionally, that you allow me to provide a substitute, and the substitute I would suggest would be the man whose substitute – and a very bad one – I am at present (cheers), and believe me, lads, if you had a few men like him there there would be more substantial legislation, and less of these disastrous labour disputes, which are simply the corrupt outcome of rotten laws, made by employers (loud cheers)". After this the men dispersed vowing to be more determined than ever to fight this battle, forced upon them, to the bitter end, and to avenge the insult to their leader.

Meanwhile, Nemises in the shape of the private secretary, was on the track of Curley. The morning after the incident at the police station, the private secretary, Scrubbs, had been instructed by Crushem (who, though confined to his bed, was not very seriously injured, except by suffering from shock; he being merely stunned by the blow), to collect some documents which were in his private desk and bring them to him, as he wished to instruct him what to do with them; also to bring the photograph upstairs.

When the secretary, Stubbs was collecting these documents, he noticed a rather bulky one, which had fallen out of a large envelope and lay half open with the blank side towards him, but through which the words "Strike, strike," in large type, were very discernable. Having seen this much, Scrubbs was anxious to see more, and unfolding the document, which proved to be none other than the famous strike poster, another small written document fell from the between the folds, which read as follows:

> Dear Mr. Crushem, – I herewith enclose you proof (just received from printer) of the poster agreed upon between me and yourself as representing the Employer's Association, which I am confident will have the effect of breaking up the Union, and discrediting its self-elected leaders. I will call for the £100 agreed upon as payment for the job to-morrow. – Yours faithfully,
>
> D. CURLEY
>
> P.S – Kindly destroy these on receipt; as my life would not be worth a moment's purchase were they to be seen by anyone but yourself.

[23 December 1893]

Chapter XXII.

The Court-house was packed to suffocation on the morning of the magisterial enquiry into the case of robbery with violence against Goodman, and the road outside with an excited multitude.

There was a full bench of magistrates, including Grindem, the senior member of the firm, Crushem, Grindem, and Co., while Garnish and Doctor Smythe sat at the side of the solicitor engaged for the defence, and Curley occupied a place set apart for witnesses.

The drunks were speedily disposed of with the stereotyped five shillings and costs or fourteen days, and the monotonous change of the court swearer – "'Struth. Nothin' but 'struth. 'Selp me God," was relieved by the calling of the case of the day.

As Goodman stepped into the box a subdued murmur of sympathy went out from the body of the court, while in the silence that followed the demand for "Silence in court," the click of Curley's teeth could be distinctly heard. Goodman had pleaded not guilty, the evidence of the police had been taken, the man who sold the hook to Goodman had reluctantly enough identified him, and ventured an opinion as to Goodman's innocence, and was curtly told to stand down and keep his opinion until asked for it.

Then Curley entered the witness box to give evidence of the bad feeling existing between Goodman and Crushem, and the threats and strong language he had heard Goodman use, and the case began to look black indeed against him, the opinion being among his friends in court that "he was sure to go ter the 'Sizes."[93]

Curley's evidence being finished, he was about to step down from the witness box, when the solicitor for the defence rose to cross-examine.

"Your name, I believe, is Curley?'

"Yes."

"H'm! Daniel Curley, I believe?"

"Yes."

"Is that the only one you've got?"

(With a click of the teeth) "Yes."

"H'm! at present, I suppose. Did you ever have any other?"

"No –o – no, not that I can remember."

"H'm! Let me refresh your memory, Mr. Curley. Did you ever call yourself Mr. —?"

"Well, yes, once."

"What! only once, Mr. Curley? Come, now, think again."

"Well, perhaps I may."

"Ah! Now that's better. Well, now, just listen carefully to my question, which may, perhaps, further refresh your memory. Did you ever live in —shire?"

"What has that got to do with this case?"

"Come, come now, my dear Mr. Curley, don't lose your temper. Answer my question."

"Am I bound to answer that question, your worship?" inquired Curley of the bench.

After consultation with the magistrates' clerk, their worships decided that the question must be answered, and Curley reluctantly replied "Yes."

"Ah! Now we're getting on very nicely," said the solicitor. "Did you know a Mr. Armitage in that locality?"

"Yes, slightly."

"Only slightly? Come now; your memory is at fault again. Didn't you work together in the same firm?"

"Yes, I believe we did."

"Do you remember while you were employed by that firm a robbery similar to the present one – a robbery, with violence – being committed on the person of your employer?"

"Yes." (Sensation, and cried by the usher of "Order in court.")

"You, I believe, were the principle witness in that case against Armitage, who was sentenced to penal servitude?"

"Yes; that is correct."

"Ah! Your memory is improving. Of course you know that Armitage went to gaol?"

"Yes."

"And that he has since escaped?"

"No (with a click of the teeth); I wasn't aware of that."

"Will you take it from me that he has?"

"Yes, if you say so; but I shouldn't think so myself."

"Why, Mr. Curley, shouldn't you think so?"

"Well, because its easier to get in than out."

"Do you speak from experience, Mr. Curley?"

"I decline to answer that question."

"Nevertheless, I press it."

"Do you think these questions relevant to the case before us, Mr. Solicitor?" asked the chairman.

"I'm willing to accept your worship's ruling on the point, but I submit that these questions are a test of the trustworthy nature of this man's evidence."

"Very well," said his worship, "we will allow the questions."

"Now, Mr. Curley," said the solicitor, "answer yes or no. Were you ever in gaol?"

"Well, yes; once." (Sensation.)

"Your memory is going again, Mr Curley. Perhaps this will refresh it. (Reading from a manuscript.) 'County sessions ... six months for robbery with violence. Town police court ... one month for petty larceny.' Is that correct?"

"Yes, I suppose so."

"Very well; now we come to the case before the court, and your evidence. You swore you heard the prisoner using threats? Where were they used?"

"On the public platform."
"Were you on the platform?"
"Yes."
"And what side did you take on that platform? Was it the side of the men or the masters?"
"The side of the men, of course."
"Do you recognise this book as the minute book of the Union of which you are the secretary?"
"Yes."
"You posted up these minutes, and this is your handwriting, is it not?"
"Yes."
"Is this yours, also?" reading out the letter advising proof of strike poster, and handing it to Curley.) (Sensation.)
"No, it is not; it is an impudent forgery."
"H'm; that will do for the present, Mr. Curley. Call Mr. Scrubbs."

As the private secretary passed Curley, and stepped into the place vacated by him, Curley's face went the colour of the wall behind him, and his teeth clicked with an unaccustomed rapidity as he made his way towards the door leading out of the court.

"Officer," said the solicitor, "will you kindly take care of Mr. Curley! We are not quite done with him yet," and so Curley was forced to stay, and while he stayed a conviction began to dawn on him that he and the prisoner Goodman would shortly change places, and so, indeed, it turned out.

The evidence of Mr. Scrubbs was to the effect that he was the Armitage, mentioned by the solicitor, convicted of a crime committed by Curley, of which he now possessed ample proof. He had been searching for him ever since he escaped from prison and had tracked him to Liverpool[94] for the purpose of exposing him. He was one of the men employed by Curley in an inland town to take the places of the men on strike, and he was denounced by Curley, who was playing a double part, when he got here, and with the assistance of credentials belonging to a dead friend of his who died in America, he secured a situation as Crushem's private secretary, and there he found further evidence of Curley's guilt, in the shape of the letters produced, and he also had possession of the receipt signed by Curley when the money promised was paid over to him.

He had taken the liberty of bringing another witness with him, in the shape of the phonograph which had registered the plot between him and Crushem, and as he placed the cylinder in its place and set the machine in motion, the phonograph rolled out in Curley's voice the history of the "Strike, strike, poster." The usher at this point had considerable difficulty in keeping silence in court, and Grindem, on the bench, nearly went into a fit.

There was more to follow. Scrubbs described Curley's nocturnal and clandestine visit; how he laid a trap for him, not expecting such results as had unfortunately followed. How surprised he was at the reception of the news at Doctor Smythe's, and his reception at the police-station. He had also fathomed the mystery of the hook with Goodman's initials on it, and how it came to be stolen, and the thief found out. It now only remained for him to be identified, and for this purpose the solicitor would ask their worships to recall Mr. Curley; and as Curley appeared again in the box, a gangway was made through the densely-packed mass in the body of the court to make way for Mrs. Goodman and her little son to give evidence.

In simple, innocent language, with his big blue eyes taking in all his surroundings, the little chap told his story; how he and his sister were playing with the hook in the lobby when Mr. Curley called to see his father; how they, getting tired of their play, had left their playthings, hook included, on the floor, and how he saw Curley stoop down, when going out, to pick the hook up, and put it in his belt. He had meant to tell his daddy about it, but a game of football in the back jigger[95] with an old tomato can drove it out of his head, and, looking across to where his father stood, he said, "I'll tell you now, daddy, and perhaps the police bobby[96] 'll let yer out."

[30 December 1893]

Chapter XXIII.

The private secretary had done his work well, and the chain of evidence was so complete that there was not the shadow of a doubt about Curley's guilt, who was remanded without bail to stand trial on the double charge preferred against him while Jack Goodman and the private secretary were lifted shoulder high by their enthusiastic admirers and carried in triumph to the club room.

Here the private secretary told to an admiring audience the story of an eventful life – how he had been suffering for a crime committed by Curley, and which he had fastened on him in a similar manner to that by which he had attempted to fasten this onto Goodman. It was a pathetic story, and when the secretary told of his suffering physically, his escape, his mental suffering at a glimpse of his wife and children, who mourned him as dead, and whom he was forced to pass by unrecognised until the task he had set himself of clearing his name was complete. There was scarcely a dry eye among that rough, uncouth crowd of men, who forgot their own sorrows in sympathising with another's. And their own troubles were not to be despised.

The fight had lasted six weeks, and still the same spirit of determination existed, though there were signs here and there on both sides indicative of a wish to end the struggle, a feature noticeable in all disputes when the intervention of a third party (if there be any such) is acceptable.

So it happened in this case

A gentleman of pronounced political views, but in great sympathy with the labour movement, was invited to intervene, and he accepted.[97] And so a deputation of dockers, headed by this gentleman, was appointed to meet the employers, who had also consented to meet the men whom a few weeks before they had indignantly refused to recognise.

So the movement had at last been educational, and so much had been gained – the recognition by the employer of the right of the men to combine.

But at what cost!

The empty homes, denuded of every stick of furniture, the thinly-clad bodies of the wives and children, and the pinched faces of all supplied the answer. This, together with the falling-off (owing to the attack on Crushem) of the very scanty contributions to the soup kitchens, which provided children only with one meal a day, was a very potent factor in the deliberations.

And the result was a compromise, the men getting a concession from the employers of a regular, recognised meal-hour, the right of combination, and an overtime wage tariff, being more than 40 per cent of their demands.

The only sore point was the working harmoniously with non-union men (this was a very sore point). However, it was the only way out of the difficulty, and was accepted, and would have been loyally acted up to if the employers had not shamefully broken their compact.

And herein lies the mischievous element in the intervention of a third party, as the intervener, however good his intention may be, is very liable to ere on the wrong side from his want of knowledge and experience of his surroundings.

This is what happened in this case. The men went back to work on a purely verbal agreement, that no one was to be singled out as a victim, and bygones forgotten.

This, by a peculiar process known only to Employers' Associations, whether verbal or written, is invariably lost sight of.

However, the strike was over, and the men went back to work, but not according to agreement. And now nothing remains to be told of my story but the sequel.

There were some men who never went back to work at all, men who could not get any work to go back to. Men who had served a life's apprenticeship in building up the firm of Crushem and Grindem, who were refused work everywhere they went to look for it because of the issuing of the hue and cry against them of the Employers' Association, of which Crushem and Grindem were the moving spirit.

These men have dropped in their tracks in the public streets from exposure and exhaustion, and have been carted to the hospital in a brewer's ambulance,[98] to whom teetotal Crushem had granted a licence, and from the hospital to the dead house, and from the dead house to a pauper's grave, their families being kept alive by the rates subscribed by dock labourers and administered by Crushem. The ward in the hospital set apart for the cripples made during the strike gradually assumed its normal position, while the majority of the cripples graduated to the cemetery, and swelled the dividends of the Funeral Company, of which Messrs. Fatpurse and Grindem were chairman and directors.

In the meantime something else was happening, which happens in the best regulated families.

Dr. Smythe had married Miss Crushem, and, as the story goes, lived happy ever after, notwithstanding the fact of the cruel par-ie-ent.[99] Mr. Garnish married Miss Smythe, and old Smythe was reconciled, had given up business on 'Change,[100] and was now developing alarming symptoms of Socialism quite shocking to his respectable friends, and might now be seen in company with his daughter and son-in-law every Saturday night distributing bowls of soup and bread and jam tarts at the Cinderella Club[101] treats, and singing comic songs and making shadows with his fingers to amuse barefooted, disgustingly ragged and dirty children of the lower orders. And then something else happened which never was known to happen before.

The Union prospered in spite of every obstacle, and Goodman, who was secretary, and Scrubbs, who had succeeded in getting a good job in one of the firms willing to work in harmony with the Union, had succeeded in forming a labour party, of which Dr. Smythe was chairman. And the doctor's wife, and Mr. Garnish's wife, and Goodman's wife, and Christie's – aye, and even Tom Curley's wife were members.[102]

And then something else happened. Crushem suddenly discovered that he had an intense love of justice to Ireland, and although he had not the slightest idea of her geographical position he felt he must do something to gratify his burning desire, especially as his time would be up in the Council next year. So he attended the Irish National Concert and became a member.[103] Some one suggested he should practice justice to Irishmen in England first if he was in earnest, but the man who made such a ridiculous suggestion was expelled the National League, without having an opportunity to defend himself at the next meeting, which was as it should be, of course – Why not?

Meanwhile Scrubbs, who was now comfortably settled with his wife and family in the neighbourhood, was acting honorary secretary of the Labour Party, and was doing wonders and making converts by the score by organising meetings, and, to use his own expression, "pegging away" and pointing out to the workers that their only hope of salvation was political action and having working men in Parliament and Town Councils to make laws which they were bound to obey. And then something else happened.

Doctor Smythe and Goodman were nominated as labour candidates for the November elections, which were close at hand, in opposition to Crushem and Fatpurse, and were vigorously denounced by the National League as being in the pay of the Tories[104] "who, if they got possession of the Town Hall, wouldn't give an Irishman or a Catholic a job o' lamplighting or scavenging in a hundred years."

And so the fun went on till the day of election and then –

An accident happened. The Labour Party mustered strong on the day of election, Scrubbs marshalling his forces manfully, while Goodman was looking after the voters with the Doctor's father's horse and trap, the horse being a somewhat restive animal.

Things went but slowly during the day, as all Crushem's employees to whom any suspicions were attached, and who had votes, were drafted to the other end of town and on the river, while the faithful few were kept working in the vicinity so as to allow them to vote at dinner time. The National League of Lamplighters were also busy canvassing for Crushem.

About six o'clock in the evening Scrubbs, who had been busy drumming up the voters as they knocked off, was just turning the corner of the street when he ran full tilt against a man coming in a hurry from an opposite direction, with a lug cap,[105] with the lugs hanging down and the peak well over a pair of eyes and a big muffler scarcely concealing a set of gleaming teeth that could belong to nobody but Curley. The force of the collision nearly knocked the breath out of Scrubbs, who, when he recovered himself, was prompted to follow the man with the lug cap, but he had disappeared. Then he remembered that Curley's time was about up; but then, again, he might be mistaken. Surely, he would never dare to venture in this neighbourhood again, he thought.

"No, it must have been imagination," he assured himself, and was about to continue his journey towards the polling-booth when a loud shout and the clatter of horse's hoofs caused him to glance down the street, and he saw Goodman in the trap accompanied by a woman voter he was taking home after having voted.[106]

The horse had bolted, collided with a lamp-post, and torn a wheel off, and the maddened beast was now dragging the light trap along on its axle, with the woman terror-stricken clinging to the high side, and Goodman, with face cut, endeavouring with the reins to check its furious career. To spring into the middle of the road and wait the approach of the horse, to fling himself at the head of the frightened brute and force him back upon his haunches, was but the work of a few moments, and Goodman and his charge were safe.

By this time the usual crowd that seems to come mysteriously from nowhere, had collected, and Goodman was kneeling in the road supporting the prostrate form of his rescuer, and wiping away the blood that was oozing from his mouth and ears.

"Some of you ring up the ambulance, quick!" commanded Goodman. "My God!" as another gush comes from the injured man's mouth, "he'll bleed to death if they're not quick. My poor old chum, what can I do for you?" asked Jack, as he bent down and silently laid his lips on the injured man's forehead, and mingled his tears with his life's blood.

"Nothing, old man; no thing," feebly whispered Scrubbs, between gasps. "Get me away to the hospital, quick! The shafts struck me hard, old man, but you – you're all right. Here come the ambulance chum; put me in, and get back to business, and keep pegging away," and with this sage advice he once more lapsed into unconsciousness, and was placed in the ambulance and driven away.

The same night, at 9.45, Goodman, the Doctor, and the injured man's wife stood by his bedside, when he returned once more to consciousness, and his first words were, "Well, what's the result?"

"Now, my dear fellow, don't excite yourself," said the Doctor. "We'll tell you later on, though." In a side whisper to Goodman, "I don't think he'll last till morning. The shaft has completely broken his chest bone, and he's dreadfully injured internally."

"No, tell me now, Doctor, tell me now at once. Do you hear? What's the result? I can bear it better then."

"Hush, my dear," said his wife. "Don't excite yourself; both the Doctor and Mr. Goodman are returned at the head of the poll and Crushem's at the bottom."

The injured man at hearing this news suddenly raised himself in a sitting position to give vent to his feelings, but was interrupted by another gush of blood from the mouth, which laid him prostrate, and looking up at Goodman and his wife, he feebly extended a hand to each of them, and then to the Doctor he said, "I know I'm done for, Doctor. A few hours more or less don't make much difference when a chap's bound to go, through I did think as this poor lass's life and my own was going to be a bit easier. There, there, my lass, don't take on like that. I've always been more or less of a scapegoat all my life, and (with a ghost of a smile) better a dead scapegoat than a dead Town Councillor, and especially a Labour Councillor. Tell me, Goodman, what made the horse bolt?"

"Well, old chap, to be correct we think it was a burr that we found under the harness, close to the cropper,"[107] said Goodman.

"Ah! Then it was him I seen after all. The scoundrel! Never mind, mate," said he, in the faintest possible whisper, "the thin end of the wedge is in. Keep – peg – peg – ging a – a – way," and another crimson streak appeared at the corner of his mouth, his hands slipped out of the custody of his wife's and Goodman's, and fell with a dull thud on the counterpane.

The blackleg was no more.

Martin Fair, 'Nan: A New Year's Eve Story' (1893)

The first time I saw her was in the dock – her forty-first appearance, the police said. She gave her age as thirty, but she hardly looked it, for her face was still fresh looking, and her hair long and wavy, or a deep chestnut colour. She lived in Jackson's PH,[1] she said, and she laughed heartily as she said it, and her long, supple fingers took a fresh grip on the dock-rails in front of her.

The usual charge was made against her. I mean her usual one – "drunk and incapable." She was never violent, but pliant as a lamb when drunk, and that was very often.

"What shall I do with you, Nan?" asked the magistrate. She was twisting the shreds of her apron when he asked the question.

"Eh, what," she queried? Then turning to the policeman in the dock she asked, "what does he say?"

"His Worship wants to know what he shall do with you," said the officer, stolidly.

"Oh, you do, do you?" she said, with a quick look at the bench. "Don't you know your duty – do you want me to teach you?"

There was a general titter among the spectators, and the police shouted "silence" stentoriously.

"Send me to prison, of course," went on Nan. "Let's see, this is the last day in this year. Yes, send me to prion; I'll begin the new year sober then."

The magistrate looked at her for a moment then he laid aside his pen and said: "No, Nan, I won't; I'm going to discharge you. You are discharged. Bring the woman to my room," he said to the policeman in the dock; then he left the bench.

Nan was hardly sober, and understood little of what the magistrate said, and when the policeman took her by the arm to lead her away, she looked up and asked, "How much has he given me?"

"You're discharged; he wants to see you in his room," the man answered.

"What," laughed Nan, "no fine; well here's luck. What an old idiot he must be." Then she seemed to think for a moment and began to smooth her hair with her hands, and try to remove the mud from her skirt as she muttered "What does he want, I wonder?"

The magistrate was looking intently in the fire as she entered his room, but, seeing her, he motioned her to a seat near the fire, and turning to the officer said curtly "Leave us." The man and woman sat there in silence for a few minutes – to Nan it was years; she was uneasy. The man was watching shadows running swiftly through the flames. Childish forms and faces, now a man's stern look, and then a woman's soft entreaty. Voices spoke in whispers in his ear, memories were recalled and he lived over again the past.

Suddenly he looked up, and leaning forward in his chair he fixed his eyes on the woman and asked softly, "Annie, where is your child?"

The woman shook like the leaves in a hurricane, her eyes opened wide with a stare of agony, her hands worked convulsively, and her lips turned ashy grey as she stammered "My child. I – I – who are you! What?"

"Yes, your boy. Yours and Arthur's," the magistrate said, but his voice was husky and faint.

"Arthur," Nan repeated in a dazed fashion, "Where is Arthur, my little Arthur? *My* Arthur's gone." She went on deliriously, "gone, my Arthur's gone, gone away, my little Arthur's in the snow; but I had to leave him; they found him, I know they did for I saw him once through the window. He's happy and warm. I –" Nan was gone. The woman sitting here was a mother, the mother breathed again, the mother wept bitter tears – hot scalding tears – but it was not Nan. It was a woman, a mother that shed them.

The magistrate let her cry. He never moved, but his face softened and a light lit up his eyes which before had been cold as glass. He sighed wearily, then touched a bell, and said to the officer who answered it, "Have a cab at the private door in fifteen minutes."

Then he turned to Nan. She was quiet by this time – her eyes were swollen and red, her hands still shook but with an anxiety to know more about her past life, of its loves and hopes, they had slipped away from her.

"Nan," said the magistrate gently, "you are ill, I am afraid very ill; you need care; I'm going to take you home."

"What home," she asked suspiciously.

"My home; to my house, of course. I am sure my wife will be glad to see you."

"Will you tell me all about Arthur, my Arthur?" she asked pitifully.

"Yes, I'll tell you all about both Arthurs. Come now."

"Both Arthurs," moaned Nan. "No, not both. Arthur's gone." But she went with the magistrate quietly, muttering and moaning as she went, unconscious of the disgust of the policeman, only conscious of the name and remembrances of "her Arthur."

The magistrate set his teeth firmly as he passed between the ranks of his subordinates; he knew their thoughts pretty well. He understood that when he had gone they would criticize him in their own fashion. But at last Nan was inside the cab, and the magistrate followed her after telling the cabman, in a clear voice, to "drive home."

Nan never asked him a question – in fact, she never said a word during the whole journey; her mind was in the past. She was only a young woman, but she had crowded a century of life in her little cycle of time. She was busy with her thoughts, and so was the man sitting opposite to her. For he did not sit beside her; he wanted to look at her, and his eyes seemed to be greedy, insatiable, for they never left the woman's mud-bespattered head for a moment. He was thinking of the time when a boy – the boy was still a boy to him, although he was now a grown up man – used to sit on his knee, and prattle childishly to him. He had watched that boy grow to manhood, had helped him in his troubles, felt for him in his disappointments, and finally, when the boy had grown reckless and dissipated, had tried to hush up all his wrong doings, and so far as possible, right the wrong.

Did I say all the boy's wrong-doings? Then I'm wrong. All but one. The wrong done could never be undone, nor repaired, it cost a life – a woman's life, and the woman was sitting in front of the father now. Her name was Annie Hawtrey, not Nan; that was all her associates could get out of her, though.

When a girl of seventeen she was an orphan, the daughter of one of the magistrate's friends, a friend from boyhood. He took her, into his house as a daughter, but she hated to be dependent, and insisted upon acting as governess and companion to the younger children in the family. Arthur, the eldest son, was away from home when she became one of the family. But her beauty, her grace, her simplicity, her sweetness, turned his head when he did see her.

He loved her – that is, he said he did, and soon gained all the love of her nature. His object may have been good at first, but the time came when Annie had to confess her wrongdoing to her lover's mother. He mother pleaded for her, blamed her son, reminded her husband of his promise to the girl's dead father; but the man was inexorable. The girl was a sinner, she was *the* sinner, she was a woman. She must go; and so she went with her unborn baby out into the world.

A year passed, and no tidings could be obtained of Annie. The young man had repented of his action after a fashion – that is, he thought the girl as much guilty as he was, and "Well," he used to say, "I'm no worse than other fellows." But the mother had never forgiven her son for his action, she had never given up the hope of some day bringing Annie back again to them.

One night, however, a little over a year from the time when Annie left the house, a warm night, but wet, for a soft, drizzling rain had been falling all afternoon, the bell rang violently, startling the servants in the kitchen, and causing their mistress to ejaculate "My God! What is that?" The servants went to the hall in a body, and the butler opened the door in trepidation.

A wailing sound greeted him as he peered out, but there was nobody on the steps. A basket was lying there – a big basket, and hearing the unusual sound he stooped to the basket, exclaiming as he did so: "Somebody's left us a kid!" Then he turned to the footman, "'Ere, fetch a policeman," he said, "this brat must go to the work'us." "Poor little thing," said the women in chorus, "please may we see it put in. Oh, let's just see it." The footman was turning to obey the butler's order, when the mistress appeared, and she was informed of the advent of a baby. "I'm sending John for a policeman, ma'am," he explained, "these beggars' brats should go somewhere else." "Beggars' brats?" said the lady, stiffly, "Never use those words again in my presence. Bring the basket into the drawing-room, Robins," and she turned to the motherly-looking cook. "You'll come with me please."

The basket was unpacked by Robins, baby bawling lustily the while, the mistress of the house watching the operation anxiously. "Here's a letter, ma'am," she said, "right in this shawl. Poor darling," and she tried to hush the baby as she handed her mistress the letter. There was only a line, and it read: "His name is Arthur, tell him I'm dead – Annie." The baby was kept as their own; its father was told where it came from, and how it came, but they never heard of Annie.

Some years after the baby had been found on the doorstep, Nan was up before the court for being drunk. While in the dock she began singing: –

> "Oh, little thought my mother
> When she first cradled me,
> That I should die so far from home
> Or hang on a gallows tree.

The magistrate listened. Where had he heard that song before? It was the ballad of the "Four Marys,"[2] his wife's favourite song, but he had a recollection of some fresh young voice singing it in his later years. Nan went to prison several times before the court thought further in the matter. But, one night after one of Nan's appearances, he said to his wife "That song of the Four Mary's is a pretty one, is it not?"

"Yes, very," she answered in surprise. He noticed it, and went on "It has been running in my head all day." "That's strange," she said quietly.

"Why strange?" he asked.

"Because that's Annie's song, you know."

He got up and walked across the room. "Annie's song. Nan – Nan – Annie," he thought. "Is Annie Nan?"

He wife followed him; she knew he was troubled. "What is it, dear?" she asked. Then he told her. The woman begged him to be sure to examine her as to her early life, and if it was Annie to bring her home to them at once. He rebelled against the thought of it. Should he bring such a vile thing as Nan into his house, a worse than beast? Then his wife settled the matter by saying, "You know, dear, that whatever she is, Arthur is the cause of it. She is more sinned against than sinning."

Then he gave his promise to bring Nan home, and he kept his word.

His wife's hands stripped the rags from the Magdalene's back, her hands bathed the bloated features of the outcast; her lips touched the lips of the woman whose name was a synonym of impurity. And as Nan slept in her own bedroom, the mother of the man who had blasted her life, knelt beside her. Nan moaned in her sleep uneasily. She wanted Arthur, "her little boy. Arthur had gone," and then she would toss about for a while restlessly. They watched her until night set in, then a doctor was sent for. He shook his head, "fine constitution," he said, "very fine. Ruined absolutely ruined by drink; a case of alcoholism. She may live a week, but probably only a day or two." Then he went away, for there was nothing more to be done or said.

But they watched Nan until midnight as she slept; they heard the bells ring in the New Year as they rang out the Old.

Then Nan awoke. She was quieter, her eyes more natural in their appearance. She looked round the room in wonder, as her eyes opened.

"Where am I?" she gasped.

"Home, dear," the old lady said, and she kissed her. "Home – don't you know me?"

"Home! Home! I ... " and she rubbed her eyes like a little child awakening. "I – oh, yes, but –"

"I'm Arthur's mother, and –"

"Arthur's mother," screamed Nan, "and I am in your house. Will you turn me out? Oh, I loved him." Then she saw the magistrate. "I'm only Nan," she said, turning to him, "drunken Nan, but tell me about my boy."

They told her he was well, strong, healthy, happy. "He doesn't know I'm Nan, does he?" she asked. Then she wanted to trace him. She wanted to get up to go and find him; she would find him and see him. To quiet her they told her the boy was in the house, that he was as their own child.

She listened quietly, and the big tears rolled down her cheeks. When they had done, she asked in a faint whisper, "Please let me see Arthur, just for a minute."

They looked at her in wonder. Her voice was changed; her face looked brighter, more peaceful than it did an hour ago – what did it mean? The mother knew. They sent for the boy, a fine lad, nine years old. He came into the room shyly, for they had told him that his mamma wanted to see him, that she was very ill.

As he came to the bedside Nan turned to look at him. "Stand there," she said as he stood by the bed. Nan put out her hand and stroked his long thick curls lovingly, murmuring softly as she did so.

'Come and kiss me, Arthur,' she said soon. And the boy jumped on the bed and threw his arms round her neck, kissing her lips and cheeks again and again, and saying repeatedly, "My mamma, my own mamma."

"Say that again, darling!" she whispered. And he obeyed her, finally laying his head beside hers, looking at her and wondering what she was crying about. Then he turned to his grandparents as if to ask whether he was doing right or not. And they smiled at him through their tears.

Suddenly a thought seemed to enter the young brain, and he turned in bed and asked, "Where's my papa?" then started and looked at the old people, and they looked at one another for a moment, and then the old man left the room.

He came back with his son, pale and agitated, for his father had told him the story. Nan simply said "Arthur" and took his hand, lifting it to her mouth to kiss now and then.

And so morning dawned. As the first grey streaks of the new year were struggling through the clouds, Nan lifted her head and said, "Arthur, kiss me." The child was asleep; he was smiling; the father stooped and kissed Nan's lips. She looked at the boy and kissed him fondly, then turning to the window she asked, "Is it New Year now?"

They told her it was, and she smiled, laid her face close to her boy's, and with her eyes looking at his father's face, she died.

Dan Baxter, 'A Terrible Crime' (1893)

"I give you a kiss as a guarantee that I shall tell it in such a manner as will save you all tragic emotions."

"Well, proceed," said she.

"In the days," began he, "when the desires of a free people were controlled by men and women who were trained from their infancy to deal only with results, and could not, or would not, look deeper than results, there lived a man who became so wealthy that neither dukes, nor even clergymen could stand upright in his presence.

"Philip Bullion was his name. He lived in a house like yours, surrounded by lawns, and gardens, and forests, and streams.

"The source of his wealth was a mystery to the whole people, until one day the report was flashed all over the world, along with the intelligence that he had been found dead on a couch.

"In each some two hundred rooms of his palace, and some outhouses, were found plaster casts and dies, and machinery of all kinds for producing every coin of the various realms of the world. Not only that, but in four of the largest rooms were found expensive photographic and lithographic[1] plants adapted for the making of all descriptions of paper money.

"Ha!" cried everybody. "Then Bullion was a maker of counterfeit coins, and notes – a forger, a scoundrel."[2]

"All that I know," cried one man, "is that had it not been for Bullion, a great many thousands of our respectable people would not be such large shareholders in the railways, mines, and other company concerns formed for the purpose of sucking the life's blood out of the people."

"Now it happened that the free, generous, good-natured slow-to-anger people, who lived in those days, were so careful to guard against any tampering with their money stamps, that they had proclaimed forgery to be one of the vilest of crimes, and punishable even by death.

"It had been made a crime to order that individuals might not become possessed of the power to command the products of the people's labour, without giving products of their own labour, or some appreciable equivalent in exchange.

"So, when it became known that Squire Bullion was not only a forger, but had made thousands of men and women wealthy by giving them gifts of the money he made, and in that way enabling them without working to procure what the people had sweated to produce, the whole population turned out, and in their wrath were preparing to burn his body, when a more highly developed man than the rest stepped on to a chair and cried:

"Friends, listen to me before you set fire to these tar barrels."

"You are cursing Mr. Bullion and his satellites. Why?

"Yesterday you would have gone, hat in hand, to beg of them to be allowed to toil for your means of life!

"Is it because thousands of your fellows have, without your knowledge, accumulated large stocks of forged coins and notes, and are going amongst you with them, forcing you to supply them with food and clothing, forcing you to dig coal and make gas and build fine houses, and repair these fine houses, and provide them with all the other comforts and luxuries, without their doing a hand's turn in the work?

"Is that what makes you angry? Is it because they are giving you *forged* money instead of good money for the products of your labour, that you are so angry?

"If these thousands, tens of thousands of idle men and women, gave you what you call 'current' coin of the realm, what would be the difference to you, you asses?

"Would they not be idle all the same?

"Would you not be doing all the work that requires to be done without their help, forged money or good money?

"There are many thousands giving you good money.

"Lord Rent, Squire Tax and Messrs. Profit and Interest and their flunkies are giving you good money. They do no work. You do it all.

"Why, then, curse Forgery without at the same time cursing Rent, Profit and Interest?

"Your anger, friends, shows that you have got a glimpse at the truth. You shall have a good look at it.

"See. Who is that at the castle door? He is no other than Squire Bullion. He was not dead – only pretending. He filled his rooms with the implements of the forger, in order that you might rise in your wrath against a system that permits a poor type of men and women to live lives of idleness and wrong-doing by obtaining large stacks of your money-stamps – the token of your labour – in a way that is no more honourable than it is to forge them.

"Mr. Bullion is a convert to the truth – to Socialism – and has taken this way of showing it to you."

"Yes," cried Mr. Bullion, stepping from the door of his castle, "I have taken this way of showing you why you should take charge of your own affairs; why you should take back to yourselves the money, the keys to the products of your own labour; the articles you, as a people, put your stamps upon; the articles that were intended to measure the value of your own labour, but which have not served that purpose since your fore-fathers introduced the use of coal and machinery. These money stamps (the money) are your own. You must take them. And if you do not need them, to make ornaments for your wives and daughters, place them under the control, the distributive control, not of irresponsible anybodies who have the cunning and greed to do nothing but keep them from your reach; place them under the control, the distributive control, of men and women whom you can trust to distribute them in such a way as to make sure that every man, woman boy, and girl, shall not only get what they need, without crime, but also be placed in a position that will enable them to give what Nature alone will force them to give."

EDITORIAL NOTES

Flestrin, 'A Tale of a Turnip'

1. *four ale and unsweetened*: 'Four ale' is ale sold at fourpence a quart, i.e. very cheap alcohol; 'unsweetened' probably refers to alcoholic spirits such as gin, rum or whisky. The brewing process for beer or ale includes the malting of the grain, producing the sugars dextrin and maltose, which makes ale sweeter than spirits and lowers the alcoholic content in relation to spirits. Face is a heavy drinker and consumes cheap beer and strong liquor.
2. *Cockney*: originally a derogatory appellation for people living in London, officially those born within the sound of the bells of St Mary-le-Bow. The association of 'Cockney' with the working-class East End of London comes from the confusion surrounding 'Bow bells', mistaking St Mary and Holy Trinity in the district of Bow for St Mary-le-Bow in the City of London.
3. *temperance reform*: The temperance movement began in the 1830s as an attempt by the upper and middle classes to reduce working-class alcohol consumption through leading by example. Temperance originally promoted moderate consumption, but in 1832 the 'Seven Men of Preston' who formed the Preston Temperance Society, including the working-class journalist and reformer Joseph Livesey (1794–1884), pledged to abstain entirely from drinking alcohol, except for medicinal purposes. There were other temperance societies, but Preston was the first to abstain entirely, and by the 1840s the movement insisted on total abstinence. The Band of Hope, formed in 1833, was a very popular organization within the temperance movement; it aimed to promote abstinence to children and was associated with the aspirational members of the working class. Many socialists supported the temperance movement, most famously Keir Hardie, who had joined as a young man, but socialists rejected the argument that alcohol was the cause of poverty, as this perspective placed responsibility for poverty on the individual rather than on the inequalities of the capitalist system.
4. *Dog and Duck*: a public house, similarly the Horn and Chequers. The Dog and Duck is a popular pub name associated with the sport of shooting fowl and the bodies being retrieved by the hunting dog. David Rothwell's *Dictionary of Pub Names* (Ware: Wordsworth Editions, 2006) notes that the reference might also be to the 'sport' of Charles II, who would pinion the wings of ducks on a duck pond and send dogs in to 'hunt' them. The ducks could only escape temporarily by diving. The Horn and Chequers may refer to the hunting horn, the post horn or the horn of the drayman signalling his arrival, and the game of chequers, or draughts, but it might also be a reference to the associations of the sign with financial exchange: 'the word "exchequer" originally meant

a kind of chessboard. Some inns may have used the sign to indicate that they were ready to change money or act as bankers' (p. 82). Both public houses are associated with aristocratic sports and wealth, the sale of alcohol providing a distraction from the surrounding inequalities and also a stick with which the wealthy could beat the poor, as they claimed the money spent on alcohol was the root cause of poverty.

5. *Bacchus and Mars*: Greek mythological figures commonly associated with wine and war. Face is expressing his enjoyment of drink and drunken brawling.
6. à Voutrance: *A l'outrance*, meaning with few or no rules, was a combat between medieval knights. For more details, see N. Evangelista, *The Encyclopedia of the Sword* (Westport, CT: Greenwood Press, 1995). The fight was to the death, and Face threatens the same with Bill Cherry as he asserts his intention to decapitate him, 'filbert' being a slang word for the head.
7. *scapegrace*: a man or boy of reckless and disorderly habits; an incorrigible scamp; *OED*. The neighbourhood required someone against whom they could measure their respectable habits and feel superior in comparison. Face was a better 'scapegoat' – meaning one who carries the sins of others – than William Cherry, who had the capacity for improvement in line with genteel society's expectations. Face fills the position of scapegoat better through his unrelenting resistance to reform.
8. *Private bar ... taproom*: Public bars would be separated into a number of smaller rooms and inhabited according to class, and sometimes gender. The private bar would be for the 'respectable' customers, and the taproom would serve the less respectable drinker. There might also be a 'Ladies Room' for women to drink.
9. *spittoon*: a receptacle for spittle, usually made of earthenware of metal; *OED*.
10. *shag*: low-grade, cheap tobacco.
11. *clay*: clay pipe; a cheap receptacle for cheap tobacco. The spittoon, shag and clay pipes, as well as their location in the tap room, suggests the lowly and unrespectable status of both Face and Legs.
12. *Pilot Point (perhaps Nunquam ... this point)*: Nunquam is the pseudonym of *Clarion* editor Robert Blatchford. Pilot Point might refer to a city in Texas of that name. The American army had banned the distribution of alcohol to its soldiers in 1865, and the British army had reduced the alcohol distributed to its soldiers. The whispered secret might be information about a supplier to the American army, who would be manufacturing illegal alcohol for American soldiers, or the recipe passed on from a soldier from Pilot Point. The call for enlightenment from Nunquam might refer to his knowledge of alcoholic drinks, his experiences as a soldier or both.
13. *badge*: a medal for honour, service or bravery during his service. Legs's consumption of alcohol had not diminished his work as a soldier, but his punishment was the removal of a visible reward for honourable service.
14. *Methusaleh*: Methuselah, the oldest man in the Bible, who lived 969 years; Genesis 5:27. Face would not have earned a medal for service, even if he lived as long as Methuselah.
15. *clay*: Legs is unsuitable for employment in the local brick-making industry and must take labouring employment on the land.
16. *basket chaise*: a small, light, open-topped carriage used for leisure travelling, usually having one or two seats and made of wicker or basket-work.
17. Tempora mutantur: Latin, meaning times change, or have changed.
18. *Loamshire*: a fictional county, but suggesting that the Captain intends to stand for election in an agricultural area.

19. *Byron's black friar... Norman stane*: George Gordon Lord Byron's (1788–1824) 'Beware! Beware! of the Black Friar' (1823), which opens with the lines 'Beware! beware! of the Black Friar, / Who sitteth by Norman stone'. Byron's Black Friar has been evicted from his Catholic church by the dissolution but remains to haunt the family of the lord, who destroyed the church at Henry VIII's command and who benefited by the dissolution by taking the land for himself. The Black Friar is existing evidence of the injustice meted out to the friars of the Catholic church, who had been living quietly before the dissolution; Legs is existing evidence of the injustice meted out to those at the bottom of society.
20. *home had gone and ta'en his wages*: the funeral song from Act IV, scene ii from Shakespeare's *Cymbeline*: 'Fear no more the heat o' the sun, / Nor the furious winter's rages; / Thou thy worldly task hast done, / Home art gone, and ta'en thy wages: / Golden lads and girls all must, / As chimney-sweepers, come to dust.' Legs was killed by the accident.
21. *the young Tobias*: In the Bible, Tobias, son of Tobit, is told to marry his cousin Sarah by the angel Raphael, but first he must destroy the demon who killed Sarah's first seven husbands. In his prayer after the demon has been driven from the house, Tobias says, 'Lord, I have chosen Sarah because it is right, not because I lusted for her. Please be merciful to us and grant that we may grow old together'; Tobit 8:7. Captain Tiplady is reminding young Gillyflower that his marriage should be considered sanctioned by God and that God should be thanked regularly. The Captain's allusions are weighted with irony, as he is revealed as the destroyer of Legs's family.
22. *Workus*: the workhouse, an institution developed through the 1834 Poor Law Act to house the unemployed and destitute but to make inhabitants uncomfortable to discourage entry. The soldier and Face would have been desperate in order for them to bear the discomfort and stigma attached to entering the workhouse. Face's hesitation to mention it suggests his embarrassment.

Carpenter, 'Saved by a Nose'

1. *Treaty of Peace*: The Treaty of Versailles ended the Franco–Prussian War after the unification of Germany and the declaration of William I of Prussia as Kaiser. The Treaty required France to pay reparations to Germany, and German troops would continue to occupy parts of France until payment was complete.
2. absinthe: a highly alcoholic drink distilled from wine and wormwood; *OED*.
3. *Commune*: the Paris Commune of 1871. The French government's attempt to remove the weaponry from the Paris militia brought about the overthrow of the government in the city, and the Parisian working class took power. The revolution lasted only seventy-two days (between 18 March and 28 May 1871) before the national government again took control of the city.
4. *Coblentz*: now Koblenz, a German city at the confluence of the Rhine and the Moselle. The Fortress Ehrenberitstein, originally built in the eleventh century and extended in the seventeenth and eighteenth centuries, commands a prominent position overlooking Koblenz.
5. *Trèves*: Carpenter uses the French spelling and pronunciation for Trier, a city on the Moselle near the border with Luxembourg.
6. diligence: a public stagecoach; *OED*.
7. thaler: a German silver coin worth about a dollar; *OED*.
8. *Burgomaster*: chief magistrate, a similar position to that of a mayor in England; *OED*.

9. parlez-voo: parlez-vous, meaning 'do you speak', used in this context to indicate that the narrator speaks a little French.
10. Nase – stumpf: nose – blunt or stumpy.
11. *A fellow-feeling makes us wondrous kind*: an unattributed proverb or saying.

M'Ginnis, 'Posterity'

1. *Marquis of Salisbury*; Robert Arthur Talbot Gascoyne-Cecil (1830–1903), Conservative politician and Prime Minister 1885–1892 and 1895–1902. He opposed Irish calls for independence, or Home Rule, and joined with the Liberal Unionists to defeat the 1886 Home Rule Bill in the Commons. He later threatened to create more peers in the House of Lords to defeat the second bill, but this was not necessary as the peers rejected the bill by 419 votes to 41 in September 1893. The story is reminiscent of Percy Shelley's (1792–1822) 'Ozymandias' (1818), as Salisbury's power is proved as transient and period-bound as Rameses's.
2. *prima donna's*: prima donna, the leading female singer in an opera. Lotta's roles in high culture (opera) and labouring work (pruning vines) are part of Blatchford's vision of a socialist society that embraces both the necessity of work and the importance of culture for all. He expands on this vision in 'The Sorcery Shop'; see Volume 4 for the complete text.
3. *immutable economic laws*: the capitalist argument that current financial systems are essential and unchangeable. Blatchford, and other socialists, argued against this perspective and, through literature, imagined worlds where priorities were changed.
4. *silver fret fan ... in return*: an example of the changed financial and economic priorities in Blatchford's utopia. Under capitalism, silver would be deemed more valuable than a rose, but in the utopia their value lies in their beauty and therefore they are equally desirable.

'Citizen', 'Little Maggie's Boots'

1. *My Grandfather's Clock*: 'My Grandfather's Clock' (1876) by Henry Clay Work. The song is about a 'grandfather clock', owned by the narrator's grandfather, which had shared the old man's life and had stopped working the moment he died. Like the clock, the London Tram is better known for stopping.
2. *Cluck, cluck*: to the horses pulling the tram, encouraging them to begin moving.

Glasier, 'Telby Torbald: or, A Socialist Transformed'

1. *shopmates*: used to indicate his fellow workers in a factory or workshop rather than the retail business.
2. ser-i-at-im: meaning consecutively or one after another; *OED*.

McMillan, 'Mary's Lover'

1. *gasalier*: gasolier, an ornamental frame to hold gaslights, usually hung from the ceiling of a room; a contraction of gas chandelier; *OED*.
2. *new-fangled women*: the New Woman. The term 'New Woman', coined by author Ouida (pseudonym of Marie Louise de la Ramée (1839–1908)) in 1894 and based on the Sarah Grand essay 'The New Aspect of the Woman Question', gives a name to the multiple demands for female emancipation in the 1880s and 1890s. The New Woman demanded

the freedom to work, to live independently, to earn and control her own money, and to make her own decisions about relationships and marriage. Commentators and subsequent historians have recognized that while coining a name went some way to cohering a set of demands into a unified movement, it also allowed critics to narrow and calcify the perimeters and to ridicule the women's aims.

3. *temperance orator*: For an outline of the temperance movement in Britain, see above, p. 359 n. 3. The young man, used to putting across his own agenda for the improvement of society, is unnerved by Mary, her confidence and her difference.
4. *drugget*: According to the *OED*, this is a heavy cloth of wool, or a mixture of wool and other cloth, used as a piece of clothing. The woman is house-proud, has created a sense of comfort in the home by the use of the material as a rug, and demonstrates a certain level of relative wealth in her ability to adorn the floor as well as herself with cloth.
5. Comic Cuts: the halfpenny comic magazine first published in 1890 by Alfred Harmsworth and which ran until 1953. In 1893 it ran the Sherlock Holmes satire 'Chubblock Holmes', which was the creation of illustrator John (Jack) Butler Yeats (1871–1957), younger brother of William Butler Yeats (1865–1939). The young man is not of a serious or intellectual frame of mind.

Becke, 'A Touch of the Tar Brush'

1. *House of Representatives*: As a part of the British Empire after the jurisdiction of New South Wales in Australia was extended to include New Zealand in 1840, the country was governed by a representative of the Queen until the New Zealand Constitution Act of 1852 created a General Assembly that included the Governor, an elected House of Representatives and a Legislative Council. The first General Assembly sat in 1854. Only male European New Zealanders and male Maoris could vote until women were given the franchise in 1893 (the first country in the world to give women the vote). Maori representation was granted in 1868 when Maori men were given the opportunity to return four Maori MPs; Rauparaha is one of these Members. There were no official political parties until the 1890s, when the Liberal Party formed a distinct social group. The Labour Party did not become an official political group until 1916, but there would be representatives of the workers in the House who would find common ground in their arguments and goals.
2. *village settlements*: The 1863 New Zealand Settlements Act confiscated land from Maori people, who were considered rebellious during what was termed the New Zealand Wars. The conflicts ran through the 1860s and 1870s, and more than four million acres of Maori land were confiscated and given to settlers. Rauparaha understands that the Bill is designed to transfer the possession of land from Maori hands into those of the European settlers.
3. *Treaty of Waitangi*: New Zealand's founding document, signed on 6 February 1840 and named after the place of signing in the Bay of Islands. This treaty between the British and 540 Maori chiefs ensured British sovereignty and prevented the annexation of New Zealand by France. The Maori were persuaded by the positive effects of British sovereignty, while the negatives were glossed over. There were two versions of the Treaty: British and Maori. The British version stated that the Maori were to yield to British sovereignty, the Crown would have the right to buy land Maoris wished to sell, the Maori would have full ownership rights to their land, and the Maori would have full rights as British subjects. The Maori version had subtle differences to the British wording, which shows some misunderstanding or misleading over British intentions; for instance, the Maori version

translated sovereignty as 'governance', believing they were to maintain the right to manage their own affairs. Whichever version Rauparaha is holding up during his speech, the Maori right to hold their land is set out in the Treaty and should be honoured.

4. *C.M.G.ship*: the Most Distinguished Order of St Michael and St George, a royal honour conferred on those who have served the Crown in foreign or Commonwealth matters. At the time, this would be an honour conferred to those serving the Empire. The short, fat man honours the Crown and the British aristocracy for his own ends and ennoblement.

5. *Te Ariri*: Helen Thornton's family home, the translation of which in Maori means 'the shellfish' and particularly the limpet, an association that positions the European inhabitants of the house as those who have battened on to the indigenous people and are weighing them down. In the language of the Micronesian area now known as Kiribati, it means the labour of the birth process, a more positive association of new relationships and new futures for the country.

6. *fustian*: in this sense meaning bombast or gibberish. To Brewster, the idea of racial equality is incomprehensible.

7. *Five thousand a year ... humoured*: Brewster's cousin has a substantial income of five thousand pounds a year; therefore she must be humoured and persuaded to marry him so he can benefit from her wealth.

8. *Waikato thirty years ago*: The Waikato War 1863–4 caused by the confiscation of Maori lands by British settlers. Rauparaha's sense of injustice and resistance has been passed to him from his father.

9. *"blithering" idiots*: Blithering is a colloquial term for talking nonsense. Here Brewster uses it as a qualifier for the idiocy he sees in his cousin and his aunt for entertaining Rauparaha.

10. *quadroon strain*: 'Quadroon' means to have one black and three white grandparents. Helen, therefore, has a one-eighth black heritage.

11. *Maori pah*: a village or settlement.

12. *The assault ... Royal Irish*: British infantry regiment garrisoned at Conmel that was involved with the Waikato and Taranaki battles during the New Zealand Wars.

13. *children of Ham*: Ham, son of Noah, was father to Canaan. Ham was cursed by Noah after Ham had discovered his father naked and drunk; Genesis 9:20–7. This story has been read as a justification for the treatment of people with black skin by white Christians.

Lowerison, 'Auld Randy'

1. *close*: an enclosure or an enclosed place; *OED*. Ewes are brought from the hills into an enclosed place near the house during lambing season so shepherds can monitor and aid the birthing process.

2. *neuk*: nook. The old man is sat inside a large fireplace that has seating on either side of the fire. This type of fireplace is often called an inglenook, ingle meaning fire.

3. *outbye*: a distant or outlying farm. The old man does not live in the farmhouse but has his own farm in the area.

4. *"natural" or half-wit*: a person with a lower than average intelligence, perhaps with learning difficulties. The implication of 'natural' is of someone who has not learned the social codes necessary for social and cultural interaction and is therefore 'natural' or unlearned.

5. *Goy bon*: Scots., possibly 'gae bond', meaning to warrant, but used as an exclamation similar to 'I'll be bound'.
6. *Old Nick*: the devil.
7. *Methodys*: Methodists, a branch of the dissenting sects of British Protestantism.
8. *half litten*: half lighted. In life, Randy's eyes were evidence of his low levels of understanding and intelligence.

'Devilshoof', 'One New Year's Eve'

1. *lock-up*: the local prison cell or gaol.

'Devilshoof', 'On the River'

1. *Cassandra*: Cassandra, daughter of Priam, was granted the gift of hearing the future by Apollo. When she refused his love, his curse ordained that her prophecies would not be believed. The word is used here to suggest Nell had anticipated the Governor's response, but the association is rejected because as Cassandra foresaw the fall of Troy and her own death, Nell does not want to imagine she could prophecy their own end.
2. *told off*: counted; Danvers is part of a small group of men set to work unloading the steamer.

C. H. V., 'One Among Many'

1. *Guardians' board*: The Board of Guardians were the administrators of the parish workhouse. Formed under the 1834 Poor Law Amendment Act, the Guardians were formed of elected and *ex officio* members. *Ex officio* Guardians were eligible because of their position as local magistrates; elected members were ratepayers of £25 p.a. or more, were appointed annually by the parish ratepayers and could include women. The Board would administer the workhouse, accounts and staff, and make decisions on the applications for relief.

Law, 'Connie'

1. *Drury Lane*: Drury Lane runs between Aldwych and High Holborn in the West End of London and is renowned for its associations with the theatre. There has been a historical association between the theatre and prostitution, as Jeffrey Kahan points out in his biography of John Kean (1811–68): 'Prostitution in London was nothing new, nor was its association with the theatre'; *The Cult of Kean* (Aldershot: Ashgate, 2006), p. 84. See also Kirsten Pullen's *Actresses and Whores: On Stage and in Society* (Cambridge: Cambridge University Press, 2005) for her consideration of prostitution and performance. Connie's position as a theatre dancer and her home's location 'in a street leading out of Drury Lane' raise assumptions of her working as a prostitute, which are countered as the novel continues.
2. *a few minutes*: Nineteenth-century London was renowned for the close proximity of extremes of wealth and poverty, as were many other large cities. In *How the Poor Live*, his investigation into the London slums published in 1883, George R. Sims (1847–1922)

alludes to the nearness of rich and poor when he set out his intention: 'In these pages I propose to record the results of a journey with pen and pencil into a region which lies at our own doors – into a dark continent that is within easy walking distance of the General Post Office'.

3. *leaves one to a stranger*: Connie's use of Received Pronunciation is unusual for a working-class woman and gestures towards the possibility of her parentage being of a higher social group. This will be echoed at points throughout the fragment: the furniture in Chapter II is described as being of a quality not usually associated with the poorest of the working class, and Humphry's sister Diana will note Connie's ladylike essence in Chapter XII. These indicators may have been included to form a revelation about her parentage in the completed novel in order for her to be able to marry the gentleman she is speaking to in this scene, Humphry Munro.

4. *four-wheeler*: a horse-drawn private cab, sometimes also called a 'growler', larger than the two-wheeled hansom cab.

5. *pulled a latchkey out of his pocket*: One of the New Woman's goals for emancipation from male control at the *fin de siècle* was to hold the latchkey allowing independent ingress and egress to the family home. Later, one of the signifiers of attaining the age of majority and adulthood – at the age of twenty-one – was to be given the key to the house, hence the song 'I've got the key of the door / Never been 21 before'. Connie's predicament is that her father, in his refusal to trust her with the latchkey to keep her dependent upon him on the basis that only he is responsible, has failed to fulfil his duty, which has left her at the mercy of another man.

6. *Horsewhips and tennis rackets*: Nineteenth-century Tory ideology was distinguished from the dour Liberal ideology by what Patrick Joyce, in *Work, Society and Politics* (London: Methuen, 1982), calls 'the politics of beer and Britannia'. Tories were associated with sportsmanship, gambling, beer and entertainment rather than Liberal decorum and improvement. Humphry is being positioned as part of the patrician land-owning class by his association with sport.

7. *pantomime*: not used in the modern sense of a theatrical comedy for children, but in the original British sense of 'a traditional theatrical performance, developing out of commedia dell'arte, and comprising a dumbshow, which later developed into a comic dramatization with stock characters of Clown, Pantaloon, Harlequin, and Columbine'; *OED*. The Theatre Royal in Drury Lane was famous for the elaborate pantomime productions of Augustus Harris in the 1880s and 1890s. Connie's work as a dancer in the pantomimes is reinforcing her youth, as pantomimes would employ a cast of working-class children as part of the show.

8. *ladder*: a tear in the fine fabric of stockings that unravels the knit.

9. *thirty shillings*: the equivalent of £1.50 in decimal currency. Maud Pember Reeves's (1865–1953) study of family income, *Round about a Pound a Week* (1913), described the difficulties of raising a family on the male's earnings of about one pound. Connie's earnings, even after she has given her father the ten shillings she promised, leaves her relatively comfortable financially and able to support herself while working.

10. *gallery from the pit*: These areas for the audience were defined by social division. The expensive gallery would be reserved for wealthier visitors to the theatre, who would sit in tiers elevated from the floor of the building and would be subject to dress codes. The pit was the cheapest area and would be populated by the working classes.

11. *antimacassars*: These were loose covers placed on the backs and arms of sofas and chairs to prevent staining the fabric of the furniture, especially from the macassar hair oil used by men during this period.
12. la petite danseuse: the little dancer.
13. *Bar*: a synecdoche referring to the practice of law by a barrister. The 'bar' is both the wooden rail surrounding the judge's seat in a court of law where the prisoner is stationed for trial and the place where the business of the court is transacted; *OED*.
14. *Lady Dacre's*: The title of Baron Dacre was first created in 1321, and the family line had two outstanding Ladies Dacre: Lady Anne Dacre (d. 1595), whose will founded the Emanuel Hospital almshouses in London, and the poet Barbarina Brand (1768–1854). At the point of publication, this name refers to Susan Cavendish, the wife of Henry Robert Brand (1841–1906) who became the twenty-fourth Baron Dacre in 1892. The reference positions Humphry and Grey as members of the British upper classes.
15. *Crœsus*: the wealthy King of Lydia in Ancient Greece (595–c. 547 BC). Humphry is making a point on the relativity of wealth, apparently unaware that his claims of poverty may be surprising or offensive to someone living on a pound a week. Neither extreme of wealth can imagine life at the opposite end.
16. *dog-cart*: a high, two-wheeled carriage drawn by one horse. A common form of transport, suggesting the squire's lack of ostentation.
17. *deshabils*: dishabille, the state of being partly undressed, or dressed in a negligent or careless style; *OED*. The farmer is saying the horse will be neither brushed nor saddled on the Sabbath day of rest.
18. *the land don't pay*: The development of a plutocratic state had brought about a decline in landed power in favour of accumulated wealth. As David Cannadine notes in *The Decline and Fall of the British Aristocracy* (London: Macmillan, 1996), pp. 88–9, business carried fewer obligations than land management and a higher turnover of profit than the seasons and harvest gave.
19. *duties attached to it*: Diana takes the Tory ideology of duty as part of the social contract as well as rights. Here, however, her notion of duty creates a material basis for marriage, privileging the acquisition of private property over emotion.
20. *diamond merchant ... Jew*: The Jewish population of Britain increased significantly through immigration after the pogroms in Russia between 1881 and 1882 following the assassination of Alexander II. The influx of Russian Jewish émigrés between 1880 and 1914 swelled the Jewish population in Britain by a third and caused a great deal of concern about the effects of this increase on British life. The Jewish population were, like the rest of Britain, divided between rich and poor, but their (understandable) reluctance to integrate into society meant that socialist criticisms of Jewish financial power, held, for instance by the Rothschild banking family, were levelled at those of the Jewish faith as a whole. Henry Hyndman was particularly virulent about Jewish financiers in many articles in *Justice*. For example, see 'Imperialist Judaism in Africa', *Justice*, 25 April 1896. Harkness's Jewish theatre manager is also part of a contemporary literary trend associating the rich and/or powerful Jew with British theatre. The 'Boss' is as sexually predatory as Wilde's (1854–1900) Isaacs in *The Picture of Dorian Grey* (1890), and the control the Boss holds over Connie's employment anticipates the control over female performance in George du Maurier's (1834–96) *Trilby* (1894). Similarly, Bram Stoker's (1847–1912) *Dracula* (1897) would have Semitic overtones and would be performed to emphasize these traits; see H. L. Malchow, *Gothic Images of Race in Nineteenth-Century Britain* (Stanford, CA: Stanford University Press, 1996), pp. 153–65.

21. *mash*: a man who makes indecent sexual advances towards women, especially in public places; *OED*. This diamond ring the Boss is offering to Connie is advance payment for sexual favours. See above, p. 365 n. 1 on the association between prostitution and the theatre.
22. *draw her on to his knee*: This image suggests William Holman Hunt's (1827–1910) 'The Awakening Conscience' (1853–4), which depicts a man at the piano with his kept mistress starting up from his lap. Connie's refusal to sit on Humphry's knee suggests that unlike Holman's woman, who is only just beginning to realize her fallen position, she has a sense of control over her actions and decisions in her relationship.
23. *little cottage at Kew ... well-known actress*: Despite the description of Humphry and Connie's unmarried cohabitation appearing to be hidden from the world, Kew is a suburb of London and was connected to central London by the District Line, which opened a station there is 1869. The association of the theatre with sexual promiscuity or laxity is perpetuated by the former owner of the cottage in which Connie and Humphry cohabit who worked as an actress.
24. *regulations and prejudices*: Marriage, 'free love' (unmarried sex) and sexual relationships were contentious issues debated by socialists during this period. See, for example, Friedrich Engels (1820–95), *The Origins of the Family, Private Property and the State* (1884); Edward Aveling (1849–98) and Eleanor Marx Aveling (1855–98), *The Woman Question* (1886); Olive Schreiner (1855–1920), *Woman and Labour* (1911); and the essay argument between Ernest Belfort Bax (1854–1925) ('Some Heterodox Notes on the Women Question', *To-Day*, July 1887; 'No Misogyny but True Equality', *To-Day*, October 1887) and Annie Besant (1847–1933) ('Misogyny in Excelsis', *To-Day*, August 1887). For recent scholarship on the subject, see, for example, S. Rowbotham, *Dreamers of a New Day* (London: Verso, 2011); Hannam and Hunt, *Socialist Women*; Hunt, *Equivocal Feminists*; and J. R. Walkowitz, 'The Men and Women's Club', in *City of Dreadful Delight: Narratives of Sexual Danger in Late Victorian London* (London: Virago, 1992).
25. *A bat flew ... garden seat*: There are a number of superstitions surrounding bats flying near or into houses, which portends evil, but Connie and Humphry are outside, so the bat flying close to them would be read as an omen of future betrayal. As the instalment ends with Connie's letter, the reader is left with the cliffhanger of whether the betrayal would be Humphry's. There is a superstition that white moths are the souls of the dead, and another that a chirping cricket in the house would signal good luck, but its position beneath the couple may suggest their own (eventual) good fortune.
26. *portmanteau*: a double-sided suitcase, hinged in the middle and opening to provide two equal spaces.
27. *gardens, to the palm house*: Royal Botanic Gardens, Kew. Created in 1759 by Lord Capel John of Tewkesbury from his exotic garden at Kew Park, the Royal Botanic Gardens now houses the world's largest collection of plants. The Palm House was built between 1844 and 1848 by Richard Turner and was designed by Decimus Burton. It is a large Victorian glass and iron structure in the manner of the Crystal Palace constructed for the 1851 Great Exhibition.
28. *shop-girl*: With the development of the department store, shopping became a fashionable pastime for women from the 1870s onwards. The female shopper and shop assistants at this time were physically moving out of the house and into the male-dominated public sphere. They were often deemed 'fair game' by predatory men and sexually lax by conservatively minded women.

29. *Temple*: either the Honourable Society of the Inner Temple or the Honourable Society of the Middle Temple. Both are Inns of Court, the professional associations for barristers. Every barrister must be associated with one of the four Inns of Court, the others being Lincoln's Inn and Grey's Inn. Neither the Squire nor Diana take Humphry's work as a barrister seriously, privileging the status of landowner and the gathering of wealth through rents over the earning of money.
30. *Ufindel*: I can find no information about this unusual surname.
31. *Jewish tailor*: The Jewish employer – especially in the clothing trade – had a reputation for 'sweating' his labour (extracting hard work from employees for low wages; *OED*), so Connie has expectations of her future as being full of work and poverty. Harkness had previously depicted the powerlessness of female employees of Jewish businessmen in *A Manchester Shirtmaker* (1890), when protagonist Mary Dillon is defrauded out of wages by her Jewish employer; see also above, p. 367 n. 20.
32. *She walked from Kew ... Piccadilly*: a distance of almost eight miles. Connie moves from leafy Kew, where her cohabitation was hidden from sight by nature, back to the theatre district, where she is again located in public view.
33. *Thames Embankment ... seat*: Opened in 1870, the Thames Embankment, the collective name for the Victoria, Albert and Chelsea Embankments, reclaimed around thirty-seven acres of marsh land at the side of the Thames between Westminster and Chelsea Hospital. The Embankment, like Trafalgar Square, had become a place where the homeless gravitated at night to sleep, and it had become a signifier of poverty in London at the end of the nineteenth century. Sociological surveys of poverty in the capital included descriptions of the Embankment homeless in works by Charles Booth, George Sims, Andrew Mearns and others. The image was also drawn into fiction by other socialist authors, including A. Neil Lyons and Robert Blatchford.
34. *Haymarket ... Charing Cross*: These areas of London were renowned for being areas where prostitutes plied their trade, and so the male inhabitant, seeing Connie walking alone, would assume she was offering her body for sale.
35. *The Beggars' Metropole*: The term is used ironically, as the Metropole Hotel in London was a luxury hotel that opened in 1885 and was used by Edward, Prince of Wales, for entertaining guests. The building is still used as a luxury hotel today, trading under the name 'Corinthia'.
36. *vivisected ... full of holes*: There was a strong anti-vivisectionist movement at the end of the nineteenth century, which included socialists such as Annie Besant and George Bernard Shaw (1856–1950). There was a belief that empathy should not be restricted to the human animal and that the power of the vivisector over the animal was akin to that of the capitalist over the worker. Flora's sympathy for the vivisected rat is extended to human beings and evident in her rescue of Connie.
37. *a very pure breed*: As this fiction is focalized through Connie's perception, the disparity between the 'mongrel' and Flora's persuasion of it being a 'pure breed' can be interpreted as evidence that Connie understands the deception, seeing this as another example of the lies men tell women, now that she thinks she has been deceived by Humphry.
38. *A bottle of champagne ... still young*: The description of Flora and Bess, their home and their 'friends' build a picture of two high-class prostitutes. The women keep nocturnal hours, they receive gifts from various 'men friends', and their use of makeup suggests God's denunciation of the harlot Oholibah in Ezekiel 23:40: 'And lo, they came – for whom you bathed, painted your eyes and decorated yourselves with ornaments'.

39. *cats'-meat man*: a vendor of cheap meat unsuitable for human consumption but used for pet food, often horsemeat. The vendor would take his wares around the streets in a wooden barrow, selling from door to door.
40. *possess his soul in patience*: Luke 21:19: 'In your patience possess ye your souls', meaning patience will preserve the soul. Humphry, impatient to see Connie, attempts to act by this teaching.
41. *cellaret*: a wooden case made to hold wine bottles for use on the table; *OED*.

Chee, 'The Bank-Manager's Girl'

1. *cr. £102 2s. 1d.*: 'cr.' means credit. Miss Jacques has a large amount of money in her account.
2. *£2 odd*: a little over two pounds; two pounds and some 'odd' pennies.
3. *dr. £25*: 'dr.' means in debit.
4. *squared the valuer*: to 'square' means to adjust or adapt; to cause to correspond to or harmonize with something; *OED*. Chapson ensures that the valuer's estimate matches his own.
5. *O.D. men ... squalls*: advice to start debt collectors working to retrieve the bank's bad debts or there would be trouble.
6. *messuages*: land occupied by or intended for a dwelling house and its outbuildings; *OED*.
7. *devil's-pool*: Australian billiards, played with three billiard balls and twelve pins. Chapson has taken to drink and gambling.

Mayo, 'A Bit of Tragedy'

1. *City Dead-House*: Before the twentieth-century development of the morgue, a dead house would be where bodies were stored before burial.
2. *He who lets ... every woe*: John Henry, Cardinal Newman, 'Verses on Various Occasions XCVII: Flowers without Fruit'. The quotation warns against useless sentimentality, while the title of the poem alludes to Thomas Reed's early death; his flowering was without fruit in the form of a happy, useful life and the begetting of children.
3. *redeeming the time ... days are evil*: Ephesians 5:15–16. The older phrasing 'redeeming the time' is taken from the King James Bible, and the 'revised version' is from the Weymouth Bible. The second version uses a vocabulary similar to that of capitalism and emphasizes the importance of purchase and being able to purchase the necessaries of life: '15. Therefore be very careful how you live and act. Let it not be as unwise men, but as wise. 16. Buy up your opportunities, for these are evil times'.
4. *robbing of Peter to pay Paul*: moving debts from one creditor to pay another without clearing the debt. Dorothea's point is that mercy must be all encompassing, otherwise it is mere superficiality.
5. *They shall look ... first-born*: Zechariah 12:10. Dorothea translates into the third person Christ's prophecy to Zechariah of the grief felt by the family of David because of the crucifixion, applying it to all who have persecuted, knowingly or unknowingly.

Martyn, 'A Mystery'

1. *purple sweets*: violets. The Victorians were fond of associating flowers with certain human attributes, and the violet represents modesty, virtue, faithfulness, love, and the willingness to take a chance on love.

Claxton, 'Nigel Grey (A Serial Story of Love and Effort)'

1. *Brierly*: There is a village called Brierly in South Yorkshire, between Wakefield, Barnsley and Doncaster, but other geographical references in the story do not suggest that the story is set here. The name of the village could be a reference to the Lancashire dialect author Ben Brierley (1825–96), famous for his 'Ab-o-th'-Yate' sketches; see *Minor Victorian Poets and Authors*, at http://gerald-massey.org.uk/brierley/index.htm [accessed 25 February 2013].
2. *furriners*: foreigners. Mrs Brenton is being positioned as rural, working class, poorly educated and untravelled.
3. *London pride, and Old Man*: London Pride or *Saxifraga urbium*, an evergreen plant that was easily cultivated. 'Old Man' is possibly a reference to Old Man's Beard or *Clematis vitalba*, a common hedgerow plant. These are plants that can be gathered from the wild and cultivated at no cost to the gardener.
4. *Tam o'Shanter*: a traditional Scottish bonnet, and also the eponymous character in Robert Burns's (1759–96) poem about the evils of drink.
5. *the cup that cheers*: the first part of a temperance maxim that completes, 'but does not inebriate'. It was used as a slogan to promote the drinking of the non-alcoholic beverage of tea as an alternative to beer and spirits.
6. *Ameriky*: the United States of America.
7. *had it pat*: She learned the language easily. Either Constance is humouring Mrs Brenton, or she is referring to the dialect differences between English and American-English.
8. *British Museum ... catalogue*: The British Museum, on Russell Street, London, was established in 1753 to give free admission to the collection of manuscripts and antiquities bequeathed by Sir Hans Sloane. Its holdings were greatly expanded over the course of the nineteenth century to include the Rosetta Stone, the Parthenon sculptures – alternatively known as the Elgin Marbles – and, until 1997, the British Library. Sir George's comment emphasizes the gulf between the classes: he has as much knowledge of the everyday objects in a working-class house as he does of the objects on display in the Museum.
9. *David and Goliath*: 1 Samuel 17, the Biblical story of Goliath, the giant Philistine, slain by the young Israelite David.
10. *'Bliaf*: This is assumed to be a childish pronunciation of 'Goliath'.
11. *ferrotype*: the process of creating a photograph on a thin metal plate.
12. *oleograph*: a type of coloured lithograph that has been impressed with a canvas grain and varnished in order to make it look like an oil painting; *OED*. The references to Mrs Brenton's possessions emphasize their cheap quality as items of mass production.
13. *All's well ... Leave well alone*: The first idiom refers to the outcome as being more important than the method and was a phrase used before Shakespeare took it for the title of his play. The second idiom advises non-interference. George is punning on the word 'well' in response to Nigel and Tom's project, but his making fun of the project also indicates his *laissez faire* attitude towards such social projects in the same manner as Mrs Brenton earlier in the chapter.

14. *temperance organisation*: see above, p. 359 n. 3. Although Keir Hardie, editor of the *Labour Leader* and chairman of the ILP, was himself an abstainer, he was not convinced that alcohol consumption was the cause of working-class poverty. In his article 'The Temperance Question' in *Labour Leader*, 17 April 1897, Hardie argued against the general theory that drink was the main cause of working-class poverty and suggested that the siphoning of profits by the capitalist was the cause. He posed the question, 'if the spending of ninety millions by the workers [on drink] can be alleged as the cause of their poverty, how much more must the abstraction of £730 millions be as a cause?'
15. *pledge-card*: a card held by those who swore to avoid alcoholic drink as part of the temperance movement.
16. *teetotaler*: one who abstains from strong drink; more usually spelled 'teetotaller' in British English. Early temperance advocates focused on encouraging the refusal to drink spirits while allowing beer, but later advocates promoted total abstinence (teetotalism).
17. *twenty shillings*: The average London workman earns one pound a week; see Fabian socialist Maud Pember Reeve's 1913 study of poverty in Lambeth entitled *Round about a Pound a Week*.
18. *Newfoundland*: a large breed of dog originally bred as a working dog.
19. *perfect Daniel come to judgement*: a reference to the Biblical character Daniel (Daniel 5:14) renowned for wise judgments. The secular use of the phrase is less complementary, meaning one who believes they can rectify a problem where others have failed.
20. *Hammersmith*: According to Charles Booth's (1840–1916) poverty map of London for 1898–9, Hammersmith was a mixed area; the red blocks indicating 'Middle class, well-to-do' were the visible housing along main roads such as King Street, but behind lay areas of light blue which Booth classified as 'Poor. 18s to 21s a week for a moderate family'. Nelly's home places her in the category of poor but not 'chronic' (dark blue) or criminal (black). For a searchable online version of Booth's poverty map, see the *Charles Booth Online Archive*, at http://booth.lse.ac.uk/static/a/2.html#viii [accessed 14 March 2013].
21. noblesse oblige: the obligations of the ruling class to the labourers. The idea that each social group has both duties and responsibilities to themselves, each other and the nation generally stretches back to the feudal period and was part of the political ideology of the Tory Party. It stood in contrast to the individualism promoted by the Liberal Party. Nigel's sympathy for Nelly is deemed 'reprehensible' because many socialists criticized the idea of *noblesse oblige* as patronising and perpetuating an unequal social structure. His attitude towards Nelly in this scene and his anonymous gift of money in the next chapter is to be compared with his reaction to Constance's gifts to his sister in Chapter V.
22. *to a T*: to be exactly right, perfectly suited; often spelt 'tee'.
23. *taboring ... table*: drumming his fingers on the table. A tabor is a small kind of drum used chiefly as an accompaniment to the pipe or trumpet; a taborin or tabret; *OED*.
24. *For a' that ... and a' that*: Robert Burns, 'A Man's a Man for a' That'. Burns is expressing the equality of human beings despite the divisions created by society through wealth or lack of it. This poem was a favourite with British socialists.
25. *Chelsea*: another mixed area according to Booth's map (see n. 20 above), but which has areas designated yellow (Upper middle and upper class. Wealthy) and red (Middle class. Well-to-do). Nigel, living 'off a busy thoroughfare', will be situated in the areas marked light blue (Poor) or possibly purple (Mixed. Some comfortable, others poor).
26. *the gallant boys ... true*: an allusion to E. O. Murden's 'Sumter: A Ballad of 1861', a Confederate ballad on the Battle of Fort Sumter during the American Civil War; Murden was listed as a Major in the Third South Carolina Infantry Regiment of the Confederates.

The reference is taken from the stanza that describes the soldiers of the Confederate army: 'From cotton- and from corn-field, / From desk and forum too, / From workbench and from anvil, came / Our gallant boys and true'. The reader is being asked to make the association of the ordinary men fighting for what they believed in for the Confederate side of the American Civil War with the socialists waging war against injustice and poverty.

27. *room of strong contrasts*: possibly also a reference to John 14:2: 'My Father's house has many rooms'. Nigel, as representative of socialism, has strong and wide-reaching concerns for others.
28. *My Dinah ... North Carolina rose*: This song is unidentified, but there is an old minstrel song entitled 'The North Carolina Rose', in which plantation slaves praise their master's lady love. She is, however, unnamed, and the lines quoted here do not appear in the song. There are also a number of minstrel songs that include the name 'Dinah'.
29. Blackwood's Magazine: *Blackwood's Edinburgh Magazine* (1817–1980), a monthly magazine published in Edinburgh and then London. It was a miscellany that published work by the greatest writers of the nineteenth century, including Coleridge, Shelley, the Brontë sisters, George Eliot and Joseph Conrad. The reference suggests Nigel's consumption of 'quality' literature despite his lack of education.
30. *nether world*: the poorest parts of London. The phrase is possibly a reference to George Gissing's (1857–1903) naturalist novel *The Nether World* (1889), and an anticipation of Jack London's (1876–1916) account of poverty in London in *The People of the Abyss* (1903).
31. *Fabian Essays*: *Fabian Essays in Socialism* is a collection of essays by Fabians such as Sidney Webb (1859–1947) and Graham Wallas (1858–1932) as well as George Bernard Shaw, who edited the collection. Edward Pease, in his *The History of the Fabian Society* (1916; Teddington: Echo Library, 2006), p. 55, describes Shaw's essay thus: 'His characteristic style retains its charm, although the abstract and purely deductive economic analysis on which he relied no longer commends itself to the modern school of thought'.
32. locum tenens: one who temporarily holds a position for another; *OED*.
33. *Three acres and a cow*: a lasting slogan from Joseph Chamberlain's (1836–1914) land reform message in the mid-1880s, which proposed land redistribution. Although the slogan is now usually associated with Chamberlain's campaign, Jesse Collings was the originator of the phrase and became known as 'Three Acres and a Cow' Collings. Hilda is challenging the Colonel's right to ownership of land.
34. *A starry night for a ramble*: from 'Starry Night for a Ramble', composed by Samuel Bagnall, tune and lyrics published 1873; see also *East Anglian Traditional Music Trust*, a thttp://www.eatmt.org.uk/tracing_tunes.htm [accessed 24 September 2012]. The song continues, 'I like to take my sweetheart out ("Of course you do", says she) / And softly whisper in her ear, "How dearly I love thee"', which is why Constance accuses Rollo of being 'vulgar'.
35. *the sanguine and the phlegmatic*: two of the four 'humours' that make up the human body: sanguine (courageous, hopeful, amorous); phlegmatic (stolid, calm, imperturbable); choleric (hot-tempered, passionate, fiery); and melancholy (sullenness, brooding, unsociability); *OED*. Sir George consists of the first two humours, Nigel of the latter two.
36. *the greatest good ... greatest number*: Jeremy Bentham's (1748–1832) utilitarian dictum that seeks the greatest happiness for the most people. Constance is affected by Nigel's questioning in Chapter II but gravitates towards Bentham's utility rather than socialism.

37. *poke bonnet*: a bonnet with a protruding brim; *OED*. The poke bonnet was part of the Salvation Army uniform. The Salvation Army, founded by William Booth (1829–1912) and his wife Catherine (1829–90) in 1865, sent men and women into urban slums to convert the inhabitants to Christianity. There was also some relief work carried out to alleviate some of the sufferings of poverty, but generally the socialist movement was critical of the Salvation Army for elevating the soul above the body's material sufferings and therefore distracting the poor from working towards social, political and economic change. See, for instance, the exchange between Henry Hyndman and John Law (Margaret Harkness) in *Justice*, March 1888, after the publication of the latter's novel *Captain Lobe: A Story of the Salvation Army* (1888; republished 1890 under the title *In Darkest London*).
38. *verbatim*: in their own words; *OED*. George quotes Graham Wallas's 'Property under Socialism', which was published in 1889 in George Bernard Shaw's collection *Fabian Essays*; George has evidently read the collection to the point of memorizing part of it.
39. *whist*: a card game for four people. Mr Cope, although professing not to be proficient at leisure activities to maintain his spiritual attitude, proves to be an experienced card player, his unworldly persona a front.
40. *extreme practices*: possibly a reference to self-flagellation or other mortifications of the body. Mr Cope appears to need extreme practices to maintain the self-imposed high expectations of himself and his renunciation of the material world.
41. *rub*: an obstacle, impediment, or difficulty of a non-material nature; *OED*. Mr Cope is alluding to Hamlet's soliloquy in Act III, scene i: 'To sleep perchance to dream, aye there's the rub', where Hamlet ponders the question of life after death.
42. *The unknown God ... unto you*: Acts 17:23: St Paul in Athens saw God-fearing people worshipping at an altar inscribed to 'The Unknown God' and brought the news of Jesus and his resurrection. Constance considers the worship of God without the material practice of Biblical teaching in the same light as ignorant worship.
43. *Humanity is the Son of God*: a reference to the birth of Christ on earth; Matthew 1:18–24.
44. *Baptismal Service*: The Anglican and Church of England baptismal service ceremoniously welcomes the child (or adult) into the Church. Mr Cope does not differentiate between being initiated into the Church of England and practising Christ's teachings.
45. *Thy kingdom come*: The Lord's Prayer: 'Thy kingdom come / Thy will be done / On earth as it is in Heaven'; Matthew 6:9–13. Constance is questioning the possibility of creating Heaven on earth with the attitude of the Church of England as it is.
46. *I had not forgotten him*: Constance (and Lilian Claxton) takes the same approach to socialism as many in the ILP: the practice of socialism was not separated from Christian teaching. The foundation of the Labour Church by John Trevor (1855–1930) aimed to join Christianity and socialism for a material impact on the world.
47. *down in the mouth*: having the corners of the mouth turned downwards, as a sign of dissatisfaction, etc.; dejected, dispirited; *OED*. This phrase is usually used to denote a negative psychological or emotional state rather than a physical change for the worst.
48. *Brierley Heath*: This spelling has changed from 'Brierly' in previous chapters.
49. *in your school*: Nigel is acknowledging not only the different standards and forms of education between the classes but also the training in strict forms of etiquette in which Constance will have been 'schooled' from an early age.
50. *patronage*: originally this meant the support of one person by another's influence or money; *OED*. However, Nigel uses the word in its pejorative form, meaning to wield superiority or condescension over another while appearing to act with kindness; *OED*. Constance's shock at Nigel's statement and her claim to 'never patronise' contradict

her claims in Chapter II that she has been taught to 'go about among the cottages' by her 'Conservative landowner' father (p. 143). The Squire embodies the Tory ideology of paternalism, as Constance describes her father paying for the education of tenants' children, keeping their rents low, ensuring his workers have 'sufficient', and 'in trouble and sickness when they go to him (as they always do) they are never sent away without sympathy or substantial aid' (p. 145). What Constance has been taught by her father as kindness, Nigel teaches her is demeaning to the receiver.

51. *monomaniac*: one with an obsession; *OED*. A form of mental illness characterized by a single pattern of repetitive and intrusive thoughts or actions; now an obsolete term. Nigel is being ironic, suggesting he has other interests as well as socialist politics.

52. A woman convinced ... opinion still: a misquotation from Samuel Butler's *Hudibras* (1660–80): 'He that complies against his will, / Is of his own opinion still'; ll. 547–8. Nobody can be compelled to take on another's opinion.

53. *Switzerland has an ideal land system*: The Swiss Allmende held land as a community and governed the land by majority decision. Even when householders claimed the land they cleared and cultivated, that land was still under the control of group regulations known as the *Flurzwang*. Friedrich Engels discusses western European common land in the appendix to *Socialism: Utopian and Scientific* (1882).

54. *Moses ... thirsty Israelites*: Exodus 17:6: Moses gives God's gift of water to the Israelites freely; modern businessmen would see the vital resource of water as an opportunity for profit.

55. *The right use of wealth ... human life*: possibly a reference to Aristotle's Nicomachean Ethics, Book IV, Chapter 1, where Aristotle differentiates between the use of wealth (spending and giving) and the possession of wealth (hoarding and keeping). Nigel is arguing that money is only useful when it is being circulated for the good of all rather than hoarded by monopolies.

56. *violets*: For the meaning of violets, see above, p. 371 n. 1. Both Constance and Nigel are associated with the violet, emphasizing their modesty and virtue despite her class status and his power as a reformer.

57. *lilies of the valley*: In Victorian flower language, lily of the valley means purity, sweet nature, chastity and happiness. The lily of the valley is also mentioned a number of times in the Bible, most frequently in the Song of Solomon, for instance Song of Solomon 2:1, where the female voice sings: 'I am the rose of Sharon, and the lily of the valleys'. The lily's whiteness and sweetness is associated with the sweetness and purity of Jesus Christ. The association of Constance with the flower suggests her growing socialism – which she has associated with Christianity in Chapter VII – and her concern for the well-being of others.

58. *Karl Marx's 'Capital' ... Encyclical Letter*: Karl Marx's *Das Kapital* was originally published in German in 1867, the French translation was published serially between 1872 and 1875, and the work was eventually translated into English by Samuel Moore and Edward Aveling (the common-law husband of Marx's daughter Eleanor), edited by Friedrich Engels and published in 1886, three years after Marx's death. Henry Mayers Hyndman, the chairman of the SDF, had begun to serialize an English translation in his periodical *To-Day* between 1886 and 1889, but did not complete the work. The 'Socialist Encyclical Letter' probably refers to Robert Blatchford's *Socialism: A Reply to the Encyclical of the Pope*, first published in the *Clarion* and then reprinted as a pamphlet by the Clarion and Labour Press Society in 1893. Hyndman and Blatchford represent the two extremes of British socialism – the theoretical Marxist socialism of Hyndman was

very different to the untheorized ethical socialism of Blatchford and the *Clarion* group. George's comment is meant to show that he would embrace every aspect of socialism to make Constance happy.

59. *Once, in Kensington High Street ... Lord Allerton's steward*: There is an echo in this scene of the original ending to Charles Dickens's (1812–70) *Great Expectations* (1860–1):

> I was in England again – in London, and walking along Piccadilly with little Pip – when a servant came running after me to ask would I step back to a lady in a carriage who wished to speak to me. It was a little pony carriage, which the lady was driving; and the lady and I looked sadly enough on one another.
>
> 'I am greatly changed, I know, but I thought you would like to shake hands with Estella too, Pip. Lift up that pretty child and let me kiss it!' (She supposed the child, I think, to be my child.)
>
> I was very glad afterwards to have had the interview; for, in her face and in her voice, and in her touch, she gave me the assurance, that suffering had been stronger than Miss Havisham's teaching, and had given her a heart to understand what my heart used to be.

Both Pip and Nigel are simultaneously aware both of the social distance between themselves and their female interlocutor and of the reduced distance between them because of personal events and history. As this is not the final scene, there is hope that the future for Constance and Nigel will be brighter than that of Estella and Pip.

60. *rookeries*: a dense collection of housing, especially in a slum area; *OED*. Nigel aims to alleviate overcrowding as well as poor housing.
61. The Police News: The *Illustrated Police News* was a weekly London paper published between 1864 and 1938, specializing in detailed reports of murders and court scenes; it had a reputation for sensational and prurient reporting. See *Dictionary of Nineteenth-Century Journalism*, ed. L. Brake and M. Demoor (Gent: Academia Press, 2009), pp. 303–4. The implication is that the taste for low culture and sensation is not restricted to the working classes.
62. *Ah well ... enter in?*: a misquoted section of John Greenleaf Whittier's 1867 poem 'George L. Stearns'. The poem should read:

> Ah, well! The world is discreet;
> There are plenty to pause and wait;
> But here was a man who set his feet
> Sometimes in advance of fate;
>
> Plucked off the old bark when the inner
> Was slow to renew it,
> And put to the Lord's work the sinner
> When saints failed to do it.
>
> Never rode to the wrong's redressing
> A worthier paladin.
> Shall he not hear the blessing,
> 'Good and faithful, enter in!'

The poem was written as a tribute to George Luther Stearns on his death in 1867, as Whittier imagines Stearns's reception in heaven. Stearns was a prominent supporter of the abolition of slavery in the United States; he had enriched himself through business and used his wealth to campaign on behalf of the slaves. Constance is making the connection between the humble births of Stearns and Nigel Grey and recognizing the potential in Nigel to do for the British working class what Stearns did for the American slave.

63. *the Row*: Rotten Row, Hyde Park, London. A corruption of 'Route du Roi' or King's Road, Rotten Row was where the fashionable rich would congregate and promenade on horseback or in horse-drawn carriages. Constance's presence on the Row serves to reinforce her class status.

64. *And they helped ... good cheer*: a misquotation of Isaiah 41:6: 'They helped every one his neighbour; and every one said to his brother, Be of good courage'.

65. *stump oratory*: The phrase means one who speaks from a platform. The 'stump' originates in US terminology, meaning one who speaks from the stump of a felled tree; *OED*. The sense of the phrase as used by the youth is that Nigel is prepared to put his words into action.

66. *heliotrope*: signifies devotion in the language of flowers.

67. *soup kitchens ... same principle*: Lady Drayton, like Constance when she first met Nigel, conflates the giving of alms through patronage with the work of socialism. She misunderstands the aims of socialism to remove the necessity of reliance on the wealthy and to build a society where all who can work will work.

68. *This is the way, walk ye in it*: Isaiah 30:21: God will guide and set the path of life out for the individual. Nigel has a more material interpretation of the path of life, following work and duty rather than God.

69. *tallow dip*: Sarah is too poor to afford a wax candle and lights her room by a burning cloth in tallow grease. Tallow is animal fat that is solid at room temperature and was originally used for making candles before wax became the most common basis.

70. *Guy's 'Orspital*: Guy's Hospital, founded by Thomas Guy and opened in Southwark, London in 1725. The hospital originally cared for the incurably ill, but by the nineteenth century it practised medicine rather than simply palliative care.

71. *Thames Embankment*: see above, p. 369 n. 33.

72. *neuralgia of the heart*: Now called angina pectoris, neuralgia is pain caused by a nerve, rather than myalgia, which is muscle pain. Angina itself is not fatal but is usually caused by coronary artery disease. Worsening and sudden attacks of angina might be precursors to myocardial infarction, commonly known as a heart attack.

73. *do what I will with mine own*: Matthew 20:15. The phrase is the response by the owner of the vineyard to the labourers who complain they are paid the same amount for a day's labour as those who have been employed for an hour: 'Is it not lawful for me to do what I will with mine own? Is thine eye evil, because I am good?' He justifies the equal payment by pointing out his freedom to distribute his money as he feels fit. Similarly, Nigel is justifying his freedom to make a decision which, although right for him personally, may not be financially beneficial.

74. *fore-and-aft cap*: usually refers to the soft military cloth cap worn on the side of the head and which folds flat, but this use suggests a deerstalker hat, which has peaks to the front and back.

75. *For the whole world ... in pain*: Sarah Chauncey (Susan Coolidge) Woolsey (1835–1905), 'The Cradle Tomb in Westminster Abbey' (1875): 'Men die, but sorrow never dies; /

The crowding years divide in vain, / And the wide world is knit with ties / Of common brotherhood in pain'.
76. *Beulah*: Isaiah 62:4: 'Thou shalt no more be termed Forsaken; neither shall thy land any more be termed Desolate: but thou shalt be called Hephzibah, and thy land Beulah: for the Lord delighteth in thee, and thy land shall be married'. 'Beulah' means married, in the Bible it was the marriage between God and his people, but here the minds and hearts of Nigel and Constance are married in a shared vision of socialism.
77. *Progress and Poverty*: Henry George's (1839–97) most famous work propounding his idea on the cyclical depressions of capitalism and the association of industrial and technological progress with the value of land. His argument for the single land tax had been read by a number of socialists early in their political reading, and although George did not propound socialism, many saw it as their first step to socialist theory. The quotation comes from George's conclusion, which was couched in religious terms referencing Bunyan's *Pilgrim's Progress*, as he denies political economy is the dismal science termed by Carlyle but describes the hope for the future through the fight of the present: 'Lo! here, now, in our civilized society, the old allegories yet have a meaning, the old myths are still true. Into the Valley of the Shadow of Death yet often leads the path of duty, through the streets of Vanity Fair walk Christian and Faithful, and on Greatheart's armor ring the clanging blows. Ormuzd still fights with Ahriman – the Prince of Light with the Powers of Darkness. He who will hear, to him the clarions of the battle call'.
78. *He either fears ... venture all*: lines from 'My Dear and Only Love' by James Graham, Marquis of Montrose (1612–50). The first part of the stanza declares the lover's intention to be the only possessor of his love's heart: 'Like Alexander I will reign, / And I will reign alone; / My thoughts did evermore disdain / A rival on my throne'.

Jeffries, 'A Shop Girl'

1. *brougham*: an enclosed carriage drawn by a single horse, having either two or four wheels and made to accommodate two or four people; *OED*. Mr Cardigan's sprightliness is enabled by his wealth and his shorter working hours.
2. *covert coat and spats*: 'Covert coat' is presumably a typographical error for 'overcoat'; 'spats' are coverings for the shoe or boot, reaching around the instep and just above the ankle; *OED*. Joe Corbett's appearance is described as that of a dandified young man who emulates the dress of the upper-class gentleman, but his appearance is as superficial as his kindness to Edith.
3. *His moustache was black and his chin bluish*: The dark-haired Corbett is unshaven, adding to the image of his attempting to be something he is not.
4. *spec.*: speculation; Corbett is a gambling man in business.
5. *give me the sack*: terminate her employment. The phrase is believed to originate in the sack a workman would use to remove his tools from a place of employment.

Bradbury, 'Guilty – But Drunk'

1. *State of Georgia*: a state in the south-eastern United States, situated between Florida, Tennessee, South Carolina and Alabama.
2. *circuit judges*: Similar to British circuit judges, these men would have responsibility for a specific area (circuit) where they would decide on cases of federal law and hear cases between people of different states. The judges would travel from town to town in their

area to hear cases at regular intervals. Circuit judges were abolished in 1912 and their jurisdiction transferred to US district courts.
3. *comfortably corned*: intoxicated, drunk.
4. *carry-all*: an American term for a single-horse-drawn carriage for two or four persons; *OED*.
5. *court*: the place of judicial hearing for those on the circuit.
6. *better half*: his wife.
7. *devious*: winding, indirect; *OED*. The judge is too drunk to walk in a straight line.
8. *a "practical"*: a practical joke.
9. nolle prosequi: a termination of criminal proceedings, an end to the prosecution; *OED*. The judge is refusing to take the case any further.

Elihu, 'Nobody's Business'

1. *pocket book*: a small book to be carried in the pocket. The merchant is keeping a record of all his financial successes, drawing more money to himself and his family and away from those who need the money desperately, such as the dying man.
2. *babbles o' green fields*: The hostess describes Falstaff's last moments in *Henry V*, Act II scene iii: "A made a finer end, and went away an it had been any christom child; 'a parted ev'n just between twelve and one, ev'n at the turning o' th' tide; for after I saw him fumble with the sheets, and play with flowers, and smile upon his fingers' end, I knew there was but one way; for his nose was as sharp as a pen, and 'a babbl'd of green fields.' Both men return to happier times before their death, but the return to nature is more poignant for the dying man in this story, as he dies in urban squalor far from the green fields of his memory.

Anon., 'A Life for a Life'

1. *Boer*: the White South African farmers who were resisting British control. This story is set during the Second Boer War of 1899-1902 which was criticised by many socialists as being a war of financial greed rather than the protection of British suzerainty the Colonial Secretary, Joseph Chamberlain, claimed when he justified the hostilities. The British government, through Chamberlain, had claimed suzerainty over Paul Kruger's (1825-1904) South African republic after gold was discovered in the Witswatersrand area of the Transvaal. Kruger had been elected president of the Transvaal by the Afrikaners in 1883 after the first Boer War when Britain gave the area limited independence. For more on Chamberlain, see above, p. 373 n. 33.

Adhem, 'Blood on the Cheap Trip'

1. *Whit-Friday*: Whitsuntide refers to the week following Pentecost, the seventh Sunday after Easter and a religious holiday for Christians. Whit-Friday is the Friday following Pentecost, and the holiday was celebrated throughout Lancashire, with towns organizing 'Whit Walks' – parades of Sunday-school children through the town – and brass band displays and competitions. The holiday from work would also be used by many to travel to the coast for a break.
2. *cheap trip trains*: Rail travel at the end of the nineteenth century was still too expensive to be used regularly by the working classes (see J. R. Kellett, *The Impact of Railways on*

Victorian Cities (1969; Abingdon: Routledge, 2007) for details on numbers of regular travellers), but there was a large demand for railway holiday excursions by factory workers in Lancashire. The growth of the seaside towns of Blackpool and Morecambe (and others around the country) were a response to the high volume of factory workers using their newly established formal holidays to escape the city and spend time on the coast. See also P. J. Cain, 'Railways 1870–1914', in M. J. Freeman (ed.), *Transport in Victorian Britain* (Manchester: Manchester University Press, 1988), pp. 92–133.

3. *we have always with us*: a paraphrase of Matthew 26:11: 'For you always have the poor with you; but you do not always have Me'. The verse, which is Christ's response to his disciples' criticism of a woman preparing him for burial by pouring on him costly perfume that could have been sold to aid the poor, is quoted out of context to justify the existence of poverty as inevitable and unresolvable. Clarke's paraphrase suggests that under capitalism some will inevitably be brutalized by the system.
4. *Jinkins's factory lodge*: The use of the term 'lodge' here refers to a reservoir of water used by a mill; *OED*. Neither child has seen the sea and can only conceive its size in terms of industrial bodies of water.
5. *slutch*: Lancashire dialect meaning mud or dirt.
6. *bobbies*: a slang term for policemen, presumed to be a reference to Sir Robert Peel (1788–1850), who, when Home Secretary, passed the 1828 Metropolitan Police Act forming the first police force.

Ashton, 'Bill Spriggs an Patsy Filligan o'er Winter Hill. Likewise Bet'

1. *Colonel Ainsworth ... across t' moors*: Colonel Richard Henry Ainsworth JP (1839–1926) closed public access to the path over Winter Hill to the north west of Bolton, Lancashire. The SDF had called on local people to gather for a mass trespass on Saturday, 12 September 1896, and the *Bolton Chronicle* estimated 8,000 to 10,000 people attended. There were further trespasses organized for 13 and 20 September. The song Teddy Ashton sings later in the story was written by Clarke for the trespassers to sing on their protests. Bolton Corporation bought the land in the late 1920s, but the road was only declared a public right of way in 1996.
2. *Trotterteaun*: Trottertown, Clarke's name for Bolton; the nickname for inhabitants of Bolton is 'Trotters'.
3. *L. & Y.*: the Lancashire and Yorkshire Railway Company.
4. *Moses Gate ... Salford*: Moses Gate was a village three miles southwest of Bolton, now part of the Bolton suburbs. Salford is a city to the west of Manchester, over twelve miles southwest of Bolton.
5. *Smiles' "Self Help"*: Samuel Smiles (1812–1904) published *Self-Help, with Illustrations of Character and Conduct* in 1859. It was a phenomenally popular didactic work on individual success and was used as a justification for *laissez-faire* politics and the refusal of aid, as illustrated here. Patsy needed money, and his 'friend' gave him a text advocating self-reliance.
6. *hauve-a-creaun*: half a crown; see Glossary in Volume 1.
7. *has he hek as like*: a northern phrase giving an emphatic negative. It is usually given as an answer to a question but can also be used, as Bill does here, to reinforce a negative quality or lack.
8. *through t' needle's eye o' Scripter*: : Matthew 19:24: 'And again I say unto you, It is easier for a camel to go through the eye of a needle, than for a rich man to enter into the kingdom of God.'

Haslam, 'Murdered by Money'

1. *card-room*: the room in a cotton or woollen mill that housed the machines used to comb and clean the cotton or wool in preparation for spinning. The gendered division of labour in the cotton or woollen mills would mean that the spinning machinery would be tended by men and the weaving machines tended by women. The carding room would have both men and women working together.
2. *flies*: the flying shuttle of the weaving machinery, invented by John Kay (1704–c. 1780) and patented in 1730. This appears to contradict Haslam's earlier positioning of Matilda in the carding room.
3. *doff*: In textile production, this term can refer either to the stripping of carding cylinders of remnants of wool or cotton, or to the removal of full bobbins or spindles in the spinning process to replace them with empty ones; *OED*. The former definition is suggested by the description of Matilda's actions in relation to the process of roving in the following paragraph. See following note below.
4. *roving*: the thin strands of carded cotton or wool ready for the spinning process.
5. *slubber-tenter*: Slubber is the processed cotton after carding and before spinning, where the employee would remove imperfections in the pre-spun cotton. The term tenter in this context is used to describe someone who looks after the machine. The dead woman's occupation is very similar to that of Matilda and a prophecy of her future.
6. *cerebellum*: the back of his head.
7. *Jack-frame tenter*: the operator of a machine for winding textiles onto bobbins, in this case the unspun cotton Matilda tends.
8. *scutchin*: scotching, meaning to beat the cotton in order to soften it.

Ashton, 'Greensauce Sketches. Georgie's Fust Day in t' Factory'

1. *yure o' t' yeard*: the hair on your head.
2. *dickey*: either a coarse workman's jacket or a false shirt front; *OED*. Georgie may mean the latter and be insinuating that the management is only superficially superior to the workers.
3. *cardreaum and weivin shed*: card room and weaving shed. For more information on the card room of a textile mill, see above, p. 381 n. 1.
4. *hobble-hole*: in this context meaning a perplexing situation; *OED*. In dialect, hobbil, meaning a dunce or idiot. Georgie is shocked by the noise and movement of the mill and considers those who inhabit such a space to be foolish.
5. *yeadwarch*: a headache.
6. *loblorry*: a mispronunciation of loblolly, meaning an unskilled assistant. Originally used to describe a non-professional assistant to a ship's surgeon in the Royal Navy, the loblolly boy would carry out the jobs that the surgeon was too busy or too superior to carry out himself. The name originated from the 'loblolly' or thick porridge stew that was fed to patients. Georgie is not to be trusted with any skilled work.
7. *gradely reet*: gradely right or all right. Charlie wonders if Georgie has all his mental faculties.
8. *baggin time*: the lunchtime break. Lancashire dialect uses 'baggin' to refer to a packed lunch prepared at home.
9. *Th' dal foo'*: either 'the daft fool' or 'the damned fool'.
10. *flust*: possibly a version of flusk, meaning a whirring sound.

Ashton, 'Th' Kock-Krow Club an' th' War. Darin Decision to Form a Kock-Krow Volunteer Corps to Batter th' Boers'

1. *Rachda*: Rochdale, Lancashire.
2. *pratoism*: a mispronunciation of patriotism.
3. *grasy*: a mispronunciation of gracious.
4. *stockin feet*: stocking feet, without shoes, in only his socks.
5. *Canidy's*: 'Canidy' is Canada. Australia and Canada were part of the British Empire, as was 'Indy' (India), which follows. Bill is aligning the importance of Tum Fowt with that of the rest of the Empire.
6. *Lanky*: an affectionate abbreviation for Lancashire.
7. *Lord Salisbury an Joe Chamberlain*: Robert Arthur Talbot Gascoyne-Cecil, third Marquess of Salisbury (1830–1903), Conservative Prime Minister 1885–6, 1886–92 and 1895–1902, a politician renowned for 'mental abstraction, aristocratic remoteness and short sight'; P. Smith, 'Robert Arthur Talbot Gascoyne-Cecil', *ODNB*. Joseph (Joe) Chamberlain, industrialist and politician, member of the radical wing of the Liberal Unionists who formed a coalition government with Salisbury's Conservatives in 1885. Chamberlain was Colonial Secretary and involved in the political manoeuvring that goaded the Boers into attacking the British to justify the war. Support for a war based on imperial acquisition was achieved by rousing national patriotism, and jingoistic mobs would violently break up any anti-war meeting. Working-class men were encouraged to fight a war that would lead not to material gain for them but instead to the reinforcement of British imperial power and control of the Rand's gold and diamond wealth by Cecil Rhodes's British South Africa Company.

Plant, 'The Absent-Minded Beggar'

1. en fete: enjoying a holiday or celebration. This celebration is for the leaving of soldiers to fight in the Boer War in South Africa; see following n. 2 below.
2. *South Africa*: For information on the origins of the Boer War, see above, p. 379 n. 1.
3. *oakum job*: Picking oakum (which meant either the separation of the woody fibres of tow from the finer fibres of hemp or flax, or the unravelling of old hemp rope; *OED*) was the employment given to the inmates of prisons and workhouses. Bill is either a habitual criminal or long-term unemployed.
4. *mash*: see above, p. 368 n. 21.
5. *quod*: slang for prison; *OED*.

Anon., 'Sunshine and Shadow'

1. *The glamour ... Arlette*: poem entitled 'Arlette' by Sarah Doudney (1841–1926) published in *Good Words*, January 1886. The memory of the Arlette of the poem brings the narrator joy and comfort: 'My old belief in truth and trust / She brings back, sometimes yet'.

'Citizen', 'The Blackleg'

1. *Revision Court*: a committee to review the lists of people eligible to vote in a particular area, parish, borough or constituency. The committee would be presided over by a member of the legal profession, and representatives of the political parties contesting the seat would be present to press for decisions in their favour. After the Second Reform Act was passed in 1867, men who owned or rented property over a value of £10 p.a. were eligible to vote in general elections, but this excluded men who lived with their parents, those employed by the armed forces and those who had been admitted to the workhouse. The exceptions here are the two men who were eligible to vote when the Revision Court made their decisions but were admitted to the workhouse before the date of the election.
2. *full week*: Casual employees at dockyards across Britain were employed on a daily basis and were often selected through favouritism. Here, Sexton is commenting on the favouritism shown to workers who shared Crushem's religious attitudes or who were content to affect religious devotion in order to secure regular employment.
3. *Be ye content ... placed ye*: Hebrews 13:5: 'Let your conversation be without covetousness; and be content with such things as ye have: for he hath said, I will never leave thee, nor forsake thee'. Sexton is following the popular argument that religion was developed and wielded by the rich to control the poor, but it has been argued by historians that religious dissent in Britain had been an important part in the development of critiques of the State, reaching back to Wilkes, Paine and others. Karl Marx stated in his *Introduction to the Critique of Hegel's Philosophy of Law* (1844) that 'Man makes religion, religion does not make man', arguing that religion was simply an inversion of reality and when reality was reorganized fairly religion would be unnecessary.
4. *purple and fine linen*: The colour purple was associated with royalty and wealth. The dye was extracted from sea snails found in the eastern Mediterranean and was very expensive to produce, being more costly than silver; hence the colour was named 'imperial' or 'royal' purple. Crushem's ability to afford purple and fine linen positions him as someone in possession of great wealth.
5. *oilskins*: waterproof material, in this instance fashioned into a cape or loose coat worn to keep the worst of the rain off the body and clothes beneath. Goodman has had to pawn his oilskins to keep his family fed and housed during his period of poor employment.
6. *nesh*: to turn soft; *OED*. In northern English dialect it means someone who is weak, delicate or faint-hearted. Goodman does not want to get used to the warmth of the policeman's hut before having to return to the cold and wet to work.
7. *bums*: abbreviation for bumbailiff, a derogatory term for bailiffs of the lowest order.
8. *T.T.*: teetotal, someone who abstains from the consumption of alcohol; see above, p. 372 n. 16, and Volume 1, p. 325 n. 78. The policeman makes the assumption that John Goodman's poverty stems from spending money on drink rather than from low pay and high costs of living. This popular assumption placed the responsibility for poverty with the poor rather than on the inequalities generated by the system of capitalist economics.
9. *old time crab-hand winch*: a hand-operated winch used to lift goods out of ships' cargo holds. Christie Kennedy worked at the docks before the use of machine-driven winches – and other motorized machinery – became standard.
10. *de ould Dutch*: his wife. Christie, despite his Irish accent, uses this cockney term to refer to his wife. Albert Chevalier's (1861–1923) song 'My Old Dutch: A Cockney Song' had been a music hall and vaudeville hit in 1892 and was a celebration of a long and happy

married life. The song was associated with working-class poverty, and Chevalier would perform it as an old man who was separated from his wife when entering the workhouse.

11. *de bit o' tommy*: their food. Christy, like many men in literature who have failed to get work, refuses to return home so that his wife and children will not need to share their food with him.

12. *cocoa room ... on spec*: Cocoa rooms were an alternative to the public house where people could meet socially without having to buy and consume alcohol. Sexton is showing that not all working men indulged in hard drink and that the provision of alternatives would be, and were, used by the workers. To have the drink 'on spec' would be to drink now and pay later: the provider would be speculating on a return on payday.

13. *scaldy*: the hot liquid; scalding.

14. *Banagher*: to beat (or bang) Banagher, to surpass everything; Bangher is the name of a town in Ireland, which is said to have become proverbial as a 'rotten borough'; *OED*. The town was known as a parliamentary seat that was 'given' to family or friends rather than elected, and the seat became the standard of corruption and nepotism against which others were measured. But Christie uses the personal pronoun, which suggests he is referring to the alternative explanation of Banagher as a minstrel famed for telling tall tales. Christie also refers to the response 'and Banagher beat the devil', but the origins of this are unclear.

15. *book larnin*: education. John and his wife are both educated beyond the usual level for working-class children. Although their ages are not given, it is assumed that they would have benefited from the 1870 Elementary Education Act, also known as Forster's Education Act. The Act ensured the provision of education for all children between the ages of five and twelve, but it was not until the 1880 Elementary Education Act, also known as Mundella's Act, that attendance at school was made compulsory up to the age of ten. John and his wife have been given the opportunity to extend that education, and their intelligent and thoughtful attitudes are evidence of the general socialist support for equal educational opportunities and the necessity of a well-educated working class.

16. *bob-lolly-boy*: possibly a mistake or mispronunciation of 'loblolly boy'; see above, p. 381 n. 6. Hoppy is given labouring work that the official timekeepers, gardeners and grooms would be too busy or superior to carry out.

17. *courtin'*: courting, paying court to someone. Goodman and his future wife are falling in love and building their relationship.

18. *a hook instead iv a pen*: Jack now works as an unskilled manual labourer on the docks rather than as a clerk in the firm of Crushem and Grindem. The 'Longshoreman's hook' or 'Stevedore's hook' was the main tool of the dockers' trade and would be carried in the belt of the docker when not being used. Curley steals Goodman's hook in Chapter XX and carries it off by hooking it into his belt. The exchange of tools, from pen to hook, is a demotion for Goodman in terms of both social standing and level of earning.

19. *reeve off ... main hatch spars*: reeve – 'to pass a rope or cable through a hole, ring or block'; *OED*. Hoppy is asking Jack to ready the hatch for hoisting and lowering cargo.

20. *span*: A span is 'a length of chain or wire rope used for suspending derricks ... to the masts of ships', while a derrick is 'a contrivance or machine for hoisting or moving heavy weights'; *OED*. Jack is working at a great height during bad weather.

21. *bowline*: a maritime term with two meanings: it is a 'rope passing from about the middle of the perpendicular edge on the weather side of the square sails (to which it is fastened by three or four subdivisions, called "bridles") to the larboard or starboard bow, for the purpose of keeping the edge of the sail steady when sailing on a wind'; *OED*; and it is

also a knot used (among other things) to winch people up – having fallen overboard or, in Goodman's case, to reach a high point in the ship – by sitting in the loop of the knot. Goodman chooses this method because of the pressures of time placed upon him by employers and management demanding a swift unloading of the cargo.

22. *Tory father ... gracious queen*: Tory ideology was centred on the importance of history and heredity, breeding, property rights, the duty of the individual to maintain civil and social order, and the importance of the monarchy and the Protestant Church of England. Smythe's father is depicted as the 'typical' Tory who is more concerned with preserving tradition, social distinction and national honour than leading or reacting to the modern world.

23. *it came to pass*: a phrase used throughout the Bible to mean 'as things turned out' or 'as things happened'. It is used here to illustrate the different experiences of the doctor and his father at the same university.

24. *Jew money lenders ... neighbourhood*: Moneylending had been a business associated with the Jewish faith for centuries. In the thirteenth century Jewish moneylending was protected from violent Gentiles who hoped to be rid of their debts by murdering their lender. The formation of *archae* or 'coffers' was decreed by the Crown, which was losing tax through the unpaid debts, and protected the debt by preserving records duplicated and held by both Jew and Gentile guardians. Oxford was an important Jewish centre and so one of the *archae* was located in the city. Despite the expulsion of the Jews in 1290, Oxford once more attracted Jewish immigrants in the eighteenth and early nineteenth centuries after Oliver Cromwell (1599–1658) relaxed the ban on Jewish settlement in 1655. As industrialization grew, Oxford became less important to the Jewish businessman, and so Smythe senior's experience of the inhabitants of the university town was different to that of his son.

25. *Praise God ... Amen!!!*: 'Praise God, from whom All Blessings Flow' (1674) was written by Thomas Ken (1637–1711) and was originally the final verse in a longer hymn, 'Awake my Soul, and with the Sun'. The verse, 'Praise God, from Whom all blessings flow; / Praise Him, all creatures here below; / Praise Him above, ye heavenly host; / Praise Father, Son, and Holy Ghost. Amen', set to the Old 100th attributed to Louis Bourgeois (*c.* 1510–61), is now part of the Protestant doxology. The 'eminently respectable member' is more concerned about his soul in the afterlife than he is about the earthly bodies of his employees.

26. *smash King Billy's portrait*: William III of England, Protestant Dutch Prince of Orange, invaded England in 1688 and deposed the Roman Catholic James II and VII. Christie's antipathy to William situates him as a Catholic Irishman, attempting to destroy the image of the man who defeated James at the Battle of the Boyne, near Drogheda, in 1690. Protestant Irish and Scots celebrate this defeat of the Catholic threat through the institution of the Orange Order or Lodge and by public marches every 12 July on the anniversary of the battle.

27. *bridewell*: literally, this means a prison or house of correction; *OED*. In this context it refers to the police station and its holding cells, where prisoners would wait to be tried at court.

28. *no vote*: see above, 383 n. 1. Curley neither owns property nor rents at £10 or above p.a.

29. *Jack Christie's*: presumably an error and should read 'Sad business, this accident of Jack's, Christie'.

30. *flywheel pump*: a mechanical device that generates and stores energy through rotation. Christie is sucking on his pipe in a regular, rhythmical way.

31. *constant number*: Crushem is offering to return Jack to a permanent position of employment at the docks rather than his reliance on the scramble for work as a casual labourer as described in Chapter I.
32. *bewwie hole*: the bury hole, the grave. The little girl has heard that her father may have been fatally injured.
33. *Poor-law Authorities*: The 1834 New Poor Law introduced a system of relief for the poor that was based on deterrence until absolute necessity. The application for financial relief, burial or admittance to the workhouse was made a stigma and was avoided by the poor until the final extremity. Crushem holds the double standards of the capitalist and Liberal who refers the woman to the Poor Law Authorities (of which he is one) to avoid having to take financial responsibility for the funeral himself, while he and other wealthy businessmen condemn workers for applying for financial relief, branding them lazy and work-shy.
34. *compensation for injury ... appeal to it*: Jack is referring to the 1880 Employers Liability Act; see n. 36 below.
35. *badger you ... be badgered*: to bait; to hound; to subject to persistent harassment or persecution; to pester, bother, (in later use freq.) to ply with repeated and irritating requests to *do* something; *OED*. The use of the word derives from the old sport of badger baiting, where dogs would be used to attack and kill a badger, usually in its sett.
36. *Employers' Liability Act*: the 1880 Act that gave employees the right to sue for compensation, but which placed the burden of proof on the employee. The Act was replaced in 1897 with the Workman's Compensation Act, which only required proof of the injury being sustained while at work.
37. *I know you can read*: Crushem's patronizing attitude is used to create a sense of class difference between himself and his workman. Crushem would not make the same statement of one of his peers, as it would be assumed that the middle and upper classes would be literate. The education acts of 1870 and 1880 (see above, p. 384 n. 15) had raised already high literacy levels in Britain to almost 100 per cent, and it was always going to be more likely that Crushem's employees would be literate.
38. *deadhouse*: see above, p. 370 n. 1.
39. *great was the rejoicing thereof*: possibly a reference to Ezekiel 7:12: 'Let not the buyer rejoice nor the seller grieve, for wrath is upon the whole crowd'. In Ezekiel, God's wrath is brought against the materialists to teach them the error of worshiping wealth rather than God. The verse refers to the joy of the buyer who gains material possession and the sorrow of the seller who loses his land in the transaction. The reference in this context is to the exchange of labour power: the employer buys labour at a greatly reduced price and gains profit in the transaction, while the labourer is underpaid for his work. The wrath here is not that of God but rather the growing discontent of the workers with a system that is heavily weighted against them. The hope is that the wrath of the crowd will be the engine of political and social change.
40. *prominent Liberal ... Tory and a shipowner*: supposedly opposing political ideologies, but both are driven to maximize profits at the expense of the worker. Neither is on the side of the worker, despite Liberal claims that they represent the working class, hence the necessity of independent labour representation in the Houses of Parliament.
41. *the exchange*: The London Stock Exchange, the world's oldest stock exchange, can trace its origins back to 1698, and John Castaing's list of stock and commodity prices in the London coffee houses is the earliest evidence of stock trading. Smythe, Grindem and Fatpurse are making their fortunes out of unearned profits through shares.

42. *William Morris*: Morris (1834–96) was the son of a wealthy City financier who first found fame as a poet and then used that talent and fame to promote the ideology of socialism. Morris was an early member of the SDF but split the group in 1884 to form the anti-parliamentary Socialist League. Morris was an important part of British socialism at this time, but he is also raised here as a wealthy, upper-class man who was working towards equality and was evidence that socialism was not merely the ravings of a violent underclass.
43. *living on the rates*: a fixed tax relating to property ownership used to fund local services, including the relief systems of the 1834 Poor Law Act. To live on the rates meant to be supported by the local authority or parish without working. There were two forms of relief: indoor, meaning to move into the workhouse, and outdoor, meaning to receive financial support to live outside of the workhouse. Because of the low pay and short supply of female occupations, many widowed women with children were reliant on outdoor relief.
44. *board of the guardians of the poor(?)*: The distribution of 'relief' collected through the rates system was overseen by a committee of local men, usually drawn from local aristocracy, industrialists, shopkeepers and other influential businessmen. Crushem's place on the Board of Guardians is awarded because of his status as an employer of a large number of local men and his role as local councillor. The question mark following the title emphasizes the irony of the man whose wealth is made by underpaying his workers being given the responsibility of distributing relief to those he had impoverished, and to the irony of the title itself, as Crushem guards nothing other than his own wealth and status.
45. *Established Church*: the Church of England rather than any of the Dissenting branches of Protestant Christianity. Prior to the Reformation and separation from Rome, the church had been an independent body, which, for instance, set its own rate of taxation. During and after the Reformation, the English Revolution and the Restoration, the Church of England was limited in its powers and its voice – outside of the pulpit – was restricted to the House of Lords, where bishops debated with the Lords Temporal. Crawthumper is aligned with, and takes the side of, the capitalists.
46. *trucks kecked up ... spars and booms*: The scene is described as having been abandoned in the midst of unloading. The trucks are in place to receive the goods, which need winching from the holds of the ships, but all the paraphernalia associated with the dockers' work lies abandoned.
47. *cocoa worm*: a typographical error that should read 'cocoa rooms'.
48. *pro tem*: on a temporary basis.
49. *sagged school*: played truant.
50. *bunced*: to gain, to profit; *OED*. Probably meaning to swap or win the marbles and buttons off one another.
51. *thrutched*: thrutch is to press, squeeze, crush; *OED*.
52. *physical force*: the use of violence to bring about social and political change. The term is usually associated with the mid-century Chartist movement, which was divided between the supporters of physical force as a method change and those who favoured 'moral force' in the form of argument and persuasion. The difference between Goodman and Curley does not suggest that the socialist movement was similarly divided over the methods of change, although the anarchist faction of the movement did advocate physical attack, or 'propaganda by deed'. Curley represents the infiltration of socialist action by police *agent provocateurs* who encouraged violence in order to discredit the action and socialism gen-

erally. See also Bramsbury's 'A Working Class Tragedy' in Volume 1 (p. 328, n. 105) and the fictional account of the 1886 Black Monday demonstration in Trafalgar Square.

53. *J.P.*: Justice of the Peace, a citizen of some local standing who sits in the magistrates' court and presides over summary cases carrying up to two years' imprisonment. JPs have no legal training and are advised on legal matters by a justices' clerk.

54. *on spec*: on the chance of being chosen to work. The men were speculating their time and rest in the hope of accumulating work and pay.

55. *Blessed are ... find peace*: an amalgamation of the opening and closing of the Sermon of the Mount in the Book of Matthew: Matthew 5:5: 'Blessed are the meek: for they shall inherit the earth'; Matthew 11:28: 'Come to Me, all you who labor and are heavy laden, and I will give you rest'; and Matthew 11:29: 'Take My yoke upon you and learn from Me, for I am gentle and lowly in heart, and you will find rest for your souls'. Crushem, with all his professional titles and wealth, is the opposite of the teachings of Christ and of what is promoted through his chapel.

56. *He that advances money ... reward hereafter*: an adaptation of Proverbs 19:1: 'He that hath pity upon the poor lendeth unto the Lord; and that which he hath given will he pay him again'. These references to Biblical teachings are evidence of the Christian basis of the ethical socialism practised by the ILP and others.

57. *car*: an abbreviation for tramcar.

58. *wideawake*: a deep-brimmed hat, also known as a Quaker hat, as worn by eighteenth- and nineteenth-century American Quaker men. Rembrandt's (1606–69) 1632 self-portrait depicts him in a wideawake hat. Curley turns down the usually upturned brim of about four inches in order to keep his face hidden.

59. *Villadom*: the wealthy part of the town. Villas were originally country dwellings owned by the wealthy, but it also became the term for large houses in towns and cities with substantial gardens.

60. *rubicon*: a boundary, a limit, especially one that, once crossed, entails irrevocable commitment; a point of no return; *OED*. The use of this word here denotes the unbridgeable gulf between rich and poor; one will have no chance (or there will be no danger) of crossing from one side of the social and economic divide to the other.

61. *lanyard ... darbies*: A lanyard is a short piece of rope or leather used to secure the truncheon to the wrist, and darbies refer to handcuffs, which is presumably a derivative from Darby's bands (also Father Darby's bands), a rigid form of bond by which a debtor was bound and put within the power of a moneylender (it has been suggested that the term was derived from the name of some noted usurer of the sixteenth century); *OED*. The policeman is readying himself for a potential arrest in the protection of capitalist wealth.

62. *half cwt*: half hundredweight. A hundredweight is a British imperial measurement representing 8 stone or around 50 kg, so a half hundred weight would be 4 stone or around 25 kg. The journalist sees the shoddy work of the jerry-built slums and the dangers of skimped work, as the mortar is inadequate and the bricks are insecure. The image is also suggestive of relentless buildings unbroken by nature.

63. *Crushem ... port*: see above, p. 384 n. 12 on the cocoa rooms; and D. Mutch, 'Intemperate Narratives: Tory Tipplers, Liberal Abstainers and Nineteenth-Century British Socialist Fiction', *Victorian Literature and Culture*, 36:2 (2008), pp. 471–87, for more on the theme of drink and socialist fiction.

64. *havanas*: cigars manufactured in Cuba. Cuban cigars are deemed to be the world's best and are priced to reflect their status. Crushem's consumption of Havanas positions him

as a wealthy man who can afford expensive cigars and as luxuriating in his wealth while promoting thrift and abstinence in his workers. His association with fine wine and good cigars depicts him as a hypocrite and a humbug.

65. *purple plush*: see above, p. 383 n. 4 on the association between the colour purple and wealth. The description of the chair covered in plush fabric both depicts the sumptuousness of Crushem's room and alludes to the plush-weavers' strike at Bradford's Manningham Mills in the winter of 1890–1. Although the strike was unsuccessful, it has been recognized as a significant moment in labour history and as the origin of the ILP.

66. *Be just, and fear not*: Cardinal Wolsey's advice to Thomas Cromwell in Shakespeare's *Henry VIII*, Act 3, scene ii, line 446. In this scene Wolsey's treachery against the king has been revealed, as he supported Henry's divorce and remarriage to Anne Boleyn to Henry but criticized it to the pope. Wolsey is urging Cromwell to be unselfish and true to his king and country. The journalist is playing the double role in this scene as he advises Crushem to act fairly, when the agreement will be that Crushem will immediately break his promise to Curley and share the information with the journalist and Hoppy.

67. *pig in a poke*: a phrase possibly originating in the late Middle Ages and which has similar phrases across Europe. It is a warning about buying without checking the goods. At a time when meat was scarce, confidence tricksters would sell a dog or cat in a bag or sack (the 'poke'), claiming it was suckling pig. Those who did not check the contents bought inferior meat, but those who did 'let the cat out of the bag'. Curley's demand for payment before giving Crushem the information is like buying a pig in a poke because the exchange is based on mutual trust, which neither of the men has for the other.

68. *I prefer cash*: Paper money or bank notes are a form of promissory note where, in exchange for the note, the bank will supply the bearer with the equivalent value in gold. The value of British currency in the nineteenth century was based on the global price of gold (the gold standard), while America and France based their currency on the price of both gold and silver (bimetallism). The exchange of paper money, which in Britain has the words 'I promise to pay the bearer on demand the sum of …', began in the seventeenth century and became the standard currency in 1844, when the exchange of metal was replaced by a note promising the bearer metal the cost of the note. Bank notes were backed by the country's gold reserves until the Great Depression in the 1930s, when Britain ended the gold standard in 1931, and now all bank notes are fiduciary, meaning the value is based on consumer confidence or on securities; *OED*. Curley's mistrust of Crushem extends to his paper money, and Curley wants more tangible wealth than a promise to pay. The physical gold in the treasury reserves is referred to as bullion, and the sovereigns Crushem gives Curley are bullion coins, meaning they are made of gold and therefore carry their own value.

69. *Looking Backwards*: a utopian novel by American author Edward Bellamy (1850–98) published in 1887. The novel, about a young man who goes to sleep in nineteenth-century Boston and wakes up in the year 2000 to find that Boston is organized on Marxist lines, was an inspiration for William Morris's *News from Nowhere*, in which Morris re-envisaged a socialist future as a pastoral anarchy rather than Bellamy's state-controlled organization. Doctor Smythe represents the anti-Marxist socialism of the ILP and so rejects Bellamy's vision.

70. *Roland for my Oliver*: In the legend of Charlemagne, the long siege at Viane is to be decided by a duel between Charlemagne's nephew Roland and Girard de Viane's champion Oliver. Neither participant is able to destroy the other, and after a long fight, depending on the version, they either agree to become loyal friends or an angel descends

and instructs them to be so. Smythe's reference to the story suggests that Miss Crushem is an adversary equal to him.

71. *free and* independent: This is a phrase used by many socialist writers and authors in this ironic way to emphasize the forces pressing on British workers who are labouring under the misapprehension that they can exercise free choice.

72. *subtenants*: Property in slum areas would initially be rented from the owner, who would usually have very little involvement in the property other than collecting rent. The buildings would be of poor quality but let at a high cost. In order to reduce the rent, the original leaseholder would sublet rooms, the subletting tenants might take in a lodger, and that lodger might also sublet to another. The reference to subtenants in this scene is used to illustrate the overcrowding of the slums as well as the range of impact caused by Crushem's deception.

73. *homes ... three times over*: The relative cost of living in the slums was considerably higher than in the better parts of a city. In the Old Nichol slum in London's East End, rents could take up to one-fifth of a week's pay and, per cubic foot, were between four and ten times the cost of the best West End properties; see S. Wise, *The Blackest Streets* (London: Vintage, 2008). Crushem's power spreads beyond employment and into the homes of 'free and independent' workers.

74. *three-decker*: Sometimes called a triple decker, this was a novel published in three parts. The three or triple decker fell out of favour at the end of the nineteenth century and was replaced by the single-volume novel. The three decker was, at this time, an old-fashioned form, and the agent is shown as both aspirational by owning the book (presumably picked up second-hand after one of the main buyers of three-decker novels – the circulating libraries such as Mudies – had finished with it) and as backward-looking at a time of new forms of publication as well as new political ideas.

75. *fever hospital*: The issue of infection control in densely populated areas was part of the sanitary reforms instigated across the latter half of the century. Advances in germ theory in the mid-century enabled doctors to recognize the causes and differences between infections. The sight of the fever ambulance and the location of the fever hospital – like the general hospital where the maimed were taken from Crushem's docks – serves to emphasize the dangerous and unhealthy conditions in which the workers lived.

76. *authorities ... protection of property*: The doctrine of first occupation is built into British law to protect the property rights of those who have taken what is deemed to be unoccupied or unowned and claimed it as their own. Ownership, which is legal under capitalist law, is seen as immoral by socialists, who argue that capitalist profit is simply the theft of the workers' time by the owners of the means of production. The irony here is that the *laissez-faire* Liberal capitalist is now demanding state assistance to defend his private property.

77. *the blood began to ooze ... afresh*: The man's blood pressure is rising through fear of being attacked again, and the pressure is re-opening the wound.

78. *not wisely, but too well*: *Othello*, Act 5, scene ii. Othello, after smothering Desdemona, wants to be remembered as one whose mistakes were the consequence of loving too much; the strike poster is the consequence of capitalist greed doing its work to smother the trade union.

79. *German pauper princes ... British elector*: Prince Albert was accused of being a 'pauper prince' when he married Victoria in 1840, but he had died in 1861. Changes to the civil list monies paid to the monarch meant that Victoria received a smaller amount than had been given to her predecessors, and she also paid income tax. However, the management

of her finances and the duchies of Lancaster and Cornwall by Albert saw an increase in her personal fortune, and she privately funded some things that had previously been funded publicly, including some of the costs of the Golden Jubilee; see W. M. Kuhn, 'Queen Victoria's Civil List: What did She Do with It?', *Historical Journal*, 36:3 (1993), pp. 645–65. The point being made by Goodman here is that Victoria's wealth – whether gained through the Civil List or through personal management – will always be gathered through the 'British elector', through either taxes or rents.

80. *missus ... help you*: Although women did not have a vote in general elections at this point, from 1869 unmarried female ratepayers could vote in municipal elections and could vote for and be members of Poor Law Boards of Guardians and school boards. Goodman's wife is ineligible to join Garnish on the Council because of her married status. The use of the word 'bull' in this context means a ludicrous jest; *OED*.

81. *land of the brave and the free*: a phrase usually associated with the United States of America, but here used to describe the United Kingdom.

82. *Rothschilds*: a Jewish European family whose wealth was based in banking. During the nineteenth century the pan-European family and their business amassed the world's largest private fortune. Garnish's point is that the supply of strike-breaking labour would exceed even the largest fortune in the world and there needs to be a more fundamental change in favour of the power of labour.

83. *told off*: see above, p. 365 n. 2.

84. *No. 9 hump*: in colloquial English, to 'take the hump' means to be annoyed or offended by a perceived slight or insult. 'No. 9' is the degree to which the offence is taken, presumably on a scale of one to ten. Therefore, Hoppy is exceedingly annoyed by Scrubbs's insistence on Hoppy counting the money in front of him.

85. *gang his own gait*: a Scottish phrase meaning to go one's own way.

86. *cotton-hook*: see above, p. 384 n. 18.

87. *put their buttons up*: Trade union members would be identified by the button or badge they wore to show their membership. Christie is ensuring that all the union men are visible by their buttons.

88. *West Injies*: West Indies, meaning the West India Dock. This is a series of three docks on the Isle of Dogs in the east of London, which were opened in 1802 and was the largest in London. There is no West India Dock in Liverpool, despite the suggestions that this novel is set in a fictional version of Liverpool; see below, p. 392 n. 94.

89. *Met a scab ... polis*: Christie has attacked a strike-breaker, and the fight is ended by police intervention.

90. *B.P.*: British Public or British People. This generalization is more usually termed the BWM – British working man – but Sexton removes the gender bias.

91. *that an enemy hath done this*: Matthew 13:28, the parable of the wheat and the tares. Goodman knows, as do his union members, that the attack on Crushem has been a deliberate ploy to discredit the union and the movement in the same way that the enemy sowing tare seeds in the wheat field was a deliberate act of sabotage. Goodman's advice is the same as that of the man who sowed the good seeds: do not enter into any rash act, as that may cause more harm than good.

92. *punch and judies*: Punch and Judy is a traditional puppet show dating back to the seventeenth century in England. Sexton's reference equates the mainstream public and their prejudices to the well-known puppets, as they are manipulated by the capitalist puppet master to respond in ways that will benefit the capitalist at the expense of the worker.

93. *'Sizes*: the Assizes, the criminal courts held periodically which dealt with the most serious cases that could not be heard by the magistrate's court. The Assizes would be presided over by judges, known as circuit judges, who would sit in different towns at different times. Assize courts in Britain were abolished in 1971 and replaced with permanent Crown courts.
94. *Liverpool*: the first time the setting for the story is placed in reality. Previous to this, the city of Goodman and of the dock strike has been referred to as Mudpool.
95. *jigger*: a specifically Liverpudlian term for an alleyway, passage. Despite the anomalous 'West India Dock', this, the prominence of the docks in the local vicinity and the large Irish population all suggest that the novel is set in Liverpool.
96. *police bobby*: see above, p. 380 n. 6.
97. *gentleman of pronounced political views ... accepted*: This could be a reference to either Cardinal Manning, who intervened to end the London dock strike of 1889, or Tom Mann, who organized the Liverpool dock strike of the same year and advised the dockers to return to work.
98. *brewer's ambulance*: a van used to transport the injured and sick to hospital, donated and maintained by a local brewer.
99. *cruel par-ie-ent*: possibly a reference to Robert Burns's (1759–96) song 'How Cruel are the Parents' (1795), which was sung to the tune 'John Anderson, my Jo'; or 'Oh Cruel were his Parents who Sent my Love to Sea', an anonymous folk ballad of a maid sent mad by the separation from her lover.
100. *'Change*: the Stock Exchange; see above, p. 386 n. 41.
101. *Cinderella Club*: Cinderella Clubs were a nationwide network of groups founded by Robert Blatchford and promoted through the *Clarion* for the benefit of poor children. In his autobiography *My Eighty Years*, Blatchford recalls meeting a young match-seller in the Manchester slums who wanted to sell her last box of matches so she could attend a Catholic Sunday School tea party: 'I remembered when as a poor child such parties gave me great delight. How easy to please a child, and a child of the poor. And why not, I asked myself, why not weekly parties for children of the slums? We founded within a few days the first Cinderella Club' (pp. 189–90). The aristocratic Smythe senior is rediscovering his duty to care for the poor by entertaining the innocent victims of capitalism.
102. *the doctor's wife ... were members*: The issue of women in socialism was a cause of much debate among the different groups in the British socialist movement during this period. Socialists such as Ernest Belfort Bax and 'Tattler' (assumed to be a pseudonym for Harry Quelch, editor of *Justice*), both members of the SDF, published strongly worded articles against female equality, while the Woman Question was supported and promoted by female SDF-ers such as Eleanor Marx Aveling and Dora Montefiore. The ILP was much more inclusive of women in its organization: it included influential female socialists such as Margaret Macmillan and Katherine Bruce Glasier, neé St John Conway, and had strong links to the suffrage movement through Keir Hardie's friendship with Sylvia Pankhurst. The involvement of the wives in the Mudpool/Liverpool labour party suggests that this is a fictional branch of the ILP.
103. *Irish National Concert ... member*: The Irish National League was formed on 17 October 1880 in the Antient Concert Hall in Dublin, but as Crushem is unaware of Ireland's 'geographical position', his attendance would be at one of the concerts celebrating Irishness and promoting Irish nationalism held regularly in Liverpool. Liverpool had a large Irish community that was rapidly expanded during the famine exodus, and many Irish settled in Liverpool permanently.

104. *in the pay of the Tories*: This was a common accusation levelled by the Liberals at socialist candidates, especially during general elections. The most famous example of the accusation was the uproar surrounding Henry Hyde Champion's financial support for Keir Hardie's campaign for Mid Lanark in the 1888 general election. Champion, Michael Maltman Barry and Margaret Harkness were all accused of taking money from the Tory party to fund Hardie's candidature in order to split the Liberal vote. Crushem and Fatpurse – like the Liberal Party did in reality – do not see the embryonic Labour Party as a significant political challenge but as a mechanism for dividing the working man's vote three ways, which would reduce their chances of election.
105. *lug cap*: usually known as a deerstalker, a peaked cap with flaps covering the ears. Most famously worn by Sherlock Holmes, the headwear is here being used to hide the wearer's identity.
106. *a woman voter ... having voted*: single women rate-payers could vote in municipal elections; see above, p. 391 n. 80.
107. *cropper*: crupper, a leather strap leading from the saddle and passing beneath the tail to prevent the saddle from sliding forward; *OED*. The burr was placed in the tenderest part of the horse's anatomy to ensure its reaction.

Fair, 'Nan: A New Year's Eve Story'

1. *PH*: public house. Nan spends so much time in the public house that she feels she might as well live there.
2. *ballad of the "Four Marys"*: an old Scottish ballad of a woman about to be executed by the king for the murder of her baby. There is some debate about the identity of the narrator; she calls herself Mary Hamilton and counts herself as one of the four maids of Mary Queen of Scots, all of whom were called Mary, but none had the surname Hamilton. In the eighteenth century a woman called Mary Hamilton was executed for killing her illegitimate child by Peter the Great in Russia. Both stories centre on illegitimate births and the death of the child at the hands of the mother. Although Nan has not murdered her child, her request for him to be told she is dead feels like the separation of death between herself and her baby.

Baxter, 'A Terrible Crime'

1. *photographic and lithographic*: A photograph is an image copied onto sensitive material; a lithograph is an engraving or print on stone; *OED*. In both senses the money produced by Bullion is only a representation of the real.
2. *paper money ... a forger, a scoundrel*: see above, p. 389 n. 68.

SILENT CORRECTIONS

Flestrin, 'A Tale of a Turnip'

p. 8, l. 17   Duckling] Duck

Carpenter, 'Saved by a Nose'

p. 13, l. 9   Englishmen] Englishman

Law, 'Connie'

p. 95, l. 20   McCannow] McCannon

Claxton, 'Nigel Grey (A Serial Story of Love and Effort)'

p. 140, l. 36   you're] your
p. 145, l. 1   where] were
p. 190, l. 2   blamable] blameable

Adhem, 'Blood on the Cheap Trip'

p. 229, l. 26   been] been on

Ashton, 'Bill Spriggs an Patsy Filligan o'er Winter Hill. Likewise Bet.'

p. 234, l. 17   Bill] I

Haslam, 'Murdered by Money'

p. 242, l. 11   chosing] choosing

'Citizen', 'The Blackleg'

p. 288, l. 37	your] you're
p. 311, l. 25	sure] sure,
p. 318, l. 38	you've] "you've
p. 321, l. 19	unlimited.] unlimited."
p. 326, l. 33	and] "and
p. 336, l. 31	track.] track."